TOTALITARIANISM RECONSIDERED

Kennikat Press
National University Publications
Series in Political Science

TOTALITARIANISM RECONSIDERED

edited by

ERNEST A. MENZE

National University Publications
KENNIKAT PRESS // 1981
Port Washington, N.Y. // London

Manufactured in the United States of America

Published by
Kennikat Press Corp.
Port Washington, N.Y. / London

Library of Congress Cataloging in Publication Data
Main entry under title:

Totalitarianism reconsidered.

(National university publications)
Bibliography: p.
Includes index.
1. Totalitarianism—Addresses, essays, lectures.
I. Menze, Ernest A.
JC481.T64   321.9   80-18926
ISBN 0-8046-9268-8

CONTENTS

PREFACE

Totalitarianism has been "reconsidered" before, and the reappraisals will continue. This volume grew out of a session at the 1977 annual meeting of the American Historical Association in Dallas. The editor wishes to thank Hans Schmitt of the program committee and Mack Thompson of the A.H.A. for facilitating that session. The editor is indebted to Professors Curtis, Nolte, and Soucy for joining him on the panel, for agreeing to the concept of this volume, and for making available part or all of their contributions. Deep appreciation also goes to the other contributors who subsequently made their work available.

Grateful acknowledgment of encouragement given and assistance rendered in planning the project and readying the editor's translations and comments is offered to friends and colleagues at Iona, especially James Caldwell, John Daretta, Edward Dramin, John Mahon, Michael Palma, Tom Smith, and Michael Zaremski. A special note of thanks goes to Michael Ledeen for suggesting the inclusion of the chapter from Alberto Aquarone's book, to John Colaneri for reviewing it, and to Donald Malanga for translating it on short notice.

Pat Larkin and the staff of Iona College's Ryan Library, time and again, were helpful in locating and obtaining sources. The cheerful assistance of Florence Alberti of the vice-president's office at Iona College, and of Mary Bruno and the staff of the secretarial center, in getting the manuscript ready for the publisher, turned the sometimes frustrating task of compiling a multiauthor volume into a pleasant experience and is much appreciated.

This volume brings together views recorded many years ago with essays written specifically for this reconsideration of a disputed concept.

The volume also includes contributions "borrowed" from other, rather recent publications—regarded particularly relevant—and a renewed consultation with the behavioral sciences. The resultant encounter hopefully will stimulate further discussion.

The durability of some of the traditional views on the subject of totalitarianism becomes apparent in continuously issuing challenges, reassertions, and new perspectives, placed alongside them selectively in these pages. Both the concerns of contemporary scholarship and the dilemmas of contemporary international politics called for a renewed airing of the on-going controversy. Ernst Nolte's initial readiness to travel far to review the issue gave momentum to the enterprise. Cornell Jaray of Kennikat Press saw the need to put it into print. K. C. M. and M. K. C. kindly and patiently sustained the effort. While its shortcomings remain the editor's responsibility, the merits, whatever they be, are gladly shared.

The editor wishes to express his appreciation to the following for permission to translate and/or publish the following selections included in this volume: Karl Dietrich Bracher for "Der umstrittene Totalitarismus: Erfahrung and Aktualität," in K. D. Bracher, *Zeitgeschichtliche Kontroversen um Faschismus, Totalitarismus und Demokratie* (Munich, 1976), pp. 33-61, and for "Terrorismus und Totalitarismus," in K. D. Bracher, *Der Weg in die Gewalt* (Munich, 1978); Martin Greiffenhagen and List Verlag, Munich, for "Der Totalitarismusbegriff in der Regimenlehre," in M. Greiffenhagen, R. Kühnl, and J. B. Müller, *Totalitarismus: Zur Problematik eines politischen Begriffs* (Munich, 1972); Stephen F. Cohen and W. W. Norton and Co., Inc., New York, for "Bolshevism and Stalinism," in Robert C. Tucker, ed., *Stalinism: Essays in Historical Interpretation* (New York, 1977), pp. 3-29; Alberto Aquarone and Giulio Einaudi Editore, Turin, for "Stato totalitario e dittatura personale," in A. Aquarone, *L'organizzazione dello Stato totalitario* (Turin, 1965), pp. 290-311; Stanley Milgram and the editors of the *Journal of Abnormal Psychology* for Stanley Milgram, "Behavioral Study of Obedience," *Journal of Abnormal and Social Psychology*, vol. 67, no. 4, 1963, pp. 371-78 (Copyright 1963 by the American Psychological Association); Robert Jay Lifton and Simon and Schuster, New York, for excerpts from pp. 283-325 of *The Broken Connection* (New York, 1979); Michael Curtis and Transaction Books, New Brunswick, N. J. for *Totalitarianism* (New Brunswick, N. J., 1979), pp. 75-90.

TOTALITARIANISM RECONSIDERED

CONTRIBUTORS

William Sheridan Allen is professor of history at the State University of New York, Buffalo.

Alberto Aquarone is professor of modern Italian history at the University of Rome.

Karl Dietrich Bracher is professor of political science and contemporary history at the University of Bonn.

Stephen F. Cohen is professor of politics and director of the interdepartmental Russian studies program at Princeton University.

Michael Curtis is professor of political science at Rutgers University.

A. James Gregor is professor of political science at the University of California, Berkeley.

Martin Greiffenhagen is professor of political science at Stuttgart University.

Robert Jay Lifton, M.D., holds the Foundations' Fund for Research in Psychiatry professorship at Yale University.

Ernest A. Menze is professor of history at Iona College.

Stanley Milgram is Distinguished Professor of psychology at the Graduate School and University Center of the City University of New York.

Hans Mommsen is professor of history at the Ruhr University, Bochum.

Ernst Nolte is professor of history at the Free University, Berlin.

Robert Soucy is professor of history at Oberlin College.

ERNEST A. MENZE

Introduction

TOTALITARIANISM
An Outmoded Paradigm?

The three parts of this book reflect the objectives governing the selection of the contributions. Part I consists of four essays on the historical dimensions of totalitarianism in its principal manifestations and as a subject of scholarly controversy. Part II presents a number of recent contributions by prominent scholars reassessing the merits of the concept of totalitarianism. Part III represents yet another effort to bring into a discussion often dominated by historians and political scientists the contribution of behavioral scientists, placed into perspective by an historian. Since each contribution is provided with an editorial preface, this introduction will allude to them only briefly.

Professor Allan Mitchell, in an article on "Bonapartism as a Model of Bismarckian Politics," takes to task a German historian for his notion of "Caesarism," concluding that the term, "overloaded with ambiguity," is "one that is likely to land sooner or later on a heap of platitudes along with the concept of totalitarianism."[1] Though aware of the "hard times" that have befallen the venerable cold war concept of totalitarianism under the onslaught of ideological critiques and serious fascism and Stalinism studies, the reader may be surprised, nevertheless, to find it relegated so decisively to so ignominious an end. The essays brought together in this volume will help to determine whether there is any merit in further use of the concept as an analytical tool, if not as an historiographical category.

In this day, when historians increasingly make use of "models" to throw light on obscure problems of the past, their cooperation with behavioral and political scientists who, so to speak, make their living building and dismantling paradigms, has become a commonplace occurrence.

Actually, the use of models by historians by no means represents an innovation. Friedrich Gottlieb Klopstock (1724-1803), listing the "guild of historians" (die Zunft der Geschichtschreiber) first among the "depicting guilds" (darstellende Zünfte) of his "German Republic of Scholars" (Die deutsche Gelehrtenrepublik), says of them that "they invent, when they depict in a novel way, and they discover, when they bring out what really happened. Whosoever wants to be justified in calling himself a historian must bring the two together. This guild would be the smallest of all, if it were not also to admit those as members, who merely occupy themselves with the examination of the bygone."[2]

Political scientists and historians, in that sense, "invented" the model of totalitarianism, borrowing the term designating it from Gentile and Mussolini. Leonard Shapiro has reminded us that the concept of totalitarianism appeared in the history of political thought long before the term was coined,[3] but that the twentieth-century totalitarian regimes were new types nevertheless because their features, though observable in the past, were now "exhibited within a framework of mass democracy," because they sought legitimacy through mass approbation and because they made use of democratic formulae and modern technological devices.[4]

It has meanwhile been convincingly shown that the doctrines linking fascism and bolshevism and fascism and capitalism both were formulated long before the beginning of the cold war—unless one dates its onset in the early twenties.[5] But there also cannot be any doubt that the bipolar confrontation of the post-World War II period greatly aided the general acceptance of the doctrinaire identification of Fascist and Communist regimes as totalitarian in the West and the similarly emphatic identification of capitalism and fascism in the East. With that, as Walter Schlangen has observed, "the concept of totalitarianism (like the concept of fascism and other social science terms), stands between politics and academic science [Politik und Wissenschaft]."[6]

While Franz Neumann, much to the relief of contemporary critics of the concept of totalitarianism, writing in 1942, did not emphasize the totalitarian nature of the Stalinist regime, other Western writers increasingly did.[7] It is unfortunate that the important contributions of Sigmund Neumann, Ernst Fraenkel, Hannah Arendt, Carl Joachim Friedrich, and Zbigniew Brzezinski were to be wedged by postwar circumstances between "Politik und Wissenschaft" and subsequently challenged unfairly by radical critiques.[8] Regardless of the insufficiencies later critics claimed to detect in their work, the lasting impact of these writers on modern political thought will be denied by few. Professor Nolte has remarked that "the alliance of the theories of liberalism and conservatism, addressing at once national socialism and bolshevism, the totalitarianism doctrine,—

corresponds most exactly to the reality and the needs of the immediate postwar epoch. . . ."[9] Challenged, the totalitarian model nevertheless became the point of departure for a renewed search for viable, but separate, theories of fascism and Stalinism. The totalitarianism doctrine has not so much been "overcome," as some would have it, as it has been transformed by the insight derived from the labors of ongoing scholarship.[10] A logical division of labor, then, led to the solidification of new distinct fascism and Stalinism theories. The turning point came with the work of Professor Nolte in the field of fascism studies and Professor Robert C. Tucker in the field of Soviet studies. These scholars demonstrated that the sustained and rigid application of a general label of totalitarianism obstructed insights that could be gained by detailed studies of chronologically, formatively, and structurally distinct regimes.[11] Unlike the passionate critics of the Left, who continued to denounce the cold war conception of "brown equals red" with sometimes counterproductive severity, these two scholars advanced the understanding of a difficult epoch by providing new conceptual models and by rigorously employing newly developed analytical tools.[12] As a result, they helped fashion solid steps in the collective enterprise of scholarship, the erection of a meaningful and comprehensible historiographical structure of the twentieth-century.

In the wake of this historiographical reorientation, then, the emphasis of scholarly discussion has been on the development of new theoretical constructs of various fascisms and divergent Communist models by a generation of younger scholars.[13]

Does all of this now mean that the term *totalitarianism* has been passed by for good? Judging by some of the writings included in this volume, this is by no means the case. It was not too long ago that Karl Dietrich Bracher, the eminent explorer of Hitler's *Machtergreifung* and *System* addressed the question.[14] One of the two selections from Professor Bracher's writings on totalitarianism is included in Part I of this anthology. Sharply critical of those who have belittled the concept of totalitarianism as a mere product of the cold war, Bracher asserts that a differentiated application of the concept today is not only possible but also pertinent. Dissatisfied with the fascism theories that have emerged in the West, Bracher proposes a further development of the theory of totalitarianism, so that it will contribute to the analysis and explication of modern dictatorship even after the demise of Mussolini, Hitler, and Stalin. To this end he proposes that left-wing as well as right-wing dictatorial regimes be examined independently of their ideological classification and self-appraisal in terms of their structures of domination and their effect on the freedom, the rights, and the welfare of man. Bracher's differentiated modern theory of totalitarianism will leave behind the "passing elements of contemporary politics" and present a much more complicated picture than the classical equation of fascism and communism. By means of its "greater elasticity" it will be able to work up typologies of the totalitarian in other historical as well as in contemporary regimes.

A more limited affirmation of the usefulness of the concept of totalitarianism is found in Martin Greiffenhagen's exposition of its evolution in political theory. Reviewing the established interpretations, Greiffenhagen finds use for the concept only as descriptive of transitional phases of government evolving—as in Stalinism—into more moderate forms. Stalinism occupies center stage in Professor Cohen's contribution to the historical section of this book. The intense controversy over the nature of Stalinism in relation to bolshevism, which led to the initial publication of this essay, forced scholars also to examine more closely their presuppositions regarding the place of Stalinism in the theory of totalitarianism. Professor Cohen's critique of a continuity theory in Soviet studies, which he considers to be fostered by the concept of totalitarianism, yet emphasizing the totalitarian character of Stalin's regime, raises important questions. Is a classificatory tool other than the term *Stalinism* needed to locate meaningfully within the outline of political theory this distinct epoch of Soviet history? How is the widespread popular support received by Stalin to be explained?

If the place of Stalinism in the context of a theory of totalitarianism presents the student with unresolved problems, the "totalitarian character" of Italian fascism has been questioned all along, notwithstanding the fact that the term was coined in Italy. By pointing to the chief obstacles in the way of a full unfolding of the totalitarian state in Italy— the Church and the monarchy—Alberto Aquarone long ago made clear that the totalitarian impetus was there. Unlike the views advanced in the —sometimes passionate—ongoing debate among Italian scholars over the nature of fascism in Italy, Aquarone's exposition remained detached and, therefore, serves well to round out the historical dimensions of the problem of totalitarianism sketched in Part I.

It is not only in Italy that the scholarly debate over the nature and classificatory affinities of twentieth-century manifestations of political radicalism continues—sometimes passionately—and largely unabated. The impact of terrorism in recent years has tended to intensify the debate and to place the historical controversy into the context of contemporary politics. Examining Professor Bracher's juxtaposition of terrorism and totalitarianism, the American reader must keep the perspectives of the European political scene in mind. By insisting on the relevance to contemporary life of the concept of totalitarianism, Professor Bracher invites those who tend to "bind" it to distinct historical epochs to reexamine their premises.

As do all the other contributions to Part II of this book, grouped under the heading of "Interpretative Contentions," Michael Curtis's essay reveals the continuous engagement of contemporary scholarship in the revising of earlier interpretations. Not above adjusting his own position in keeping with insights gained from recent research, Professor Curtis has come increasingly to see the need for a common appellation in the vocabulary of political science, categorizing twentieth-century mass-movement regimes of totalitarian character.

Even more emphatic in the recognition of this need, and concerned in detail with the application of scientific rigor to the theoretical and methodological problems connected with the enterprise, Professor Gregor's essay clearly pleads the cause for the retention of the totalitarian paradigm. Detecting in it not only mnemonic and taxonomic capacities, but also pedagogic merit, Gregor is confident that interdisciplinary cooperation will advance causal explanations which a theoretical framework devoid of the totalitarian paradigm would not necessarily supply.

Whereas the "interpretative contentions" alluded to so far were marked by a spectrum of views ranging from qualified support for the retention of the concept of totalitarianism to its emphatic endorsement, Hans Mommsen's essay denies its usefulness both for the analysis of past Fascist and Communist regimes and for that of possibly forthcoming mass-movement regimes whatever their legitimization. Professor Mommsen's careful analysis of Hitler's regime and his advocacy of a comparative theory of fascism as more promising of classificatory exactness and causal elucidation clearly present a challenge to the upholders of the totalitarian paradigm. In the same vein, Professor Allen's essay depicts totalitarianism as, in the main, a dictator's boast. Basing his analysis on recent research in the conduct of daily life in a small town under totalitarianism, Professor Allen contrasts concept and reality and warns of the conceptual confusion resulting from a facile reliance on the totalitarian paradigm. Professor Mommsen's and Professor Allen's essays make clear that a general consensus of scholars on this question is not soon to be expected.

If a "breakthrough" in the apparent stalemate of scholarly contention regarding the concept of totalitarianism is to come about, it might likely come from the pen of Ernst Nolte. Long engaged in the struggle to shape a new historiographical foundation accounting for the epochal transformations of the modern world, Professor Nolte here takes a stand intended to correct mistaken perceptions of his work. Though his endorsement of the notion of totalitarianism as the opposite of pluralist democracy may come as a surprise to those who see him as the preeminent phenomenologist of fascism, his argument fortifies nevertheless the position of those who find the upholding of the theory of totalitarianism—even if under another term—essential to a meaningful explanation of contemporary political options.

A deliberately provocative dimension is brought into the debate by Professor Soucy's essay, forcing the reader to focus his view on the political center as a source of totalitarian attitudes. Shifting the scene from the three countries commonly identified as the loci of historical totalitarian regimes to France, Soucy demonstrates that not enough attention has been given to the totalitarianism of the center and that important insights may be gained from intensive research in this area in a variety of national settings. The interpretative contentions presented in Part II of this volume, then, make clear that the question of whether the paradigm of totalitarianism is outmoded has by no means been conclusively answered.

This conclusion is reaffirmed by the contributions of Part III, linking once more the behavioral dimension to the historical and political problems connected with totalitarianism. The introductions to Professor Milgram's and Dr. Lifton's work and the editor's epilogue endeavor to place the components of this interdisciplinary exercise into perspective.

PART ONE

HISTORICAL DIMENSIONS

KARL DIETRICH BRACHER

THE DISPUTED CONCEPT OF TOTALITARIANISM
Experience and Actuality

Professor Bracher's views on totalitarianism were summed up in an article published in volume 4 of the Dictionary of the History of Ideas *(New York, 1973, pp. 406-11). Taking issue with mid-century critics of the concept of totalitarianism who denounced the term as purely polemical, Professor Bracher asserted that comparative studies of totalitarian regimes, notwithstanding the denial of their feasibility by leftist critics, produce a wealth of pertinent information and sharpen a differentiated perception of contemporary political phenomena.*

A product of the twentieth-century, totalitarianism, in Bracher's view, goes far beyond earlier manifestations of absolutism and autocracy in its complete and uniform control of political, social, and intellectual life. The total mobilization and terrorist regimentation of all aspects of life in totalitarian states, Bracher holds, was "primarily conditioned and facilitated by modern industrialism and technology in the 'age of the masses,'" especially the crisis following the First World War.

Unlike the critics of the concept, who judge political systems on the bases of the ideologies governing them and the socio-economic structures sought, Bracher considers the methods and practices of ruling, the technique of domination, instrumental for any meaningful classificatory scheme.

Conceding the imperfections of an ideal-typical definition of totalitarianism characteristic of shortcomings found in all ideal types, Bracher nevertheless finds the ideal type useful in capturing the universal and exclusionary claims to power and infallibility asserted by all totalitarian

---

Translated by Ernest A. Menze

regimes. Differentiation between them, in turn, is possible if their rise to power, their self-perception, and their development in contrast to other, transitory dictatorships are closely viewed. The differences between regimes such as Italian fascism, German national socialism, and Stalinism revealed by an examination, nevertheless, do not eliminate the common denominator, described by Bracher as "absolute, exclusive ideology, legalized terror justified by chiliastic promises, control of state and society by means of force, the forming of a 'new man' to arise from such a perfect order, the negation of further conflicts, and the suppression of opposition in favor of ideo-political unity and technological efficiency, and the irrational equation of oligarchical leadership with the interests of the 'whole,' the Volksgemeinschaft *[community of the people] or the workers and peasant class."*

Reviewing the historical development of totalitarianism in distinct national environments, Bracher finds similar thrusts toward "totality" even where totalitarian goals are not openly acknowledged. In effect, it is precisely the pseudo-democratic element, present in all totalitarian regimes, which sets them apart from traditional dictatorships and authoritarian regimes.

Rejecting the simplistic equation of Fascist and Communist systems, Bracher calls for a differentiated typology, incorporating the distinctions between as well as the common features of totalitarian regimes.

The continuing debate and the effects of the ideological aberrations connected with totalitarianism on the contemporary world, as perceived by Professor Bracher, are reflected in two selections from his recent writings translated from the German by the editor.

The longer selection incorporated into the introductory part of this volume represents a historical exposition of the controversy over the concept of totalitarianism. Professor Bracher's essay linking contemporary terrorism and totalitarianism is found in Part II.

To this day, the controversy over the idea and concept of totalitarianism has lost nothing of the political actuality and scholarly import characterizing it for over half a century. The fascist seizure of power in Italy caused the first concrete formulation of modern concepts of totalitarian order and government. Its application to comparable dictatorships (e.g., the National Socialist system in Germany) and above all its use in reference also to the ideologically opposite Stalinist dictatorship and other Communist regimes, from the outset encountered objections motivated in quite a variety of ways. Viewed in the context of this historical debate, the current critique of totalitarianism, endeavoring to explain and do away with the concept as merely a product of the cold war, does not appear to be by any means so novel and original as it presents itself. It is part of a more general assault on liberal-democratic traditions and positions. This assault against the liberal-democratic state is carried out by right-wing conservative critics of democracy in the tradition of Carl Schmitt as much as by Marxist and neoleftist polemicists.

Nevertheless, now as then, differentiated application of the concept of totalitarianism appears not only possible but to the point, as long as it is used to characterize the totalitarian claims of a monopolistic—not necessarily monolithic—power structure, based on the historical and political premises specific to that type of regime. The current renaissance of a general theory of fascism, with its one-sided approach to the ideological and socioeconomic components of modern dictatorship, cannot take the place of studies examining totalitarian politics and structures of government. Moreover, the general theory of fascism slights the legitimate question as to the comparability of right- and left-wing dictatorships—a question that cannot be dismissed as a mere excess of anticommunism. This essay presents a critical account of the discourse concerning the historical and political dimensions of the question. It also undertakes to clarify theoretically the feasibility of systematic comparative analysis and conceptualization. In the process it addresses an ongoing problem of immediate importance also to the current conflict over the standards of political education.

DEFINITIONS AND CONTROVERSIES

Totalitarianism became a political term and a theoretical concept after the First World War. Although the revolutionary intensification of political domination or the conduct of war had occasionally been characterized earlier as "total" or "totalitarian," the term was applied, hence, above all, to the three radical dictatorial governmental systems of the interwar period: Italian fascism, German national socialism, and Stalinism in the Soviet Union. The major factors differentiating particularly the nationalist authoritarian systems from communism were subordinated to a general concept, characterizing the modern, radical form of dictatorship. Here lies the essential claim, but at the same time the problem of totalitarianism as a concept and as a reality. Generated in the context of a specific form and during a specific phase of modern dictatorship during the twenties and thirties of our century, the term underwent a transformation after the termination of the Fascist and National Socialist regimes (1945). However, it was especially due to the changes within the Communist systems after Stalin's death that the concept was increasingly questioned. Was it, and is it still, permissible and meaningful to compare past Fascist regimes with Communist systems still in the process of development?

The intensified doubts and controversies over the question of the comparability, or even equation, of regimes so pronounced in their contrasts was caused not least by the political scale of values and the use of totalitarianism as a polemical fighting concept. Indeed, it was preeminently on the part of those representing a conception of liberal democracy that the difference between Western democracies on the one side and modern dictatorships of the Left as well as the Right on the other was defined by the term *totalitarianism*: not the ideological "quality" but the totalitarian demands appeared to be the most decisive criterion setting them apart.

The problems of conceptualization were complicated further by the linking, since the Second World War, of theories describing totalitarianism and their critique with the confrontations of the cold war. Indeed, a large share of the most important literature on totalitarianism appeared under the impact of the global conflict between East and West: the bipolar world of freedom-oriented democratic and dictatorial Communist regimes. No wonder that many contemporary critics view the concept of totalitarianism as a polemically employed instrument, an "anti-ideology," rather than as a usable tool of political analysis.

Now it is correct, of course, that the specific political connotation of the concept merits critical examination as much as the fact that profound differences do, indeed, exist between fascism, national socialism, and communism. By the same token, however, it is also correct that modern dictatorship, in its most pointed and consequent manifestations, constitutes indeed a particularly important subject of comparative analysis. The search for characteristics common to such regimes and for a general theory elucidating their structure and operation has yielded a plentitude of relevant data and interpretations, facilitating the recognition of similarities as well as differences. It seems meaningful, therefore, to differentiate types or versions of totalitarianism, but not to reject completely the concept of totalitarianism.

The general concept of totalitarianism characteristically has been rejected, all along and most emphatically, by Communists—who in turn make efforts to use a most extensive and all-inclusive concept of fascism, applicable to non-Communist states and "capitalist" societies of the most divergent character.

These controversies over the topic of totalitarianism, governed obviously by political-ideological and propagandistic considerations, are set apart from scholarly dialogue. Scholarly dialogue proceeds above all from the question whether, and in which points, the structure and function of "totalitarian" regimes differ essentially from those "classical" dictatorships which, in the form of despotism and tyranny, have been experienced and described time and again ever since Plato and Aristotle. Most definitions of totalitarianism depict modern dictatorships in terms of a model governed by complete centralization and uniform regimentation of all aspects of political, social, and intellectual life. This tendency transcends by far earlier manifestations of absolute or autocratic rule and their capacity to control politically, socially, and technologically the mass of their subjects.

In this sense totalitarianism truly is a phenomenon of the twentieth century, differing fundamentally from the capacities of earlier dictatorial regimes. Modern industrialism and technology in the "age of the masses," their expansion and mobilization, constituting the inherent basis and legitimization of total rule, are its essential precondition. Organization, communication, and propaganda, perfected in the modern world, provide the instruments for and facilitate the all-encompassing controls, the total mobilization and coordination of the citizen's life and thought of a type—based on the coercion of terror or seductive persuasion—not experienced in history before.

Totalitarianism, in this context, is the immediate product of the crisis brought about as a consequence of the First World War. The development of fascism and national socialism as well as that of communism is connected closely with the political and socio-economic consequences of that war and the ideological confrontations caused and intensified by it. The regimes tending toward totalitarianism differ essentially from earlier dictatorships and absolutist forms of government also in that they have a thoroughly ambivalent relationship to modern democracy. This relationship constitutes an important support for each totalitarian movement and its rule; for, although they reject the pluralist system of representative democracy, they simultaneously present themselves as a higher manifestation of popular sovereignty, of the people's democratic consensus and unity.

Totalitarianism, therefore, is inconceivable and unrealizable without the democratic notion of popular sovereignty and its concrete realization in the modern state. For the totalitarian claim to legitimacy by means of plebiscitary acclamation, pseudodemocratic though it is, remains essential because, unlike real democracy, it merely manipulates assent to the exercise of power by a leader or a monopolistic party. These, in turn, claim to represent totally the general will of state and society. As different as the historical conditions, the social and national framework, and the ideological positions and ends sought by totalitarian movements may be, they undoubtedly possess significant common features as far as the use of power, the techniques of government, manipulation, and oppression are concerned. Though not uncontroversial, the efforts to determine the common denominator for totalitarian systems have helped significantly to elucidate the character and functioning of these systems.

Fundamental to all totalitarian regimes is the claim to exclusive leadership on the part of one party and ideology. The activity of rival political parties and groups is precluded, and the fundamental claim to individual liberty and civil rights is denied. In that sense, its pseudodemocratic legitimization notwithstanding, totalitarianism is a blow against the democratic creed of human and civil rights—whether it denies them explicitly (as was done by fascism and national socialism), or undermines them by manipulation (as in the case of Leninist and especially Stalinist communism). The ideological trappings of a totalitarianism presenting itself as "democratic," setting apart in particular its leftist manifestation from that of the Right, vanish in the face of this clear distinction between totalitarianism and democracy: the dictatorship of a monopoly party and the ideological-doctrinaire suppression of human rights make clear that democratic principles, fostering the free unfolding of the individual personality and the autonomy of various aspects of life and culture, for totalitarian systems, constitute a *contradictio in adjecto*.

This statement may be met by the objection that totalitarian principles of order, in the form of one-man dictatorship or the dictatorship of the proletariat, are justified by their ideological ends, aiming at a higher and ultimate mode of "freedom" for all (or consoling them with that hope). Such justification of the means of dictatorship by reference to their higher ends is part of the classical repertory of totalitarian apologetics; however, for the concretely affected individual, oppression is not rendered less burdensome by the mere presentation, in the garb of popular democracy, of a grandiosely and radically styled people's dictatorship. The actual consequence still is the abolition of personal liberties and the negation of all socio-political activities outside the regime, while the mostly utopian, ultimate end justifying oppression is raised to become the common standard of thought, action—and suffering, with equal brutality. Individuals as well as groups are meant to be integrated into a tightly knit, all-encompassing system, incorporating or preparing the future order of state and society; in this process individuals are to be made into "new men" whose assent, enthusiasm—yes—whose revolutionary dynamic is founded on and fed by a sense of ideological mission. It is a manipulated, obligatory faith in one's own greater and superior nation, class, and race whose claim to power is to be realized by any means, domestically (dictatorship of the party and the leader) as well as abroad (expansion, world domination).

The total monopoly of the party, the leading elite and the leader, of power and control over state and society, is sanctioned and elevated not only pseudodemocratically, but also pseudoreligiously. Equipped with the attitude of infallibility, these highest echelons of totalitarian systems demand glorifying veneration on the part of the masses which are being organized, indoctrinated and mobilized to this end and led, in gigantic parades and public spectacles minutely ritualized and theatrically staged, to deafening orgies of mass adulation. The aim is total consensus, manipulated in terms of social psychology to the point of exalted submission, planned in every detail by an opera buff and devoté of architecture like Adolf Hitler. This dogma of total consensus, formulated in the motto "The leader, the party is always right," aspires to solve definitively the perennial and basic problem of all government by insisting on the full identity of leadership and people.

Such a generalized fixation of totalitarianism in terms of Max Weber's ideal type, of course, can only provide a framework for the concrete analysis of empirical phenomena. But this limitation applies to most terms and concepts of social and political science. The applicability to reality and heuristic merit of such general concepts is most clearly revealed when measured against their usefulness in the determination of similarities and differences in totalitarian systems. To this end these major areas, in particular, present questions:

1. How do such dictatorial regimes come to power?
2. How do they interpret themselves?
3. How do they develop in comparison to transitional dictatorships and dictatorships in developing countries, nontotalitarian in character?

The "legal seizure of power," Fascist-National Socialist style, appears to be completely different from Communist "revolution." Nevertheless, this rather conceptual difference is diminished by closer analysis in view of the fact that, in all cases of totalitarian seizure of power, the technique of the *Putsch* associated with the *coup d'état* played the decisive role. This applies to the open use of force in the October Revolution as much as the more or less concealed and legalized terror and coerced coordination associated with national socialism and fascism (though applied more gradually in the latter case). The differences are not so much a matter of substance and effect as they are a matter of form: concealment and legalization on the basis of ideology. Much more important are the similarities viewed in the framework of a concrete sociological analysis of the seizure of power: here the incense of the revolutionary myth does not suffice to alter the facts. An approach such as this is more appropriate to the political upheavals of the twentieth century than the conventional "sociology of revolution," with its interpretation of leftist revolutions as progressive and Fascist seizures of power as "counterrevolutionary."

Unlike Communist systems, fascism and national socialism have, in legitimizing their unfolding claim to power, episodically at any rate acknowledged or made use of totalitarianism as an aim and framework of reference. The fact that Communist ideology did not, in the same manner, employ totalitarian terminology to justify and legitimize the exclusive and preemptory claim to power may indeed indicate a difference: that between totalitarianism as end (fascism) and as means (communism). The awful facts of real life, however, must render this difference academic: the citizen subject to totalitarianism is hit as hard by one as by the other, for the ends sought remain unattainable, the permanence of domination remains undiminished. Means and end become one, the totalitarian present cannot be alleviated by the nontotalitarian future. This became clear most unequivocally when Stalin was able to transform the presumably collectivist party leadership of Leninist communism into his one-man leadership, personality cult and all. That remained the governing fact for thirty years, exceeding the regimes of Mussolini and Hitler and rendering the exculpation of communism (as unlike fascism in its nontotalitarian self-perception and conduct) by the critics of the concept of totalitarianism an unhistorical bagatellization of Stalinism.

The chief problem is contained in the third great question against which the similarities of and differences between totalitarian systems are to be measured—the question examining their development, tenure, and function. But here, too, it is not the evaluation of the ideologies with the well-known major differences between the doctrines of the Right and the Left, but the concrete examination of structures of government, which supplies useful criteria. It must be established, first of all, that not only Soviet communism, referred to in terms of its post-Stalinist development by critics of the concept of totalitarianism, is marked by various stages in the development of its mode of government: fascism and national socialism, lasting only one-half or one-quarter of the time, respectively, were also marked by various stages of development. But in their case the development was interrupted prematurely due to military defeat and the violent death of the leaders, whereas the Stalinist regime appears essentially as a central stage within a long-term process; after Stalin's death in 1953, the one-man regime again turned into a one-party regime. Whether that means that one therefore may no longer speak of totalitarianism is as disputed as the question how decisive the role of the totalitarian leader is to be considered. The more recent versions of the theory of totalitarianism, incorporating Mao's China into the concept, particularly insist on the central role of the totalitarian leader (R. Tucker, L. Shapiro). Indeed, the triangular relations of party, leader, and people within the totalitarian system remain of importance even when the leadership cult is replaced temporarily (or for a sustained period of time?) by oligarchical collective leadership. The central role of the charismatic leader legitimized by plebiscitary and pseudoreligious factors, in the rise of all totalitarian systems to date, cannot be denied. The temporary receding of this component, however, does not do away with totalitarianism itself any more than it eliminates the stringent, antiliberal and exclusivist character of dictatorship as such.

The definition of totalitarianism and the use of a theory of totalitarianism, therefore, are not only based on an evaluation of the relation between party and leader, but also, and essentially so, on questions of historical periodization. One may speak of an epoch of totalitarianism limited in time from Mussolini's assumption of power (1922) to Stalin's death (1953): here the role of the totalitarian leaders and the character of their rule, rooted in the time after the First World War and conditional upon their life span, stands in the foreground. Other interpretations stress the supposedly Fascist character of totalitarianism; they either link it closely to an "epoch of fascism" in the interwar period (Nolte) or extend it to all "Fascist" tendencies and rightist dictatorships up to the present time. In an even broader sense, totalitarianism is defined as a tendency inherent in practically all modern states—that is, insofar as they strive for a perfectionist management of socio-economic crises and the efficient guidance of national development by means of the political and ideological monopolization of power, be it in the name of capitalist or socialist solutions.

Indeed, totalitarian politics may be reduced to a syndrome of characteristic features. There are above all four elements that give shape to the social and political structure as well as the ideological justification of a totalitarian regime.

An official ideology with all-encompassing and exclusive claims, resting in part on the rejection of traditional values and a demonstrative abhorrence of the past, in part on the conjuring up of chiliastic expectations of the future.

A centralized, unity-oriented, uniformed mass movement, conceived as the instrument of the most total politicization and integration of the citizens and the overcoming of class society. These ends are to be attained either through the monopoly of one class and the exclusion of all others or through the fusion of all groups in the proclaimed "community of the people." In reality, however, the totalitarian movement remains strictly and hierarchically organized, a politically thoroughly one-sided, monopolistic, and official party under strictly authoritarian leadership.

Complete control of the media and all relevant instruments of coercion is considered of particular importance. It is here that the distinction from earlier forms of dictatorship, with their less developed potential to coordinate and terrorize society, becomes particularly apparent. It is here, too, however, that the similarity of the instruments and processes used in all totalitarian systems to coordinate information, guide public opinion, and enforce total obedience is impressively demonstrated. It is not the ideological "quality" of the various regimes, but their capacity to indoctrinate and exert pressure, that provides standards to compare and evaluate their totalitarian character.

Lastly, the bureaucratic control of economic life and social relations, implemented by means of centralized government, socialization, and nationalization, plays a major role.

Of course, a differentiated theory of totalitarianism will take exception to the simplistic thesis representing totalitarianism as a monolithic, conflict-free form of public order and government: such an order is a fiction not ever reflected in historically-empirically verifiable political and social reality. The new criteria, setting apart modern totalitarianism from earlier forms of dictatorship, nevertheless are clear: an absolute and exclusive ideology; legalized terror legitimized by chiliastic promises; thorough control of political and social life by means of pressure and threats, fear and coercion; the creation of the "new man" to fit the new and perfect totalitarian order; the preclusion of future conflict by means of suppression of all opposition in favor of ideological political cohesion and effective technological function; lastly, as the basis for a legitimization of this unprecedentedly brutal extermination of individual freedom, the identification of oligarchic dictatorial leadership with the interests of the "whole," the "community of the people" (*Volksgemeinschaft*) or the "class of workers and peasants," an identification as fundamental as it is fictitious; moreover, this identification represents a throughly irrational postulate disproving, in the first place, the Marxist claim to a rational-scientific exposition of government and once again affirming the comparability of "left-wing" dictatorships even with excessively irrational "right-wing" tyrannies.

DEVELOPMENT AND SELF-PERCEPTION

The story of the development and stages of modern totalitarianism reflects throughout also the problems of interpretation and the controversies over the use of the concept in the fields of history, philosophy, and the social sciences. Conceptions of the total state and totalitarian rule, from the beginning, were fundamental to the self-perception of fascism and national socialism; the application of these concepts to Communist systems in the sense of the analogy of right- and left-wing dictatorships, on the other hand, encounters terminological problems. Viewed historically, the concept (beginning with the French Revolution), has appeared only rarely and then in the context of popular mobilization, the *levée en masse* of total war (Robespierre, Ludendorff, Goebbels). On the other hand, German philosophers of the state like Adam Müller and Hegel attribute "totality" to the concept of the state—that is, an all-encompassing quality and obligation transcending the individual and social groupings. Rousseau's *volonté générale* also reflects the notion of totality. In the end one finds it also in the expectation of total transformation or revolution on the part of Marx and Lassalle.

Such vague and general thoughts, however, were for the first time transformed into a systematic terminology in Italian fascism: the terms *totalitarian* and *totalitario* and *totalitarita* were meant to designate a radically new phenomenon that is the postulate of total unity of theory and action, of thought and deed, of compulsory organization and complete consensus within the state as much as in society. It was in this sense that Mussolini applied the notion of totalitarianism to the Fascist state, as for example in the widely known formulation in his speech of 28 October 1925: "Tuto nello Stato, niente al di fuori dello Statos, nulla contro lo Stato." This formulation went beyond a mere absolutist or authoritarian statism. Its true meaning was revealed in connection with other basic formulations used by the Fascist leaders at the time to proclaim their "feroce volontà totalitaria" and their decidedly totalitarian program. This early vocabulary of fascism perceives "total" and "totalitarian" above all as a political style devoted to the use of force, a cult of violence, a style stressing rapidity of decision making and implementation ("decisionism"), of unconditionally carried-out actions, of radical demands and of emphatically uncompromising intolerance.

Already at this point the concept's ambivalent dual character revealed itself as clearly as it did later in the context of developments outside Italy: first of all full and absolute power, comprehensively organized, secured and applied; subsequently, however, and often apparently in contradiction thereto, a political dynamic based on dictatorial decision and unceasing actions as the consequence, confirmation or modification of the unlimited control of power. Both aspects presently are part of the concept of totalitarian politics: on the one hand the totalitarian statist aspect, asserted by the Hegelian philosopher Giovanni Gentile, who was a member of Mussolini's cabinet and his dogmatizer; on the other hand the dimension of totalitarian dynamism leading via dynamic-imperialistic and destructive-terroristic policies in the end (especially in national socialism) to radically racist policies of conquest and extermination.

German national socialism, too, even if under ever-so-different national conditions, entails a similar combination of statist absolutist and radical revolutionary elements. However, whereas the Hitler regime put into being a dictatorship of the utmost radical nature, the rhetorical use and philosophical formulation of the notion of totalitarianism remained on the whole in the domain of the Italian Fascists. This was done, at first, more in the sense of an elaboration of the statist institutionalist interpretation; beginning in 1933, under the impact of Hitler's revolution and rule, the concept was articulated more strongly in the sense of the dynamic radical, revolutionary meaning of totalitarianism. The dominant role of the party as a dynamic "movement" and the continuity of a never-completed permanent revolution are at the core of the idea of totalitarianism, set apart pointedly from the traditional structure of party and state as well as from bureaucratic and bourgeois dictatorship.

Added to this must be the fact that, already in the early twenties, critical commentators and analysts compared Fascist and Communist dictatorships in terms of the concept of totalitarianism. It is, therefore, incorrect to say that one deals here with a mere manifestation of the cold war, as the present opponents of the theory of totalitarianism have it. Above all, distinction ought to be made between the negative application of the concept on the part of liberal writers and scholars, and its indeed positive, at times even emphatic use, by political movements and regimes striking totalitarian poses of their own: explicitly and boastfully the Italian Fascist, with varying accents in the case of national socialism. Hitler himself, especially during the early days of the Third Reich, preferably used the term *authoritarian*, whereas Goebbels the propagandist, as well as the regime's eager scholars of public law and government, men like Carl Schmitt, on the other hand, preferred the emphatic Italian version. Simultaneously, Communist theoreticians and propagandists were engaged in the effort to reduce the phenomenon of totalitarianism to the confrontation of so-called revolutionary and counterrevolutionary systems, identifying them in pointedly partisan simplification with either their own or the Fascist camp. The Fascist theory (and self-perception) of totalitarianism, on the other hand, clearly does not recognize the Soviet Union as a totalitarian state, but views it as a class dictatorship diametrically opposed to the Fascist idea of unity and the classless society.

Unlike the situation in pre-Fascist Italy, the idea of the total state in Germany had substantially taken shape before it was applied to Hitler's dictatorship after the National Socialists seized power. Alongside the political propagandists, there were at the time also respected theoreticians and scholars of public law and government like Carl Schmitt and Ernst Forsthoff who did much to call attention and give credence to the idea of totalitarianism in circles beyond that of the National Socialists. They saw in this idea the antiliberal, antipluralistic consequence of the parliamentary Weimar Republic shaken by crisis. The earlier and at the outset rather apolitical bureaucratic-antidemocratic concept of a strong monocratic state, then, was linked during the decisive months of 1932-33, to the impending new reality of the Hitler regime. But it is precisely for this reason that this quasi-administrative version of the theory of totalitarianism, generated outside the movement, produced only a short-term inflation of pamphlets and hymns of praise on behalf of totalitarianism but (unlike fascism) never became official doctrine. A few conservative protagonists of state absolutism in the tradition of Hegel were even suspected of playing out, with reactionary intent, the concept of totalitarianism against the revolutionary and racist dynamics of national socialism.

In structure and policies the Third Reich, on the other hand, did indeed reflect the idea of totalitarian organization, concentration of power, and ideological monopoly like no other dictatorial system. To be sure, the external structure was revealed by an apparent dualism of party and state; on one side there was a pseudolegal continuity of the legal and constitutional system, and on the other systematic revolutionary coercion and terror. This "dual state" was also in line with tactical calculations, as the resulting confusion of competencies of party and state offices reenforced, at the same time, the omnipotence of Hitler's leadership, of the supreme arbiter presiding over the "guided chaos."

Simultaneously monolithic and pluralistic, saturated on all levels of political and social life by an exaggerated form of the leadership principle, the confusing dictatorial system of the Third Reich nevertheless was marked increasingly by a reduction of the traditional political and legal systems and—behind the facade of governmental structures—the creation of radically ideological instruments of domination and destruction. This rise of the so-called SS-state was accelerated and intensified under the conditions of the National Socialist war effort. The policies of mobilization and expansion, elaborated and perfected in this system, the persecution and liquidation of entire peoples and races, the emphatically total conduct of war, were conceived of in the utmost totalitarian terms even when this ran counter to all morality and logic and had to be carried out at the expense of rational and effective policies—as in the case of the equally ghastly and senseless murder of millions of Jews.

The results of the historical experience reveal that totalitarian policy in this ultimate and excessive form, indeed does not reflect what passes for monolithically ordered planning and efficiency, but essentially consists of a system of arbitrary decisions and conflicts, controlled exclusively by a leadership that is in itself uncontrollable. If, then, the totalitarian concept of monolithic order was not reflected in reality, it was nevertheless real in the sense that the transformation and revolutionary reconstruction of state and society was modeled on the will of a single leader. Even though we know much more today, and in more detail, about the chaotic and at times improvised state of the Third Reich, the fundamental totalitarian intent and orientation, the thrust toward ideologically absolute total organization and mobilization as the basis of government still represent the most suitable point of departure for an analysis of national socialism.

There is of course the more sharply disputed question whether a similar interpretation of governmental structure and the leadership principle may be validly applied to a critical analysis of the Stalinist system, as well as to the Communist subsystems, satellite and successor regimes. Communist theoreticians never made use of totalitarian terminology to explain or legitimize the actual domination by the dictator or the supposed dictatorship of the proleteriat. But the substitute notion or claim—that of their dictatorship as representative of a more perfect and genuine form of democracy—does not in any way contradict the totalitarian character of a political movement or a corresponding governmental system. Even Hitler at times insisted that compared with the parliamentary "plutocracies" of the West, the new Third Reich, its leader legitimized by plebiscite and governed by a consensus of 99 percent, represented a more democratic— yes, a "total-democratic"—form of government, an interpretation which in the end also led to the scholarly derivation of a concept of "totalitarian democracy" from the excesses and ideological make-up of modern mass democracies as they evolved, beginning with the French Revolution (J. L. Talmon).

Indeed, totalitarianism differs from earlier types of dictatorship by its capacity to apply manipulated formulations and fictions of democracy, by simultaneously using the entire range of modern communications and technology to compel or obtain surreptitiously the consent and the submission of the masses. However, this pseudodemocratic basis of totalitarian systems ought not to be misunderstood as real democracy, as time and again and right up to this day is the case in the classification of real Communist dictatorships, claiming total democratic structure and legitimization—that type of misinterpretation leads to grave consequences: the seduction, deception, and disappointment particularly of democratic intellectuals and young politicians.

Fundamentally, both major controversial interpretations of pseudodemocratic totalitarianism equally miss the mark: the conservative interpretation by simplistically conceiving of totalitarianism as the consequence of democracy, the apologists of Communist as well as those of Fascist and related systems by praising not least, especially, the democratic quality of plebiscites and acclamations, of political mobilization and the manipulated participation of all citizens. The ruling clique's or the leader's attempt to legitimize dictatorship in action by reference to mass support or identification with the people or class, respectively, does not really confirm the democratic quality of the regime, but signifies rather the specific form of mass dictatorship in a democratic age.

All of these stipulations and controversies make clear that the problem with the concept of totalitarianism is not merely one of definition, or of excessively restrictive or extensive application. The concept's range as a theoretical concept and tool in social science and historical inquiry, rather, depends quite essentially on two questions. One, whether it is limited, in keeping with the more recent critique of the theory of totalitarianism and the disappearance or transformation of the relevant political systems, to those regimes perceiving and proclaiming themselves as totalitarian or in the process of becoming so. The other, whether the concept is applied also, as a means of critical analysis and for the purpose of comparative study, to regimes employing different terminologies and marked by dramatically opposite ideological dogmas. This latter model appears justified since it more realistically accounts for the totalistic claim to and exercise of government and for the purposeful omnipresence of dictatorial systems in action. The validity of this application is not affected by the deceptions and self-delusions of a system, whatever form they may take.

In the first case (that of limitation of the concept to regimes perceiving themselves to be totalitarian), the idea of totalitarianism indeed would not represent much more than a rather curious example of an exaggerated, overblown aspiration to power of the kind found in Nietzsche's superman. Such a concept of totalitarianism fits the self-characterization and superman pose typical of Mussolini's theatrical fascism, but it is of little value to the deciphering and explanation of a Fascist system's actual functioning, even less of Hitler's regime.

In the second case, on the other hand, it will undoubtedly be necessary to develop further the older theory of totalitarianism in such a fashion that it will be rendered fit to contribute to the analysis and explanation of modern, postdemocratic dictatorship also after the demise of Mussolini, Hitler, and Stalin. Moreover, that contribution might rest, not least, in the examination of left-wing as well as right-wing dictatorial rule, regardless of their ideological classification as Fascist or Socialist and their self-appraisal as progressive, democratic or revolutionary, in an examination of their real structures of government and their effect on the freedom, the rights and the well-being of man.

POSSIBILITIES OF APPLICATION

Since the idea of totalitarianism as a critical concept serves the comparative study and analysis of modern dictatorship, it cannot be fully grasped and defined by a mere listing of its usage and various meanings. But the majority of efforts at establishing a typology incorporating the most important elements of systems understood to be totalitarian, too, fail over the differences and contradictions revealed between the findings of historical analysis and those of systematic analysis. This is also the major objection voiced against the well-known and influential—but also intensively criticized—theory of totalitarianism, developed in the fifties by C. J. Friedrich and Z. K. Brzezinski. The rigid form of this typology, indeed, remains subject to criticism, especially the overestimation of the Fascist claim to totalitarianism when viewed against the reality of Mussolini's defective dictatorship.

Subsequently, differentiated empirical analyses of the relationships on which Friedrich and Brzezinski based their findings have revealed some factual discrepancies and led to greater caution; scholars now are wary of a too-general equation of heterogeneous sets of circumstances to further the axiomatic schema of an exactly defined totalitarianism syndrome. Quite evidently, it is impossible to reduce, with regard to their structure and functioning, complex modern dictatorships to a small number of variables. More promising approaches are offered by a synopsis and the combining, on the basis of the comparative method, of various typological approaches rooted in the evolution of the totalitarianism concept, with the findings of contemporary scholarship, in the study of democratic and dictatorial systems. A number of research designs of the fifties and sixties, in this context, still are quite useful, as for example the early works of Sigmund Neumann, Franz L. Neumann, and Hannah Arendt, more recently especially the contributions of Hans Buchheim, Robert Tucker, and Leonard Shapiro.

In the process, one will note that these historians and political scientists proceeded with less ideological and partisan distortion than many of the total critiques of the theory of totalitarianism which currently are as popular as they are short-lived. Some of these "total" critics throw out the baby with the bathwater by exchanging an undifferentiated form of anticommunism for an even more undifferentiated, warmed-over version of a theory of fascism and anticapitalism saturated with slogans. This latter theory is also applied to parliamentary democracy, while the dictatorial reality of "Socialist" systems is preferably overlooked: considered not comparable to other "bourgeois" forms of dictatorship, they are not subjected to critical analysis. Other critics differentiate on the basis of intellectual history and philosophy, in terms of ideological positions; for example, Ernst Nolte and his quite far-ranging extension of a phenomenological theory of fascism. Others, such as H. J. Spiro, criticizing C. J. Friedrich's schema in particular, focus on constitutional and sociological issues. However, like other purist attacks on the general concept of totalitarianism, they do not give credit to the historic services rendered by the concept in bringing out the novel aspects of modern dictatorship relating to political control and social organization.

A summary of research done so far and a continuation of that work will open up a wide field of study. Characteristic traits and variables revealed in the comparative analysis and systematic ordering of very different historical and intellectual, economic and social conditions must be fixed. A further development and modification of the theory of totalitarianism certainly requires the disregarding of transitory contemporary political problems; a scholarly theory of totalitarianism is not guided by a deductive, politically and ideologically determined schema, but proceeds in the manner of a genuinely empirical theory, constantly testing anew and revising its criteria in the face of a reality exactingly explored. Insofar as it proceeds to attempt an encompassing typology, it will take account of the various distinctions established by comparative studies and produce a more complex, less conveniently unified picture than the classical equation of fascism and communism, which is the product of a fixed historical and political constellation, both in its simplistic and its pertinent aspects.

The effort to reconcile social theory and historical accuracy, an effort in my judgment both promising of success and desirable in terms of scholarship, also calls for the preservation of a functional theory of totalitarianism. This holds true in the face of heated attacks as well as uncritical support which, in either case, is at times too much motivated by political considerations. It is clear, first of all, that today a neat and precise definition of totalitarianism, a definition which still was fully applied to the classical cases of Fascist Italy, Hitler's Germany, and Stalinism, no longer suffices. Rather, efforts must be made to loosen this almost dogmatic usage and to incorporate into the theory other, even though more rudimentary, forms of totalitarian politics, their prehistory and consequences, and an indication of the varying levels of totalitarian content. This greater elasticity facilitates the determination of "typical" traits of totalitarianism which, to a degree anyway are indeed functional also in other systems, especially in still-conventional or incomplete dictatorships in developing countries. Historically, for example, they may be found in Latin America, in the Balkans, in Spain, more recently in Mao's China and the North Korea of Kim-il-Sung.

The chief characteristic, in all cases, still is the extraordinary position of the leader. His rise, of course is tied to general political, economic, and cultural conditions, allowing or facilitating, or almost calling for, a dictatorial regime. But the actual character, the intensity and prestige of a totalitarian system, domestically as well as in foreign policy, still seems inseparable from, indeed completely unthinkable without the figure and capacities of the leader. So it was really not just Stalin, but already Lenin, who assumed the role of the totalitarian leader and thereby initiated the development of the Soviet Union into a totalitarian system: the essential role played by his pseudoreligious glorification to this very day confirms its importance for the Communist system and ideology, especially in its dogmatically totalitarian and exclusionist opposition to modes of socialism and communism deviating from the Marxist-Leninist brand of the Soviet Union.

The totalitarian leaders Mussolini and Hitler as well as Franco, Salazar, Lenin, Stalin, Mao, and even more lesser figures like Castro, Ho Chi Minh, or Kim-il-Sung by virtue of their extreme cult of leadership occupy, historically and politically, positions transcending every other aspect of the dictatorships they embody. They also transcend, above all, the ideologies and doctrines invoked by them at will, adhered to and dropped arbitrarily, then again declared as unalterable, exclusively binding and to be violently reinforced; this, not least, also applies to the use made by Stalin of Marxism. The role of leadership also contradicts those arguments brought forth emphatically time and again by critics of the theory of totalitarianism, asserting the incomparability in principle of Fascist and Communist systems—arguments which are justified in the main by references to radical differences of ideology. Totalitarian leaders indeed are fitting subjects of comparative study; it is they who constitute essentially the core of the governmental system and its sociopolitical and human reality, not the letter of pure doctrine subject to interpretation and application by them. One needs to think only of the disregard for and reversal of fundamental National Socialist "teachings" by Hitler, for example, in the case of his pseudoparliamentary politics of legality before 1933, or in reference to the Hitler-Stalin Pact of 1939; or one need think only of Stalin's ideology, or his introduction of the leadership cult into Marxism, and its grotesque imitations by other Communist leaders: unmistakable evidence of the dominant, all-important role of the leader.

This role also becomes apparent in the relationship of the leaders to the party. The party, after all, also is proclaimed infallible and dominant. In the Third Reich, as well as in the Soviet Union and Mao's China, the coexistence of power centers, defined as omnipotent, constitutes a characteristic source of possible conflict. However, even more important as indictators of rival power centers are the purges guided by the leader, the show trials, the cultural revolutions and the "permanent revolution" of the totalitarian system. By means of such euphemistically legitimized purges as much as by the proven tactic of *divide et impera*, the monopoly position of the leader, the visible manifestation and core of totalitarianism as such, is further developed and protected. Least successful here, again, was Mussolini, who as Duce had to reckon with considerable rival powers existing beside himself, in the military, the monarchy, and the Church which, in the end, even prevailed over his dictatorial power. Hitler and Stalin, on the other hand, in respect to rival powers within their systems, revealed equal virtuosity in devising a strategy of totalitarian leadership. They made all other powers and authorities dependent upon themselves by forcing them to recognize the leader as the ultimate source of power; even the apparently and ostentatiously omnipotent monopoly party was dependent on their arbitrarily exercised will.

As indispensable and fundamental as the one-party system may be to any totalitarian regime, it still and nevertheless is the "one-leader" principle which determines the real power structure of such dictatorial systems—and this largely independent of the question of what qualities one wishes to attribute to the aims and doctrines of the respective systems. The common or comparable totalitarian component clearly is of greater significance—and more in this context than any other—than any ideological differentiation made between leftist and rightist, progressive and reactionary regimes. One may draw the conclusion that the totalitarian character, making possible the comparison, is rooted in a constellation of power in which the leader not only largely controls party and ideology, but indeed takes their place and surmounts them. In view of the pre-eminent position of the leader, the totalitarian character of Lenin's dictatorship, as well as that of the regimes following Stalin, must also be examined in more detail and in a more differentiated manner. It also appears advisable that the extension and modification of the concept of totalitarianism, defining it in terms going beyond the now historical precedents of the thirties and forties, be subjected to the same kind of examination. This project appears to be as necessary as it appears to be complicated.

The definition of totalitarianism in terms of a charismatic totalitarian leader legitimized by plebiscite does not only involve his control over and manipulation of the ruling party and ideology, but also his sovereignty over state and law. The coincidence of radically arbitrary acts and apparent due process, manifested also in the facade of the legitimate constitutional state, is characteristic of both Hitlerism and Stalinism. Order and chaos, stability and revolution, are joined in the totalitarian "dual state," but only insofar as this joining safeguards the pseudolegal cover of the arbitrary leadership policies; there are not any of the guaranteed rights customary in the state-of-laws, nor is there any predictability exempt from the will of the leader. The rather superficial difference which existed in this regard between Hitler's and Stalin's regimes was rooted in national tradition and ideological factors, setting apart the more strongly legalistic German and the more emphatically revolutionary Russian camouflage. Mussolini, here, was less successful, much as he wanted to pursue the same course by compromising: powerful residues of monarchy, the Church and the army, in a society both individualistic and critical of the state, were in his way and in fact allowed hardly more than partial totalitarianism.

A further important criterion, setting apart totalitarianism and earlier forms of dictatorship, is found in the level to which the private life of the individual citizen is controlled and subordinated to a "new morality" of collective conduct, to the primacy of total social and political coordination. The regime quite openly and insistently demands the complete politicization of every aspect of life; its success in realizing this dimension of totalitarian control, involving simultaneously a reorientation of values, is a measure of the regime's capacity to reach its aim of fusing totally state and society, party and people, individual and collectivity into the ideal of total unity. Here, too, the leader as the ever-present yet, at the same time, distant model, plays a central role: he looks down from walls and placards and epitomizes the new man, reflecting the unity of state and party, of individual and society.

The most important function of the movement's ideology also is defined in terms of its influence in controlling the people. It justifies and even glorifies, in the name of "higher" national, racial, social, or political ideals, the violation and circumvention of existing laws and constitutions, of justice and morality. The new man and the new community hereby are ideologically legitimized and contradict absolutely all previous concepts and standards of values, again in the sense that a totality of means and ends transcends individual human sacrifices. Thus terror and millionfold crimes, initiated and legitimized by leaders like Hitler and Stalin, are sublimated in the name and service of the "whole" on which totalitarian ideology draws. The perversion depicting crime as merit, murder as preservation, brutality as humanitarianism, most excessively demonstrated in the attempts to justify mass murder by Himmler's SS, but also in the purges and deportations, show-trials and brainwashing processes of Communist systems, is part of the pathetic consequences of this modern totalitarian reorientation of values.

It has become clear, time and again, how important a role was played, in this context, by the fiction of what was made to appear as democracy. A regime legitimizing itself by reference to the total consensus of the population and, to that end, setting up "elections" rigged to yield 99% assent will, in one way or another, always fall back on the fundamental fiction expressed classically in Rousseau's *volonté générale*. In the modern version of totalitarianism it is the fiction of the total unity of leader, party, and people which is diametrically opposed to the principles of democratic pluralism and differentiated parliamentary representation. The Communist notion of "democratic centralism," too, is part of the false front behind which is hidden a "unity" extinguishing the autonomous individual. This unity, by its nature, must assert itself violently, for it contradicts the empirical reality of society in which individuals and groups are concerned with representation in various parties and the decentralization of power. Totalitarian regimes, therefore, cannot be served sufficiently by traditional methods of autocratic government, military suppression, or religious sanctions, effective as these may be in pertinent situations. Only as a government pretending to be representative of the people can modern dictatorship expect the more or less voluntary support of the masses called for, if complete mobilization and effective function is to be the result. The effort is sustained by the extensive use of modern means of communication, directed particularly to the glorification of the leader and the manipulation of the charismatic and pseudoreligious, emotional qualities of idealized models. Here, again, a pseudodemocratic fiction is a fundamental precondition of totalitarian dictatorship, the fiction of a direct connection of the individual with the leader by means of mass meetings and other emotionally charged and guided communication processes, making unnecessary (indeed, revealing as redundant to the point of insult to both sides) intermediary institutions like parliaments, interest groups, or a multi-party system. This is the basic fiction of direct mass democracy. It envisions direct participation and direct representation as realized in an identity of the leader and the led. It proves to be an always effective fiction, finding to this day much support and sympathy also in Western democracies, especially among students and intellectuals, when portrayed as "town-meeting democracy" or the democracy of soviets. This has been so even though modern history, ever since the French Revolution, the Paris Commune uprising, and the German November Revolution, time and again has contradicted it. The perversion of the democracy of soviets, its rapid transformation into one-party and one-man dictatorship, after all, has been the record of the Russian Revolution of 1917/18. The experience of the Russian Revolution demonstrates, at the same time, to what extent the perfectionist appeal to direct democratic, rather than representative democratic, structures and legitimizations, in the age of complex, technological mass-society, is not only unrealistic, but may even lead directly into the reality of a totalitarian system, by concealing it pseudodemocratically and, thereby, by facilitating its growth and giving it substance.

Taking into account the entire scope of the controversy and independent of its use (and occasional political abuse) during the era of the cold war, the legitimacy, appropriateness, and usefulness of the concept of totalitarianism, even today, appear to be clear. As significant as the differences between fascism, communism, and other dictatorial regimes may be, as far as ideological aims and social policy are concerned, the real divergences between leftist and rightist systems are far less pronounced when viewed in terms of their actual functioning and their totalitarian aspects; rather, the similarity of fundamental methods and processes of government still appears striking, now as then, even though our knowledge is tempered by more differentiated and detailed analytical data not available to the earlier pioneers in the scholarly study of totalitarianism.

To be sure, the classical systems of totalitarianism appear to be part of the past, and history may not repeat itself. But in this age of crisis-prone mass democracies, mass movements, and profound social change, some fundamental premises and components of totalitarianism remain of contemporary concern. They constitute a potential which may be mobilized by future leaders whenever social crises, the emotional need for security and order, the idealistic longing for a political creed ideologically compact and capable of solving all problems, and the craving for power and the resulting worldwide tensions become too strong. These stimuli, then, may be tied to the conviction that only the concentration of all energies in *one* power center and the complete subordination also of individual liberty—sublimated as a "moral sacrifice"—to the chiliastic visions (the "Thousand-year Reich," the "withering away" of the state) of a total movement and its quasi-deified leader will solve the problems of modern society.

In this sense the precepts and claims of the totalitarian organization of state and society are not a phenomenon of the past, due exclusively to the unique constellation of historical circumstances during the interwar period. Rather, totalitarianism, even today, is and will remain for the foreseeable future a possible consequence of and peril attendant upon the modernization process. It is a threat to nations and societies even in the second half of the twentieth century, in the era of mass democracies, superbureaucracies, and pseudoreligious ideologies. The totalitarian vision, conjured up more than three decades ago, by George Orwell's *1984*, has not yet vanished.

MARTIN GREIFFENHAGEN

THE CONCEPT OF TOTALITARIANISM IN POLITICAL THEORY

Published in Germany in 1972, Professor Greiffenhagen's essay took issue with the conceptual imprecision of the term totalitarianism *in view of its widespread use under the conditions of the cold war. Unlike radical critics of the concept, who wish to ban the term* totalitarianism *from the language, Professor Greiffenhagen set out to clarify its meaning within the context of traditional theories of government. In doing so, he endeavored to render it applicable as a classificatory tool to certain strictly limited phases and aspects of government.*

Professor Greiffenhagen reviewed what he considered to be the five established interpretations of totalitarianism. The first of these portrays totalitarianism as an extreme form of traditional, autocratic government. While the second depicts it in terms of gnosticism, the third gives a Machiavellian interpretation. Next, totalitarianism is used as an extension of Rousseauism. Finally, the concept is interpreted as strictly a manifestation of the twentieth century. Of these five, Greiffenhagen found the latter two to deserve closer scrutiny, if the concept were to be made useful for the purpose of political science as a modern academic discipline.

Examining the evolution of the concept of the total state, Greiffenhagen sees its German manifestation as derived from nineteenth-century racial and folk notions of homogeneity, sharply opposed to Western style pluralistic democracy as well as to what he perceives as the "radical democracy" of Marxism. Observing that national socialism did not transform the core of traditional German social life, Greiffenhagen determined that any concept of totalitarianism applicable to both national socialism and

Translated by Ernest A. Menze

Communist states must take account of these significant differences.

Greiffenhagen also expresses doubt about the validity of the generally accepted distinction between totalitarianism and authoritarianism. He points to the fact that some of the characteristics commonly assumed to be exclusive to totalitarianism are shared by modern authoritarian regimes. In view of the fact that ideological self-legitimization, compulsory demonstrations of solidarity, and the fusion of state and society are attributes also of contemporary authoritarian states, Greiffenhagen concludes that only a definition focusing on the governing precepts of totalitarianism as aspiring to a completely new system of values and social order will make sense. But such an attempt at an ideal-typical definition, as well as the efforts to fashion a sociology of "totalitarian societies," must account for the fact that both correspond to the reality of national socialism only conditionally and found fulfillment exclusively in the Stalinist phase of "democratic centralism."

Continuing his reappraisal of the justification for the joining, under one common theory, of national socialism and communism, Greiffenhagen presents his evidence for the authoritarian rather than totalitarian makeup of the National Socialist state in terms of the people's perception of that state and its policies and aims. On the basis of his evidence Greiffenhagen therefore prefers to discuss national socialism in the context of a theory applicable to authoritarian regimes. He is not persuaded to the contrary by those pointing to the similarity of governmental methods employed by the National Socialist and Communist regimes. Rather, he finds significant differences here, too—for example, in the fact that the Stalinist regime directed its terror against all with the aim of completely reshaping society, whereas Nazi terror focused on selected groups. To Greiffenhagen, only a concept which attributes to totalitarianism rational ends appears meaningful and useful in the study of political systems. This he finds in a concept viewing totalitarianism as always a transitional phase of government—as in Stalinism—necessitated by the tension between aspired aims and obstacles to their implementation but, in the long run, evolving into more moderate forms.

The concept of totalitarianism is today generally accepted. All encyclopedias list it. It appears without fail in specialized works of reference and political science texts. Textbooks in the field of social studies make use of it. The Conference of Ministries of Cultural Affairs (of the West German federal states) has issued specific "Guidelines for the Treatment of Totalitarianism in the Classroom."[1] However, there does not exist an unequivocal definition commensurate with the generality of the term's acceptance. Moreover, theoreticians discussing the concept lack confidence in the prospect of such definitional clarification. Though there were some attempts made, in the early sixties, to create a frame of reference for the subject and concept of totalitarianism, the observation that no coherent theory of totalitarianism had been presented up to that time still is valid.[2] The effort to clarify the concept sociologically also proceeded from the observation that the concept of totalitarianism had not yet come of age.[3]

Meanwhile a plethora of monographs examining the National Socialist and Communist systems of government have appeared. All of these studies employ the term *totalitarian*. Nevertheless, it is true that "the definitive clarification of the question "What is 'totalitarian'?" becomes more urgent "as the works examining a totalitarian system undoubtedly deserving to be so designated increase in depth and scope."[4] Whether one searches after "building blocks for a general theory of totalitarian systems of government and society,"[5] whether one views the possibility of conceptualizing an ideal type skeptically,[6] whether one at last, by and large somewhat recklessly, advances definitions, it is certain that "none of the more or less promising theories of totalitarianism have gained acceptance, and even a generally accepted operational definition is lacking."[7]

This is an awkward situation for a variety of reasons. The daily references to totalitarianism, the totalitarian state, and totalitarian regimes tend to obscure the fact that perhaps none of the currently existing political systems correspond in concrete terms to such concepts. This may have fateful effects on practical politics. Whoever employs, in everyday politics, inadequate concepts as fighting slogans, may possibly tie his own hands. At any rate, up to now, the concept of totalitarianism has been a fighting concept, and the question arises whether it ever will be freed of this polemical accent. The decrease in number, beginning in the early sixties, of theoretical treatises examining the concept of totalitarianism is due, probably, to considerations like these. Polycentrism in the Eastern Bloc and the differentiated political and social systems of the peoples' democracies today hardly allow any longer what once was called the first condition governing a scientific formulation of the totalitarian phenomenon: "The interlocking makeup of the Eastern Bloc makes it necessary for analysts of totalitarian systems and societies to look at and evaluate the Eastern Bloc, with its internal causal and functional dependencies, at all times as a whole, going beyond the consideration of historical-national particularities. At the same time, however, the historical, political, and social particularities of each single totalitarian governmental and social system must also be recognized."[8] The question whether "integral totalitarianism will prove to be a temporary historical interlude,"[9] raised as early as 1957, was countered by the suggestion that the process leading to the integral acceptance of totalitarian rule is likely to take generations.[10] This long-term development of the phenomenon of totalitarianism will be matched by a corresponding long-term development of an applicable theoretical concept of totalitarianism.

It remains to be seen whether sufficient time has elasped for commentary to advance theoretical understanding beyond a mere reaction to contemporary political conditions in East and West. After all, political conceptualization, as a rule, lags behind political reality. Those who feel that sufficient time has elapsed to make the formulation of theories possible are likely to think in terms of the period since the onset of de-Stalinization. The volatile discussion of totalitarianism carried on from 1958 to 1963 stood under the impact of the political realities of Stalinism. Meanwhile, a more pluralistic development appears possible, and a renewed discussion of the totalitarian phenomenon seems meaningful. Skepticism about attempts to grasp and classify the phenomenon of totalitarianism as such will, of course, further increase; and one risks now, just as in the early sixties, though more time has elapsed, the historical relativizing of definitions offered.

It is the purpose of this essay, first of all, to present the most important concepts of totalitarianism so far developed. However, this effort at cataloguing is guided by the approach governing the essay as a whole, examining the possibility of clarifying the concept of totalitarianism within the framework of traditional theories of government—that is, in terms of autocratic models. The concern here is not with a sociological theory of societies under totalitarian rule; rather, it appears that the concept of totalitarianism may find application within the context of contemporary political theory (though limited to certain phases and certain aspects of government). Thus classified, the concept ought to be useful even in terms of future political developments.

FIVE MEANINGS OF TOTALITARIANISM

Totalitarianism as an Extreme Form of Traditional Autocratic Government. Ever since the first appearance of the concept of totalitarianism, efforts have been made to apply it not only to modern, but also to earlier autocratic regimes. These efforts usually lead to an identification with such concepts as tyranny, despotism and dictatorship. In the preface to his *Ortsbestimmung der Gegenwart*, Alexander Rüstow asks for "the specific nature and the historical origins of that tyranny which threatens us today . . ."[11] His point of view, reconstructing overlapping patterns of oppression, permits him to classify totalitarianism as a subspecies of other forms of government. In that sense he conceives of absolutism as the precursor of Hegel's "totalitarian idolization of the state."[12] Aiming at sociological generalization, cultural sociology is apt to apply historical concepts to times in which they were not known and which, as historians critically object, do not, strictly speaking, permit of their application. Just as Rüstow speaks of Hitler's "Catilinarianism,"[13] he in turn employs the term *totalitarianism* in reference to each extreme form of oppression in history. Pitirim Sorokin applies the concept to the political regimes of ancient Egypt, China, and the Incas.[14] Franz Neumann calls Sparta and Diocletian's rule early experiments in totalitarian dictatorship.[15] Such theoreticians of international relations as Robert McIver and Guglielmo Ferrero also tend to place totalitarianism within the context of a general, historically consistent theory of the abuse of power.[16] Specialized works of reference, too, view totalitarianism as "a most extreme manifestation of the tendency to centralize, make uniform, and regulate one-sidedly all of political, social, and intellectual life."[17] A prominent German *Lexikon* describes it as a concomitant of dictatorship, "only too often turning into despotism."[18]

The effort to view totalitarianism in the context of traditional concepts of governmental theory is reflected clearly in the passage by Wilhelm Hennis quoted below. It documents the determination of the author to situate the phenomenon of totalitarianism within the tradition of political autocracy. The strong emphasis on ethical elements is uncommon in the prevailing spectrum of views:

The embarrassed perplexity shown by contemporary political science in the face of modern tyranny has made clear how little awareness there is of the ever-present threat to lawful political life. Political science had at its disposal no concepts adequately defining what was happening; as a rule even the capacity to recognize what really was evil in the regime was lacking. Of course, modern tyranny is not simply identical with what tyranny once was understood to be by theoreticians: modern tyranny, as any modern system of government, uses technological and ideological tools which, in the past, were inconceivable. But the core of its success did not lie in the way it shaped political attitudes (as implied by those who designate the regime as authoritarian or dictatorial), or in the realm of ideology (the "totalitarian state"), but in the realm of morality: the disregard for human life and human dignity, the baseness of those wielding power, the perverse falseness of the "aims" supposedly pursued by them, the moral degradation imposed by them upon the governed, the spreading at large of lie and fear, finally the prevention of even the martyrdom of the opponent by the preclusion of all publicity. Traditional political theory defines all of these manifestations with precision. The chapter on tyranny in Book 8 of Plato's *Republic* and in Xenophon's *Hiero* reveal more about the nature of the National Socialist regime than most of the sociological or socio-psychological attempts at explanation.[19]

If Hennis runs the risk, by sticking too closely to Aristotelean criteria, of missing the uniquely ideological as a chief characteristic of the totalitarian phenomenon, Karl Popper, searching for precursors of totalitarian ideology, does the opposite by calling Plato's conception of the state simply totalitarian.[20]

The common element in these interpretations of the term *totalitarian* (cited here only selectively) lies in the effort to convey a political phenomenon peculiar to the modern world by means of concepts and in terms of models no longer current in political theory. Thus the formulation of theories establishing "precursors of" or "budding forms of" modern totalitarianism is facilitated. The term *totalitarian* in each case conveys the meaning "despotic," "dictatorial"—tyrannical rule in the most oppressive sense. At times the literal meaning of the word *totalitarian* is brought out by emphasis on the intensity of despotic rule. On the whole, the interpretation of totalitarianism as a traditional historical phenomenon portrays it as rather a quantitative acceleration of autocratic excesses in the exercise of power. This applies also to Wittfogel's doctrine of hydraulic societies. Wittfogel attempts to find the causation for the Chinese manifestation of totalitarianism in terms of world history and cultural sociology. With that he endeavors, like the other authors cited in this section, to view totalitarianism under historically continuous and consistent aspects.[21]

Totalitarianism as Gnosticism. Eric Voegelin[22] undertook to interpret the phenomenon of totalitarianism in terms of intellectual history by envisioning the intellectual foundation of totalitarianism in a connection between Gnostic thought and modern ideologies of the Left and Right. The thirst for power, the systematization of political violence, and the prohibition of philosophical speculation, according to Voegelin, were the basis of Marx's and Nietzsche's political philosophies. Both these "deicides" based their philosophies on an axiomatic prohibition of inquiry, "substituting man for God" and thus making man the omnipotent shaper of his world and the most powerful, all-pervasive political ruler. Gnostic thought has its origin in the loss of that cosmos "in which Hellenic man feels at home." Gnosticism represents one of the many efforts to endure and interpret the world as the experience of an alien realm. Voegelin traces these efforts all the way up to Heidegger and detects in them fateful consequences especially for political philosophy. The Gnostics' escape from alienation through knowledge, resulting in salvation through the self, has in Voegelin's view, also produced those political systems in which total knowledge becomes the basis for total rule and total planning.[23] If Popper saw Plato as the precursor and trailblazer of totalitarian ideologies, Voegelin endeavored to discover totalitarian elements in Gnosticism. It is true that Voegelin expands the traditional concept of Gnosticism to the point where, historically, it includes the works of modern political philosophers. Whether this method is helpful will not be decided here. Rather, the point must be made that Voegelin interprets the modern phenomenon of totalitarianism by referring back to an ancient religious teaching. In the end, it remains questionable whether Gnosticism explains totalitarianism, or whether the effort to capture the ideological form of totalitarianism has led to a completely novel, considerably stretched understanding of Gnosticism.[24]

Totalitarianism as Machiavellism. Erwin Faul's book on modern Machiavellism reflects an effort to understand totalitarianism as a system of Machiavellian politics in the overall context of modern history. According to Faul it was Machiavelli who gave rise to an understanding of political conduct that made possible, in the end, the "excessive Machiavellism" of totalitarian movements. Machiavelli's view of man reflects his psychology of government, and his detailed instructions serve as the historical basis of "Contemporary Machiavellism."[25] Hitler later translated into action those visions entertained by other Machiavellians before him "only as intellectual temptation."[26] In drawing his analogy, Faul concentrates mainly on certain similarities of atmosphere between the period of Hitler's so-called seizure of power and the Renaissance: "The unfulfilled longings, caused not only by expectations of life come to naught, but also by the general demystification of the world, to which the Germans in their attachment to romantic visions seem to be particularly prone, were vented in the formation of manifold political sects. Within these sects a need for myths revealed itself, responding strongly to the illusions developed in modern Machiavellism."[27]

Faul thus tends to see in modern Machiavellism not so much a political theory as a political situation, a crisis involving the intellectual and social foundations of politics: "Viewed from the social point of view, this development appears as a revolutionary breakthrough of strictly material forces; viewed intellectually, it appears as the unmasking and reduction of ideologies. On such doubly shaken foundation, Machiavellism appears as the autonomous blueprint of power applied and the mind's subordination to it; moreover, Machiavellism also inevitably and concretely leads to violence and deception, here to be considered not as merely incidental, but as the political means tied intrinsically to a viewing of the world exclusively in terms of the 'naked struggle for existence.'" Totalitarianism is presented as the product of a cultural-historical process initiated during the Renaissance and "connected with the experiment of contemporary human existence, its revolutionary greatness and great anxiety." Totalitarian politics is "politics under the scepter of death" for, after the destruction of intellectual and institutional certainties, only considerations of power count. The fear of purges and mass arrests reflects that "disquietude of life" which points to a deeper, metaphysical insomnia. Cesare Borgia and the modern totalitarian dictators thus are brought into a parallel cultural-historical course. The modes of exercising power employed by such Machiavellian dictators, then, even over a span of centuries, appear comparable. Since the legitimizing principles of political government, ever since the appearance of Machiavellism, have become shaky, there is no guarantee of the end of modern Machiavellism even after the collapse of national socialism and the transformation of the Communist systems of government.[28] Unlike the two concepts of totalitarianism as historically continuous, presented in the foregoing, Faul conceives of it as a phenomenon of modern history and politics. Specific modes of consciousness, revealed for the first time in the fifteenth century, make their effects felt in the present. In contrast to efforts to interpret totalitarianism in terms of universal history, Faul restricts his historical interpretation of the phenomenon to the chronology of his epoch. To him, Machiavellism will clear up the problem of totalitarianism, not vice versa.

Totalitarianism as Rousseauism. Ever since the appearance of Jacob L. Talmon's work,[29] Rousseau is considered by many as the father of totalitarianism. His doctrine of the *volonté générale* supposedly provided the theoretical preparation of that totalitarian democracy implemented by Robespierre as the first totalitarian dictator. The Jacobin phase of the French Revolution ushered in the "Age of Revolutions," creating the conditions necessary for totalitarian rule. This view is widely accepted and frequently encountered in the pertinent literature.[30] In the early stages of the Communist movement, Russian Marxists themselves saw their historical role in terms of an analogy to the French Revolution. "But these comparisons, so convincing before 1917 and completely governing Trotsky's imagination even into the twenties and thirties have over the span of time assumed an increasingly unreal and scholastic connotation; today, no Soviet leader and hardly any serious critical observer would think of basing his interpretation of the Soviet present and future on such parallels."[31] The paralleling of Rousseau, Robespierre, and Babeuf, on the one hand, and modern totalitarianism on the other, is limited exclusively, as Talmon specifically emphasizes, to the Marxist-Communist mode of modern totalitarianism.[32] The notion of total and radical democracy hails from the tradition of European rationalism. Progress, virtue, justice, classless society, and natural order are concepts of the Enlightenment. National socialism, on the other hand, tied itself to the romantic countercurrent and deliberately stayed clear of Enlightenment influences, embracing a "new barbarism." Aside from the limitation of totalitarian "Rousseauism" to the leftist modes of totalitarianism (a limitation not suffered by the three interpretations previously discussed), the theory locating the origins of Communist totalitarianism in the intellectual, economic, and political situation of the French Revolution entails a number of interesting parallels. For not only the ideological implications, but also certain techniques of government (the employment of terror by Robespierre, the principle of "critique and self-critique," the function of the secret police, and the attempts at establishing a *religion civile*) may support the thesis that totalitarian phenomena already revealed themselves in that first great revolution.

Totalitarianism as a Phenomenon of the Twentieth Century. The phenomenon of totalitarianism would not have received such heavy attention had not the majority of theoreticians held the view expressed by Gerhard Leibholz in the sentence frequently cited: "The total state is *the* political phenomenon of the twentieth century."[33] The notion of precursors and historical parallels to modern totalitarianism was rejected by Stammer: "Considered as a sociopolitical phenomenon, totalitarianism, on the other hand, does not merely represent an intensification of traditional dictatorial methods of government. Notwithstanding inherent differences between various systems of modern totalitarian government, they may be called so only as long as they tend toward centralization, are based on a monopoly of power and government, and have developed, by means of a mass movement—autocratically led by a political minority with the aid of a dictatorially ruled state—a bureaucratically stabilized apparatus of government pervading all domains of society. Totalitarian rule aims at . . . the most complete possible politicization of society."[34] Compared to revolutions of the past, totalitarianism represents a "novel type of revolution."[35] The dynamics of totalitarianism, perceived by many as completely unprecedented, are reflected in such book titles as *The Permanent Revolution* and *The Permanent Purge.*[36]

The most categorical characterization of totalitarianism as an entirely new political phenomenon has come from the pen of Hannah Arendt. Totalitarian politics, according to her, is not old-style power politics, not even in the sense of a heretofore unknown radicalization of the striving for power for the sake of power, but behind their politics is hidden an entirely new and unprecedented concept of power, just as behind their *Realpolitik* lies an entirely new and unprecedented concept of reality. Supreme disregard for immediate consequences rather than ruthlessness; rootlessness and neglect of national interests rather than nationalism; contempt for utilitarian motives rather than unconsidered pursuit of self-interest; "idealism," i.e., their unwavering faith in an ideological fictitious world, rather than lust for power—these have all introduced into international politics a new and more disturbing factor than mere aggressiveness would have been able to do.[37]

The reasons given to substantiate the thesis presenting totalitarianism as unique are varied. Whereas some concentrate on ideological aspects and speak of a "reintroduction of the sacral into politics,"[38] others emphasize more strongly the changed technological prerequisites of political rule. Karl Mannheim, for example, sees in them the decisive cause

for the assumption of totalitarian forms by modern dictatorships. None of the older forms of dictatorship and planned societies manifested totalitarian control of individual members to the extent exercised by contemporary dictatorship. We know of the older forms of despotism that no one, not specifically standing in the focus of political or intellectual resistance, at any given time was as strongly under the control of central authority as is the case today. Thus, Czarist Russia comparatively never was as "totalitarian" as modern dictatorships. Even intellectual guidance by the Church of the Middle Ages, much as it penetrated the individual conscience, was not as coercive as modern thought control. The cause appears to me to rest in two essential factors. For one, in that modern means of communication and news media such as railways, the telephone and radio make centralistic domination much more feasible than earlier; the other, and more so, however in the fact of the "fundamental democratization of the masses."[39]

A significant suggestion is found in the reference by many authors to the process of "full democratization." All totalitarian regimes, so the argument goes, require at the very least pseudodemocratic legitimization.

The thesis that totalitarianism finds no comparable phenomenon in history is supported, not least, by references to the atrocity of the National Socialist crimes of violence, never before experienced in human affairs. Our language does not suffice to describe these crimes:

But which language can do justice to large-scale genocide, carried out on the basis of the division of labor? What kind of murder is that, not only suffered by thousands, but committed by thousands? Concepts taken from the penal codes of individual justice, such as culprit and accessory, do not really measure up to the facts. How would one describe the social relationship of culprits within the group of culprits? . . . . When we accept terms from the dictionary of the inhuman such as "final solution," "deportation," "selection," and "special treatment," we do so because we feel, to begin with, that here crimes more ghastly, other than those covered by traditional terminology, are defined. We have not yet found terms for the ghastly, enabling us to grasp it by designating it. For the time being there is only the gangster language of the perpetrators.[40]

The uniqueness of the totalitarian form of government, to Hannah Arendt, is also at the root of a psychological condition not known before. The totalitarian instrumentality of terror forces the individual into a condition of absolute loneliness—a condition differing fundamentally, in her view, from the wonted state of solitude.[41]

Meanwhile, the criteria determining totalitarian rule, established by Carl Joachim Friedrich in the mid-fifties, have long since gained acceptance. Friedrich shares the view "that totalitarian dictatorship is historically unique and *sui generis,*"[42] and represents "a developmental stage of political life tied to certain features of contemporary industrial society."[43] The six criteria (ideology, party, terroristic secret police, monopolistic control of mass communications, monopolistic control of operational weapons, and a centrally guided economy), having fully become part of common consciousness in the interim, together determine the character of "totalitarian dictatorship."

A comparative view of the interpretations of totalitarianism presented here in paradigmatic fashion[44] reveals that the last two, totalitarianism as Rousseauism and as a phenomenon of the twentieth century, must be given special consideration if the concept is to be rendered useful in terms of political science and applicable to the contemporary teaching of government. In the following, national socialism and its self-styled theory of the total state, together with Mussolini's theory of the *stato totalitario* as the initiators of the concept of totalitarianism, will be examined.

THE THEORY OF THE TOTAL STATE

The concept of the total state was developed as the antipode to that of the liberal state.[45] This critical attitude toward liberalism evidently was present at an early date in Germany. The substance of the concept appeared in the work of Adam Müller, who defined the state as the "totality of human affairs, their fusion into a living entity."[46] In contrast to the liberal conception of the constitutional state, the theory of the total state proceeds from the notion of folkish homogeneity, conceiving of the body politic in terms of organic substance.[47] Political life, by its very nature, has always entailed totality; insofar as the individual cannot be conceived of separately from the state, the community, in principle, has been given precedence over the individual: "The totality of the political must find its expression in the total state. The erroneous notion still is widespread that the total state must be fitted into the preexisting condition of total politicizing. This notion cannot be opposed sharply enough."[48]

The concept of the total state entails the idea of the leader state (Führerstaat). The political system of the total state is defined, above all, by its contrast to the democratic principle of legitimacy. This point cannot be emphasized strongly enough. As will be shown further on, it represents one of the most important divergences from communism. Almost all theoreticians of totalitarianism observe that totalitarian regimes, in our day, require democratic pseudo-legitimization. Strictly speaking, this does not apply to national socialism. The dichotomy of leader and followers in national socialism was intentional from the beginning. The National Socialist leadership principle differs fundamentally from Rousseau's idea of democratic government. Forsthoff made this unequivocally clear:

Each form of government is based on the distinction between those leading and those led, between ruler and governed. All forms of government, therefore, necessarily are undemocratic, for democracy is the polity essentially shaped by the equating of governors and governed. This equating necessarily must suspend the authority of the government, for such authority can only be exercised by governors over the governed. Authority cannot flow from the imminence of democratic functionalism. A government exercising its authority only because it has a mandate from the people is not an authoritarian government. Authority is possible only on the basis of transcendence. Authority calls for rank considered as valid by the people, because it is not bestowed by the people but accepted.[49]

In contrast to Rousseau's doctrine of democratic equality, Forsthoff insists on the distinction between the governors and the governed, a distinction "not only outward, but resting on real differences and factually negating the democratic doctrine of equality." Total government represents itself sociologically as "an upper class privileged to lead the state," as an aristocracy, however, not allowing of equality within the ranks. Its chain of command organization is the characteristic feature of authoritarian order.[50]

Probably not without intent, Forsthoff employed the terms *authoritarian* and *total*. Achieving a cumulative effect without detracting from their meaning he used both concepts in the following sentence. "For only a state marked by personal rule also on the lower levels of government, free in principle to initiate, but curbed by the awareness of full responsibility and obliged to the will of the Führer, is truly authoritarian and may be thought of as a total state."[51]

The total state is based on the premise of the people's political homogeneity.[52] The elements of homogeneity stressed by national socialism are strongly tied to national origins. Racial notions increasingly became the criteria determining the folk community. Forsthoff emphatically rejected democratic-egalitarian factors as the basis of homogeneity: "People, in this sense, does not stand for the *volonté générale*, not for the majority, not for the mass, but for a differentiated community. Democracy, presuming to bring the people to power in terms of the general will and the mass, in reality deprived the people of power, for the power of the people is not based on the obligations of the common will born of egalitarian principles; rather, it is based on the energies derived from the orderly relations of the component parts of the community to each other. The German people must overcome its impotence by overcoming Rousseau's democracy."[53] That national socialism opposed not only representative democracy, but also radical democracy, is reflected in one of Hitler's comments, comparing both forms with the racial doctrine: "The presumption of the equality of the races, then, becomes the basis for an equivalent presumption in the evaluation of peoples and, moreover, individual human beings. International Marxism, therefore, is only the rendition by the Jew Karl Marx of long-existing ideological attitudes and conceptions, in the form of a definitive political confession of faith."[54]

The National Socialist version of the total state is, by design, a state governed by the leadership principle (Führerstaat) and racial criteria (Rassestaat). Whatever Socialist and democratic ideas there were in national socialism initially, they mattered little in the long run. Nor were they conceived along lines corresponding to the traditional German perception of the state. The totality envisioned for this German state was one conceived in terms of the folk. Equality was based, ideologically, on "Germanness" or "racial pride." Efforts to revive the corporatism of medieval crafts[55] were carried on in the spirit of a political theory that viewed the state organically.

If National Socialist ideology, in that sense, was antidemocratic and guided by traditional German notions of organic development, there are nevertheless authors who perceive the National Socialist regime as having led to a measure of democratization and as having facilitated, at any rate, the development of modern industrialized society. "Hitler needed modernity, little as he liked it."[56] Ralph Dahrendorf stresses this "contradiction between the National Socialist ideology of the organic and its mechanical practice of coordination," observing that the National Socialist leaders had no choice but "to leave the state or to set into motion a social revolution in Germany with all brutality."[57] Viewing it in retrospect, there is no denying that national socialism, indeed, constituted a decisive step in the direction of modernity. Dahrendorf's thesis, in the meanwhile, has received additional support. David Schoenbaum speaks of two revolutions making up the National Socialist movement: "It was at the same time a revolution of means and ends. The revolution of ends was ideological war against bourgeois and industrial society. The revolution of means was its reciprocal. It was bourgeois and industrial since, in an industrial age, even a war against industrial society must be fought with industrial means, and bourgeois are necessary to fight the bourgeoisie."[58] Whether Dahrendorf's statement that "where the *Volksgenosse* prevails, the subject cannot return"[59] is correct in a conclusive sense becomes doubtful once it is realized that the socio-economic structure of pre-National Socialist Germany remained almost untouched. The revolutionary pathos celebrating the National Socialist seizure of power was not matched by real revolutionary change in the field of economics. In effect, the National Socialist version of the total state fully adopted the existing capitalist system of economics. Before seizing power, Hitler had already concluded agreements with industry and financial capital, and he did not for a moment consider initiating a real revolution in the economic realm, neither in the direction of socialism nor in the sense of a return to an antimodern agrarian constitution called for earlier during the "conservative revolution" no matter how that seemed to conform to the logic of National Socialist ideology. The core of social life was not touched. This fact is often overlooked in comparisons between national socialism and communism.[60] Nevertheless, for the development of a theory of totalitarianism, it is of decisive importance. Before this critical distinction may be examined more closely, problems of definition must be cleared up.

CRITERIA OF THE CONCEPT OF TOTALITARIANISM:
"Authoritarian" and "Totalitarian"

Among all the definitions of totalitarianism, the one most suitable for discussion, and therefore the one most discussed is advanced by Drath, depicting totalitarianism as a primary phenomenon:

What distinguishes totalitarianism from authoritarianism is its intention to introduce a system of values completely different from those prevailing in society. This is not meant to be just a side effect; rather, it is designed to attract adherents and to legitimize the regime. It is the aim of totalitarianism to realize, based on this new system of values, an order thus radically differing from prevailing systems of value. As a rule, therefore, totalitarianism is tied to a new social ideology; whereas authoritarianism, in this respect, too, is conservative, totalitarianism here is instead emphatically revolutionary. The new system of values, first of all, gives birth to new criteria of the ought-to-be; it puts up against the values actually governing conduct within a society a system of values determined by the objectives sought and by the problems of their realization. The primary phenomenon of totalitarianism, determining its uniqueness and shaping its every aspect, therefore, appears to be its aim of implementing a new system of social values substantiated even in metaphysical terms.[61]

Drath's definition essentially stands on the differentiation of *authoritarian* from *totalitarian*. This differentiation has gained acceptance in the teaching of government, especially since the appearance of Loewenstein's *Verfassungslehre*. While the authoritarian regime settles for political control of the state "without claiming dominance over all aspects of society's socioeconomic life or endeavoring to shape intellectual attitudes in its own image," the concept of totalitarianism encompasses "the entire political, social, and moral dynamics of the state. It is not a mere apparatus of government, but a creative force. The governmental methods of a totalitarian state are necessarily authoritarian. But the regime strives for much more than merely to deprive the governed of their legitimate share in forming the public will. Rather, it attempts to fashion the private lives, the souls, the minds, and the mores of the governed in accordance with a prevailing ideology, an ideology imposed by various coercive processes upon those not willing to adhere to it freely. The prevailing ideology of the state enters every nook and cranny of public life; its claim to power is total."[62] Notwithstanding the general acceptance and almost unquestioned status of the differentiation of authoritarian and totalitarian regimes, some doubts remain concerning its justification. These will be briefly mentioned in the following, though not for the purpose of suspending the conceptual distinction.

First of all, the question may be asked whether it is really true that authoritarian regimes never depend on ideologies.[63] Loewenstein himself observed that authoritarian states always also entail an ideology, for no polity can exist without self-legitimization. However, he continued, this ideology commonly is not uniformly expressed, nor is consistent adherence insisted upon.[64] It may be shown without much effort that a number of authoritarian regimes of the past and present required ideological bases in order to maintain their power.

Another frequently invoked criterion differentiating authoritarian from totalitarian regimes also does not bear out what at first sight appears to be at hand. It is the differentiation between required "spontaneous" and sustained demonstrations of political solidarity in totalitarian regimes and the abstention from political activity supposedly tolerated in authoritarian states. Research has shown that the call for compulsory demonstrations of solidarity in contemporary authoritarian regimes may indeed be very high. In authoritarian states governed by one party, political passivity, as a rule, does not suffice to prevent conflict with those in power. Whether and when the regime will find political abstinence on the part of potential opposition acceptable depends on the domestic and foreign political situation.

In the face of conditions in modern, dictatorially ruled developing countries, the third, often employed mark of differentiation, the presumed separation of state and society in authoritarian states, appears totally useless. Created essentially with reference to Franco's Spain and Salazar's Portugal, this criterion was modeled on reactionary regimes of the Right. They differ from contemporary leftist dictatorships in that, for reasons of ideology, they must face a more comprehensive restructuring of society if they are to industrialize sufficiently. The declining fruitfulness of attempts to differentiate between authoritarianism and totalitarianism is shown by Theo Stammen's study of governmental systems. After having defined the traditional differentiation he never again referred to it.[65] Instead he discussed in turn the Communist teachings of the state and government systems of the USSR, the German Democratic Republic, and the peoples' republics. Whether and in what respect these systems of government merit the general label "contemporary totalitarian Communist governments" he leaves open. Other authors completely avoid any attempt to differentiate authoritarianism from totalitarianism. Maurice Duverger thus speaks of the "Russian-type regime,"[66] and Eleonore Sterling discusses the "dictatorship of the proletariat," the "corporative state [Italy]," and the "racial state."[67]

These objections notwithstanding, the definition of totalitarianism as distinct from authoritarian regimes may make sense when it stresses, as it does in the case of Drath's definition, the realization of a completely new system of values and a new social order as the governing precept and aim of totalitarianism. Indeed, an ideology encompassing all of society is needed if the totalitarian revolution is to be justified and the intellectual foundations of a new social homogeneity are to be laid. The totalitarian model of society, therefore, presents from the outset a novel catalogue of the ought-to-be, addressing all of society.

The second distinguishing mark of totalitarianism, its coercive character, proceeds necessarily from the political aim of the planned and rapid relocation of a timeworn society into new socio-economic channels: "It is the resistance arising against a totalitarian system in an existing society, or that to be expected, which renders the system really total in the first place."[68] Loewenstein, too, wants to see the concept of totalitarianism limited to those political processes "in which the rulers impose a dominant ideology upon the governed." On the other hand, if the governed accept the state's ideology without objection, the "essential element of planned coercion," marking the system as totalitarian, is lacking. Pharaonic Egypt does not fall within the category of totalitarian regimes, because political coercion there had become part of common custom to the point "that the governed no longer perceived it as such, and it did not arouse any resistance."[69] With that the third significant criterion comes into view, the one depicting all totalitarian regimes as revolutionary. The acceptance of this precept rules out a general, historically consistent application of the concept of totalitarianism.

The publication of Drath's definition was followed by a lively discussion of the question of whether and how it represented totalitarianism in the sense of an ideal type. Drath himself claimed that the concept of totalitarianism represents an instance of ideal-typical conceptualization in Max Weber's sense. With that, the premise is established "that a system designated as totalitarian does possess significant totalitarian features, not that it is fully totalitarian."[70]

The fact that a new system of values must be imposed by force, defined by Drath as the primary phenomenon, gives the concept of totalitarianism its determinative characteristic, whereas the "secondary phenomena" do not need to appear explicitly in the ideal type. Therefore, neither "multi-dimensionality" nor the particular situation giving rise to the system are essential to the development of the concept of totalitarianism as ideal type.[71] This goes also for the formulation of other ideal types in political theory—for example, absolutism.

In his critical discussion of Drath's definition, Ludz objected that Drath's concept of ideology "is still guided by the definitiveness of Marxist-Leninist ideology and by the homogeneity of the ideological dogma embodied in the party." But ideology, Ludz maintained, is subject to change itself, so that one cannot speak of "the" ideology of totalitarian governmental systems. Moreover, the ideal type does not take into account the developmental processes of such systems. Changes in social structure bring about "variations in the application of sanctions," sanctions which, in turn, may be regarded as symptoms as well as causes of profound structural change and consequently render questionable Drath's primary phenomenon of totalitarianism. Ludz thus suggests, and I think rightly so, that a Bolshevik system is transformed to assume authoritarian features as soon as it becomes subject to the conditions governing modern industrial society.[72]

Ludz's effort to fashion a sociology of "totalitarian societies" is not essentially served by an ideal-typical definition of totalitarianism. Such a definition would have to account for all possible transformations of the regime. The ideal type cannot provide such comprehensiveness. No matter how totalitarian any given society may be, it cannot possibly live up sociologically to all the criteria of the ideal-typical definition. Ludz himself has provided sufficient evidence to substantiate this fact. The question occurs whether it is meaningful at all to create a sociological theory of totalitarian societies. Perhaps it is no accident that his essay endeavoring to do so has been his last word on the subject.

The matter looks different in the teaching of government. Here it seems meaningful to focus on the significant characteristics of a given regime on the basis of the ideal type. Political theory is not charged with exploring its subjects empirically in their totality in order to fix them subsequently theoretically. Nor is political theory able to fully account for changes in organization and in the structure of government, for the dynamics of strife, or for newly developing conflicts, not to speak of the complete restructuring of society. This is borne out in the treatment in political theory of liberalism, absolutism, constitutionalism, Caesarism, or any other ideal-typical designation of political regimes. If the field of public law and government is to retain the concept of totalitarianism at all, only an ideal-typical perception will serve. With that it becomes clear, however, that there has never been in reality a society constituted along totalitarian lines, nor a totalitarian state. In using the concept of totalitarianism, therefore, one never deals with a concept applicable in the strict sense of one hundred percent correspondence, but with only a tendency toward totality.[73] As long as totalitarianism is viewed only in terms of political theory and defined in line with the criteria developed by Drath, it follows that the concept of totalitarianism applies to national socialism only conditionally (see section IV below) and that it applies to the Stalinist phase of "democratic centralism" (section V).

NATIONAL SOCIALISM–A TOTALITARIAN REGIME?

The question of whether national socialism and communism may be joined under one common theory of totalitarianism depends entirely on the criteria set up to govern such a theory. Quite apart from the criticism thus far leveled against the complete likening of national socialism and communism,[74] the acceptance of Drath's definition represents a decision in principle against any parallelisation under the terms of a theory of totalitarianism. If totalitarianism aims at implementing, by means of coercive governmental measures, a completely new system of social values, diverging from the established social order, this definition cannot seriously be applied to national socialism. Folk and racial notions were current in

Germany long before the appearance of national socialism. The National Socialists, however, did not at all intend to really overturn, by means of these racial notions, the social order prevailing at the time. The leadership principle, anticipated by the conservative revolution, had already imparted to the Weimar Republic, in its waning years, strong authoritarian accents. The vast majority of the people welcomed this authoritarian form of government and followed Hitler into a Führer state, not perceiving it as a completely new system or an alien order of political values, because a democratic tradition did not exist in Germany. The question of how "the almost complete absence of resistance and, with that, the evident acceptance by the population of the National Socialist regime" was "possible" also permits, however, of a different answer. Dahrendorf observed that the German people followed national socialism without resisting because it represented—though not ideologically, nevertheless in fact—a liberation, a "thrust into modernity."[75] I am not very confident about the correctness of this point; rather, it seems that Hitler's regime was attractive as an authoritarian alternative to a real reordering of socioeconomic structures. The call for a leader was already current during the twenties, but in terms of an antiliberal longing for authoritarian, not totalitarian rule.

The most important justification for the classification of the National Socialist regime as not a totalitarian, but an authoritarian regime must be seen in the fact that the National Socialist movement, in principle, was "not a revolution in the sense of profound structural social change."[76] Hitler never touched the governing feature of the German economy, private ownership capitalism, nor can the restrictions due to wartime armament needs in any way be compared to the complete restructuring of the socioeconomic base in the Soviet Union. The great majority of the people, therefore, did not labor under the fear called for by the definition, that of being rerouted, under threat or application of force, from the established course of social life to a new social order and value system. German history had fully familiarized the German people with national, imperialistic, and racial notions.[77] Moreover, National Socialist ideology, as a conglomeration of fragmented ideas, was not at all capable of representing an image of sought-for social change. "All that remained was the quite vulgarized late-Wilhelmian concept of man and history expressed in the notion of the strong leader and of a form of competence unique to the German people."[78]

Dahrendorf, too, recognizes the authoritarian character of the National Socialist regime: "Notwithstanding all tendencies to the totalitarian, National Socialist Germany in 1938 was still marked by authoritarian features of equal intensity, including particularly the unprotesting indifference of the many. Coordination was the prevalent tendency, it is true, but up to the beginning of the wars of conquest it surely was not consistently reflected in reality."[79] The war, however, brought to the fore in all belligerent states certain totalitarian tendencies characteristic, in the sense of "total mobilization," of modern war.

National socialism, therefore, ought preferably to be discussed within the context of a theory applicable to authoritarian regimes. This proposition appears to be contradicted by the far-reaching similarities in the methods of government in the Communist and the National Socialist regimes. Those who, with Buchheim, consider it a merely formalistic viewpoint "to attribute more significance to the differentiation of political movements than to that of governmental forms"[80] will continue to parallel these two systems of government and thereby, to a certain extent, identify them with each other. Considerations of the social psychology of individuals living in such states are also likely to reveal similarities rather than differences. Individual autobiographies written by people who suffered under both regimes, however, also reveal interesting differences.[81] Psychological studies also reveal rather a parallelizing tendency: "The extremely prejudiced person tends toward psychological totalitarianism, something which seems to be almost a microcosmic image of the totalitarian state at which he aims."[82]

However, once Friedrich's criteria of the prevalence of ideology, of the one-party state, the secret police using terrror, the monopolies over communications and operational weapons, and of a centrally directed economy are applied, the observant critic finds significant differences even in the methods of government. The use of terror may serve as an example. Whereas Communist terror served the coercive reeducation of an entire people, National Socialist terror was directed against the Jews; it therefore lacked the intent to alter the manner of human conduct: "No one will be able in all seriousness to relate the persecution of the Jews by national socialism, unparalleled in extent and effect and constituting undoubtedly a significant part of its system of terror, to any of the phenomena governing the Soviet system, little as that system, in turn, shrinks from the destruction of humans. National socialism revealed a measure of the inhuman, of an anonymous, satanical will to exterminate human beings retaining, in its specific style of bureaucratic perfection and in its ghastly results, a uniqueness transcending by far even the extent of cruelties during the wars in China and the Spanish Civil War."[83] In reference to the most important instruments of terror, the Gestapo and S.D., the Cheka and G.P.U., and later M.V.D., too, Schulz feels, notwithstanding undeniable similarities, that there are sufficient differences "warning us to refrain from summarily identifying the Soviet institution, tied to the tradition of the czarist secret police, the Okhrana, with its widely distributed system of informers, with that of National Socialist Germany."[84] In view of the softening of massively coercive methods in the Eastern European Bolshevik systems and in the USSR, Siegfried Jenkner suggests that a theory of totalitarian government based centrally on the element of terror loses credibility.[85] As far as the criterion of the centrally directed economy is concerned, an identification of National Socialist Germany, governed by private ownership capitalism, with the radically Socialist system governing the Soviet Union cannot in any way be defended.

The National Socialist system of government was characterized by a measure of pragmatism, the extent of which has been confirmed time and again by recent researches.[86] Given the degree to which the interests of the National Socialist leadership were governed by considerations of foreign policy rather than domestic political goals, the National Socialist state was not suited to bring about a totalitarian transformation of society. Such a transformation was also impossible even in terms of ideology. Since homogeneity was defined not in terms of a common goal, but in terms of folk origins, the end sought could only be the restoration of ethnic and racial purity, not the shaping of a fundamentally different form of society. Operating within a framework of ideas based on historicist, organicist, and racial notions, national socialism was unable to effect a totalitarian transformation of society in the sense of developing democratic elements.[87]

A number of authors endorse the thesis articulated by Herbert Marcuse in his noted essay on liberalism and the totalitarian conception of the state: "The transformation from the liberal to the total-authoritarian state takes place on the foundation of an unchanging social order. In reference to this unchanging economic basis, it may be said that liberalism 'creates' the total-authoritarian state out of itself, as self-consummation on a higher stage of development. The total-authoritarian state brings with it the organization and theory of society corresponding to the monopoly stage of capitalism."[88] The thesis has much to say from various points of view[89] not of concern here. Of significance in the context of this essay is the insight gained from it that the National Socialist "revolution" does not meet the conditions set by Drath in his definition of totalitarian revolution.

TOTALITARIANISM AS A PHASE OF DEMOCRATIC CENTRALISM

A rebuilding of society—carried out on the basis of public policy— measures up to Drath's definition of totalitarianism in action, when such a compulsory rebuilding effects simultaneously the ideological and the economic foundations of the society in question. Viewed in terms of its aims, communism consistently measures up to the premises of such a total rebuilding. In the preface to the English edition of the *Communist Manifesto* (1888), Engels wrote: "The section of the working class convinced of the insufficiency of mere political transformations and insisting on *the necessity of a total transformation of society*, that section at the time called itself Communist."[90] The most significant example of such a totalitarian transformation is found to this day in Stalinism. All authors agree, therefore, that Stalinism represents a form of totalitarianism. With the end of the Stalinist epoch, however, the viewpoint representing this totalitarianism as a historical interlude has gained preponderance.[91] Considering the question in general, Ludz suggested that the analysis examining totalitarianism on the basis of the Stalinist model has fulfilled its function in historical and political terms.[92] The declining cohesiveness of the Soviet Bloc, the beginning of liberalization in economic life and other changes and dynamic trends within the Soviet system no longer permit, in the view of many authors, continued references to totalitarianism as such or, at the least, make necessary a significant broadening of the concept.[93]

Conceiving of the Stalinist epoch as "the quarter century from the end of the N.E.P., the transition to centralized planning and enforced collectivization (toward the end of the twenties) to Stalin's death (1953)," Werner Hofmann arrived at this definition: "Stalinism, first of all, must be understood as representative of a society openly in transition to socialism, guided excessively by the use of force in domestic and foreign affairs." The three lasting historical achievements of Stalinism, notwithstanding the terror of the epoch, were seen by Hofmann as "(1) the industrialization of the entire country; (2) the corresponding transformation of society, bringing not only many millions of Muzhiks vegetating near the level of animals to the perimeter of industrial civilization, but also opening to that doubly oppressed half of humanity, to women, a new world of active development; (3) the cultural revolution transforming a people of illiterates, in the briefest possible time, into the vehicles of a historically novel conception of education."[94]

If a concept of totalitarianism usable in the field of political science, that is a value-free concept, is to be arrived at, it is urgently necessary that totalitarianism first of all be understood in its own terms. "Only an 'imminent' critique of Stalinism promises results. It must proceed from the Marxian theory of the 'proletarian dictatorship,' that is from the intentions, aims and expectations of those who made the claim to consciously shape society."[95] This demand, in the meantime, is gaining greater and greater acceptance. No doubt, the concept of totalitarianism was developed initially to serve as the opposite of that of pluralistic democracy: "Totalitarianism, however, also entails a political-ideological principle; it also calls for political alternatives, commitment to opposition on the basis of principle, an opposition which is irreconcilable and leaves nothing but consequent rejection. This concept embodies the horrible image of a society afflicted by the disease of evil."[96] But the concept becomes significant in terms of a useful contemporary theory of government only when simplistic anti-Communist implications are dropped. Once the historical manifestation of Stalinism is understood as "the fundamental tension between the Marxian teaching of future society and the conditions of its implementation,"[97] a determining characteristic of totalitarianism comes into view: the intensified application of political coercion serves a future political end and is not an end in itself. Here is found a significant difference from national socialism. Its tools of coercion, ideologically and in practice, were permanent fixtures, aiming less at the "reeducation" of the people than a differentiation, in principle, between the rulers and the ruled. A concept of totalitarianism based on national socialism would thereby assume a tautological meaning: its *raison d'être* would be found in itself. "The struggle against the freedom and dignity of the individual, then, turns out to be the substance, and all declared purposes (liberation of the people or of the class, elimination of influences destructive of culture, keeping step with worldwide developments, etc.) are revealed as mere facade. Totalitarianism understood in these terms may be denied the special 'sympathy' that is, according to the teaching of classical German historiography, a necessary precondition of objectivity, in that it enables the observer to recognize in the observed the fulness and identity of the human. For the adversary is found not really in the will of a few men, but in the inexorable coerciveness of an antihuman system."[98]

The concept of totalitarianism viewed not tautologically but—in a broad sense—as guided rationally by ends, leads to the realization that totalitarian phases necessarily are phases of transition, developmental epochs, not representative of a permanent state of affairs. It is therefore problematical to speak of totalitarian "systems of government," if one attributes to such systems, in terms of political theory, together with their general characteristics, a degree of permanence. Totalitarianism, unlike other dictatorships, by its nature aims at self-disintegration. It carries within itself the germ of self-destruction. This applies, as indicated, only to the so-called leftist mode of totalitarianism, to which alone we would like to reserve this concept, in distinction to the rather authoritarian Führer and "racial" state which, from the outset, pledged its brutal rule as permanent and did not know even the beginnings of democratic self-government. Stalinism, on the other hand, not only ideologically, but also in practice on the lower levels of political decision making, never completely abandoned the element of democratic policy formation. In order to avoid semantic confusion, therefore, a restrictive use of the concept may be recommended: that is to say, it may be applied in terms of totalitarian phases, methods, and phenomena, and totalitarian ideology may be viewed as the inaugurator, the totalitarian party as the motor of socio-economic change.

Once totalitarianism is conceived of along these lines, the connection between democracy and totalitarianism appears as a necessary relationship. Even if democracy and totalitarianism occupy, in the eyes of many, the opposite ends on the scale of political alternatives,[99] some authors nevertheless point to the necessity of democratic legitimization in totalitarian regimes.[100] However, such democratic legitimization can be valid only in Socialist regimes, not in Fascist regimes developing their concept of the total state—be it in their bourgeois or in their radical mode of existence—in terms critical of democracy. Whoever sets up a thorough transformation of society as a political end can do so only if this end is justified democratically—that is, as serving simultaneously society and the individual and sought by the entire body politic. Of the initially cited concepts of totalitarianism, only "Rousseauism" and "the phenomenon of the twentieth century" hit the mark, because only they manifest the radical democratic implications as determining factors. A conservative transformation of society, in this "age of revolution" appears as a contradiction in itself, and Japan, the one and only precedent running counter to the trend, is not likely to find repetition in our day. In view of increased political enlightenment, owing to the steadily intensifying flow of information, total political involvement may be demanded only if legitimized democratically and not without reference to the people's social needs. In the foreseeable future, political homogeneity will always encompass the idea of and demand for democratic equality.

STEPHEN F. COHEN

BOLSHEVISM AND STALINISM

*Professor Cohen's essay was first published in 1977 in a volume on Stalinism, edited by Robert C. Tucker (*Stalinism: Essays in Historical Interpretation, *New York, 1977) which, in turn, grew out of an international symposium held in Italy in the previous year. The inclusion of Professor Cohen's essay in this volume so soon after the original publication was called for by its particular relevance to the reappraisal of totalitarianism, going beyond the scholarly controversy over the nature of Stalinism. Representing an important contribution to the comparative study of communism, this essay also has much critical to say regarding the viability of a theory of totalitarianism incorporating both Communist and Fascist systems. In effect, Professor Cohen's sharp distinction between Stalinism and the phases of the Soviet regime preceding and following it made a more searching reappraisal of the problem of totalitarianism necessary. That the comparative study of Communist systems called for by Professor Tucker has not eliminated the theory of totalitarianism was argued by, among others, Leszek Kolakowski, in his contribution to the same volume (pp. 283-98). Professor Kolakowski holds that not only Stalinism, but Russian communism on the whole is inherently totalitarian, that there is indeed continuity from Marx to Lenin to Stalin, and that only a system entailing state control of the means of production is fully suitable to realize the totalitarian principle.*

Professor Cohen sharply disagrees with Kolakowski's contention that there is fundamental continuity of totalitarian intention and practice throughout the evolution of the Soviet system. Cohen sets out to discredit the scholarly axiom of Stalinism as the inevitable outcome of bolshevism. For Professor Cohen, the continuity theory distorts Soviet history; it prevents us from understanding the history, dynamics, and social consequences of Stalinism as a distinct phenomenon, and it clouds our perception of earlier and current Soviet affairs. Professor Cohen observes that the theory of totalitarianism, as evolved by Western scholars, in effect has strengthened the continuity thesis in Soviet studies by interpreting Stalin's totalitarianism as the inevitable offspring, in intensified form, of the Bolshevik totalitarianism of the Russian revolution.

Reviewing the emergence of views disputing the continuity thesis, Cohen feels that the impact of these studies so far has been limited. The fundamental difference of Stalinism—that is, of the Soviet regime after 1929—from the phases preceding and following it, in terms of the extraordinary excesses of sustained repression, of terror over millions—this difference still is obscured by the insistence of scholars to see it merely as an acceleration of Soviet authoritarianism before 1929, or even in terms of the presumably dominant autocratic streak in Russian history throughout the centuries.

Much of Professor Cohen's essay is devoted to the task of marshaling evidence for his perception of Stalinist politics as fundamentally different from the phases of the Soviet system preceding and following it. If the theory of totalitarianism, then, has helped to obscure the real nature of Stalinism, that nature still is marked by the characteristic commonly associated with and described by that term. Given Professor Cohen's determination to avoid the totalitarian label in describing the Stalinist system, the question of the manifestation of similar characteristics by Fascist regimes nevertheless is raised. Moreover, the question of what explains the broadly based popular support of Stalinism, briefly alluded to by Professor Cohen in his conclusions and discussed in a broader context in Part III of this volume, certainly suggests the need for a comparative examination of Fascist and Communist systems, even if they are not classified under one common concept.

Every great revolution puts forth, for debate by future scholars and partisans alike, a quintessential historical and interpretative question. Of all the historical questions raised by the Bolshevik revolution and its outcome, none is larger, more complex, or more important than that of the relationship between bolshevism and Stalinism.

It is, most essentially and generally, the question of whether the original Bolshevik movement that predominated politically for a decade after 1917, and the subsequent events and social-political order that emerged under Stalin in the 1930s, are to be interpreted in terms of fundamental continuity or discontinuity. It is also a question that necessarily impinges upon, and shapes the historian's perspective on, a host of smaller but critical issues between 1917 and 1939. With only slight exaggeration, one can say to the historian of these years: Tell me your interpretation of the relationship between bolshevism and Stalinism, and I will tell you how you interpret almost all of significance that came between. Finally, it is—or it has been—a political question. Generally, apart from Western devotees of the official historiography in Moscow, the less empathy a historian has felt for the revolution and bolshevism, the less he has seen meaningful distinctions between bolshevism and Stalinism.

A reader unfamiliar with Western scholarly literature on Soviet history would therefore reasonably expect to find it full of rival schools and intense debate on this central issue. Not only is the question large and complex, but similar ones about other revolutions—the relationship of Bonapartism to 1789 being an obvious example—have provoked enduring controversies. Still more, the evidence seems contradictory, even bewildering. If nothing else there is the problem of interpreting Stalin's "revolution from above" in the 1930s, an extraordinary decade beginning with the abrupt reversal of official policy and the brutal collectivization of 125 million peasants, witnessing far-reaching revisions of official tenets and sentiments, and ending with the official destruction of the original Bolsheviks, including the founding fathers and their historical reputations.

All the more astonishing, then, is the fact that the question has produced very little dispute in our scholarship. Indeed, during the great expansion of academic Soviet studies (I speak here mainly of the Anglo-American school) between the late 1940s and 1960s, a remarkable consensus of interpretation formed on the subject of bolshevism and Stalinism. Surviving various methodologies and approaches, the consensus posited an uncomplicated conclusion: No meaningful difference or discontinuity was seen between bolshevism and Stalinism, which were viewed as being fundamentally the same, politically and ideologically. Inasmuch as the two were distinguished (which was neither frequent nor systematic since the terms *Bolshevik*, *Leninist*, and *Stalinist* were used interchangeably), it was said to be only a matter of degree resulting from changing circumstances and necessary adaptation. Stalinism, according to the consensus, was the logical, rightful, triumphant, and even inevitable continuation, or outcome, of bolshevism. For twenty years this historical interpretation was axiomatic in virtually all our major scholarly works.[1] It prevails even today.

The purpose of this essay is to reexamine this scholarly axiom, to suggest that it rests upon a series of dubious formulations, concepts, and interpretations, and to argue that, whatever its insights, it obscures more than it illuminates. Such a critique is long overdue for several reasons.

First, the view of an unbroken continuity between bolshevism and Stalinism has shaped scholarly thinking about all the main periods, events, causal factors, actors, and alternatives during the formative decades of Soviet history. It is the linchpin of a broader consensus, also in need of. critical reexamination, about what happened, and why, between 1917 and 1939.[2] Second, the continuity thesis has largely obscured the need for study of Stalinism as a distinct phenomenon with its own history, political dynamics, and social consequences.[3] Finally, it has strongly influenced our understanding of contemporary Soviet affairs. Viewing the Bolshevik and Stalinist past as a single undifferentiated tradition, many scholars have minimized the system's capacity for reform in the post-Stalin years. Most of them apparently share the view that Soviet reformers who call upon a non-Stalinist tradition in earlier Soviet political history will find there only "a cancerous social and political organism gnawed by spreading malignancy."[4]

Two disclaimers are in order. A single essay cannot explore fully all the dimensions and aspects of this long-standing interpretation. I can do so here only elliptically, with the purpose of raising critical questions rather than providing adequate answers. Nor do I wish to devalue the many important scholarly works which adhere to the continuity thesis. Indeed, it is testimony to their enduring value that many contain rich materials to refute it.

The history and substance of the continuity thesis warrant closer examination. Controversy over the origins and nature of Stalin's spectacular policies actually began in the West early in the 1930s.[5] For many years, however, it remained a concern largely of the political Left, especially anti-Stalinist Communists, most notably Trotsky. In the mid-1930s, after an initial period of inconclusive and contradictory statements, the exiled oppositionist developed his celebrated argument that Stalinism was not the fulfillment of bolshevism, as was officially proclaimed, but its "Thermidorian negation" and "betrayal." By 1937, Trotsky could add: "The present purge draws between bolshevism and Stalinism . . . a whole river of blood."[6]

Unequivocal, though somewhat ambiguous in its reasoning, Trotsky's charge that Stalinism represented a counter-revolutionary bureaucratic regime "diametrically opposed" to bolshevism became the focus of an intense debate among Western radicals, and among Trotskyists (and lapsed Trotskyists) themselves. The discussion, which continues even today, suffered from an excess of idiomatic Marxist labeling and ersatz analysis— Was the Stalinist bureaucracy a new class? Was Stalin's Russia capitalist, state capitalist, Themidorian, Fructidorian, Bonapartist, still Socialist? —and from some understandable reluctance, even on the part of anti-Stalinists, to tarnish the Soviet Union's legitimacy in the confrontation with Hitlerism.[7] Nonetheless, the debate was interesting and has been unduly ignored by scholars; it anticipated several arguments, favoring both discontinuity and continuity, that later appear in academic literature on bolshevism and Stalinism.[8]

Academic commentary on the subject began in earnest only after the Second World War, with the expansion of professional Soviet studies. The timing is significant, coinciding with the high tide of Stalinism as a developed system in the Soviet Union and Eastern Europe, and with the onset (or resumption) of the cold war. This may help explain two aspects of the continuity thesis that are not easily documented but seem inescapable. One is the dubious logic, noted by an early polemicist in the dispute, that "Russian communism *had* to turn out as it has because it now can be seen to have, in fact, turned out as it has."[9] The other is that early academic works were, as a founder of Russian studies once complained, "too often written in the atmosphere of an intense hatred of the present Russian regime."[10] These perspectives undoubtedly contributed to the scholarly view that the evils of contemporary Stalinist Russia were predetermined by the uninterrupted "spreading malignancy" of Soviet political history since 1917.

The theory of a "straight line" between bolshevism (or Leninism, as it is regularly mislabeled) and major Stalinist policies has been recently popularized anew by Aleksandr Solzhenitsyn.[11] But it has been a pivotal interpretation in academic Soviet studies for many years, as illustrated by a few representative statements.

Michael Karpovich: "Great as the changes have been from 1917 to the present, in its fundamentals Stalin's policy is a further development of Leninism." *Waldemar Gurian*: "All basic elements of his policies were taken over by Stalin from Lenin." *John S. Reshetar*: "Lenin provided the basic assumptions which—applied by Stalin and developed to their logical conclusion—culminated in the great purges." *Robert V. Daniels*: "Stalin's victory . . . was not a personal one, but the triumph of a symbol, of the individual who embodied both the precepts of Leninism and the techniques of their enforcement." *Zbigniew K. Brzezinski*: "Perhaps the most enduring achievement of Leninism was the dogmatization of the party, thereby in effect both preparing and causing the next stage, that of Stalinism." *Robert H. McNeal*: "Stalin preserved the Bolshevik tradition" and approached the "completion of the work that Lenin had started." *Adam B. Ulam*: Bolshevik Marxism "determined the character of post-revolutionary Leninism as well as the main traits of what we call

Stalinism." (Elsewhere Ulam says of Lenin: "His own psychology made inevitable the future and brutal development under Stalin.") *Arthur P. Mendel*: "With few exceptions, these attributes of Stalinist Russia ultimately derive from the Leninist heritage. . . ." *Jeremy R. Azrael*: "The 'second revolution' was, as Stalin claimed, a legitimate extension of the first." The recitation could continue; but finally *H. T. Willets* confirms that non-Soviet scholars regard Stalinism "as a logical and probably inevitable stage in the organic development of the Communist Party."[12]

What is being explained and argued in this thesis of "a fundamental continuity from Lenin to Stalin" should be clear.[13] It is not merely secondary features, but the most historic and murderous acts of Stalinism between 1929 and 1939, from forcible wholesale collectivization to the brutal incarceration or execution of tens of millions of people. All this, it is argued, derived from the political—that is, the ideological, programmatic, and organizational—nature of original bolshevism.[14] The deterministic quality of this argument is striking, as is its emphasis on a single causal factor. Characteristic of our scholarship on Soviet history generally, social and political development after 1917 is explained almost exclusively by the nature of the party regime and its aggression upon a passive, victimized society. Authentic interaction between party-state and society is ignored. Not surprisingly, the literature of academic Soviet Studies contains little social history or real social studies; it is mostly regime studies.

None of this is wholly explicable apart from the "paradigm" that dominated Soviet studies for so many years. Much has been written in recent years critical of the "totalitarianism" approach in terms of political science. But its unfortunate impact on our historiography has gone relatively unnoticed. In addition to obscuring the subject by using *totalitarianism* as a synonym for Stalinism, the approach contributed to the continuity thesis in two important ways.

While most Western theorists of Soviet "totalitarianism" saw Stalin's upheaval of 1929-33 as a turning point, they interpreted it not as discontinuity but as a continuation, culmination, or "breakthrough" in an already ongoing process of creeping "totalitarianism." Thus Merle Fainsod's classic summary: "Out of the totalitarian embryo would come totalitarianism full-blown."[15] As a result, there was a tendency to treat the whole of Bolshevik and Soviet history and policies before 1929 as merely the antechamber of Stalinism, as half-blown "totalitarianism." The other contribution of the approach, with its deterministic language of "inner totalitarian logic," was to make the process seem not just continuous, but inevitable. To quote one of many examples, Ulam writes: "After its October victory, the Communist Party began to grope its way toward totalitarianism." He adds: "The only problem was what character and philosophy this totalitarianism was to take."[16]

The continuity thesis was not the work of university scholars alone. A significant role was played by the plethora of intellectual ex-Communists (Solzhenitsyn being among the more recent) whose intellectual odyssey carried them first away from Stalinism, then bolshevism-Leninism, and finally Marxism. As their autobiographical thinking developed, once-important distinctions between the first two, and sometimes all three, faded. Armed with the authority of personal experience (though often far from Russia) and conversion, lapsed Communists testified to the "straight line" in assorted ways. Some became scholarly historians of "totalitarianism."[17] Others, including James Burnham and Milovan Djilas, produced popular theories presenting Soviet communism in a different light—as a new class or bureaucratic order. But they, too, interpreted the Stalinist 1930s—the victorious period of the new class (or bureaucracy)— as the "continuation" and "lawful . . . offspring of Lenin and the revolution."[18] Historiographically, their conception differed chiefly in terminology: an unbroken continuity from half-blown to full-blown new class or ruling bureaucracy. Finally, there was the unique contribution of Arthur Koestler, whose novel *Darkness at Noon* presented Stalin's annihilation of the original Bolsheviks as the logical triumph of bolshevism itself.[19] The continuity thesis was fulsome, the consensus complete.

Just how complete is indicated by the two major historians whose work otherwise fell well outside the academic mainstream—E. H. Carr and Isaac Deutscher. Neither shared the mainstream antipathy to bolshevism: Deutscher was a partisan of the revolution, and Carr viewed it with considerable empathy. Both presented very different perspectives on many aspects of Soviet history.[20] And yet both, for other and more complex reasons, saw a fundamental continuity between bolshevism and Stalinism. Carr's great *History of Soviet Russia* concludes before the Stalin years. But his extended treatment of 1917-29, and the alternatives to Stalinism, is consistent with his early judgment that without Stalin's revolution from above, "Lenin's revolution would have run out in the sand. In this sense Stalin continued and fulfilled Leninism. . . ."[21]

Deutscher's views on the subject were more complicated and interesting, partly because he, almost alone, made it a central concern in his historical essays and biographies of Stalin and Trotsky. He carefully distinguished between original bolshevism and Stalinism. He described major discontinuities, even a "chasm between the Leninist and Stalinist phases of the Soviet regime," and he was an implacable critic of scholars who imagined a "straight continuation" between the two. On balance, however, because the nationalized foundations of socialism were preserved, because Stalin's regime had carried out the revolutionary goal of modernizing Russia, and because the Bolshevik alternative (Trotskyism for Deutscher) seemed hopeless in the existing circumstances of the 1920s, Deutscher believed that Stalinism "continued in the Leninist tradition. . . ." Despite Stalinism's repudiation of cardinal Bolshevik ideas (chiefly internationalism and proletarian democracy, according to Deutscher) and grotesque bureaucratic abuse of the Bolshevik legacy, the "Bolshevik idea and tradition remained, through all successive pragmatic and ecclesiastical re-formulations, the ruling idea and the dominant tradition of the Soviet Union."[22]

In short, for all their other disagreements, an "implicit consensus" on an "unbroken continuity of Soviet Russian history from October 1917 until Stalin's death" joined the mainstream scholarship and the counter-tradition represented by Carr and Deutscher.[23] On this issue at least, the only dispute seemed to be whether the inexorable march of Stalinism should be dated from 1902 and the writing of Lenin's *What Is to Be Done?*, October 1917 and the subsequent abolition of the Constituent Assembly, 1921 and the ban on party factions, or 1923 and Trotsky's first defeat.

Scholarly consensus, even in Soviet studies, is unnatural and impermanent. The first sustained revision of the historiography of the reigning "totalitarianism" school came in the early 1960s from mainstream scholars who looked at Stalinism in the broader perspective of underdeveloped societies and modernization. Their achievements are not to be minimized. They began to see Stalinism in terms of Russian history and social change, and as being historically limited. But rather than challenge the continuity thesis, they embraced, or reformulated, it. Stalin's social policies of the 1930s—sometimes including even the purges—were interpreted as *the* Bolshevik (or Communist) program of modernization, functional in the context of Russia's backwardness and the party's modernizing role, and thus the "logical conclusion" of 1917.[24] In a kind of amended version of the "totalitarianism" view, Stalinism was portrayed as full-blown bolshevism in its modernizing stage.

A direct challenge to many aspects of the continuity thesis has finally developed in the last few years. Benefiting from the availability of new Soviet materials, the scholars involved are less dependent on a single approach than on a critical reexamination of Soviet history and politics from 1917 onward. But although these few revisionist books have been reviewed respectfully,[25] their impact on scholarly thinking evidently remains limited. The academic consensus on bolshevism and Stalinism is no longer intact. But the great majority of scholars, including the new generation, still believe that "Stalin epitomized the Communist mind . . . ," that his acts were "pure, unadulterated Leninism," that "Lenin was the mentor and Stalin the pupil who carried his master's legacy to its logical conclusion."[26]

The voluminous scholarship devoted to the continuity thesis has certain tenacious conventions. They are, loosely defined, of two sorts: a set of formulations, historical approaches, and conceptual explanations of how and why there was a political "straight line" between bolshevism and Stalinism; and a series of interlocking historical interpretations said to demonstrate Bolshevik programmatic continuity between 1917 and Stalin's upheaval of 1929-33. Both need to be reexamined fully, though I can do so here only very briefly and, again, elliptically. I leave the question of programmatic continuity to the next section and begin with conceptual matters.

The problem begins with the formulation of the continuity thesis. Among its most familiar assertion is that bolshevism contained the "seeds," "roots," or "germs" of Stalinism. To this proposition even the most ardent proponent of discontinuity must say—Yes, of course.[27] Unfortunately, this is to say very little, indeed only the obvious. Every historical period—each political phenomenon—has antecedents, "seeds," in the preceding one: 1917 in czarist history, the Third Reich in Weimar, and so forth. In itself, however, this demonstrates nothing about continuity, much less causality or inevitability.

The bolshevism of 1917-28 did contain important "seeds" of Stalinism; they are too fully related in our literature to be reiterated here. Less noted, and the real point, is that bolshevism also contained other important, non-Stalinist "seeds"; and, equally, that the "seeds" of Stalinism are also to be found elsewhere—in Russian historical and cultural tradition, in social events such as the civil war, in the international setting, etc. The question is, however, not "seeds," or even less significant continuities, but fundamental continuities or discontinuities. Moreover, to change metaphors and quote Victor Serge on this point: "To judge a living man by the death germs which the autopsy reveals in a corpse—and which he may have carried in him since birth—is that very sensible?"[28]

Even less helpful are the three definitional components of the continuity thesis: bolshevism, Stalinism, continuity. In customary usage, these terms obscure more than they define. The self-professed *raison d'être* of the "totalitarianism" school was to distinguish and analyze a wholly new kind of authoritarianism. Yet precisely this critical distinction is often missing, as illustrated by the familiar explanation of Stalinism: "authoritarianism in prerevolutionary Leninism naturally and perhaps inevitably gave birth to Soviet authoritarianism."[29] Variants of this proposition explain that Stalinism continued the illiberal, nondemocratic, repressive traditions of bolshevism.

This argument misses the essential comparative point. (It also assumes, mistakenly, I think, that some kind of democratic order—liberal or proletarian—was a Russian possibility in 1917 or after.) Bolshevism was in important respects—depending on the period—a strongly authoritarian movement. But failure to distinguish between Soviet authoritarianism before and after 1929 means to obscure the very nature of Stalinism. Stalinism was not simply nationalism, bureaucratization, absence of democracy, censorship, police repression, and the rest in any precedented sense. These phenomena have appeared in many societies and are rather easily explained.

Instead, Stalinism was excess, extraordinary extremism, in each. It was not, for example, merely coercive peasant policies, but a virtual civil war against the peasantry; not merely police repression, or even civil war-style terror, but a holocaust by terror that victimized tens of millions of people for twenty-five years; not merely a Thermidorian revival of nationalist tradition, but an almost fascist-like chauvinism; not merely a leader cult, but deification of a despot. During the Khrushchev years, Western scholars frequently spoke of a "Stalinism without the excesses," or "Stalinism without the arrests." This makes no sense. Excesses were the essence of historical Stalinism, and they are what really require explanation.[30]

Similar problems arise from the customary treatment of original bolshevism, which is to define it in such a selectively narrow fashion as to construe it as Stalinism, or "embryonic" Stalinism. I have tried to show elsewhere that bolshevism was a far more diverse political movement—ideologically, programmatically, generationally, etc.—than is usually acknowledged in our scholarship.[31] Another related convention of the continuity thesis should also be protested: the equating of bolshevism and Leninism. Lenin was plainly the singular Bolshevik; his leadership, ideas, and personality shaped the movement in fundamental ways. But bolshevism was larger, and more diverse, than Lenin and Leninism. Its ideology, policies, and politics were shaped also by other forceful leaders, lesser members and committees, nonparty constituents, and greater social events, including the First World War, the revolution, and the civil war.[32] I am not suggesting that Leninism, rather than bolshevism, was nascently Stalinist. Those who do rely similarly upon an exclusionary selection of references, emphasizing, for example, the Lenin of *What is to Be Done?* and 1919, while minimizing the Lenin of *State and Revolution* and 1922-23.

What, then, of formulating continuities and discontinuities? It is among the most difficult problems of historical analysis. Most historians would agree that it requires careful empirical study of historical similarities and dissimilarities, and that the question of degree, of whether quantitative changes become qualitative, is critical. Not surprisingly, perhaps, this venerable approach plays a central role in our thinking about differences between czarist and Soviet political history, and almost none in our thinking about bolshevism and Stalinism. Thus a major proponent of the continuity thesis warns against equating the czarist and Soviet regimes: "It is important to stress that there is a deep gulf dividing authoritarianism and totalitarianism, and if we treat the two as identical political formations, we end by revealing our inability to distinguish between continuity and change."[33] But if we were to apply this sensible admonition to Soviet history itself, it would be difficult not to conclude, at the very least, that here, too, "differences in degree grew into differences of kind . . . what had existed under Lenin was carried by Stalin to such extremes that its very nature changed."[34]

As our scholarship stands, however, it appears that special approaches are reserved for interpreting Soviet history. One is the extraordinary determinism and monocausal explanations on which the continuity thesis so often depends. The vocabulary used to posit a direct causal relationship between the "political dynamics" of bolshevism and Stalinism, especially collectivization and the great terror, may be unique in modern-day political and historical studies. It abounds with the language of teleological determinism: "inner logic," "inexorably totalitarian features," "inevitable process," "inescapable consequences," "logical completion," "inevitable stage," and more. Or to give a fuller illustration, a standard work explains that Stalin's collectivization campaign of 1929-33 "was the inevitable consequence of the triumph of the Bolshevik party on November 7, 1917. . . ."[35]

Serious questions about historical approach are involved here. For one thing, our language betrays a rigid determinism not unlike that which once prevailed in official Stalinist historiography, and which was properly derided by Western scholars.[36] For another, while claiming to explain so much, this sort of teleological interpretation actually explains very little. It is, as Hannah Arendt observed many years ago, more on the order of "axiomatic value-judgment" than authentic historical analysis.[37] And it is vulnerable logically. Replying to similar arguments circulating in the Soviet Union, Roy Medvedev has pointed out that if Stalinism was predetermined by bolshevism, if there were no alternatives after 1917, then 1917 and bolshevism must have been predetermined by previous Russian history. In that case, "to explain Stalinism we have to return to earlier and earlier epochs . . . very likely to the Tartar yoke." He adds, on a political note, "that would be wrong . . . a historical justification of Stalinism, not a condemnation."[38]

Implicit in all this is, I think, a Sovietological version of what Herbert Butterfield called the Whig interpretation of history. The past is evaluated in terms of the present, antecedents in terms of outcome. Or as one in-terpreter of continuity in Soviet political history has argued, "sometimes the past is better understood by examining the present and then defining the relationship of the present to the past."[39]

The approach is modified here by "sometimes," but it is clear and widespread. It is not wholly indefensible. The historian, as Carr reminds us, is unavoidably influenced by the present and by established out-comes.[40] In addition, careful application of contemporary insights may illuminate the past. But the Whig tradition in Soviet Studies has given rise to unsatisfactory conventions on the subject of bolshevism and Stalinism. Accompanying the teleological determinism, there is a tendency, project-ing outcome backward upon the past, to Stalinize early Soviet history and politics; to ignore, for the "straight line" to 1917, the actual period (1929-33) when historical Stalinism first appeared; and, throughout, to interpret the party ahistorically, as though it acted above society and out-side history itself.

Two familiar, and equally questionable, lines of analysis are among the corollaries of our Whig historiography. One argues that the inner "political dynamics" (or "nature") of the Bolshevik party predetermined Stalinism. The other insists that changes in the Soviet political system under bolshevism and Stalinism were superficial or secondary to con-tinuities which were fundamental and observable. Whatever the partial truths of the first argument, it suffers from the implicit ahistorical con-ception of a basically unchanging party after 1917, an assumption easily refuted by evidence already in our literature. What is meant by "the party" as historical determinant when, for example, its membership, com-position, organizational structure, internal political life, and outlook underwent far-reaching alterations between 1917 and 1921 alone?[41]

The causal "dynamic" cited most often is, of course, the party's ideology.[42] Several obvious objections can be raised against this expla-nation of social and political development. It is even more one-dimensional. It ignores the fact that a given ideology may influence events in different ways. Christianity having contributed to both compassion and inquisition, socialism to both social justice and tyranny. And it relies upon a self-serving definition of Bolshevik ideology as being concerned mainly with the "concentration of total social power."[43]

More important, the nature of Bolshevik ideology was far less cohesive and fixed than the standard interpretation allows. If ideology influenced events, it was also shaped and changed, by them. The Russian civil war, to take an early instance, had a major impact on Bolshevik outlook, reviving the self-conscious theory of an embattled vanguard, which had been inoperative or inconsequential for at least a decade, and implanting in the once civilian-minded party what a leading Bolshevik called a "military soviet culture."[44] Above all, official ideology changed radically under Stalin. Several of these changes have been noted by Western and Soviet scholars: the revival of nationalism, statism, anti-Semitism, and conservative, or reactionary, cultural and behavioral norms; the repeal of ideas and legislation favoring workers, women, schoolchildren, minority cultures, and egalitarianism, as well as a host of revolutionary and Bolshevik symbols; and a switch in emphasis from ordinary people to leaders and official bosses as the creators of history.[45] These were not simply amendments, but a new ideology which was "changed in its *essence*" and which did "not represent the same movement as that which took power in 1917."[46]

Similar criticisms must be leveled against the other causal "dynamic" usually cited, the party's "organizational principles"—the implied theory that Stalinism originated with *What Is to Be Done?*[47] It, too, is one-dimensional and ahistorical. Bolshevism's organizational character evolved over the years, often in response to external events, from the unruly, loosely organized party participating successfully in democratic politics in 1917, to the centralized bureaucratic party of the 1920s, to the terrorized party of the 1930s, many of whose executive committees and bureaus no longer existed.[48]

Moreover, the argument is, in effect, an adaptation of Michels's "iron law of oligarchy," which was intended to be a generalization about all large political organizations and their tendency toward oligarchical rather than democratic politics. This may suggest a good deal about the evolution of the Bolshevik leadership's relations with the party-at-large between 1917 and 1929, as it does about modern parties generally. But it tells us nothing directly about Stalinism, which was not oligarchical but autocratic politics,[49] unless we conclude that the "iron law of oligarchy" is actually an iron law of autocracy.

The party's growing centralization, bureaucratization, and administrative intolerance after 1917 certainly promoted authoritarianism in the one-party system and abetted Stalin's rise. To argue that these developments predetermined Stalinism is another matter. Even in the 1920s, after the bureaucratization and militarization fostered by the civil war, the high party was not (nor had it ever been) the disciplined vanguard fantasized in *What is to Be Done?* It remained oligarchical, in the words of one of its leaders, "*a negotiated federation between groups, groupings, factions, and 'tendencies.*' "[50] In short, the party's "organizational principles" did not produce Stalinism before 1929, nor have they since 1953.

There remains, then, the argument that discontinuities were secondary to continuities in the working of the Soviet political system under bolshevism and Stalinism.[51] Though ideally an empirical question, here, too, there would seem to be a critical methodological lapse. The importance of distinguishing between the official, or theatrical, facade and the inner (sometimes disguised) reality of politics has been evident at least since Bagehot demolished the prevailing theory of English politics in 1867 by dissecting the system in terms of its "dignified" and "efficient" parts. The case made by Western scholars for fundamental continuities in the Soviet political system has rested largely on what Bagehot called "dignified," merely apparent, or fictitious parts.

Looking at the "efficient" or inner reality, Robert C. Tucker came to a very different conclusion several years ago: "What we carelessly call 'the Soviet political system' is best seen and analyzed as an historical succession of political systems within a broadly continuous institutional framework." The Bolshevik system had been one of party dictatorship characterized by oligarchical leadership politics in the ruling party. After 1936 and Stalin's great purge, despite an outward "continuity of organizational forms and official nomenclature," the "one-party system had given way to a one-person system, the ruling party to a ruling personage." This was a ramifying change from an oligarchical party regime to an autocratic "Führerist" regime, and was "reflected in a whole system of changes in the political process, the ideological pattern, the organization of supreme power, and official patterns of behavior."[52] The apparent continuities regularly itemized—leader, the party, terror, class war, censorship, Marxism-Leninism, purge, etc.—were synthetic and illusory. The terms may still have been applicable, but their meaning was different.[53]

Tucker's conclusion that Stalin's terror "broke the back of the party, eliminated it as a . . . ruling class," has been amply confirmed by more recent evidence.[54] After the purges swept away at least one million of its members between 1935 and 1939, the primacy of the party—the "essence" of bolshevism-Leninism in most scholarly definitions—was no more. Its elite (massacred virtually as a whole), general membership (in 1939 70 percent had joined since 1929 or after), ethos, and role were no longer those of the old party, or even the party of 1934. Even in its new Stalinist form, the party's political importance fell well below that of the police, and its official esteem below that of the state. Its deliberative bodies—the party congress, the Central Committee, and eventually even the Politburo—rarely convened.[55] Accordingly, the previous and different history of the party could no longer be written about, even to distort: between 1938 and 1953, only one Soviet doctoral dissertation was written on this once hallowed subject.[56]

It is sometimes pointed out, as a final defense of the continuity thesis, that "Stalinism" was never acknowledged officially during Stalin's reign, only "Marxism-Leninism." With Bagehot's method, of course, this tells us nothing.[57] Moreover, it is not entirely accurate. As the cult of the infallible leader (which, it should be said, was very different from the earlier Bolshevik cult of a historically necessary, but not infallible, party) grew into literal deification after 1938, the adjective "Stalinist" was attached increasingly to people, institutions, orthodox ideas, events, and even history. This was a departure from even the early 1930s, when they were normally called Leninist, Bolshevik, or Soviet. It reflected, among other things, the sharp decline in Lenin's official standing.[58] Catchphrases such as "the teachings of Lenin and Stalin" remained. But less ecumenical ones arose to characterize the building of Soviet socialism as "the great Stalinist cause," Stalin alone as "the genius-architect of communism," and Soviet history as the "epoch of Stalin."[59] The term "Stalinism" was prohibited from official usage; but the concept was ingrained, tacitly and officially.[60]

If symbols can tell us anything about political reality, we do best to heed Leonid Petrovsky's commentary on the statue of Dolgoruky, which Stalin built on the spot where Lenin had once unveiled a monument to the first Soviet constitution. "The monument to the bloody feudal prince has become a kind of personification of the grim epoch of the personality cult. The horse of the feudal prince has its back turned to the Central Party Archives, where the immortal works of Marx, Engels, and Lenin are preserved and where a beautiful statue of Lenin stands."[61]

Underlying the other arguments of the continuity thesis is, finally, that of a programmatic "straight line" from 1917. It is the view, widespread in Soviet studies literature, that Stalin's wholesale collectivization and heavy industrialization drive of 1929-33, the paroxysmic upheaval he later properly called "a revolution from above," represented the continuation and fulfillment of Bolshevik thinking about modernizing, or building socialism in, Russia. In other words, even if it is conceded that the events of 1936-39 were discontinuous, what about those of 1929-33?

The argument for programmatic continuity rests upon interlocking interpretations of the two previous periods in Bolshevik policy: war communism—the extreme nationalization, grain requisitioning, and monopolistic state intervention effected during the civil war of 1918-20; and NEP—the moderate agricultural and industrial policies and mixed public-private economy of 1921-28. In its essentials, the argument runs as follows: War communism was mainly a product of the party's original ideological-programmatic ideas (sometimes called "blueprints"), an eager crash program of socialism.[62] These frenzied policies collapsed in 1921 because of the population's opposition, and the party was forced to retreat to the new economic policy of concessions to private enterprise in the countryside and cities. Accordingly, official Bolshevik policy during the eight years of NEP—and NEP itself as a social-political order—are interpreted in the literature as being "merely a breathing spell," "a holding operation," or "a strategic retreat, during which the forces of socialism in Russia would retrench, recuperate, and then resume their march."[63]

How these two interpretations converge into a single thesis of programmatic continuity between bolshevism and Stalin's revolution from above is illustrated by one of our best general histories. War communism is presented as "an attempt, which proved premature, to realize the Party's stated ideological goals," and NEP, in Bolshevik thinking, as "a tactical maneuver to be pursued only until the inevitable change of conditions which would make victory possible. . . ." The author can then marvel over Stalin's policies of 1929-33: "It is difficult to find a parallel for a regime or a party which held power for ten years, biding its time until it felt strong enough to fulfill its original program."[64] The problem with this interpretation is that it conflicts with much of the historical evidence. Having discussed these questions at some length elsewhere,[65] I shall be concise.

There are three essential points to be made against locating the origins of war communism in an original Bolshevik program. First, odd as it may seem for a party so often described as "doctrinaire," the Bolsheviks had no well-defined economic policies upon coming to office in October 1917. There were generally held Bolshevik goals and tenets—socialism, workers' control, nationalization, large-scale farming, planning, and the like—but these were vague and subject to the most varying interpretations inside the party. Bolsheviks had done little thinking about practical economic policies before October, and—as it turned out—there were few upon which they could agree.[66]

Second, the initial program of the Bolshevik government, in the sense of officially defined policy, was not war communism but what Lenin called in April-May 1918 "state capitalism," a mixture of socialist measures and concessions to the existing capitalist structure and control of the economy.[67] If this first Bolshevik program resembled anything that followed, it was NEP. And, third, the actual policies of war communism did not begin until June 1918, in response to the threat of prolonged civil war and diminishing supplies, a situation that immediately outdated Lenin's conciliatory "state capitalism."[68]

None of this is to say that war communism had no ideological component. As the civil war deepened into a great social conflict, official measures grew more extreme, and the meaning and the "defense of the revolution" became inseparable, Bolsheviks naturally infused these improvised policies with high theoretical and programmatic significance beyond military victory. They became ideological.[69] The evolution of war communism, and its legacy in connection with Stalinism, require careful study (though the similarities should not be exaggerated). But the origins will not be found in a Bolshevik program of October.

The question of NEP is even more important. Not only were the official economic policies of 1921-28 distinctly unlike Stalin's in 1929-33, but the social-political order of NEP, with its officially tolerated social pluralism in economic, cultural-intellectual, and even (in local soviets and high state agencies) political life, represents a historical model of Soviet Communist rule radically unlike Stalinism.[70] In addition, the standard treatment of Bolshevik thinking about NEP is more complicated because all scholars are aware of the intense policy debates of the 1920s, a circumstance not easily reconciled with a simplistic interpretation of NEP as merely a programmatic bivouac, or the antechamber of Stalinism.

Tensions inherent in the interpretation are related to secondary but significant conventions in our literature on NEP. The programmatic debates of the 1920s are treated largely as an extension, and in terms of, the Trotsky-Stalin rivalry (or, perpetuating the factional misnomers of the period, "permanent revolution" and "socialism in one country"). Trotsky and the Left opposition are said to have been anti-NEP and embryonically Stalinist, the progenitors of "almost every major item in the political program that Stalin later carried out." Stalin is then said to have stolen, or adapted, Trotsky's economic policies in 1929. Having portrayed a "basic affinity between Trotsky's plans and Stalin's actions," these secondary interpretations suggest at least a significant continuity between Stalinism and Bolshevik thinking in the 1920s, and underlie the general interpretation of NEP.[71] They are, however, factually incorrect.

The traditional treatment of the economic debates (we are not concerned here with the controversy over Comintern policy or the party bureaucracy) in terms of Trotsky and Stalin bears no relationship to the actual discussions of 1923-27. If the rival policies can be dichotomized and personified, they were Trotskyist and Bukharinist. Stalin's public policies on industry, agriculture, and planning were Bukharin's, that is, pro-NEP, moderate, evolutionary. This was the cement of the Stalin-Bukharin duumvirate that made official policy and led the party majority against the Left oppositions until early 1928. During these years, there were no "Stalinist" ideas, apart from "socialism in one country" which was also Bukharin's.[72] If "ism" is to be affixed, there was no Stalinism, only Bukharinism and Trotskyism. This was understood at the time. As the opposition of 1925 complained: "Comrade Stalin has become the total prisoner of this political line, the creator and genuine representative of which is Comrade Bukharin." Stalin was no prisoner, but a willing adherent. He replied: "We stand, and we shall stand, for Bukharin."[73]

Bukharin's economic proposals for modernizing and building socialism in Soviet Russia in the 1920s are clear enough. Developing the themes of Lenin's last writings, which constituted both a defense and further elaboration of NEP as a road to socialism, and adding some of his own, Bukharin became the party's main theorist of NEP. Though his policies evolved between 1924 and 1928 toward great emphasis on planning, heavy industrial investment, and efforts to promote a partial and voluntary collective farm sector, he remained committed to the NEP economic framework of a state, or "socialist," sector (mainly large-scale industry, transportation, and banking) and a private sector (peasant farms and small manufacturing, trade, and service enterprises) interacting through market relations. Even during the crisis of 1928-29, NEP was for the Bukharinists a viable developmental (not static) model, predicated on civil peace, that could reconcile Bolshevik aspirations and Russian social reality.[74]

But what about Trotsky and the Left? Though his political rhetoric was often that of revolutionary heroism, Trotsky's actual economic proposals in the 1920s were also based on NEP and its continuation. He urged greater attention to heavy industry and planning earlier than did Bukharin, and he worried more about the village "kulak"; but his remedies were moderate, market-oriented, or, as the expression went, "nepist." Like Bukharin, he was a "reformist" in economic policy, looking to the evolution of NEP Russia toward industrialism and socialism.[75]

Even Preobrazhensky, the avatar of "superindustrialization" whose fearful arguments about the necessity of "primitive socialist accumulation" based on "exploiting" the peasant sector are often cited as Stalin's inspiration, accepted the hallmark of NEP economics. He wanted to "exploit" peasant agriculture through market relations by artificially fixing state industrial prices higher than agricultural prices.[76] Both he and Trotsky, and the Bolshevik Left generally, thought in terms of peasant farming for the foreseeable future. However inconsistent their ideas may have been, neither ever advocated imposed collectivization, much less wholesale collectivization as a system of requisitioning or solution to industrial backwardness.[77]

The debates between Bukharinists and Trotskyists in the 1920s represented the spectrum of high Bolshevik programmatic thinking, Right to Left. The two sides disagreed on important economic issues, from price policy and rural taxation to the prospects for comprehensive planning. But unlike the international and political issues which most embittered the factional struggle, these disagreements were limited, falling within the parameters of "nepism," which both sides accepted, though with different levels of enthusiasm.

In fact, the revised Bukharinist program adopted as the first Five Year Plan at the Fifteenth Party Congress in December 1927, and calling for more ambitious industrial investment as well as partial voluntary collectivization, represented a kind of amalgam of Bukharinist-Trotskyist thinking as it had evolved in the debates of the 1920s.[78] When Stalin abandoned this program a year and half later, he abandoned mainstream Bolshevik thinking about economic and social change. After 1929 and the end of NEP, the Bolshevik programmatic alternative to Stalinism, in fact and as perceived inside the party, remained basically Bukharinist. From afar, the exiled Trotsky leveled his own accusations against Stalin's regime, but his economic proposals in the early 1930s were, as they had been in the 1920s, far closer to, and now "entirely indistinguishable from," Bukharin's.[79]

NEP had originated as an ignoble retreat in 1921, and resentment at NEP economics, politics, and culture continued throughout the 1920s. It was perpetuated in the heroic Bolshevik tradition of October and the civil war, and probably strongest among cadres formed by the warfare experience of 1918-20, and the younger party generation. Stalin would tap these real sentiments for his civil war reenactment of 1929-33. But, for reasons beyond our concern here, by 1924 NEP had acquired a general legitimacy among Bolshevik leaders. Not even Stalin dared challenge that legitimacy in his final contest with the Bukharinists in 1928-29. He campaigned and won not as the abolitionist of NEP, or the proponent of "revolution from above," but as a "calm and sober" leader who could make it work.[80] Even after defeating the Bukharin group in April 1929, as NEP crumbled under Stalin's radical policies, his editorials continued to insist that "NEP is the only correct policy of socialist construction," a fiction still officially maintained in 1931.[81]

The point here is not to explain the fateful events of 1928-29, but to illustrate that Stalin's new policies of 1929-33, the "great change," were a radical departure from Bolshevik programmatic thinking. No Bolshevik leader or faction had ever advocated anything akin to imposed collectivization, the "liquidation" of the kulaks, breakneck heavy industrialization, and a "plan" that was, of course, no plan at all.[82] These years of "revolution from above" were, historically, and programmatically, the birthperiod of Stalinism. From this first great discontinuity others would follow.

In treating Stalinism as "full-blown" bolshevism, and the Soviet 1930s as a function and extension of 1917, the main scholarly disservice of the continuity thesis has been to discourage close examination of Stalinism as a specific system with its own history. I am persuaded by Tucker's argument that essential, even definitive, aspects of Stalinism, including critical turning points in its history and the "excesses," cannot be understood apart from Stalin as a political personality.[83] Nonetheless, the agenda of what remains to be studied by way of broader political, social, and historical context and factors is very large. The present would seem to be a good time to begin this kind of innovative research. In addition to the availability of new materials and longer perspectives, the same questions are now being discussed in the Soviet Union, though for the moment largely by *samizdat* writers.

It is important, first of all, to shed the ahistorical habit of thinking of the Stalinist system as an unchanging phenomenon. The historical development of Stalinism must be traced and analyzed through its several stages, from the truly revolutionary events of the early 1930s to the rigidly conservative socio-political order of 1946-53.[84] The 1930s themselves must be divided into periods including at least the social upheaval of 1929-33, the interregnum of 1934-35, when future policy was being contested in the high leadership, and 1936-39, which witnessed the final triumph of Stalinism over the Bolshevik tradition and the political completion of revolution from above.

The years 1929-33, obscured in both Western and official Soviet theories of Stalinism,[85] are especially important. They were the formative period of Stalinism as a system; they presaged and gave rise to much that followed. For example, several characteristic *idées fixes* of full Stalinism, including the murderous notion of an inevitable "intensification of the class struggle," first appeared in Stalin's campaign to discredit all Bukharinist and NEP ideas in 1928-30. Stalin's personal role in unleashing imposed collectivization and escalating industrial targets in 1929, when he bypassed councils of party decision making, augured his full autocracy of later years.[86] More generally, as Moshe Lewin has shown in a social history of 1929-33, many administrative, legislative, class, and ideological features of the mature Stalinist state took shape as makeshift solutions to the social chaos, the "quicksand society," generated by the destruction of NEP institutions and processes during the initial wave of revolution from above. In Lewin's view from below, the first in our literature and rich testimony to the need for social history, the Stalinist system was less a product of Bolshevik programs or planning than of desperate attempts to cope with the social pandemonium and crises created by the Stalinist leadership itself in 1929-33.[87]

As for subsequent events, it would be a mistake to interpret Stalin's terrorist assault on Soviet officialdom in 1936-39 as a "necessary" or "functional" byproduct of the imposed social revolution of 1929-33.

A very different course was advocated by many party leaders, probably a majority, in 1934-35. More telling, there is plain evidence that the purges were not, as some scholars have imagined, somehow rational in terms of modernization, a terrorist Geritol that accelerated the process, weeding out obsolete functionaries, etc. The terror wrecked or retarded many of the real achievements of 1929-36.[88]

Nevertheless, there were important linkages between these two great upheavals, and they require careful study. The enormous expansion of police repression, security forces, and the archipelago of forced labor camps in 1929-33 were clearly part of the background and mechanism of 1936-39. There were also less obvious, but perhaps equally important, consequences. Even though forcible wholesale collectivization had not originated as a party, or even collective leadership, policy, the entire party elite, and probably the whole party, was implicated in the criminal and economic calamities of Stalin's measures, which culminated in the terrible famine of 1932-33. Every semi-informed official must have known that collectivization was a disaster, wrecking agricultural production, savaging livestock herds, and killing millions of people.[89]

In official ideology, however, it became obligatory to eulogize collectivization as a great accomplishment of Stalinist leadership. This bizarre discrepancy between official claims and social reality, uncharacteristic of original bolshevism, was a major step in the progressive fictionalization of Soviet ideology under Stalin. It must have had a profoundly demoralizing effect on party officials, contributing to their apparently meager resistance to Stalin's terror in 1936-39. If nothing more, it implicated them in the cult of Stalin's infallibility, which grew greater as disasters grew worse, and which became an integral part of the Stalinist system.[90]

The few authentic attempts to analyze Stalinism as a social-political system over the years have been mostly by Marxists who offer "new class" or "ruling bureaucracy" theories of the subject. This literature is fairly diverse and features wide-ranging disputes over whether the Stalinist bureaucracy can be viewed as a class or only as a stratum, and of what kind. It also contains valuable material on the sociology of Stalinism, a topic habitually ignored in academic studies, and reminds us that the new administrative strata created in the 1930s strongly influenced the nature of mature Stalinism, particularly its anti-egalitarianism, rigid stratification, and cultural and social conservatism.[91]

As a theory of Stalinism, however, this approach is deeply flawed. The argument that a ruling bureaucracy-class was the animating force behind the events of 1929-39 makes no sense, logically or empirically. Quite apart from the demonstrable role of Stalin, who is reduced in these theories to a replaceable chief bureaucrat, it remains to be explained how a bureaucracy, which is defined as being deeply conservative, would have decided and carried out policies so radical and dangerous as forcible collectivization. And, indeed, Stalin's repeated campaigns to radicalize and spur on officialdom in 1929-30, and after, suggest a fearful, recalcitrant party-state bureaucracy, not an event-making one. Nor is it clear how this theory explains the slaughter of Soviet officialdom in 1936-39, unless we conclude that the "ruling" bureaucracy-class committed suicide.

We are confronted here, as elsewhere, with the difficulty inherent in applying Western concepts, whether of the Marxist or modernization variety, to a Soviet political and social reality shaped by Russian historical and cultural tradition. One reason Western-inspired theories apply poorly to the Stalinist administrative elites created in the 1930s is that the latter were more akin to the traditional czarist *soslovie*, an official privileged class that served the state—in this case a resurgent Russian state[92]—more than it ruled the state. Arguably, there is today a Soviet ruling class or bureaucracy which has emancipated itself; but during its formation and agony in the Stalin years, for all its high position and great power over those below, it did not ultimately rule.

Approaches that take into account historical-cultural tradition are therefore essential, though they, too, sometimes have been abused in Western scholarship. Early studies of Stalinism in historical-cultural terms tended to become mono-causal interpretations of a revolution (or communism) inevitably undone or fatally transformed by history. Instead of viewing tradition as contextual, they treated it as virtually autonomous and deterministic.[93] As Carr has said, however, "every successful revolution has its *Thermidor*."[94] But the outcome is not predetermined; it is a problematic admixture of new and old patterns and values, and the nature of this outcome depends upon contemporary social and political circumstances as well. In 1932-33, for example, the Stalinist regime reinstated the internal passport system, once thought to typify czarism and despised by all Russian revolutionaries. Here was an instance of revived tradition, but also of contemporary policy and crisis, since the retrogression came about in direct response to the social chaos, particularly wandering peasant masses in search of food, of 1929-33.

Cultural approaches can contribute to an understanding of many things, from Stalin's personal outlook and political autocracy, as Tucker has shown, to the social basis of Stalinism as a system. There is, in particular, the important question of Stalinism's popular support in Soviet society, a problem largely ignored and inconsistent with the imagery of a "totalitarian" regime dominating a hapless, "atomized" population through power techniques alone. Though the coercive aspects of the Stalinist system can scarcely be exaggerated, this seems no more adequate as a full explanation than would a similar interpretation of Hitler's Germany.

While its nature and extent certainly varied over time, it seems evident that there was substantial popular support for Stalinism, inside and outside officialdom, from the beginning and through the very worst. Some of this sentiment probably demands no special explanation, though it must be taken into account. Revolution from above was an imposed upheaval, but it required and obtained enthusiastic agents below, even if only a small minority, from the cultural to the industrial and rural fronts.[95] In addition, revolutions from above (a little studied category) are by definition a great expansion of the state and its social functions, which means a great proliferation of official jobs and privileges. While many were victimized, many people also profited from Stalinism, and identified with it. Not just the "whole system of smaller dictators" throughout Soviet administrative life, but the millions of petty officials who gained opportunity and elevation of status.[96] Even the purges, Medvedev suggests, elicited the support of workers, who saw in the downfall of bosses and bureaucrats "the underdog's dream of retribution with the aid of a higher justice. . . . Impotence seeks the protection of supreme avenging power."[97] And there can be little question that the wartime patriotism of 1941-45 translated itself into considerable new support for the increasingly nationalistic, and victorious, Stalinist system.

Other aspects of Stalinism usually regarded as only imposed from above and without social roots also need to be reconsidered in this light and in longer perspective. The main carriers of cultural tradition are, of course, social groups and classes. In the 1930s, as Lewin has shown, the "petty bourgeois" majority of Russia swarmed into the cities to become large segments of the new working class and officialdom, the Drozdovs of tomorrow. In this context, is it sufficient to view Stalinist popular and political culture as merely artifices of censorship? Did not the literature, or the state nationalism, of 1936-53, for example, also have authentic social roots in this newly risen and still insecure officialdom, whose values, self-perceptions, and cultural babbittry it so often seemed to reflect?[98]

Finally, a dramatic example of cultural tradition and popular support was the Stalin cult, in some ways the major institution of the autocracy. Stalin promoted it from above, but it found fertile soil, becoming (as many Soviet sources tell us) an authentic social phenomenon. It grew from an internal party celebration of the new leader in 1929 into a mass religion, a "peculiar Soviet form of worship."[99] Neither Bolshevik tradition, the once modest Lenin cult, nor Stalin's personal gratification can explain the popular dimensions it acquired. For this we doubtless must return to older values and customs, to "unwritten mandates borne by the wind."[100] Not surprisingly, these popular sentiments have outlived Stalin himself.

ALBERTO AQUARONE

THE TOTALITARIAN STATE
AND PERSONAL DICTATORSHIP

*Although published many years ago and highly regarded in the field,
Professor Aquarone's* L'organizzazione dello Stato totalitario (The Organization of the Totalitarian State) *has been available in English translation
only in part (see "The Rise of the Fascist State" in Roland Sarti,* The Ax
Within: Fascism in Action *[New York: 1974], pp. 101-105). The final
chapter of Aquarone's balanced survey, abridged and translated by Professor Donald Malanga of Iona College for inclusion in this volume, still
stands as the most fitting summary of totalitarian aspiration and reality in
Mussolini's Italy.*

*Professor Aquarone does not so much question the reality of totali-
tarianism as the manifestation of twentieth-century mass movement
regimes as he questions its realization in Mussolini's Italy. Never leaving
doubt about Mussolini's aspiration to integrate all aspects of Italian
society within the wholeness of the totalitarian state, the author defines
the institutional obstacles as well as the deficiencies of Mussolini's character in the way of attaining the desired goal. Pointing to the Fascist
regime's inability to develop the institutional and ideological cohesion
requisite to settling relations with the monarchy and the Catholic church
in its favor, the author demonstrates how these twin obstacles helped
prevent the totalitarian integration of Italian society.*

*An interesting comparative dimension may be found in fascism's in-
capacity to gain the consistent and unambiguous adherence of the officer
corps and the corresponding situation in Germany. Whereas German
officers had to make do with the memory of monarchy, fond as it was,*

Translated by Donald Malanga

the Italian military still was very much tied into the reality of the ruling house as the symbol of the unified nation.

Viewed in the context of the hold exercised by the Catholic church over large segments of Italian society, the magnitude of Mussolini's task in breaking down sectional and institutional loyalties and replacing them with a new unifying principle becomes apparent. Singling out the very wording of the 1929 Lateran Treaties as evidence of the rival position assured to Catholic dogma in a regime claiming universal dominion for Fascist principles, Aquarone makes clear that Mussolini never came close to penetrating all of Italy with his ideas. The outline provided here of complex relations between men of refined culture, steeped in tradition and torn by aspirations of nationalism and modernity, to a regime essentially vulgar and not too remote from the Socialist underpinnings of its founder, challenges the reader to be aware of simplistic explanations of the Italian "face of totalitarianism."

The difficulties of interpretation presented by Italy's institutional makeup and ideological pluralism are complicated further by the incoherence of Mussolini's personality. Though never underestimating the considerable talents and achievements of the Fascist dictator, Aquarone also does not fail to analyze sharply the essentially "ad hoc" modes of Mussolini's government and their disintegrating effect on an order aspiring to total unity. The fundamental contradiction between the ends sought and the means to attain them, between the holistic vision and the centrifugal forces unleashed to realize it, indeed, is compelling as presented in Aquarone's by now classic analysis of the Fascist regime. The fact that the personal dictatorship of a man so disorganized and even dissolute was acceptable to many Italians who were disinclined to fascism as such raises important questions about the nature of totalitarianism and man's need to submit.

Under fascism the totalitarian state, aspiring to the complete integration with society, never succeeded in attaining its goal. Even in those moments of its greatest success abroad and of its greatest penetration into internal affairs, the regime remained essentially very distant from its aim of identifying completely with Italian society; even for a large number of sincere Fascists, to be good Fascists did not mean total involvement in the formalities of public life; often this was of secondary importance in the hierarchy of values, less important than other, more binding loyalties—the feeling of belonging first of all to other groups and to other organizations (that is to say, to other systems of socialization).

A first and partial explanation of this fact is found in Karl Mannheim's statement: "Fascism is a form of group integration which is effective principally in the emotional domain. However, it makes no attempt to direct the flow of emotion in directions in which it might be able to unite its forces with reason, judgment, and responsible action."[1] Fascist nationalism, tending to be strongly irrational in nature, was not supported by a correspondingly solid ideological structure and to an even lesser degree by a strict moral discipline, which might filter down to the masses. The pretense of building a totalitarian state found its ultimate expressions in a continual appeal to passion, activism in and for itself, and an unthinking acceptance of the mandates of an irresponsible order: obviously this could not suffice.

However, what revealed more than anything else the consummate weakness of Mussolini's totalitarian aspirations was an often-demonstrated inability to confront, with conscious steadfastness and with effective totalitarian determination supported by a coherent ideological structure, the crucial problem of the relations of fascism with the monarchy on the one hand, and with the Catholic church on the other. The Fascist state constantly proclaimed itself, in great and exuberant tones, a totalitarian state; but it remained up until the end a dynastic and Catholic state as well, and therefore not a totalitarian one in the Fascist sense.

It had been seen on a number of occasions that the neutralization of influence of the crown under fascism was far from absolute. Rather, it continued to be, all during the years of the regime, a source of authority and possible political influence and, therefore, also unavoidably a disintegratory element in reference to the homogeneity and the compactness of the Fascist ruling class. The latter, moreover, was never outstanding in this respect. For fascism, there existed in truth, as Mussolini himself wrote after the 25th of July in his *Storia do un anno*, a "drama of the diarchy."[2] To be sure, Mussolini at that time, under the direct and burning impression of his fall and of the manner in which it had occurred, exaggerated perhaps the degree of that drama and exaggerated the intensity of his quarrels with the king.

There remains, however, the fact that the dynasty and fascism, the monarchy and the totalitarian fascist state, were in substance, and in the final analysis, incompatible. Therefore, as such, at least in their latent state, they could not enjoy any mutual loyalty. During its entire history fascism was burdened by the heavy ball and chain of this incompatibility. This was for fascism one of the basic weaknesses, one which would appear in all its weightiness at the most critical moments. More than a single crack, but rather a very real break in the totalitarian concept of the Fascist state, was represented in particular by the fact that the process of "fascistization" of the army always remained, within certain limits, incomplete—

so much so that, for the majority of the officers at every level, devotion to the king continued to prevail over loyalty to fascism. Mussolini himself had to declare in one of his outbursts against the king, which were becoming more and more frequent with the passage of time, "it is the monarchy with its idiotic exaltations which impedes the fascistization of the army."[3] Indeed, even some of the highest ranks of the party did not hesitate to manifest, on occasion—and not always privately—their attachment to the monarchy, letting it be fully understood that it took precedent, as far as they were concerned, over attachment to fascism itself. Above all else, this was due to their desire to secure for themselves an aura of respectability with the upper social classes and to free themselves from the image of plebeian coarseness and petit bourgeois vulgarity, under which fascism had always appeared in the eyes of the upper bourgeoisie and aristocracy. These divided loyalties were due to polemics within the party, to the needs to achieve a separate identity from this or that faction, and to secure specific alliances for themselves.

At still other times divided loyalties were due to preoccupation with the need for protection from upheavals which might result from an eventual premature demise of the dictatorship; for, as a consequence of such a development, it was most probable that the monarchy would once again acquire a decisive role in the political life of the nation.

In addition to the monarchy there was still another institution which had even deeper roots in Italian society and which exercised an even greater influence over the masses requisite for the realization of a genuine program of totalitarian government. Fascism, however, never dared to come to a final reckoning with the Catholic church, notwithstanding the sometimes violent encounters it had with her. With the "conciliation," fascism aimed at using the Catholic church for the purpose of increasing its own prestige and reinforcing its own position at home as well as abroad. To some extent this goal was realized. By the same token, however, fascism renounced most definitely its dominance over the spiritual formation of the Italian people and thereby accepted perilously divided spheres of influence with the church. In so doing, fascism was merely deceiving itself of the nature of prevalent power relations, wrongly convinced that control over the church could be maintained in all confrontations and under any circumstances. One might object at this point that, after all, the regime had no choice and that finding it impossible to unleash an in-depth struggle against the church with the aim of pursuing a complete integration of Italian society within the Fascist state, the only recourse left was that of accord with the Holy See, even at the price of major concessions. No doubt such an objection would have a good basis; there remains, however, the fact that another vast break was made in the system of Fascist totalitarianism, and one of such dimension as to undermine its very foundation.

Mussolini could claim for the Fascist state "its own spirit, its own morality, which confers strength to its laws, and by which it succeeds in assuring obedience on the part of the citizenry."[4] But with Article 1 of Mussolini's 1929 Lateran Treaty with the Vatican, Italy, or in fact the regime, recognized and reaffirmed the principle consecrated in Article 1 of the Constitution, on the basis of which the Catholic Apostolic Roman Religion was the sole religion of the state. Fascism could work tirelessly to realize an absolute monopoly in the education of the young, and it could break the reins of the Catholic Youth Organizations, but in Article 36 of the agreement Italy, or rather fascism, stated it would consider "the foundation and the highpoint of public education, the teaching of Christian doctrine according to the form handed down in Catholic tradition,"[5] that is, the teaching of a doctrine which in certain aspects would be radically incompatible with the moral and ideological premises of fascism itself. Moreover, the doctrine would be imparted under the strict control of an authority completely alien to the state and the party, that is to say, under the direction and supervision of ecclesiastical authorities. And Article 43 of the Lateran Treaty established that organizations dependent on Catholic action were to evolve their activities "outside of any and all political parties and under the immediate direction of the hierarchy of the church for the dissemination and realization of Catholic principles." In addition, the Fascist state recognized that organizations dependent on authority taken out of its sphere of control and inspired by principles and values different from its own had a right to exist, to proselytize, and to engage in activities shaping the minds of the young and others. These could easily become—if not centers of active resistance (which, in fact, they did become)—at the least institutions in which those who would assume future responsibilities in public life were trained and upon whom the regime thus had only a limited possibility of exercising its influence.

Two years after the signing of the Lateran Treaty, a scholar of ecclesiastical law, dealing with the problem "of the juridical qualification of the Italian state in ordering its relations with the Church," basing himself on various contradictory ordinances as well as on comparison with the positive rights of other states, arrived at the following conclusion: "There is no doubt that if it is believed useful to group contemporary states empirically and to designate them in traditional terms, our state will not be classifiable among the separatist countries but rather among those considered confessional."[6] But the Italian state, by the very fact of its being confessional, could not be totalitarian in a Fascist sense.

At issue were not merely terminological or purely theoretical questions;

above and beyond the definition of the Italian state as confessional or less so, there was a concrete reality which was anything but reconciled to the claim of fascism to the totalitarian control of all society. Especially in the provinces, rural areas as well as small and moderate size municipalities, it was a fact that at times the cross and not the "fasces" set the tone in public life and drew devotion and obedience. This was a bitter pill for those leaders—and they were not few in number—in whom there ardently remained that anticlerical component which had left its imprint on early fascism. These men looked with the greatest revulsion at the competition which the ecclesiastical authorities offered on the level of local power and influence.

It is also necessary to note, as we pass to another level, that while the "conciliation," with all its confessional and anti-Risorgimento aspects, favorably impressed the majority of Italians and contributed heavily to reinforcing the prestige and internal strength of fascism, it also created a state of profound hardship in a substantial number of men of culture and of different intellectual and political background. Notwithstanding their differences, they all were united in their feelings of repugnance to any abdication on the part of the lay state in its confrontations with the Catholic church. Men who, contrary to those who had seen and still saw in the treaty "a tract of refined political art, to be judged not according to ingenious ethical ideals, but as politics in conformity with that hackneyed saying 'that Paris is well worth a mass,' still held that hearing a mass or not was something worth infinitely more than Paris, because it was a matter of conscience."[7] The stipulation of the Lateran pact had a negative influence particularly on the relationship of the philosophy of actualism to fascism; for, as has been observed already,[8] with the "conciliation," fascism ceased to be the practical manifestation of what in philosophy was actualism, and a good number of the actualists finally joined the opposition, leaving their master Gentile almost alone in his loyalty to Mussolini. Some, such as Ugo Spirito, united together in that fascism of the Left, at times turbulent and at other times slimy, from which later on the Communist party would draw some of its best elements. Others, however, joined the anti-Fascist ranks right away.

The Concordat of 1929, on the other hand, was destined to work to the detriment of the Catholic church and to Catholicism itself, by appearing in the view of many as the handmaiden of fascism, associated with its methods and ends.[9] And if fascism often bore the heavy burden of severe judgments, condemned as a bourgeois instrument of class oppression depriving workers and peasants of their due, such a negative appraisal was often made also of the church and its hierarchy, closely linked as they were to the regime.

Fascism did not only fail to solve completely in its favor the crucial problem of relations with the monarchy and the Catholic church, in order to secure totalitarian control of the masses; it also did not succeed for the most part in its effort to create a truly compact and homogeneous ruling class, competent on the technical and administrative level, truly convinced on the political level, and elevated on the moral one. A little more than five years after the "march on Rome," the foreign observer noted that the majority of the Fascists had remained essentially Socialist if their background had been a Socialist one, Catholic if they had belonged to the Popular Party, liberal, if such was their origin. And although the Fascist label, as a matter of course, applied to all these various contradictory tendencies, it nevertheless operated under the surface, and each political faction criticized the regime insofar as it did not follow a policy in conformity with its own original program.[10] Doubtless, this was true principally for all those who, after 1922, had approached fascism with some reluctance or who adhered to it with varying degrees of conviction and enthusiasm even after it had attained power and had demonstrated its ability to hold that power.

But an analogous deficiency of ideological homogeneity and analogous contrasts in the perception of fascism's concrete ends also characterized, as they had always characterized, the ruling nucleus of the Fascists of the "pre-March" era, who controlled the key posts in the regime. Obviously, this situation could only aggravate the eternal confusion of the regime. Under these circumstances it is no wonder that one of the major weaknesses of fascism was the absence of a well-integrated political class capable of serving as its solid pivotal point, capable of mediating clearly and perceptively its very goals and means, capable of articulating the conflicting issues preoccupying the different social and economic groups, and capable of revitalizing them, specifically in keeping with the overall vision of the regime. Fascism never had such a political class because, among other things, it lacked a sociologically coherent base, a class, an order, a group which might identify totally with it. As Stefano Jacini observed: "The regime did not have any compact group to rely on, a group whose interests, both moral and material, might coincide in full with its own, or at least might be such as to link it indissolubly to its own fortunes. To be sure, in theory the entire nation, in reality here and there a few small groups of the faithful, and more often a few influential individuals, were ready to be called on; yet these groups did not generally represent the best but rather the worst of their respective categories."[11]

Corporate capital, whether industrial, financial, or agrarian, had always had an essentially instrumental concept of fascism, one which therefore excluded any inherent identification of its representatives with the regime.

Therefore, all indiscriminate or blind support of the regime was also out of the question. Such an identification had existed without any doubt, to a certain degree, as far as petit-bourgeois and middle-class sectors of society were concerned. These groups were more open to the violently nationalistic tendencies of fascism and saw in fascism a political force and ideology which had blunted the charge of the proletariat and curbed the excessive ambitions and immoderate greed of the capitalists. It is really of little consequence that this conviction had virtually no basis in reality. Nevertheless, in the long run, it became clear that the advantages the regime assured to the majority of the various sections of the middle class remained negligible while, at the same time, the militaristic policies were not formulated to please them in any fashion whatsoever—since mere oratory might well materialize into a call for real sacrifices. At a certain point, for many of these individuals, involvement with fascism—as truly convinced followers of the movement—was transformed into mere atonic acceptance, due principally to simple inertia on their part. It was an involvement which did not stand up to the test of the first serious crisis. Concerning the social policies by which the regime tried to win over the masses, both the limits of their programmatic base and the shortcomings in their concrete implementation have already been pointed out. Without any doubt, these policies succeeded on a number of occasions in making a favorable impression, either by that psychological suggestion which Fascist propaganda used so well in a number of domains—angered nationalism, for example, never missed finding both workers and citizens vulnerable—or because the balance was not necessarily negative on the level of material benefits. Nor did the regime appear to the proletariat only in the context of wage cuts due, in part, to the worldwide economic crisis.

On the whole, however, class repression aimed at the proletariat remained one of the basic characteristics of fascism and most of the people affected reacted in consequence.

However, fascism's greatest failure probably falls into the cultural domain, and it was a failure which inevitably was to have profound consequences in relation to its aims of molding Italian society into a totalitarian unit. The regime existed at all times in the context of a cultural milieu to which it was essentially alien, notwithstanding individual concessions and episodes of rather grotesque servitude. Unable to create a dynamic cultural program which might succeed in elucidating convincingly its ideology and its most characteristic features, fascism did not even succeed in preventing Italian culture from gradually assuming, in its most meaningful manifestations and in its best men, an attitude which was more and more openly anti-Fascist. It was anti-Fascist at least on the level of cultural values, even if not so on the level of political action—which, to be sure, was lacking. In generating militant antifascism, the contribution of the intellectuals was proportionately the highest. The divorce between fascism and culture was certainly one of the main weaknesses of the regime, a regime which was always confronted by a "great moral force for decision and action," a force it never succeeded in overcoming.[12]

What ought to have been the main unifying and integrating element of the idealistic inclinations and the material interests of groups and individuals—that is to say, the party—was, as has already been shown on a number of occasions, absolutely unequal to its task. To its original defect of lacking a true consensus among its ruling elements concerning the basic goals of fascism (a lack which did not diminish with time) there was later added, in an increasingly stressed manner, its bureaucratization linked to patronage which was both consequence and cause of its own progressive "depoliticization"; this phenomenon can be traced to fascism's inability to create for itself a ruling class of the highest level and is typical of every authoritarian regime based essentially on personal rule, as Mussolini's fascism most definitely was. Under these conditions the very power and influence which the party enjoyed had a most negative effect. Giuseppe Bottai has observed: "Given the central and dominating position of the party, maintained in the regime more in practice than by any right to it, and given its ubiquitous pretensions, the infectious paralysis and fateful consequences brought about by the absence of critical rigor and political inactivity were reflected in the administrative structure of the state and its governmental policies, making functionaries out of cabinet ministers. But, above all else, there was the irreparable damage done to the corporative order."[13]

In part because of the force of events, in part as a consequence of that same stressed and ever-increasing indulgence of "self-divinization," Mussolini found himself obliged to face almost alone all the many centrifugal stimuli to which the regime was constantly subject, even if not always under pressure. A few days before July 25, in a conversation with an old friend from his youth, Ottavio Dinale, a party revolutionary of an earlier generation, a man with whom he had maintained sincere friendship, Mussolini described himself as the dictator of a regime that he had never succeeded in making totalitarian.[14]

The task which Mussolini had thus assumed would have been perhaps of insurmountable difficulty for even the greatest of statesmen. It was an impossible task for someone like him! Despite notable mental abilities and a command over individuals and masses which might be labeled magnetic, he was far from possessing those gifts of intelligence and character necessary for a truly great and creative statesman.[15]

Concerning the duce's political qualities, one of his most perspicacious collaborators has written, in his reflections on fascism: "I remember of him the characteristic of a technician: an electrical focal point which lights up one solitary bulb. Paradoxical but exact; an energy without guiding feeder cables transforming it into a system; an energy which breaks up and volatilizes, owing to a lack of uniting centers or connections capable of bringing them together. Intense illumination for the moment: then, darkness!"[16]

Because Mussolini, with the passing years, more and more tended to avoid the detailed study of problems and meticulously prepared and organized work, he compensated by approaching everything boring and unattractive to him with fiery temperament and personal magnetism. Whether his supposedly incoercible influence over given interlocutors was real or not, he dealt with them with a magniloquent and improvised gesture. Concerning his persistent inability to lay the foundations enabling him to implement his policies, even in questions of major importance, Giuseppe Bastianni, undersecretary at the Ministry of Foreign Affairs (1936-1939), has left an exact picture in reference to the period prior to the Second World War.[17]

Mussolini's taste for improvisation and to act on the basis of intuition was not limited to the area of foreign policy, a domain in which a measure of justification might be found for it, fraught with danger though conditions were apt to be. However, it was applied as well to the less clearly defined issues of domestic and administrative policies. Precisely because of the dictator's susceptibility "easily subject to the suggestions of others, in keeping with the impulsiveness of his character and the superficiality of his knowledge of the many issues with which he wanted to involve himself personally in order to demonstrate his own supremacy," there prevailed that "superficiality in passing laws in order to resolve quickly serious and complex problems, improvisation in keeping with the disposition to change one's mind, and a return to the *faits accomplis* while laws and decrees were modified only a short time after they had taken effect.[18]

The superficiality with which Mussolini so often approached the biggest and the most delicate problems of government had its roots not only in his innate tendency for the extemporaneous, but also in his intolerance for methodical work and the lack of basic preparation prior to reaching decisions.[19] This was also a direct and unavoidable consequence of his mania for centralizing in himself all the powers, of accumulating in his own person an absurd number of ministries and functions; moreover, he refused to delegate to others a share of his many offices or else delegated them amidst the greatest confusion.

THE TOTALITARIAN STATE AND PERSONAL DICTATORSHIP / 91

In this continual confusion of power, responsibilities, and attributes, the tragic element was perpetually a part of the comic and vice versa, and it was not uncommon for Mussolini, the head of government, to find himself in a state of agitation owing to chaos created by one of the ministries of which he himself was in charge. Thus in April of 1939, Mussolini, speaking in the Council of Ministers, complained about the inefficiency encountered in the military sector. "I must say," he explained, "that this administration of the army is not at all workable. Indeed, one cannot ever count on it. The statistics are never exact. As far as weapons are concerned, the numbers are all fraudulent. Our gunners are old, and their number is insufficient."[20] Bottai, reporting the episode in his diary, noted the following: "These are surprising confessions coming from the minister of war."[21] From a minister of war, moreover, who had been in charge for about ten years.[22]

In causing such situations, the nature of Mussolini's temperament no doubt played a major role. One of his closest collaborators of many years candidly admitted that this nature seemed made to be disobeyed.[23] To be sure, there was present in him, beyond all external attitudes and premeditated poses, an internal weakness in dealing with others, one which often influenced negatively his accomplishments in governing. It was precisely such a weakness which on occasion impeded him from freeing himself of inept and pernicious collaborators and induced him to tolerate methods often underhanded, if not downright ludicrous, in nature.[24] At the base of his imprudent choices there was also a substantial and somewhat determined indifference, deriving from his conviction that he was fully able to dominate all problems, including the most complex and extremely technical ones, without any need to seek help from others. Therefore, the fact that someone might go to this post or that, or assume this or that particular function, was of little importance to Mussolini. The function of his collaborators was not to be that of advising him in accordance with their particular experience in their analysis of the concrete problem at hand, but merely that of executing his orders without contradicting him. His own intuition, however, would be sufficient in any case.[25]

In an atmosphere of this kind, it was therefore quite logical for administrators to see themselves catapulted rather unexpectedly into positions calling for capacities exceeding their competence or even unrelated to their training and individual talents. This happened to Allessandro Lessona, as to so many others, when, at the start of his career in the government, he was named undersecretary in the Ministry of Economics.

Mussolini, on the eve of his fall, confided to Ottavio Dinale how enormous the task of coordinating and balancing the various antagonistic powers within the regime had been and that he never succeeded in amalgamating and curbing them completely. But this great problem had grown and was made insurmountable by Mussolini himself—that is to say, by his own deficiencies as a political leader and by the megalomaniac isolation in which he had chosen to settle. He created around himself a vacuum while surrounding himself in large measure with men of mediocrity or inadaptability to the functions allotted to them, and he constantly appointed new ones. Often there prevailed an incredible isolation between him and his closest collaborators, not to speak of the general gap between himself and the mechanisms of the totalitarian state itself. Indeed, isolation was such that he deceived himself into believing that he dominated the state in all its most minute operations, whereas, more often than not, he was the cause of awkward obstructions.[26] The regime approached the supreme test of the war at a moment when the structures of the state and the bureaucratic rigidity of the party were rendered evermore incapable of providing for the state the needed political and ideological substance.[27] Its institutions were tied to the intellectual and physical involution of the dictator. There could be but one result, catastrophe!

It might be tempting at this point to ask whether, even without the war and its disastrous outcome, the numerous internal and ideological contradictions of fascism would not have been sufficient in themselves, in the long or short run, to cause the collapse. In other words, was the downfall of the regime inevitable at any rate because of causes much deeper and more corrosive than the military defeat?

Considering separately the fact of the very concept of inevitability, one which is unacceptable on the basis of history, it seems difficult to consider the internal deficiencies and contradictions—certainly present in the regime at the start of the Second World War—sufficient in themselves to bring about its dissolution. If the symptoms of discontent discernible in the various sectors of Italian public opinion were numerous, it is also a fact that the great mass of the population, though not adhering enthusiastically to fascism, was not ready to consider the regime a mortal enemy, one to be thrown down at any cost, and was ready even less to run serious risks to achieve this objective. Even many of those who, within the various social classes, were uncompromisingly hostile to individual aspects of Fascist policy were not therefore especially opposed to the dictatorship of Mussolini as a solution to the problem of government and power in Italy. There was some exaggeration, but also a basis of truth—greater than one would like to admit today—in the words which Mussolini, almost at the end of his career and of his very life, addressed during the night of March 9, 1945, to the journalist Ivanoe Fossane: "In point of fact, I have not been a dictator, because my power of command coincided perfectly with the will to obey of the Italian people."[28]

In a certain sense, the very fact that the regime never succeeded in assuming a rigorously totalitarian character and that, nonetheless, individuals continued to be allowed a certain margin of autonomy in the private sphere, acted as a safety valve to the benefit of fascism, insofar as it prevented the forming of irrepressible focal points of tension. Moreover, the police power of the dictatorship was efficient and harsh enough to keep in check the efforts at liberation, often dearly paid for, by the militant anti-Fascist movement. This police power was effective to the point that the anti-Fascist movement could not cause any meaningful break between the regime and the majority of the Italian people. Such a rupture, with a potential to act as a positive historical force, one with a single, irreversible direction, came about only with fascism's tragic collapse. Beyond this factual statement one enters into the domain of arbitrary suppositions, mistaking various forms of resistance, vivid in their generic and specific discontent as they might have been, for a concrete and determined will to struggle and rebel. At the same time, one could also mistake certain internal deficiencies of the Fascist totalitarian regime for deep causes of disintegration and for an inevitability which is not verifiable.

PART TWO

INTERPRETATIVE CONTENTIONS

WILLIAM S. ALLEN

TOTALITARIANISM
The Concept and The Reality

Professor Allen's observations, like those made by a number of other contributors to this volume, proceed from the fact that the concept of totalitarianism issued from "the boast of a dictator," not from theoretical constructs. Unlike those who feel that the concept was actualized elsewhere and subsequently became a useful tool in the taxonomic repertoire of political science, Professor Allen concludes that it essentially remained a boast, becoming real only in part and temporarily.

Professor Allen arrives at this conclusion by surveying the evolved theoretical framework and then testing its validity against the model of a German town under Nazi rule, previously discussed by him in a separate monograph (see his note 12). The theme of Professor Allen's paper is found in the contrast between the claims to "total" power and its reality in totalitarian regimes.

Claiming an inner dynamic resulting in total control of all aspects of life, the totalitarian regime depended much more on legitimation than its practitioners and theoreticians have been apt to admit. Stressing the programmatic "self-legitimation" of the Nazi regime and linking it to prominent strains of the traditional German value system, Professor Allen shows the discrepancies between claims to total power and its reality in the German case.

Turning to the model of one German town, Professor Allen suggests the overall accommodation of the regime to reduced dynamism and elements of disenchantment by depicting daily life on the local level in the conduct of party officials. Echoing the distinction employed frequently in contemporary nazism studies between "movement phase" ∟ *and "regime phase," Professor Allen sees accommodation by the regime—*

97

far short of totalitarian claims—as mandated by the realities of power. Though emphasizing the role of manipulated legitimization, and not overlooking the role of terror, in the attainment of a sometimes superficial consensus, Professor Allen does not rule out the causative function of deeper structures. Unable to obtain complete control, subject to the debilitating effects of excessive bureaucratization, the Nazi regime could not, Professor Allen shows, afford to challenge unnecessarily the always present and significant elements of German opposition.

Originally the term *totalitarian* was not a concept developed by some theoretician but the boast of a dictator. Mussolini coined the term to describe his regime and to distinguish it from others. Yet though Mussolini's Fascist Italy was never thought by the subsequent theoreticians of "totalitarianism" to be an adequate example of what they meant, barely in the same league with Hitler's Germany or Stalin's Russia, the term was still well-suited to Fascist Italy because Mussolini's dictatorship was something new and demonstrably different from other dictatorships.

While previous and current dictatorships asserted control over political decision making and the instruments of force, what they required from their subjects was noninvolvement. Traditional dictatorships sought to prevent criticism or any challenge to the dictator's supremacy, but apart from that they generally left their subjects alone. Their motto was not unlike what the king of Prussia told his people after the Prussian army's defeat by Napoleon at Jena and Auerstädt: "The first duty of the citizen is to remain quiet."

But Mussolini's Fascist regime aspired to much more. It laid claim upon social organization, economic interrelationships, even cultural policy, and it attempted to mobilize the masses, to compel their positive involvement on behalf of the state. That was new, and for it a new term seemed appropriate: the "totalitarian" dictatorship, because it was not limited to the partial goal of a monopoly over only political decision making and organized force.

This useful term was soon taken over by theoreticians, however, and explored for all its implications. As it was expanded it proceeded to lose its connection with reality. It became primarily a label for two ideologically conflicting states, Nazi Germany and Soviet Russia, with the point being stressed that their structural similarities transcended their ideological differences.[1] In these two systems the word *totalitarian* was thought to describe accurately what Mussolini had boasted but never achieved: total control over the individual in all his actions.[2] Furthermore, "totalitarian" systems were said to have their own inevitable inner dynamic. They would grow progressively more expansionistic, more terroristic, more domineering over the individual personalities of their subjects. Mass murder, exemplified by the fate of the kulaks in Russia and the Jews under Nazi control, was a predicted characteristic.[3] Finally, the "pre-totalitarian society" was described: it was supposed to be a "mass society" in which individuals were "atomized."[4]

But the chief point of the "totalitarianism" theorists was that such systems succeeded in carrying out their claims. The individual living under such a system was totally at the mercy of the dictator, while the latter was subject to virtually no restraints from within. To put it another way: once a system of "totalitarian" rule was established, *politics* came to an end.[5]

This extreme, theoretical claim regarding the nature of "totalitarianism" is refuted by the reality of events—at least with respect to Nazi Germany, where we have extraordinarily full records of the regime and the party to test the concept with. In the first place, the dictator is not ubiquitous except through his agents, and when the ideology is imprecise and the party members are diverse or in conflict with one other, then there will be diversion of the dictator's intentions and at least a lack of uniformity in the actions of his agents.[6] Thus Hitler's government did not exert the same amount of control at all times or over all its subjects equally. Control progressed in intensity, reaching its apex during World War II in physical terms, though the wartime period also saw a relaxation of other demands, because of practical necessity. It was also applied differently to the different segments of society. Traditional conservatives were hardly bothered; workers were regarded with suspicion and closely watched, but also wooed by the regime through conscious self-restraint because Nazi leaders were afraid of engendering another labor uprising as in November 1918.[7] In fact one can say that control was completely exerted only over Germany's Jews.

The basic reason for this differential treatment of Germans according to group and over time is that the Nazi regime was a plebiscitarian dictatorship: it claimed to represent "the people." But more importantly it was dedicated to imperialistic expansion through war, and the Nazi leaders believed that this would be impossible without popular support. It is equally true that the Nazi leaders were willing to use manipulation and coercion to insure popular support. They were ruthlessly savage in their treatment of implacable opponents, such as the Socialists and Communists. Their propaganda was based upon contempt for the intelligence of the masses, as Hitler had explicitly and blatantly recommended in *Mein Kampf.* But they also believed that the German people must not be pushed too far or too crudely because that might lead to disaster. In short, they believed that despite all the force and propaganda, their rule was tenuous and could become delegitimized.

Thus even Hitler's willingness to employ terror had built-in limits. It was precisely Nazi dependence on brute force as the preferred "first resort" that made Hitler wary of direct confrontations on unpopular issues such as the attempted prohibition of Corpus Christi processions in the Rhineland. Overt popular opposition, even in nonfundamental matters, might break the myth of authority by compelling the Nazis to respond with pure violence. If naked force were needed in too many instances, Germans might begin to wonder whether the emperor had any clothes at all. Reckless repression, especially against the Nazi constituency of Center and Right, might also destroy the image of Nazi legitimacy as a government by popular demand. Terror had to be spent carefully, upon selected targets, for fundamental issues, and this drove Hitler to restrain his savagery.

Another way to view this is to look at the ways the Nazis won uncoerced support, because these were also areas where they could not act arbitrarily. Thus the promise to end the depression prevailed over the wishes of Nazis to act against department stores and the Jews: Hitler had to bail out the Tietz department store chain in 1933 because new unemployment might hurt his popularity.[8] There were many Nazis who were fervently anti-Christian, but Hitler fired one *Gauleiter* (Dinter) and threatened to shoot another (Wagner) rather than risk losing the support of Christians by permitting overt anti-Christian talk or action by Nazis. And, of course, the most famous Nazi retreat was over euthanasia; the reason for the backdown was fear that the allegiance of Germany's Catholics might otherwise be lost.

Conversely the Nazis also built support through other ways that were basically political: through programmatic self-legitimation. Their general espousal of nationalism, antibolshevism, and authoritarianism associated them with the goals of the traditional Right in the German political spectrum and made it difficult for conservatives to disavow the Nazi party. With effort, the moderate rightists could find cause to oppose the Nazis, but as long as Hitler spoke their language, the more likely response of German rightists was ambivalence or qualified support. This goes a long way toward explaining the quiescence of precisely those organizations within the Third Reich that continued to enjoy semi-autonomy: the army and the churches, whose leaders were traditionally nationalistic, anti-Bolshevist, and proponents of authoritarianism. Terror and propaganda were used by the Nazis against the churches and the army, but the first and most effective weapon was political legitimation.

Another political factor was the apparent absence of acceptable alternatives to nazism. Many moderates and conservatives supported the Third Reich because they believed that both the monarchy and the democratic republic had failed, and the only other option would be a Soviet Germany. This apparent political dilemma affected even the men of the 20th of July, and there were others, too, who came to abhor Hitlerism but saw it as less evil than communism or chaos. It was a powerful aid to the maintenance of Nazi rule.

A third political legitimizing element in the Third Reich was the widespread assumption that national socialism had overcome Germany's endemic pluralistic disintegration. Both the Wilhelmine and Weimar governments had been unsuccessful in developing a political system to unite the Reich's diverse social, religious, and regional groups. Meanwhile, an official "mandarinate" unceasingly promoted the ideal of national fusion.[9] But nazism convinced many that it was an integrative movement; it seemed to harness the masses into the "folk community." Thus those who opposed it were often accused of being reactionaries, or at least antimodern. The regime's mass basis, coupled with its espousal of many traditionalist tenets—no matter how ultimately spurious both might be in reality—were arguments transcending and reinforcing its dictatorial weapons. The point is that the Third Reich legitimized itself politically in ways that were perhaps as important as its control mechanisms, or at least paralleled them.

None of this ignores Hitler's desire for totalitarian control and his attempt to establish a monopoly over information and social organization. Yet here, too, the regime was clearly not omnipotent. Nazi censorship and propaganda, for example, could not prevent exchanges of information or access to non-Nazi sources of information through the radio—though these methods had to be used cautiously. Beyond that, the subjects of the Third Reich rapidly learned to "read between the lines" in the controlled press rather than simply swallowing propaganda whole. The conspicuous failure of many Nazi propaganda campaigns, as revealed in the government's own internal reports, shows that information manipulation did not lead to mind control.[10] Goebbels did manage to convince most Germans that he was exerting control over the minds of most other Germans, however. To this extent many subjects of the Third Reich felt isolated and powerless even if they opposed nazism. But whether they did or did not approve of the regime, Gestapo surveillance and official terrorism compelled outward conformity as a survival tactic. Yet on those rare instances when isolation was momentarily absent (the almost universal criticism of "Reichskristallnacht" in 1938 provides a startling example)[11] one can note that non-Nazi values instantly reasserted themselves. Totalitarian thought control remains a myth.

Similar points can be made about the Nazi claim to exercise a monopoly over organization. It is true that through "coordination" (*Gleichschaltung*) virtually all types of formal social organization were either destroyed or controlled by the Nazis, excepting the churches (though it has been argued that they underwent "auto-coordination" voluntarily).[12] But there were important exceptions. They included informal centers of traditional cohesion: friendships and families, neighborhoods or factories, or small villages. In short, there were primary loyalties that predated the Third Reich and proved impervious to its pretensions. Only the Nazi use of force and fear held them in check, but since they abided below the surface of outward conformity, they could also reemerge and affect even the Nazi party itself, as will be evidenced below.

Thus on several counts the extreme "totalitarian" theory does not hold up.[13] The Nazis did try to control all aspects of human life within the Third Reich, but their efforts failed. What they managed to achieve was largely due to terrorist tactics and political legitimation, plus frequent opportunistic accommodation, rather than a "totalitarian" system. As in so many other things, the Nazi claims here, too, were fundamentally fraudulent.

To reach such conclusions about the general limits of "totalitarianism" in Nazi Germany is one thing; it is quite another issue to look at the actual impact of the Third Reich upon daily life and to see how Hitler's agents behaved at the local level. Where that has been done[14] the evidence shows that Nazi rule was by no means either uniform or all-encompassing. On the contrary: at the lowest level, the Hitler dictatorship definitely showed signs of accommodating itself to reduced dynamism, political maneuvering rather than pure force, and concern with external compliance rather than true popular involvement.

New evidence for these assertions comes from the Nazi party files of *Ortsgruppe* Northeim, a town of 10,000 which was previously the subject of a monographic study by me and about which, therefore, detailed prior information is already on record.[15] This is of some importance, since only a knowledge of the actual personalities involved permits an accurate evaluation of the significance of the events.

The first point to note is that the character of Northeim's Nazi party underwent a significant change once the Third Reich had been firmly established. Up to 1933 and for the first two years of Hitler's dictatorship the Nazi party of Northeim was an extremely dynamic movement, reflective of the fanatical vigor of its local leader, Ernst Girman. By spring 1935, however, Girman had firmly established himself as mayor of

Northeim and found ample scope for his energies in that office. Hence he decided to give up the office of "Local Group Leader" of the Nazi party in Northeim. But he had no desire to share power or create a potential competitor. Hence he arranged to divide the party office. For Northeim's 1,000 Nazis there were created "Local Group I" and "II," each with an *Ortsgruppenleiter*. That Girman wanted administrators rather than politicians is also clear from the persons he selected as his "successors": they both were accountants and pallid personalities.

The new managers of Northeim's Nazis were also obviously mandated to bring the party's affairs into businesslike order, for their first set of actions involved replacing most of the basic Nazi cadre leaders with capable bureaucratic types. Most of the "old fighters" who had previously been "cell leaders" or "block wardens" were now retired, and their functions were assumed by "March hares"—people who had jumped on the Nazi bandwagon after Hitler had established the dictatorship in March 1933. These new leaders were *appointed* to office (sometimes clearly against their will) and were expected to collect dues promptly and regularly, make sure that there was full attendance at meetings and rallies, and above all solicit contributions on a weekly basis for the various ventures the Nazi party promoted, such as the "Winter Relief" fund.[16]

The significance of this changing of the guard in Northeim is that it marked a clear retreat from fanatical aspirations. The new party leaders were timeservers, and their goals were limited and easily measured by standard bookkeeping practices. Yet these were crucial members of the party's apparatus: each of the eighty block wardens was responsible for dealing with approximately forty-four households in Northeim on a day-to-day basis, and for most of the townspeople they *were* the Nazi party.

Nothing illustrates the consequences of the party's bureaucratization better than the "political evaluations of individuals" that the new block wardens produced in ensuing years. For all sorts of reasons the Nazi party required checks into the political reliability of Germans, and in the end these were supplied by the block wardens. A careful analysis of those submitted after 1935 in Northeim shows that they routinely declared individuals to be "politically reliable" on the sole basis of whether or not the person in question contributed a few coins regularly and cheerfully to the block warden when he took up his weekly collection. Ex-Communists, former monarchists, erstwhile *Reichsbanner* militants, or whatever—all received a clean bill of health as long as they had sense enough to ease the block warden's life by enabling him to meet his collection quota. And virtually nothing more was demanded of Northeimers who did that— at least not by the new Nazi subofficials, who themselves had joined the party from convenience rather than conviction.[17]

Of course it is one thing to note that the controls exerted over Nort-heimers had become routine and perfunctory as long as the citizen kept up appearances, but it is quite another question to ask how far Nazi officials could go in forcing their policies upon the people. Here we find the fear-some Ernst Girman, once notorious for his fanatical ruthlessness, turning to skillful politics rather than raw force. One of Girman's deepest ideological commitments was to anticlericalism: he hated the churches and was privately determined to replace "the faith of the preachers with our faith in Hitler."[18] Consequently he set out to destroy the religious schools in Northeim and eventually did so. But the way he succeeded reflects on the nature of the Third Reich, at least as it was experienced in Northeim.

Shortly after Easter, 1937, Mayor Girman summoned the parents of pupils at the Catholic school to a meeting. He told them that their children were getting an inadequate education since the Catholic school, with only seventy-seven pupils and two teachers, offered an insufficient variety of courses. The parents were urged to transfer their children to the Evangelical-Lutheran school, with its thirteen hundred pupils and ample teaching corps.

A few Catholic parents complied immediately, but in the following months the mayor brought personal pressure on the parents one at a time so that there was a slow but steady exodus from the Catholic school. The bishop of Hildesheim protested vigorously, but Mayor Girman defended his actions by asserting that his sole argument was the superior educational opportunities available at the Protestant school. By Christmas, 1937, Northeim's Catholic school had only sixteen pupils left, and Girman successfully petitioned the provincial school authorities to close it as a "dwarf school," which they did, in accordance with standing regulations. Thereupon the Nazi mayor petitioned the authorities (in February 1938) to declare the Evangelical school "nondenominational," since it now had a substantial minority of Catholic pupils; this, too, was according to the book, and so his request was granted. By April 1938, Northeim had no more religious schools.[19]

But note how this year-long campaign worked. It was not dictatorial fiat but skillful maneuver that enabled Ernst Girman to reach his ideologically motivated goal. Admittedly a heavy measure of informal intimidation in the personal interviews with Catholic parents was a critical component (no matter how "correct" Girman was in his solicitation for the welfare of the children), but essentially this Nazi leader got his way through bureaucratic politics. His actions hardly fit the "totalitarian model."

Such examples could be multiplied, but they boil down to a central point. What the minions of the Third Reich required of the people of Northeim was external compliance with Hitler's dictatorship, and, in touchy matters, they were careful not to overstep self-defined boundaries of behavior. The townsperson who conformed outwardly to the Nazis was otherwise left in peace or else manipulated into making a minimal contribution to the Third Reich.

Northeimers who refused to play the game quickly felt the wrath of Ernst Girman: his correspondance abounds with scathing letters to persons who failed to contribute to the "Winter Relief."[20] And overt indifference awakened the brutal qualities that Girman had shown in his rise to power, as exemplified by the following letter he wrote to a young woman in May 1935.[21]

It has been reported to me that on the occasion of the Führer's birthday ceremony you did not raise your arm during the singing of the Horst Wessel song and the national anthem. I call your attention to the fact that you put yourself in danger of being physically assaulted by doing this. Nor would it be possible to protect you because you would deserve it. It is singularly provocative when people still ostentatiously exclude themselves from our racial community by actions like that. Heil Hitler!

Yet when it came to matters affecting the well-being of his town, Girman was even willing to overlook or argue against official Nazi ideology—for example, the regime's campaigns against the Free masons or the Jews.[22] That Girman had limited goals emerges from a comment he made concerning a former political enemy, a social democrat who applied for a job with the state-owned railroad: "I do not believe that Herr Strohmeyer will ever become a follower of the National Socialist regime, but he also will not say anything against it."[23] With that he endorsed this man's job application.

Of course evidence from a single case can never suffice to prove a general proposition. Yet to date there has been no counterevidence but only theory to substantiate the "totalitarianism" claim. While Northeim's Nazis might be exceptional, they are more likely to reflect an exceptionally well organized "totalitarian" structure because of the extent of support given Hitler's party prior to 1933. By July 1932, some two-thirds of the town's voters cast their ballots for the Nazis, and this was clearly because their general rightist proclivities were being appealed to by the stance Northeim's Nazi adopted at that time (most notably anti-Marxism). Yet even with this amount of voluntary backing as a starting point, the Nazis still felt their rule to be tenuous. By 1935 the district

Regierungspräsident was drawing up a list of opponents to the regime that included virtually all segments of the population, including the early Nazis;[24] by 1937, the lowest officials in Northeim's Nazi party were actually being given training in the use of small arms.[25] If this was the situation in a Nazi stronghold, what must it have been like in areas where the recorded opposition prior to the Third Reich exceeded half the population?

Such nervousness helps us understand both the repressiveness of the Nazi regime and its reticence. In discussing the "totalitarian" theory we must not lose sight of the terroristic elements of Hitler's dictatorship nor the general Nazi desire to organize the German people completely. But we should also note that the Nazis were unable to accomplish completeness of control, that the party could succumb to the laws of bureaucratization, that even the most fanatical leaders found it necessary to be circumspect lest they stir up unwanted opposition.

The authoritative *International Encyclopedia of the Social Sciences* put it this way in its second edition: "The greatest problem for future research on the topic of totalitarianism is the utility of the concept itself." It raised the possibility that a third edition, "like the first one," might not even list the term.[26] But if we see "totalitarianism" in its original meaning as a *claim* of the new-style dictatorships, as a quality that set them apart from traditional authoritarian regimes, then perhaps something of its core idea can be saved. Certainly the Nazis smashed formal societal bonds and compelled overt demonstrations of support from their subjects. But as for the rest, "totalitarianism" remains what it originally was—the boast of a dictator.

KARL DIETRICH BRACHER

TERRORISM AND TOTALITARIANISM

Professor Bracher's essay, linking terrorism and totalitarianism, must be viewed in the context of contemporary politics in West Germany. Both the bitter division of Germany into two ideologically opposite countries and the brazen conduct of terrorists in the western part of Germany make for quite a different perception of the relationship of terrorism and totalitarianism among German defenders of pluralist democracy than among those in societies less affected by terrorism and the perils of Soviet domination. However, not all West German democrats perceive these dangers as acutely as Professor Bracher does, and some see in the insistence on the concept of totalitarianism a threat in turn to pluralist democracy (see the essay by Professor Mommsen).

Read in conjunction with the more extensive contribution of Professor Bracher on the history and nature of the conflict over the concept of totalitarianism, this essay takes the concept out of the historical epoch to which it is assigned by some scholars and endeavors to relate it to current trends. As one of the foremost students of the Weimar Republic's collapse in the face of the twin threats of Communist and Fascist totalitarianism, Professor Bracher is struck by the "total" hostility demonstrated on the part of the Left against those insisting on the continued relevance of the concept of totalitarianism to right- and left-wing political extremism. Addressing particularly the "false front" of the Left, which—under the guise of antifascism—endeavors to erode the foundations of democracy and representative government in the Federal Republic of Germany, Bracher leaves no doubt about his convic-

Translated by Ernest A. Menze

tion that the threat of totalitarian terrorism is a worldwide one. Dissatis-fied with the classification of left-wing terror as a variable of the Right, Bracher considers the imputation of constructive ends to unacceptable means an incredible deception. He denounces the image of terrorists as aimless and unpolitical as not in keeping with reality and demonstrates their determined adherence to political creeds.

Detecting, now as then, terror and chiliastic promises in the armory of modern-day radicals, Professor Bracher here issues a stern warning to the defenders of Western pluralist democracy.

The Federal Republic of Germany continues to live under the impact of two experiences which were essential in giving it shape: the destruction of Weimar democracy by the National Socialists in 1932-33 and the establishment of a second dictatorship in Eastern Germany after 1945. In both cases one-party rule with totalitarian claims was imple-mented. Totalitarianism of the Right and of the Left were the funda-mental experiences. The founders of the Second (West) German Republic, therefore, insisted on open democracy and a constitutional structure devised to protect the state from totalitarian tendencies. The creation of the West German Basic Law was governed by this fundamental consensus, shared by the principal political forces. To prevent a repetition of the Weimar catastrophe it was first of all necessary to avoid an erosion of democracy by the polarizing effects and obstructionism of antiparliamen-tary movements, for these ultimately lead to those "false majorities" of the right- and left-wing totalitarian parties, parties whose only common purpose is the destruction of the free state-of-laws.

An anti-Fascist orientation alone did not suffice to accomplish this task; an anti-Fascist orientation could even serve as a deception (as it did in the case of the Soviet Occupied Zone of Germany—later the German Democratic Republic), if it was not based on a conception of democracy which opposed both threats: that of another self-destruction under pseudodemocratic conditions, as in 1933, and that of left-wing dictator-ship modeled after the people's democracies, such as were carried on in the name of antifascism under the protection of the Red Army. To meet these twofold dangers meant to recognize the totalitarian in right-wing as well as left-wing radicalism, while simultaneously resisting the tempta-tion to adopt a restrictive approach to democracy.

Against this background the much-practiced substitution in the course of the sixties, in academic and public discourse, of the concept of fascism for that of totalitarianism had to bear significantly on the self-image of the Federal Republic of Germany. This was not a mere academic or publicistic squabble over concepts, as it was condescendingly characterized in the lingo and spirit of the times. Rather, it was a political issue of first-rate psychological import which could lead to a shifting of political standards and values and bring about a real change of systems. With the transformation of institutions a simultaneous transformation of terminology began.

The substitution of the anti-Fascist for the antitotalitarian conception of democracy made it possible also for liberal minds to turn to Marxist-Communist modes of thought. Theories of fascism became quite fashionable, the Soviet formula of "German fascism" was widely copied, and an overly generalized view of fascism was advanced to the detriment of the proper differentiation between totalitarian and democratic politics. The intellectual consequences are incalculable. For here, simultaneously, a gradual breakdown of restraints as well as of the protective mechanisms of "steadfast democracy" took place. These restraints and mechanisms had been intended to protect democracy from renewed polarization and pervasive extremist ideologies. They were meant to prevent pluralistic democracy from falling captive again to that undemocratic alternative which once seduced and destroyed it: the supposedly sole alternative of "communism or fascism," of a left- or right-wing solution which had entrapped so many contemporaries of the thirties (see Arthur Koestler's *Memoirs*).

The decisive element enabling the antidemocratic movements of the sixties and seventies to ostracize or taboo the concept of totalitarianism—even in serious publications—appears to have been their capacity to do so in two ways: they were able to relate the concept to exaggerated anti-capitalist conspiratorial theories (thereby making the parliamentary principle of representation itself suspect), and they were able to use it to establish monolineal, neototalitarian modes of thought and action fitting into the range of specifically German concepts of power or, at any rate, appealing to the sources that sustain them. The critique of capitalism and parliamentarianism was intensified and absolutized. In addition, the distinction between democracy and dictatorship was belittled by theories of government reducing the state to a mere tool of groups and classes—the epitome of "structural power." The use of "counterforce" against this "structural power," disregarding democratic rules and the institutions of the state-of-laws, was advocated as legitimate on the basis of democracy "in a higher sense." All of this has been going on now for a decade under the label of concepts categorized as anti-Fascist, particularly in the Marxist sense. But the campaign is turned against Western democracy and yields significant effects in broader circles considered "radical-democratic": these radical democrats absolutize the struggle against capitalism, colonialism, imperialism, and racism—in other words, against phenomena which undoubtedly call for criticism. But the critique is carried out in a spirit of *total* hostility to free democracies. What this struggle looks like to the strategists of the "worldwide Communist movement" is revealed with sufficient clarity—and with constant reference to Lenin's authority—in the book by Wadim Sagladin, the deputy head of the International Department of the Soviet Communist party's Central Committee.[1] Unfortunately, this self-revelation is not taken note of sufficiently, even though its essential features have been excerpted by the Journal *Osteuropa*, with commentary by a Soviet scholar.[2]

Having eliminated the concept of totalitarianism, one then is able to ignore identical repressive governmental policies, especially in Communist regimes, as long as they call themselves anti-Fascist and Socialist. Just as the concept of freedom governing the liberation movements of the Third World does not reveal anything about their democratic or dictatorial character, the concept of socialism, used in this sense, may serve to justify —or rule out—almost any conceivable ideology or form of government. With the disappearance of the criteria of dictatorship and totalitarian rule there also disappear the fundamental distinguishing characteristics governing the structure and control of power; the barrier between the liberal and the totalitarian concepts of democracy disappears.

The loss of the initial antitotalitarian orientation in the Federal Republic of Germany coincided with the resurgence of ideologies and resulted in the temporary rise of the NDP (the Neo Nazi movement), most significantly, however, in the rise of the "New Left" movements; the effects of this loss have become noticeable in the generation gap, in the student movement, and also in the media.

The much lamented ennui resulting from dissatisfaction with and weariness of the state, the destructive irony towards and distortion of democratic values, the relativizing of Communist doctrines *vis-à-vis* presumed Fascist threats, as well as the diabolizing of any form of anti-communism, all of these are, not least, effects and consequences of that disorientation, especially in the growing generation. Contributing factors are here just as much the actual or supposed changes in the Communist domain after Stalin as the ostentatious democratic image of the "Euro-Communists" and the eternally renewed longing for a genuine socialism, reunited and cleansed of its impurities. A half-century of differentiation between democratic and totalitarian socialism, so it is proclaimed, must finally be done away with.

Domestic political consequences of détente in foreign affairs—a policy that in itself probably was unavoidable—are part and parcel of this erosion of democratic thought. Such domestic political consequences certainly did not have to come about, as shown by the example of the United States or England. However, divided Germany finds itself in a peculiar situation. And, unfortunately, the ideological and intellectual reverse of détente led many publicists to overlook carefully and repress the antidemocratic characteristics of communism: the totalitarian label now was found inappropriate; it even appeared essentially no longer applicable, since convergence appeared to be in the making, and was becoming an exciting symbol of progress, confirmed by actual policy changes and concessions. The absence of free elections, of a pluralistic party system, and of the separation of powers, then, could no longer remain the decisive criteria. These basic principles and major characteristics of free democratic systems, in the process, gradually lost their fundamental importance as positive guideposts in the political education and commitment of young people: now, these principles in turn became suspect as ideological and were subjected to rigorous, undifferentiated criticism and ridicule as "formalized democracy" or even "F.D.G.O." (the "freiheitliche demo-kratische Grundordnung"–the free democratic basic order. According to Article 21, Section 2 of the Bonn Constitution, political parties may be outlawed as unconstitutional when their aims or the conduct of their membership imperils the free democratic basic order of the Federal Republic of Germany). The campaign against "occupational discrimina-tion" (*Berufsverbote*–the prohibition to carry on one's profession because one's loyalty to the state is in doubt) is carried on, for example, under a slogan affixed to the walls of universities. It aims at the core con-cept of the constitution, the free and democratic basic order, and sharply opposes obligatory loyalty oaths to the F.D.G.O. Ridicule of the Basic Law is tied to malevolent allusions to coercive National Socialist policies.

At the same time, uncertainty has increased because of the internal conflicts in and weaknesses of the West, especially in consequence of the Vietnam War. American democracy, formerly a model, lost prestige, and its image was twisted into its opposite; its place was taken by those ideologies of liberation which aim at domination rather than compromise. The concentration on the struggle for national emancipation in the Third World, often brought into living rooms by television without the requisite clarification of political circumstances, provided dictatorial socialism with a fascinating novel quality. That it led, in apparently successful cases, such as China and Cuba, Vietnam and Cambodia, to Communist regimes, totalitarian in organization and ideology–though under nationalist prefixes–made the dictatorial character of the liberation movement appear as a lesser evil or at times even gave it a positive aspect. It repre-sented a pure and simple idea–progress and liberation from all ills. Thus the perversion of morality characteristic of totalitarianism could come about. Injustice became justice, suppression became liberation, and coercion and terror were justified by the higher goal to be attained: the end sanctifies the means. How dissonant and even sanctimonious appeared, in contrast, the position taken by the West in defense of the democratic creed; here the means dishonored the end, especially in view of the West's irresponsible deportment in the cases of CIA actions in Cuba or Chile, in the shifting stands taken on apartheid policies, and in the ambivalence *vis-à-vis* Palestinian terrorist activity.

What is meant by the term *totalitarian* now? And of which "totalitarian syndromes" must one speak in order to evaluate the nature of such trends in the democratic West, especially in the Federal Republic of Germany? Though it has become fashionable during the past two decades to forget about earlier statements made relating to the subject, quoting my own remarks from the year 1957 may be in order: A totalitarian mode of thought and government denies in principle "the right to exist of various competing political groups and creeds, as well as the autonomy of non-political elements of society . . . Everything must be made subordinate to and placed into the service of a restrictive, absolutely binding ideological conception of state and society . . . A totalitarian mode of thought and government is based on a militant ideology, functioning simultaneously as substitute religion and infallible political gospel. It seeks to account for and justify, historically and in terms of future expectations, the suppression of opposition and the total 'coordination' of the citizen."

The tempting yet totally unscrupulous fiction of the people's complete identity with the leadership, indeed, the fictitious identity of idea and reality, is the essential factor in the face of which all differentiation between democracy and dictatorship fades away. Of course, the various theories of totalitarianism that have been advanced over the past fifty-five years are marked by weaknesses subject to criticism as are, in the end, all political and social theories that are not merely descriptive. But it is equally certain that there still is now, even after Hitler and Stalin, the manifestation of totalitarian rule, the tendency towards the totalitarian, the totalitarian temptation recently sketched in Francois Revel's book of the same title as a worldwide, but also as a French problem, especially of the Left.[3] The criticism of theories often serves only as the pretext for the curtailment of free thought and argument. This has been evident in academic and literary circles ever since the New Left proclaimed the concept of totalitarianism historically fallacious and representative of the cold war mentality. This thesis has been repeated uncritically by many people not really belonging to its immediate circle of adherents because it seemed sympathetic to détente and because, removing irksome anti-Communist labels, it stood in a way for progressivism.

A twofold connection between the problem of totalitarianism and the spread of doctrines advocating the use of force, therefore, is discernible. On the one hand the readiness of democracy to defend itself is undermined by the disparagement as mere "formal democracy" of the principles governing the state-of-laws. This is done in the name of political expediency, social change, and thought processes that relativize political and moral standards under the guise of social science terminology. On the other hand, however, totalitarian modes of thought and conduct are actually used to account for and justify doctrines advocating the use of force. The doctrines are appealed to as representing the identity of theory and practice, genuine popular sovereignty or the total absence of government in the pseudodemocratic, utopian sense. Intellectual pliability and the cult of action dovetail. An important role is played in the process by the tantalizing thesis of "counterforce" warranted and called for when applied against the "structural powers" of the state and allegedly class-bound society. It provides the intellectual armor for breaking out from the confinement of society and facilitates the first steps on the road to condoning terrorist deeds. Twentieth-century seizures of power by Lenin, Mussolini, and Hitler as well as analyses from Hannah Arendt to Leonard Shapiro have made clear that coercion and terror, whatever their ideological garb, are integral parts of totalitarian movements and regimes. Moreover, each political act of terror has totalitarian roots and motivation. The terrorist mentality calls for the complete destruction of the political enemy and the elimination of compromise and the state-of-laws, to be achieved by any means. To this end it uses the truisms of the *terribles simplificateurs*, which promise, as the one and only solution of all problems, the totalitarian temptation in a complex world, totalitarian salvation.

With that the question of the "totalitarian syndrome" has been raised, of conditions which facilitate the unleashing of force, indeed, make it necessary and justify it. The sociological and psychological dimensions of the use of force and terror have been discussed by others. Here the political and ideological components are addressed. Pertaining to those there also seems to prevail a perilous tendency to underestimate the political substance and ideals of totalitarian movements. The pseudolegal National Socialist revolution and the sympathy accorded the movement by broad layers of society were made possible, in the first place, by the misperception of its racist core, the misjudgment of its revolutionary claims, and the disregard of its devotion to the use of force. By the same token, due to the attraction of vaguely defined utopian ends, bourgeois intellectuals to this day are deceived by the Leninist doctrine of revolution with its attendant coercion of the majority and destruction of all opposition. The effects of the seizure of power are belittled or "humanistically" dressed up and glorified. The action-oriented theses of Maoism and the literature of guerrilla warfare are fitting additions. The internationalist makeup which distinguishes leftist-Communist radicalism from the rightist-Nationalist version helps to rouse revolutionary expectations even in countries not in the slightest marked by a "revolutionary situation." The coercive character reveals itself in the pronounced effort of the Communist world movement to bring into being a "political army of the Socialist revolution" (as it does in the military tenor of Communist terminology in general); it is underscored effectively in the designation of the R.A.F. (*Rote Armee Fraktion*) as a "fraction" of the Red Army. The worldwide slogan of "the struggle for peace" emphasizes and legitimizes, in the first place, all aspects of *struggle* per se, leaving "peace" to the tactical discretion of revolutionary strategy. As Sagladin's official handbook says it: "The struggle for peace, democracy and national liberation is one of the most important tools employed by the Communist parties in leading the masses to the revolution."[4] Peaceful coexistence, therefore, in a Marxist-Leninist perspective, is considered but a specific form of class struggle.

The disparagement of the totalitarian substance contrasts strangely with the evident, even understandable attraction the younger adherents of such movements in particular find in precisely such monolithic theories and ideologies. The disparagement of the totalitarian substance is also contradicted by the stimulating effect such ideologies at times have in shaping the self-image of and motivating their representatives and advocates. The refusal to classify politically contemporary coercive movements and their associates, and to take seriously their revolutionary slogans (for which they are ready to do anything, including committing collective political suicide) runs counter not only to political experience but also to the clear empirical evidence provided by the shocking statements of the Left, not least of leftist elements in the universities.

Although not free of unorthodox variations, this terrorism clearly is part and parcel of the Left and stands, in its socio-political conceptions and aims, on Marxist-Leninist foundations. Two principal objections are raised against this analysis: one portrays the terrorists as Fascists in disguise, the other denies them any political aims, picturing them as the incarnation of criminal destructive tendencies. But the designation as Fascist, first of all, confirms the totalitarian syndrome that is at hand here—it confirms that right-wing, as well as left wing, totalitarianism exists and that the two versions are comparable. Indeed, the *Freikorps* and Vehmic mentalities of the twenties, right up to the infamous murder of Potempa in 1932, reveal a mixture of fanaticism and confusion similar to that characterizing contemporary terrorists. In those years the slogan of the destruction of the bourgeois and capitalist system came readily from the lips of right-wing radicals. If, all similarities in the use of force and terror notwithstanding, the "German socialism" of Hitler with its racist-revolutionary claims was distinct from Lenin's class-revolutionary political doctrine, there were, nevertheless, in either camp those who changed sides. Moroever, there were other links demonstrating the common elements in the totalitarian concept of power and government: attitudes fundamentally antidemocratic and inimical to law and liberty, which frequently appeared to be interchangeable. One only has to think of Mussolini, the Socialist transformed into the Fascist, of his and Lenin's admiration for George Sorel's doctrine of violence, of National Bolshevism and the National Socialist Left, or of appeals by radicals from the Left and Right to Carl Schmitt's "either-or" concept of politics and his antiparliamentarianism (warmed over by the New Left under the doomsday label "late-bourgeois").

But the classification of leftist terrorism as a variant of that of the Right—fashionable today and sounding strange at any rate, coming from the mouths of those denying the concept of totalitarianism—is out of order also because its allies and many of its sympathizers belong to the leftist spectrum and, after all, identify themselves as such. On the international stage this becomes visible in the demonstrations for the self-proclaimed "red" brigades and armies, for Croissant and his imagined antifascism of violence. Presented as a means to putative liberation, the attacks on the democratic state-of-laws are thereby equated, in incredibly deceptive fashion, with resistance to its autocratic opposites. Moreover, with the manipulation of the anti-Fascist concept, even the classical doctrine of the right to resist unjust government is invoked—a right recognized as little by the dictatorships of the Left as it is by those of the Right.

Concerning the second objection, the supposed unpolitical character and aimlessness of terrorists, their allegiance to radical socialism and communism speaks loudly and clearly enough for itself. Not much concrete about the future was said by Marx, Lenin, Mao, or Castro, either. Concrete and real, however, is the program of destruction, of total hostility and devastating criticism, whereas the image of the future, aside from promises of general happiness, remains as vague and noncommittal in the new Marxism as it was in the old. Could it be that the neoleftist authors to whom one appeals, from Marcuse to Guevara, Fanon and Marighella, could it be that these self-proclaimed anti-Fascists and Marxists in the end are Fascists themselves? If so, the concepts of fascism and totalitarianism could indeed be used as synonyms. In that case, however, they would include dictatorial movements of the Right and of the Left, fascism and communism. Pluralistic democracy based on the concept of the state-of-laws and the separation of powers would remain the antagonist. But that certainly is not the intent of this most recent misrepresentation and shift in the political and ideological classification of terrorism. Rather, one is reminded of the apologetic efforts of politicians of the Right like Papen to set themselves apart, after 1945, from national socialism, by classifying it as leftist.

The acknowledgment of a Marxist-Leninist root in terrorism constitutes neither an overall defamation of Marxism in its varied manifestations, nor a denial of the labor movement's ideational roots. Rather, the achievement and importance of social democracy, especially of its German branch, rest in the repulsion of Marxist class struggle and the dictatorship of the proletariat by means of a freedom-oriented and democratic perception of politics and, notwithstanding a Marxist party program, the implementation of a democratic-parliamentarian system which was at last also conceptually confirmed in the Bad Godesberg program. To safeguard this freedom in the face of totalitarian socialism and neo-Marxist currents is the continued challenge to social democracy. It calls for clear demarcation from the Leninist concept of Marxism which continues to characterize all Communist parties in East and West. Anticipated as the totalitarian version of socialism already in Marxian theory, Leninism constitutes an important foundation of left-wing revolutionary and dictatorial movements as such. In this sense contemporary doctrines of violence are inconceiveable without the Marxian component.

Consideration also must be given to the connection between doctrines advocating violence and those democratic theories which promise both the attainment of total freedom and total social cohesion. Here, too, a symptom of totalitarian temptation reveals itself when, in the name of democratization, the human person is disregarded and a complete reconciliation of the opposites of individual and society—that is, perfect socialization—is promised.

What is at stake here is the relation between the concept of conflict and that of the exercise of power. With the overemphasis on solution by conflict at the expense of institutional solutions—a basic problem of democratic life—expectations are roused which, in the end, may turn against any type of authority and government. Processes are thereby put into motion which may lead to conversion of conduct based on an understanding of conflict into conduct governed by violence, and the pluralistic conception of politics may turn into a totalitarian one. In the process the fundamental difference is skipped over: democracy thrives on conflict; dictatorship eliminates conflict by force. This lapse is confirmed also by the experience of the past few years. Extremist and terrorist impulses came to the fore, especially at the universities and in some citizens' initiatives; the "bending of the rules" was turned into violation of the law and finally into direct militant action, all in the name of democratization.

Such thought and conduct, departing from traditional modes of conflict resolution, seek to justify the use of force by conjuring up utopian gospels and certainties which promise to solve the individual's and society's problems the world over, and by creating visions of progress and emancipation, universal socialism, and total democracy. After all, it is Communist Marxism which, though basing its all-encompassing claims on supposedly scientific certitudes, strives for them on the basis of a fervent faith that the course of all history must lead to its own triumph. The use of force is permissible and even called for as long as it serves ends in accordance with ideological mandates: no more and no less. Foremost among these mandates are Lenin's, who called it the international obligation of Communists "[to do] the utmost of that which is possible in one country to prepare, support and unleash the revolution in all countries."[5] Contemporary Communist criticism of left-wing radical terrorists and deviants, in this respect, represents a deception. For this criticism is directed expressly against premature and so-called individual terror alone. It therefore leaves to collective revolutionary terror its higher justification and does not at all reject violence in principle. Moral or humanitarian criteria are subordinated to the overall expansive strategy, notwithstanding the appeal made to them in individual cases or for the sake of philosophical self-justification.

Neither the use of force in foreign policy nor open warfare now has the role each plays in fascism, and total disarmament is advocated. Unlike fascism, communism continually speaks of worldwide peace. But it also speaks of world revolution and advocates violence in other countries. In the final analysis everything boils down to a kind of "domestic politics" covering the world, a unified process preparing and advancing revolutionary situations.

What in the Fascist and National Socialist cases was the pseudolegal revolution in the Communist context reads "that the political forms of bourgeois democracy may be used in the interest of revolutionary forces."[6] The fact that in both cases the use of force is fully legitimized renders them nevertheless subject to comparative analysis. In view of the totality of the solutions desired, peaceful conflicts are no longer possible. By the same token, standards governing conflict resolution and compromise, the conduct of strikes and political opposition as such, no longer exist. The supposedly higher and stronger order, brought about and sustained by force and even terror, conjures up the chimera of an apparently ultimate harmony, which is held up as superior to conflict-prone pluralistic democracy. But this chimera does not correspond to the universal experience of the manifoldedness and complexity of human existence. What is proclaimed as progress, at the very best, is utopia. In truth, it is regression into ancient forms of despotism and arbitrary rule which, to this day, as Solzhenitsyn laments, have characterized most of human history. This regression represents a reaction against the dynamic world of the modern polity and a return to the impersonal, archaic system of the collectivized states of the past.

The fundamental problem in the development and spread of extremism and violence lies in the meaning certain concepts have assumed due to the reintroduction of ideology into social and political thought during the past fifteen years. The close connection of language and politics clearly reveals itself in the relationship of terrorism and totalitarianism.

In conclusion these theses are proposed:

Political terrorism is a form and method of political extremism even if, in the course of its activity, it is able to divorce itself from formal political organizations and may be disavowed by them.

Political extremism contains a totalitarian root and inclination insofar as it promises the direct and total solution of all political problems and endeavors to do so by any means.

The questioning of the concept of totalitarianism and the substitution in its place of an overly extended concept of fascism during the past 10 or 15 years has caused the blurring of the fundamental difference between democracy and dictatorship and its replacement by absolutely phrased alternative formulas like "socialism *vs.* fascism."

With that the fundamental kinship of right-wing and left-wing extremist organization and conduct is denied. However, at the same time and in clear contradiction, left-wing violence is called Fascist, and an interchangeability of right-wing and left-wing extremism thus is really suggested.

The tabooing of the concept of totalitarianism rests on pseudo-scientific foundations, expressed in the most resentful rejection in principle of any comparison of Left and Right, of red and brown as such; in the process differences in ideology, aims, and social context are cited, and the supposedly humanistic essence of Communist politics is pointed out.

In contrast, seven common characteristics of totalitarian policies, of so much more importance to the people affected, are overlooked or denied:

(1) their methods of political fighting employ violence whether open or cloaked in pseudolegality; (2) their exclusive claim on truth and the right to govern; (3) the monolithic character of their ideologies; (4) their promise of total solution of all problems; (5) their destruction of the individual as person and their fiction of a new man who, fully coordinated, fuses with community and society; (6) their chimera of total liberation brought about by the coerced total identity of the governed and the government, citizen and party, people and leadership; and (7) their fundamental denial of free criticism and opposition.

The relevance and explosiveness of this relationship between terror and dictatorship lies in the fact that, even after the demise of the Hitler and Stalin regimes, ever-new manifestations of the totalitarian temptation and totalitarian impulses in extremist groups must be expected. These manifestations, like those of an earlier day, may occur under right-wing as well as left-wing radical prefixes. Their occurrence is not precluded by the apparently definitive refutation of fascism and national socialism in the catastrophe of 1945, nor by the transformation of communism under the constellation of "peaceful coexistence"—which, after all, evidently does not mean ideological coexistence, does not mean an end to the confrontation between the democratic and the totalitarian conception of politics. These still are the points of departure from which modern radical groups and movements advocating violence have proceeded. The major changes of course initiated in 1917 affect our own day, as shown by their ready impact on student movements, the New Left, and terrorism.

Even if the relative dimensions seem to render the present situation harmless, caution demands that democracy's readiness and willingness to defend itself be taken seriously. To this end the citizen must be aware that the ever-present totalitarian threat ought not to be underestimated and that the available means to refute and overcome it must be fully utilized: the constitutional and political principles as well as the insistence on the conceptually antitotalitarian nature and substance of free democracy. Proper use of language and concepts here play a decisive role. On them depends the effective coming to grips with the intellectual origins of terrorism in our society.

MICHAEL CURTIS

TOTALITARIANISM
A Monolithic Entity?

*Professor Curtis gave the principal paper at the session reconsidering totalitarianism at the 1977 annual meeting of the American Historical Association in Dallas, Texas. His contribution to this volume is based on this paper, which has been published in its entirety elsewhere. (*Totalitarianism, *New Brunswick, N.J., 1979). Writing more than a decade ago, Professor Curtis made clear his conviction that "the concept of totalitarianism is no longer the most useful classificatory device for the study of current Communist systems," and that "it does not serve the cause of comparative political analysis or of political understanding to cling to the concept of totalitarianism." ("Retreat from Totalitarianism," in Carl J. Friedrich, Michael Curtis, Benjamin R. Barber,* Totalitarianism in Perspective: Three Views, *New York, Washington, London, 1969, pp. 112, 116.)*

Limiting his discussion to the question whether the assumption of a monolithic entity, with clearly outlined jurisdictions and decision-making processes, as a governing feature of totalitarian systems is in order, Professor Curtis concludes here that the characteristics shared by the three principal regimes commonly designated as totalitarian are significant enough to "justify a common appellation." He arrives at this conclusion even though he is aware of the pronounced differences between these regimes, and he finds the assumption of underlying monolithic entities not entirely justified. In effect, the internal strife evident to Professor Curtis in all three regimes, belying the notion of monolithic entities, appears to strengthen the case for a concept incorporating the three systems under one common term. Pointing to jurisdictional, regional, and nationality-oriented disputes running through the entire history of the

Soviet regime, Professor Curtis finds even more internal strife in the multitudinal forces contending for power within Mussolini's Fascist state. Less obvious and therefore more striking are his examples of internal divisions in the Nazi regime, which have been the focus of attention in recent Third Reich scholarship and which have revealed a bewildering variety of competing feudal party fiefdoms. Since efforts to centralize were hampered in all three regimes by internal disunity, the role of the charismatic leader and head of the party in manipulating the contending forces is brought into focus. Examining the, to him, most puzzling problem of the relationship between party and state—a problem more pronounced in Italy and Germany than in the Soviet Union— Professor Curtis here, too, finds the notion of totalitarian regimes as monolithic entities wanting. Professor Curtis observes that there were, indeed, signal differences between party claims and the realities of power in Italy and Germany. Setting apart the bureaucratic world of cross-purposes revealed in the party-state relations of Fascist regimes from the plain deterioration of the Communist party in the Soviet Union under Stalin's heavy hand, and recognizing the party's revival as the central force in Soviet society under Stalin's successors, Professor Curtis points to noteworthy differences between the Fascist and the Soviet regimes in this area.

However, neither the functional differences revealed, nor the evident dichotomy in ends sought persuade Professor Curtis to deny the merits of a common appellation for all three systems. His "retreat from totalitarianism" of 1969, then, has been halted, and he must be considered among those who see a need for a concept encompassing the totalitarian character of twentieth-century mass movement regimes regardless of their locus in the political spectrum.

The concept of totalitarianism was formulated to suggest a qualitative difference between three regimes—Nazi Germany, Fascist Italy, and the Soviet Union at least until the death of Stalin—and the countless dictatorial and authoritarian systems that have existed in time and space.

Embedded in the concept of totalitarianism, perhaps more implicitly than explicitly, is the assumption of a monolithic entity with clarity both in jurisdiction and in decision making. But the experience of the regimes suggests that such an assumption is not wholly justified. The supposed monolithic entities suffered power struggles within the ruling group, diffusion of decision making, and a complex, often unclear, relationship between party and state.

Less is known about Soviet affairs in this regard than about the other two countries, but even there practice seems to have differed from theory. The Soviet Union could be characterized as a monolithic system, with its centralization of party organization and loss of autonomy by local parties, minimization of the power of the Red Army through purges, through isolation of its leaders from the party organization, and through the allocation of responsibility for ideological indoctrination and control to political commissars or political officers, withdrawal of any real independence in important decision making from the constituent republics of the country, neglect and minimization of the Soviets, and elimination of the party leadership by Stalin.[1] Yet in the Soviet Union there were always divisions between those concerned with technical and those with verbal matters, between industrial and agricultural experts, and between geographical areas and nationalities. Inner conflicts after Stalin's death led to the postponement of some decisions like the virgin soil issue in 1954. An intense, violent, and divisive power struggle occurred over the Berlin crisis of 1961.[2] The Cuban missile crisis brought Khrushchev down.

Divisions existed from the beginning within the Italian Fascist movement with its mixture of revolutionary syndicalists, futurists, nationalists, and military desperadoes, the *squadristi*. The goals of the latter group—an elitist organization, local power for the *ras*, the communal fascist leaders, a military spirit to be imposed on all—were not those of the syndicalists, who wanted class cooperation and national solidarity. In the early years Mussolini, who could not control the provincial *squadre* which had developed spontaneously, turned the movement into a party, the Partito Nazionale Fascista.

The party itself experienced a series of internal crises—on local matters, on policy, on the role of the militia, on party organization, and on differences between the northern and southern branches.[3] There were differences between the nationalists like Federzoni and the more extreme Fascists like Farinacci, between the early and late Fascists, between the militia and the squads. In 1924 Rocco lost his fight for technical councils against the *ras*. Usually more extreme, the *ras* fought against the revisionists, who were willing to accept an authoritarian system with limited pluralism.[4] There were disagreements between the syndicalists led by Rossoni, wanting to retain separate workers' and employers' organizations and to concentrate on labor problems, and the corporativists, wanting an integrated working community and concerned primarily with production. The influence of the party and the quality of its leadership varied throughout the country.[5]

Mussolini maintained control by mediating among the rival forces and by subordinating the party to the state after 1926. He disagreed with some of his close associates: Federzoni, who was an authoritarian nationalist,

Rocco, a corporativist, and Bocchini, a political police chief.[6] "After the revolution," remarked Mussolini, "there is always the question of the revolutionaries." He put an end to any revolutionary expectations that more radical Fascists may have had of the creation of a new society and of a new type of man. The syndicalist element early lost its influence. The much-discussed corporations, which were to be the cornerstone of the new society, did not come into existence until 1934 and never really functioned as intended, if they functioned at all.

Fascism was always constrained by the presence of the old conservative or traditional groups and personnel. The retention of the monarchy meant that it could be seen as an alternative, if not a source of power, with senior officials and even some party leaders pledging devotion to the king. It took only a simple act of the king to legitimize Mussolini's ouster in 1943. The army supported the regime in return for virtual autonomy. The militia did not remain a Fascist tool; rather, it became an adjunct of the army. The judiciary largely remained unchanged until 1941, though it did not oppose the regime or offer legal resistance.[7]

Mussolini soon came to terms with the Church, allowing religious teaching in the primary schools, increasing the salary of the clergy, and saving the Vatican's Bank of Rome from bankruptcy. But it was the Lateran Pacts of 1929 that allowed the Church to provide an alternative set of values. Not only was the independence of the papacy and its sovereignty in the Vatican recognized, Catholicism accepted as the state religion, and religious instruction imposed on the schools, but also Catholic Action was allowed to survive and compete with Fascist cultural and social groups. The Church never became a focus of opposition to the regime, but the protection of its authority belied the possibility that fascism could be seen as an "ethical state" in Gentile's phrase or a "total state" in Rocco's, or that there was a total identification between state and society.

The economic and social system emerged virtually unchanged from the Fascist era. The only major problem that was solved was that of the Church. The Mezzogiorno was not integrated into the rest of the country, nor were Southern attitudes changed.[8] The policy of population increase had little perceptible effect. There was little improvement in the standard of living of the Italian people. There were no long-term reforms.[9] Economic growth was modest, though more rapid in the 1930's, the attempt at autarky failed, and the country became virtually self-sufficient in wheat only at the expense of other products.

There were similar differences among the Nazi leaders, on the degree of desirable change, on the movement as an elitist or mass organization, on the respective authority of the *Gauleiter* and the center, on whether the party should merge with other organizations or remain as a control instrument, on the independence of the paramilitary organizations and later of the Labor Front. There were divisions even over anti-Semitic policy between the Ministry of Economics and the SS, and between the SD and the Gestapo. A bitter conflict occurred during the war between the Party Chancellory under Bormann and the SS.

Peterson has shown that at the different political levels, national, regional, and local, there was confusion in performance of jobs, over-lapping of administrative jurisdictions without coordination, personal conflict, organizational disputes, and competition both between officials of party and state and between different party organizations and local leaders. Hitler clearly employed the classic device of divide and rule and limited the authority of subleaders to their particular spheres.[10] But his indolence and dislike for administration left a vacuum. The intrigues and divisions continued to the end, with leaders directing autonomous empires staffed by loyal supporters who fought off the attacks on their domain.[11]

Striking examples of this conflict were evident in propaganda and in economic policy as well as in many other areas. In propaganda, struggles were rife between Goebbels, supposedly in charge of all publications, and intruders like Goering in art, Rosenberg in literature and culture, Amann in the press, and Dietrich, the Reich press chief. In economic policy Schacht, when Minister of Economics, managed to prevail over the Nazi demand for control of banks and big business, defended the strongly attacked department stores, and resisted anti-Semitic measures as bad for the economy.

In all three countries the emphasis on the exercise of strong power entailed centralization. Constitutionally the Nazis centralized with the abolition of state parliaments, the subordination of the *Länder* to the Ministry of the Interior on January 30, 1934, the abolition of municipal diets on January 30, 1935, and the unification of the police for the whole of the Reich on June 16, 1936. In Italy the provincial executive committees were reformed, and the powers of prefects were extended in 1926. Within the party the Grand Council was nominated from the top, and it in turn chose the party secretary who appointed provincial secretaries.

Yet the process of centralization was less complete than these con-stitutional reforms suggest. Local loyalties in Germany remained strong, and the *Gauleiter* tended to reinforce these loyalties to expand their own power and defy central authority. In practice local administration had considerable autonomy from central authority. The *Reichsstatthalter* appointed in 1933 by Hitler to rule over local areas became independent of Berlin.[12] Not surprisingly, Goering refused to subordinate Prussia to the Reich Minister of the Interior. In Bavaria the state authorities saved the Church from the party.[13]

Administration was itself haphazard. Even if his laziness and impatience were not major factors, Goering could not but neglect the multiplicity of offices he held. The Cabinet met infrequently and policy was often made without its knowledge. Hitler encouraged competition between ministers or appointed new agents to do work already assigned. The technical ministers like von Ruebenach might be nonparty members or like Fritz Todt, the builder of the *Autobahnen*, remarkably independent. The Minister of War was able to reach a compromise by which his officials would not engage actively in party work or party office.

PARTY AND STATE

Perhaps the most confusing element in at least two of the three systems is the relationship between party and state. The lack of clarity and of consistency in the relationship suggests even further qualifications of the idea of the systems as monolithic entities.

The tactical compromises between Mussolini and the existing influential groups in Italy before he came to power meant that the monarchical, military, administrative, judicial, and clerical hierarchy retained their positions, for which the Fascist militants were not technically qualified. Continuity was maintained in the bureaucracy and judiciary. The traditional elite, some of whom later joined the party,[14] coexisted with a Fascist leadership. Parallel party institutions were created: the Grand Council alongside the Council of Ministers, the militia with the army, the party police with the regular police force, the *federale* (provincial party secretaries) with the prefects.

Fascist leaders had spoken of the need for hierarchy, authority, and strong government, and expected these to be provided by their movement. But Mussolini soon decided that the party must not only be tamed but also be subordinated to the state. On July 13, 1923, he stated that "all party representatives are subordinate to the prefect": in the 94 provinces the *federale* were made subject to the prefect. The prefects were informed by Mussolini in 1927 that they, and not the party organs, were the official interpreters of the will of central government. The militia, which had the task of maintaining public order and premilitary training, had an ambiguous status in relation to the army. It increased in size, reaching about 750,000 by 1938. Its units fought in Spain and in Ethiopia in separate units from the army. Yet in spite of the tension that could be created by the militia, the army remained the strongest military force.

The party was to be an instrument of rather than the leader of the state. The party did not itself take part in determining the purposes of government or the framing of policy. Party national and provincial leaders were appointed by the head of the government. Intransigent or extreme leaders were removed, and the power of local party secretaries curbed. The experiment in 1923 by which the *alti commissari* exercised both political and paramilitary authority was soon abandoned when Mussolini perceived it as a threat to his own position. [15] The Grand Council was created in 1922 as the supreme body of the party and became in December 1928 the constitutional organ "responsible for the coordination and integration of every activity of the regime," with a voice in the determination of the succession to the throne and the preparation of the list of deputies to be elected and union leaders to be appointed. In fact, however, it was accorded little power by Mussolini.

Although Hitler on March 22, 1933, said that "the work done outside the state organs was decisive," there was a confused picture on legislation, decision making, appointments, and jurisdictional boundaries between party and state. Although the party was able to veto governmental appointments and it was prominent at the district and local levels, it rarely initiated policies at the national level. About 60 percent of all governmental positions were held by party members, but two-thirds of these members had joined after 1933. The old fighters themselves, fanatical though they were in support of Hitler, lacked the necessary technical skills and administrative ability for state positions. Few in the party apparatus became governmental leaders except the *Gauleiter*, who held dual positions at the local level. At the national level, apart from Hitler, the chief examples of dual leadership were Hess, Himmler, Rust, Ley, and Schirach.

Party as well as state was given legal power to act. The March 1933 Enabling Act, which handed over all legislative power to the government, was the basis for the legalizing of Nazi actions. The April 1935 law on local government, the January 1937 law on the civil service, the Nuremberg laws, and the occupancy and then abolition of the presidency by Hitler in 1934, all supposedly gave legal approval to party intervention in state matters. The 1935 law made communal officials subject to supervision by the local party leader as well as by the Reich Ministry of the Interior. The 1937 law made the appointments and promotions of civil servants subject to party approval. Civil servants who were party members were also subject to party courts. In spite of the law, however, the civil service was never completely a Nazi instrument; many senior civil servants never joined the party. Control over the life of officials was incomplete.

The December 1, 1933, law for the unity of party and state made the party the only political organization in Germany. The state accepted the party's definition of the racial issue: the office of Hess supervised the enforcement of the anti-Semitic legislation. Yet Hess's attempt as Deputy Führer to claim party superiority over the state and over decision making was only partly successful. In addition, the 1938 Nazi plan to control the personnel and budgets of the localities was a partial failure. By a 1937 law officials would report not to the party but to the minister, who could then inform the party. On the whole, ministers successfully defended their administrative integrity.[16] The party could approve official appointments, and it influenced the administration of legislative and judicial matters, but it took little part in major political decisions and never controlled national legislation. Practice did not bear out Hitler's declaration at the 1934 party convention that "the state does not command us, we command the state . . . we created the state." The very complexity of the party structure, with its large number of officials, with the *Gauleiter* mostly opposing centralization, with its feuding factions and bitter personal conflicts, both complicated relations with the state and also helped prevent the direct subordination of the civil service.

Conflicting or overlapping jurisdictions were a cause of confusion, as in the judicial field. In 1933 a special court, the *Volksgerichtshof*, was created to try alleged treason cases, including listening to foreign broadcasts. The Reich Minister of Justice in November 1935 accepted the right of judicial review by Hess,[17] who argued in 1938 that the party could not be bound by legal norms in judging an individual. During the war the minister also allowed the party the right to deny permission for its leaders to testify in court proceedings. A special judicial system was established in October 1939 to deal with cases concerning the SS. In police matters more harmony existed because of the formal amalgamation in June 1936 of the party post of Reichsführer-SS with the new office of Chief of German Police, with Himmler occupying both positions.

This confusing and sometimes, as in the powers of the HSSPF and the RSHA, bewildering pattern of relations existed in the context of two other complications. The first was the ultimate and final power of Hitler, who in 1934 had transferred the presidential powers to himself as Führer. Under the February 28, 1933, ordinance for an emergency situation, he could use the Gestapo as an instrument of his personal authority and permit protective custody, a political police force, and concentration camps. The claim of the party to represent the political will of the people was always secondary to the will of the Führer and his fulfillment of the German mission. The second complication was the rapid rise of the SS to a position of dominance which transcended both party and state. Its armed groups were not part of the police, the party, or the Wehrmacht. The SS gradually superseded the state, making policy in foreign, military, and agricultural affairs and exemplifying the new elite, the biologically pure, obedient fighter. The SS became the executive agent of the will of the Führer, to whom it was completely loyal, while the official machinery of the state concerned itself with routine business.[18] Its leader Himmler not only controlled all the local political police from 1934 and the national police from 1936, but was also Reich commissar for the strengthening of Germandom, the party representative for racial questions, and from 1943 also the Minister of the Interior. The nature of his offices demonstrates that the SS was concerned with what was important to Hitler: the maintenance of his own power, anti-Semitism, *Lebensraum*, the creation of a pure, strong *Volk*, and the elimination of opponents.

The problem of party-state relations in the Soviet Union was different from that in the other two countries: it was the elimination of the party as a policy-making body. From Lenin's theory of party organization, the concept of the dictatorship of the proletariat became transmuted into that of the dictatorship of the Bolshevik party. Lenin in his *"Left-Wing" Communism—an Infantile Disorder* and Stalin in his *Foundations of Leninism* claimed that no important political or organizational question was decided by any state institution without the guiding instructions of the Central Committee of the party. In addition the party was needed, according to Stalin in 1924, to maintain the dictatorship of the proletariat, to consolidate and expound it in order to achieve the complete victory of socialism.[19] Unlike the Nazi party, which was to be the master of public opinion, the Communist party would lead the masses, disseminating and enforcing the goals of the regime.[20] Under Lenin the party leadership, a talented group who agreed on the need for party unity, dominated the making of major policy decisions.[21] The party itself grew from 23,000 in January 1917 to 576,000 by January 1921. But the highly personal dictatorship of Stalin meant rule through cronies rather than through regular party channels.

The party was not reinstated to a prominent role until after Stalin. Between 1953 and 1958 Khrushchev managed to reassert the authority of the party in the face of possible challenge by the secret police, the army, and the state ministries. But after becoming prime minister in 1958, he too attempted to reduce the authority of the Central Committee, by inviting outside experts to its meetings. He increased the insecurity of party officials by his policy of a one-third turnover of the membership of party committees at elections, and he caused confusion by the 1962 division of the regional committees into industrial and agricultural bodies. In addition, his reliance on a few advisers in a number of policy areas meant that both party and state were sometimes bypassed.[22] But Krushchev's general view was that "the party should play a strictly political role while technical questions should be left to the experts."[23]

Under Brezhnev the party has again been restored to a prominent position, asserting more control over the economy. In the new constitution passed in 1977, the party is defined as "the force that leads and directs Soviet society; it is the central element in the political system and in all the state and social organizations."

The party controls not only appointments in the party itself, but also, through the *nomenklatura* procedure, in industry, agriculture, education, and culture. Its responsibilities extend to all political, economic, and cultural activities in its area. The influence of local party organs on industry depends on the interests of the first secretary of the party, on the type of industry, and on the particular issue of decision making.[24]

The key variable in the relationship between party and state is the territorial level. At the local level the party is strong: it is concerned with long-range policy,[25] though not with administrative details. Nor can it force a higher state official to act. The party function of checking the performance of the managers and providing guidance has been enhanced in recent years by the better technical training of party functionaries.

But the theory of the directing role of the party conflicts with the industrial principle of one-man management. Lower Soviet administrators themselves are not always clear about the proper relationship of the party organization to the plant management.[26] In the complex Soviet administrative arrangement the essential image is that of a policy-making team within the enterprise.[27]

There are other problems raised by the classificatory concept of totalitarianism: the differences between ideological convictions and the purported objectives of the three systems, the discrepancy between ideology and actual practice in the regimes, and the limits on total control over economic activity. Yet the characteristics the three regimes shared in common, in organization, in techniques, in the relationship between the political elite and citizens, in the stress on the need for sacrifice on behalf of the whole, in the destruction of free institutions, and in the degree of penetration of the private lives of citizens, are sufficiently significant to justify a common appellation.

A. JAMES GREGOR

"TOTALITARIANISM" REVISITED

Professor Gregor clearly is not prepared to see the concept of totalitarianism eliminated from the repertoire of classificatory tools available to the political scientist. Pointing to recent uses made of the concept by colleagues in the field, he detects in this much-criticized concept a "remarkable vitality" that reinforces his conviction of its heuristic, classificatory, and empirical importance in comparative politics. Notwithstanding the frequent emotive abuse of this concept—as in the case of others like "class," "democracy," or "revolution"—by people more concerned with action than thought, Professor Gregor observes that the historical reality of totalitarianism contains much-needed critical cognitive potential.

Conceding the weakness of earlier attempts at typologizing or categorizing totalitarian regimes under a necessarily general criterial definition which, at best, led to partial explanations of causation, Professor Gregor points out that these were heuristic efforts that did not result in the establishment of a rigorous, testable theory. Professor Gregor feels that earlier students of totalitarianism, unfortunately attributing—even if only implicitly—the quality of scientific "models" to descriptive theories suitable only for taxonomic purposes, failed to come to grips with the fundamental problem of concept formation. The evolving conceptual schemata of totalitarianism, based on vaguely defined but discernible traits, so far have not resulted in a theoretical framework very helpful in the causal explanations of the totalitarian phenomenon.

Professor Gregor feels that these discernible traits are too vaguely defined to be placed into the service of a truly scientific taxonomy, not to speak of a viable, general theory of totalitarianism. Nor were such results to be expected or even desirable at the stage of concept formation.

Explicit definitions identifying necessary and sufficient conditions are hard to come by—at least in the social sciences, Professor Gregor observes. Until such definitions are established, attempts at closing off the open-textured categories currently governing the conceptual schemata of totalitarianism would prove to be counterproductive.

Incomplete as efforts at establishing a viable theoretical framework governing totalitarianism so far have been, the pedagogical and cognitive yield is undeniable, and it in turn has stimulated further theorizing, resulting in advances in subsidiary fields with salutary results. Far from being an impediment to the researcher, the loosely textured ideal-type conceptual schema of totalitarianism will in its disaggregated state give rise to a variety of alternative empirical theories of varying degrees of generality.

There is no doubt in Professor Gregor's mind that the traits attributed to totalitarian systems in the ideal type are observable in reality, though he finds the operational definitions to measure and evaluate them wanting. Lack of access to existing totalitarian systems will make the task of the researcher even more difficult, so that Professor Gregor does not expect that development of viable theories of totalitarianism in the foreseeable future. But he is struck by the realization that many of the critiques leveled against the concept of totalitarianism really were theoretical propositions adding to the overall totalitarian schema, even if they do not employ the term. These critiques, in effect, seem to confirm to Professor Gregor the considerable heuristic and cognitive power of the concept.

Rejecting the contention that the concept was devised to serve as a counterideological tool of the Cold War, Professor Gregor insists on its mnemonic and pedagogical merits and its yields as a historical clearinghouse. To Professor Gregor, it was inevitable that the historical record of fascism, national socialism, and Stalinism eventually was reflected in a notion such as that of totalitarianism. Social scientists must present it more scientifically and categorize it more systematically and, if they are to arrive at acceptable causal explanations, they must cooperate with historians and scholars in other fields. The selections in Part III of this volume suggest that there is interest in such collaboration in fields like psychology, psychiatry, and history.

Irrespective of the sometimes acerbic and wide-ranging criticism directed against it, the concept "totalitarianism" shows remarkable vitality. Recently, both Leonard Schapiro and Juan Linz have insisted on its heuristic, classificatory, and empirical importance in the study of comparative politics.[1] In 1976, Domenico Fisichella published his insightful analysis of the concept and reasserted its utility.[2] In 1978, *The Review of Politics* republished Waldemar Gurian's instructive "The Totalitarian State," and in 1979, Stephen Whitfield lamented the progressive "disintegration" of what had been a classificatory and cognitive concept in the service of immediate and contingent political purpose.[3]

It is quite clear, of course, that the concept "totalitarianism" carries any number of politically sensitive connotations in its train. There is little doubt that it has been frequently employed for emotive and persuasive rather than cognitive ends. But concepts like "class," "democracy," and "revolutionary" (to allude to those that come readily to mind) have been similarly used and abused, but few would recommend either their abandonment or pretend that there is nothing in the empirical world to which they, in some significant fashion, correspond. Much the same can be said of the concept "totalitarianism." There are, in fact, "classes" in the real world, however imprecise the definitions proffered by sociologists and political scientists, just as there are "democracies" in the world. However open-textured the notions, it would be difficult to provide an account of the modern history of the Western World without reference to the concept "class." Similarly, it is equally doubtful if a convincing narrative of contemporary political history could be forthcoming without the invocation of the concept "totalitarianism."

The issue here is not one that turns on the potential for abuse. Terms like *class*, *democracy*, or *totalitarianism* can be marshaled to any number of uses. They can serve as terms of abuse, or as clarion calls to resistance. The question is, rather, whether such concepts, independent of their abuse, serve a significant cognitive purpose or not. If not, their abandonment is recommended. Their exploitation can be left to advocates, politicians, and rabble-rousers, more occupied with sentiment than sense, more committed to activism than understanding.

The evidence, however, indicates that the concept has critical cognitive potential. It can serve a didactic, heuristic, and classificatory purpose, quite independent of whatever its evident emotive uses.

The term *totalitarianism*, in fact, originally made its apperance innocent of any immediate political connotations in the work of Giovanni Gentile. As early as 1916, Gentile spoke of the "identity" of the individual and the state, a seamless identification predicated on a Hegelian "universalism" that absorbed the "elements" of society into the "totality" of the state.[4] He pressed it into comparative service to distinguish between "liberal" and "totalitarian" states, the one predicated on the empiric and moral reality of the "individual," antecedent and independent of the state, and the other committed to a conviction that the "individual" was to be understood exclusively as a function of the complex ensemble of relations that constitute the real substance of political society.

In effect, the first uses of the concept "totalitarianism" were philosophic, analytic, and comparative. And it is to the concept's cognitive serviceability that attention should be addressed. The fact that the concept has been marshaled to political purpose is irrelevant. The question is whether the concept has any cognitive yield, not whether it, like so many other concepts, has been abused for political purposes.

Critical to any such assessment is the pioneering work of Carl Friedrich and Zbigniew K. Brzezinski. In *Totalitarian Dictatorship and Autocracy*, Friedrich and Brzezinski offered what they took to be a catalog of defining traits that would identify a class of political systems they referred to as "totalitarianisms." They spoke of a set of "basic features or traits" that are "generally recognized to be common to totalitarian dictatorships." "The 'syndrome,' or pattern of interrelated traits, of the totalitarian dictatorship," they went on to indicate, "consists of an ideology, a single party typically led by one man, a terroristic policy, a communications monopoly, a weapons monopoly, and a centrally directed economy." It was equally clear to them that the political systems explicitly or implicitly included in the set were not "identical" (whatever that might be taken to mean), and that the syndrome of traits conceived as defining the class could not be considered definitive in any sense. What was offered, according to the authors, was "a general, descriptive theory of a novel form of government," a "general model of totalitarian dictatorship and of the society which it has created," which could "fit into the general framework of our knowledge of government and politics."[5]

What such a "descriptive theory" or "model" seems to involve, essentially, is pretheoretical conceptualizing, an attempt to provide a loose (and consequently general) criterial definition of a critical concept, conjoined with an indeterminate number of attendant propositions that might afford social science practitioners the occasion to store, retrieve, and employ a large body of information that might otherwise not be cataloged or might be cataloged differently and, consequently, retrieved only with considerably more effort.[6] The authors clearly imagined that the provision of a preliminary conceptual schema constructed around the concept "totalitarianism" would provide a convenient storage bin for a wide range of "reasonably well-established matters of fact," as well as serve as a didactic aid of some consequence. (They hoped to "provide a basis . . . for more effective teaching. . . .") What such a "descriptive theory" or "model" was clearly not intended to achieve was explanation. While there is, as we shall suggest, considerable confusion on this count, it seems that the authors were consciously aware that they could not "explain why this dictatorship came into being . . . ," since they were convinced that "such an explanation is not feasible at the present time, though some of the essential conditions can be described." "At the present time," they continued, "we cannot fully explain the rise of totalitarian dictatorship. All we can do is to explain it partially by identifying some of the antecedent and concomitant conditions."[7]

Logically (but not necessarily chronologically) speaking, what we have is a pretheoretical effort at typologizing or categorizing. We have an incomplete set of attributes that provide *prima facie*, nonrigorous, but plausible, criteria for admission into the class "totalitarian," and a first, and admittedly modest, attempt to generate a taxonomic schema. "Totalitarianisms" are, for example, a subset, or a "species," of the "genus" "autocracies." The "logical opposite" of "autocracy" is, apparently, another "genus," i.e., "responsible or constitutional government." We have, then, a primitive taxonomy: two genera, "heterocracies" and "autocracies," one species, "totalitarianism," subsumed under one genus, "autocracy," and several subspecies lodged under the species "totalitarian."[8]

Clearly, Robert Burrowes's basic judgments concerning Friedrich and Brzezinski's *Totalitarian Dictatorship and Autocracy* are well taken. The book is not the product of a "rigorous typological approach" that "would facilitate comparison," nor does it contain "a solid core of theory."[9] The work contains a nonrigorous, essentially pretheoretical preliminary conceptual schema calculated to serve, primarily, as a device that assists in fostering ready recall, a didactic aid, and a storage convenience. Such schemata (and there are many in the informal social sciences) also serve to provide suggestions for further research. The fact that some discrete collection of entities displays certain overt properties may imply the presence of antecedent common causes. For example, Friedrich and Brzezinski insist, in a number of places, that they are "primarily" concerned with "the fact" of one or another attribute, rather than "its explanation." This is not to say that they do not, on occasion, attempt "partial explanations" of the attributes to which they allude. "Expansionism," or "the struggle for world conquest," for instance, is spoken of as "the outward thrust of the 'passion for unanimity' " that is supposed to be characteristic of totalitarian systems. The "passion for unanimity," on the other hand, is "at least partially" explained by the "totalitarian belief in the big lie as a propaganda technique," but in "the last analysis, the passion for unanimity seems to spring from the pseudoreligious fervor of the totalitarian ideology." Clearly such "explanations" are at their very best "partial." Most are offered as "suggestions": "The history of the Communist party of the USSR suggests that the leadership of the party, operating in context devoid of democratic devices for assuring efficiency . . . is faced with the dilemma of resolving the problem . . . while maintaining the elite status of the party" and so forth, or, "The purge accordingly appears to be inherent in modern totalitarianism. It is produced both by the existential conditions of the system and by the subjective motivations of its leadership."[10] These kinds of schematic explanations are at best suggestive of vaguely characterized causal factors and their interconnection. Their merit could only be heuristic—serving to orient researchers.

It is unfortunate that contemporary social scientists should continue to use terms like *theory*, *model*, and *explanation* as cavalierly as they do. Most of the objections directed against the work produced by Friedrich and Brzezinski are the consequence of having misinterpreted the major thrust of their effort. Alexander Groth's interesting article devoted to the issue of totalitarianism focuses on what seem to be the predictive pretensions assumed by Friedrich and Brzezinski. Groth seems to conceive the principal, or at least one of the major, thrusts of Friedrich and Brzezinski's work as an attempt to enable social scientists to "be able to predict the future course of [totalitarianism] from the common model."[11] It seems reasonably clear that whatever "predictions" Friedrich and Brzezinski permit to escape are advanced without much conviction—"there is no present reason to conclude that . . . though this possibility cannot be excluded," and so forth.[12] Again, the efforts are heuristic, not theoretical. A theoretical proposition is one that can be, in principle, confirmed or disconfirmed by some determinate public procedure. A theory is a collection of systematically related theoretical propositions, containing one or more lawlike assertions, capable of affording explanations and making time-conditioned predictions or retrodictions. At best, Friedrich and Brzezinski offer "partial explanations": that is to say, they present a partial catalog of seemingly necessary or contingent conditions for the occurrence of any specific event or collection of events, but they do not undertake systematic predictive or explanatory efforts. Thus William Ebenstein is wrong when he maintains that the authors sought to "develop a general theory . . . of totalitarian dictatorship."[13] The same kind of mistake has become a commonplace in the literature. Otto Stammer, Peter Christian Ludz, and Oskar Anweiler, among many others, continue to talk about "a general theory of totalitarianism" when the very best that Friedrich and Brzezinski offered was a partial and primitive taxonomic scheme and some schematic accounts of some of the seemingly necessary and contingent conditions for the manifestations of some of the species, or subspecific, properties with which they were concerned.[14] It makes very little sense, for example, to charge them, as Ebenstein does, with the error of failing to explain why it is that if "modern technology" is the "key characteristic of totalitarianism," the most "technologically advanced" political systems are not totalitarian, when the best Friedrich and

Brzezinski claimed was that some of the manifest traits of totalitarianism were "technologically conditioned." "Modern technology," they insisted, cannot be understood to have "caused" totalitarianism, but rather to have "made it possible."[15] Since they do not specify whether technology is a contingent and substitutable condition of totalitarianism, it is hard to challenge their claim. There is no serious theoretical claim imbedded in such a discursive and descriptive account. One simply does not know how to conduct a verification study of such general claims. Such claims are neither true nor false: they are vague and general, and perhaps theoretically suggestive. Hopefully research might grow out of them. But a great deal of preliminary work would have to be done first.

That Friedrich and Brzezinski's work has been criticized for not being explanatory is at least partially the consequence of their disposition to talk about possessing a "descriptive theory" and a "model." The fact that they modify the term *theory* with the adjectival qualifier *descriptive* should have been enough to suggest that what they were attempting was not to produce a "model" or a "theory" but to typologize or taxonomize. It was not an attempt at "theorizing" in any strict empirical sense. Their use of the word *model* to identify their account was unfortunate. The word *model* is generally used in empirical science to suggest that some lawlike assertions characteristic of some range of inquiry can be successfully mapped over another (less well understood) range—one theory is imagined as "modeling" another. Since, as Frederic Fleron suggests, there is "a general lack of integrative theory" about specific Communist societies and totalitarianism in general, the use of the terms *theory* or *model* is confusing and misleading.[16] In treating "totalitarianism" we are not dealing with "theories" or "models" but with a problem in concept formation: employing a set of linguistic strategies designed to begin to sort some relatively stable constants out of the wealth of experience. Concept formation, in fact, begins characteristically with "initial vagueness" and is subject to "consequent frequent redefinition."[17] At the commencement of our work we begin to note, in an unself-conscious and nondeliberative way, some things that strike us as "hanging together"—what Friedrich and Brzezinski refer to as "a cluster of interrelated traits. . . ."[18] For recall and storage convenience we give such a trait-complex a name—in this case "totalitarianism." The cluster of traits may or may not suggest a number of vague and painfully unspecific researchable problems.

All of this indicates that we are not dealing with "theories" or "models" of totalitarianism. Fleron is obviously correct in stating that "the studies in the large literature on totalitarianism cannot, with few exceptions, be viewed as building blocks in the construction of an empirical theory of totalitarianism. Rather, they have contributed to the formation of a conceptual scheme. . . ."[19] What Friedrich and Brzezinski have provided is, at its best, a "descriptive syndrome of discernible characteristics" that seemingly "hang together" in historic space.[20] Friedrich himself indicates that even with the availability of such a conceptual schema, there has been no "significant advance in causal explanation of the totalitarian phenomenon."[21] We have, in effect, no "general empirical theory" or "model" of totalitarianism. What we have is a preliminary criterial definition of a political construct composed of an indeterminate set of vaguely defined traits.[22] The possession of at least one of those traits would seem to be logically necessary for entry into the class "totalitarian." We are not sure, given the account provided by Friedrich and Brzezinski, whether they are content with such a modest admission requirement. Do they imagine that a political system must display all or some of the traits to qualify as "totalitarian"? If only some are required, which ones?

If we consider the trait-complex that characterizes totalitarian systems, it becomes obvious immediately that what we have is no more than a set of programmatic suggestions intended to serve as preliminary guides to inquiry. To be told, for example, that in "totalitarian" systems we can anticipate an "official ideology" that "covers" all "vital aspects of man's existence to which everyone living in that society is supposed to adhere" is not to tell us how to specifically or exhaustively distinguish totalitarian from nontotalitarian ideologies. To say that such ideologies are "chiliastic" and anticipate a "perfect final state of mankind"—that such a system of beliefs entertains a "radical rejection of the existing society and conquest of the world for the new one"—does not significantly distinguish, in principle, Leninism, or fascism from the political system advocated by Plato, Calvin, Mao, Castro, or Nkrumah. There is no hard or precise distinction that one could argue with any objective conviction. To talk of a "technologically conditioned near complete monopoly of control . . . of all the means of effective mass communication . . . , of effective armed combat . . . , [and] the entire economy"[23] is not to tell us how to rigorously distinguish the controls effected by nontotalitarian as distinct from totalitarian systems. We are provided no "cutoff points and threshold levels"[24] that might distinguish "near complete monopoly of control" from any other control.

The fact that the principal work on totalitarian systems, that of Friedrich and Brzezinski, is a preliminary conceptual schema rather than an effort to produce a scientific taxonomy or a specific guide to empirical research, much less a "general theory of totalitarianism," seems to have confused most commentators. Thus even as astute a commentator as Fleron suggests that Friedrich and Brzezinski should have provided "explicit definitions"[25] for their construct, when everything we know about such preliminary conceptual schemata suggests that they could not, and to be effective should not, attempt such closure. Explicit definitions specifically identify the necessary and sufficient conditions for the employment of a term—and as such are generally the exclusive product of closed or formal systems of thought—most characteristically mathematics and logic, or a formally developed science like physics that employs calculi to carry out its research.[26] The concepts in a quasi-experimental and informal science are not—and in general cannot be—other than "porous" or "open-textured" in order to accommodate the openness of on-going empirical inquiry. At the moment we simply do not know what the measure of "near monopoly control" might be that would explicitly and effectively distinguish totalitarian and nontotalitarian systems. We do not, on the basis of best evidence, know if such systems are to be plotted on a continuum from "open" or "constitutional" systems to "closed" or "totalitarian" systems, or if such systems can be discretely characterized in terms of mutually exclusive and exhaustive categories. To attempt to provide anything like an "explicit," or as another commentator states it "connotative," definition is to pretend to possess information we simply do not have.[27] The "ambiguity"[28] to which critics allude is intrinsic to such preliminary and essentially cataloging efforts. Burrowes seems to intuit as much. He maintains that "despite the illusion of theory it conveys, the totalitarian syndrome is perhaps most appropriately viewed as a set of general categories in terms of which a vast amount of data can be cataloged."[29] Until such time as social science has developed a defensible body of theory that will permit the fairly rigorous distinctions required to support explicit and stipulative typologies or taxonomies, totalitarianism can only be assessed in terms of open-textured categories that are regularly revised, amplified, and explicated. To attempt closure at this point would be counterproductive.

In this sense most of Benjamin Barber's extended critique of the construct "totalitarian" misses the point.[30] Preliminary efforts like that of Friedrich and Brzezinski invariably either summarize and/or prompt the production of a vast body of work characterized by different perspectives, varying assessments, diffuse meanings, and frequently mutually incompatible claims. One could hardly have developed, for example, an explicit and rigorous taxonomy of organic life until one had at his disposal the vast amount of detailed empirical evidence, the rudiments of a generally accepted theory of organic evolution, and the relatively precise empirical theory concerning the transmission of genetic particles that we now possess. Before all those elements were available one could only produce preliminary and corrigible taxonomies like those of Aristotle or

Linnaeus, schematic and general categories in which information that was available could be conveniently stored and retrieved. One could not talk about the "essential," "real," or "defining" properties of any species until one had the solid substance of an empirically viable theory on the basis of which one could effectively make such distinctions. Without such theoretical leverage on political life, one can allude, as Barber does, to "the barrenness of the assumptions about political life that underlie" the preliminary concept of "totalitarianism," but to no purpose. Preliminary conceptual schemata in informal disciplines are generally the products of commonplace assumptions. That is why they are preliminary. But one must begin somewhere—until one has a reasonably well-confirmed theory at his disposal—and commonly accepted wisdom seems as good a place as any to start.

All commentators agree that we possess little in the way of defensible theories about political life in general, much less about a particular form of political life. Thus Herbert Spiro,[31] in his summary discussion of "totalitarianism," indicates that we have various proposed interpretations of totalitarianism, but none of them are, in any systematic sense, competent. All of which is perfectly true. Friedrich and Brzezinski are clear in their judgment: the conceptual schema they suggest is, in and of itself, incapable of affording explanatory or predictive leverage. The question is whether such abstract and general cataloging and sorting strategies are productive of anything other than loose typologizing and discursive, incomplete, and partial explanation sketches. The only way to answer that would be to survey the literature of which the construct "totalitarianism" is a summary and the purposes to which the concept has subsequently been put. The construct summarizes, at a high level of abstraction, much of the material that found its way into the literature devoted to revolutionary political systems between 1930 and 1950. Almost all commentators have alluded to a class of totalitarian political systems that have shared certain general species properties. Marxists and non-Marxists alike have identified, at a discursive and general level, attributes shared by the Soviet Union, National Socialist Germany, and Fascist Italy. A conceptual schema that conveniently summarizes these kinds of discursive judgments obviously has pedagogical and mnemonic merit. The question is, can this kind of cognitive effort lead to more specific and consequently empirically significant results in the effort to produce defensible empirical explanations and reasonably competent predictions? The fact is that Friedrich and Brzezinski's initial work has generated attempts at more rigorous and inclusive taxonomies,[32] as well as efforts aimed at producing "theories of middle range"—that is to say, for example, an empirical theory of how "bureaucratic controls" might operate in particular socioeconomic environments (and then it might be part of a more inclusive "organization theory"). The efforts to produce such theories have been spoken of as moving from the "static and classificatory" character of the original conceptual schema via the "operationalization" of critical terms to the level of "dynamic" or "causal" accounts.[33] Such efforts at theory construction, both rigorously taxonomic, self-consciously experimental, quasi-experimental, and historically detailed, necessarily feed back and modify the loosely characterized formulations of the preliminary schema. All of this is both expected and salutary, and is the reaction to the availability of the original preliminary formulation. That is, apparently, how a social science proceeds.

When Michael Curtis warns that one should not expect to predict political and historic trends on the basis of conceptual typologies, particularly of the kind we are dealing with, he is perfectly, and obviously, correct.[34] One can only deplore the fact that Friedrich and Brzezinski permitted their minor interest in prediction to confuse the essential character of their enterprise. The schema they proposed affords little, if any, predictive leverage. If a typology or a taxonomy has predictive capabilities it is because, by and large, it rests on a body of competent theory. Since neither Friedrich nor Brzezinski claimed to possess such a body of theory, their "predictions" could be no more substantial than the theories they entertained. Most of their suggestive judgments about the "future" of totalitarian systems are so vague and general that almost anything would be compatible with them. They generally did qualify all their explanatory and predictive suggestions with allusions to vague causes of error, historical contingencies, and personality factors. We are "uncertain" as to the "real effect of ideological motivation upon the actual policy maker"; "it is difficult to prove" that a consensus has been established in one or another totalitarian system; the "historical record" "suggests" that there are cycles of intensification and relaxation of "autocratic power"; we have no "satisfactory general genetic theory which would truly explain why totalitarianism appeared in the twentieth century." It is clear that at best "we are moving on the rather abstract level." We are dealing with a construct which like most political terms is "surrounded by a haze of vaguer and conflicting notions. . . ."[35] The principal business of their work is not prediction mongering or explanation fobbing—it is the provision of a preliminary conceptual schema that has didactic, storage and retrieval, and perhaps heuristic, utility.

Once this is granted, we are left with the very complicated question of heuristic utility. Does a term like *totalitarian* identify some collection of phenomenological or observable traits with sufficient open-textured specificity to permit "a reasonable degree of correspondence"[36] with available evidence? Most commentators agree that "totalitarianism" is a heuristic construct, an "ideal type" that suggests something about the empirical reality of some loosely characterized class of political systems. Every science begins with such schemata which, at best, are calculated to summarize, store, and efficiently retrieve whatever funded information we have about our universe of inquiry.[37] A science needs points of view and problems to be solved. From that initial point the research scientist, concerned with a variety of issues that may overlap with those embedded in the conceptual schemata made available in the literature at his disposal, may disaggregate a general construct (such as "totalitarianism") into a variety of dimensions. He may develop categories devoted to "freedom of political opposition," measured in terms of a voting system or "vulnerability of elites"; or to the means available in any political system for "interest aggregation" and "interest articulation"; or to techniques for the "transfer of effective political power"; or he may undertake a content analysis of published political literature to determine some measure of "ideological rigidity."

It is obvious that the disaggregation of such a construct can take a multiplicity of forms and will give rise to a variety of alternative empirical theories of varying degrees of generality. Factor analytic work might inform the research scientist if any of these constituents "load" on any more general factor and how much of the variance in any political system is to be attributable to any specific factor or cluster of factors. Professional interest in the history of ideas, on the other hand, may produce accounts that attempt to provide a catalog of argument forms that seem to characterize "totalistic" ideologies. These can range from loosely argued literary treatments that identify Plato or Aristotle as articulating a "totalitarian belief system" to more systematic, scholarly exegeses identifying totalitarian currents in "democratic thought."[38] A preliminary schema such as the one in which the concept "totalitarianism" is housed can serve as a goad to research, a cataloging convenience, a suggestion of the multi-dimensionality of political systems, and a point of departure for academic scholarship.[39]

One question seems to be obscured by all this. Does the concept "totalitarian" refer, with any degree of plausibility, to an identifiable collection of observable traits displayed by some past or present political systems? Are there, or have there been, political systems that are, or were, individually animated by a reasonably formal collection of ideas that might, with some legitimacy, be called "official"? Are there, or were there, political systems in which executive responsibilities are, or were, discharged by a "charismatic" or "pseudocharismatic" leader who was, or is, identified as "a world historical genius," a "telluric force," or some such hyperbolic characterization? Are there, or were there, political systems that do not, or did not, permit formal and voluntary "opposition"? Are there, or were there, political systems that "control" information flow? that develop an elaborate "bureaucratic infrastructure"? that "control" in "significant" measure the educational, productive, and distributive processes? that have the potential for the exercise of "violence" and/or "terror" against their own citizens without providing them with institutionalized agencies of defense and/or redress? that seek to "inculcate" uniform and general political and moral opinions among their citizenry? that legitimize rules by appealing to an identifiable body of social, political, and economic argument?

The answer is obviously yes, but the information such an account affords is clearly insufficient. We need fairly rigorous operational definitions, for example, of what might count as "official," "charismatic," "opposition," "control," "bureaucratic infrastructure," "significant," "violence" or "terror," and "inculcation." We need reliable and stable intersubjective indices that might be appropriate for measurement. We need competent content analyses and surveying strategies, systematic data collection, and adequate sampling procedures. We require the formulation of testable generalizations, and the discharge of subsequent verificational studies. We need, in effect, rigorously formulated empirical theories that begin to provide defensible generalizations about some of the issues central to the problems suggested by the preliminary conceptual schema. All this will be constrained by a lack of creditable data, the passing of some of the historic exemplars of the class of "totalitarian systems," and our inability to conduct any serious research in most of them (our lack of research access to systems such as those in the Soviet Union, China, or Cuba). Under such constraints, much of our inquiry will be the consequence of rank speculation couched in the ordinary language of the intelligent layman. As a consequence, we probably will not be in the possession of viable theories of totalitarianism for the foreseeable future. For the time being what we have are reasonably competent historical and discursive accounts of various systems that can be spoken of with some cognitive merit as "totalitarian." Such accounts are not "theoretical" in any serious empirical sense. They are classificatory and typological and, at best, invoke vague and ambiguous low-order generalizations. One cannot pretend to reliably explain how such systems arose or what course they might subsequently follow.

Most of the criticism that has collected around the discussion of "totalitarianism" is, in fact, devoted to the ventilation of competitive explanatory efforts. Robert Burrowes, for instance, is convinced that "modernization" and "industrialization" are perhaps somehow crucial to the "understanding" of "totalitarian systems," while Michael Curtis seems to deny their significance.[40] Robert Tucker, in turn, suggests that under critical conditions it is the psychology of "charismatic leaders" that is of overriding significance.[41] Alexander Groth, on the other hand, maintains that it is the analysis of groups, in terms of their economic interests and political strength, that is critical.[42] All of these accounts are alternative attempts at theory construction, and they are undertaken under the spur of the work provided by Friedrich and Brzezinski. Many simply attempt to provide theoretical propositions to flesh out the totalitarian schema. Some tighten up the lexical definitions of critical terms. In fact, the bulk of the "criticism" directed against the concept of "totalitarianism" constitutes evidence that the concept has significant heuristic and cognitive merit.

The notion "totalitarianism" finds a place in a pretheoretical conceptual schema that at its best summarizes, for recall convenience, a large body of funded material of a wide variety of sorts. The notion, and the schema it inhabits, attempt to suggest broad lines of historical, experimental, and quasi-experimental research. One would hardly expect a pretheoretical schema to tell us more about "totalitarianism" than we already know, for Friedrich and Brzezinski's clear intention was to summarize at a rather "abstract level" the substance of the literature devoted to fascism, national socialism, and bolshevism produced over a thirty-year period. In this sense the recent discussion by Herbert Spiro and Benjamin Barber[43] concerning the "ideological uses" to which the concept "totalitarianism" has been put is quite beside the point. The concept "totalitarianism" was not coined during the cold war to satisfy some political or ideological interests. The concept "totalitarianism" was a summary of the judgments contained in the bulk of literature devoted to fascism, national socialism, and bolshevism. In effect, the concept "totalitarianism" was not minted to serve "counterideological" purposes (however the concept was used by those who attempted to exploit it). It was articulated to serve primarily as a storage convenience, a mnemonic aid, and a pedagogical tool. As a consequence it reflected antecedent work.[44] In the original work of Friedrich and Brzezinski, the concept "totalitarianism" served primarily as a pretheoretical convenience. There was little pretense that what was being advanced constituted an explanatory "theory."

There can be little doubt that Friedrich and Brzezinski accomplished what they had set out to do. They provided a storage, recall, and pedagogical aid of no mean significance—and they precipitated a great deal of interesting discussion. They have left us richer as a consequence.

It is hard to suppress the conviction that any reading of the literature devoted to fascism, national socialism, and Stalinism could have done

anything other than produce a generic concept "totalitarianism" to refer
to the prevailing similarities that characterize the overt behaviors of these
regimes. The informal and discursive evidence that prompted such judgments provides the public warrant upon which the notion of "totalitarianism" must ultimately rest. The task of contemporary social scientists
is to attempt to provide a reasonably competent theory in which such
funded and discursive evidence can be rendered more precise and systematically housed. The work requires the collaborative effort of historians
patient enough to scour the tons of documentary evidence now available.
For that purpose they will require relatively clear selective criteria as to
what they should seek out in that mass of material. All selective reporting
requires fairly specific criteria of relevance and significance. A collaborative effort between historians, empirically oriented analysts, and generali-
zing social scientists is required if we are ever to lift our comprehension
of totalitarianism above the level of commonplaces and ordinary language
interpretation.

It is clearly not enough, for example, to say that Mussolini's Fascists
had near-monopoly control over the Italian economy. One needs to know
what "near-monopoly" might be taken to mean and how one might begin
to measure it. It is not enough to suggest that fascism was a "syncratic"
system in which established agricultural and industrial elites "collab-
orated" with the Fascist movement in order to produce the kinds of
surface features to which the concept "totalitarianism" alludes. We must
search the documentary and statistical evidence to attempt to establish,
with some degree of empirical plausibility, the nature and intensity of elite
interests and how they were, in fact, negotiated. When we receive judgments that the Fascists did not "tame" established elites, other judgments that they did, and still others that Fascists sometimes did and
at other times did not,[45] one can only hope to have more documentary
and empirical evidence to make a reasonably probative judgment.

But, for all that, the fact that any number of commentators are prepared to characterize Mussolini's fascism as "pretotalitarian," or "quasi-
totalitarian"[46] clearly implies the cognitive importance of the concept
"totalitarian." That Fascist Italy never succeeded in creating an effective
totalitarian system is all but uniformly recognized. Such recognition
necessitates that just such a system can be identified in fact, and that such
recognition can be accorded, be it to the Soviet Union under Stalin,
National Socialist Germany under Hitler, or revolutionary China under
Mao Tse-tung.

The fact is that "totalitarianism" refers to an "ideal case," just as
"capitalism" or "democracy" do. That few, if any, political systems
satisfy all the criteria for admission into the "ideal" class does little to

discredit the cognitive significance of the category. "Totalitarian political systems" do occupy a place on the continuum from "open" or "democratic" systems, characterized by "pluralistic" institutions that allow for interest articulation and interest aggregation, and those that are "closed" or "totalitarian," in which individuals and groups are mobilized into state- or party-dominated "capillary" institutions, which provide the factitious consensus that finds expression in "people's," "centralized," "guided," or "folkish" "democracies."

For all the efforts to discredit its use, the concept "totalitarian," or its equivalent, will continue to perform yeoman service in our efforts to analyze contemporary political reality. The "totalitarian" concept will continue to serve our efforts to come to understand some of the most important realities of the twentieth century.

HANS MOMMSEN

THE CONCEPT OF TOTALITARIAN DICTATORSHIP
VS.
THE COMPARATIVE THEORY OF FASCISM
The Case of National Socialism

Professor Mommsen examines the assumptions on which both the traditional Western theory of totalitarianism and the Comintern's interpretation of fascism as an extension of monopoly capitalism were based. He finds that both the attribution of a high degree of rational efficacy to totalitarian regimes by Western political scientists and the assertion, on the part of the Comintern, of an immediate identity of interests between state-monopolist capitalism and Fascist ruling cliques, represent unacceptable rationalizations of quite complex cause-and-effect relations.

By exploring the shortcomings of the theory of totalitarianism in coming to grips with the complexity of cause-and-effect relations in the rise to power and policies of Fascist regimes, Professor Mommsen presents his model of a more useful theory analyzing their nature and meaning. He finds that the theory of totalitarianism, generated in an age of ideological combat, depicts Hitler's national socialism in static terms, failing to account for the dynamics of internal change. The temporarily dominant neo-Marxist critique of the theory of totalitarianism, determined to bring out the socioeconomic roots of fascist power seizures, is also found wanting by Professor Mommsen. It continues to rely on the thesis of a direct correlation between the policies of organized capitalism and the triumph of fascism which, he observes, has been disproven by modern scholarship. By asserting the justification and fruitfulness in terms of scholarship of the comparative study of fascism and of a typology distinct from Communist studies, Professor Mommsen takes direct issue with those defending a more comprehensive theory of totalitarianism. He finds that

Translated by Ernest A. Menze

the outward similarities between Communist and Fascist movements and regimes wane under closer scrutiny, giving way to a perception of quite distinct approaches even in terms of once readily equated techniques of terror and propaganda, party organization, one-man leadership, etc.

Professor Mommsen sets apart the inherently unstable and self-destructive Fascist regimes, based on internally fragmented mass movements united only in their mobilizing function, from the Communist regimes unquestionably marked by greater capacity to stabilize themselves internally and to function under a clear chain of command.

A system such as Hitler's National Socialist regime, characterized from its inception by "polycratic decentralization" and all along lacking a center controlling policy decisions routinely and consistently, in Professor Mommsen's view, was bound to be plagued by internecine rivalries, rendering Hitler's supposedly all-pervasive dictatorial control in many ways fictional. But it is not only the fact that the theory of totalitarian dictatorship fails to account for the internal divisions of the National Socialist system that make it unacceptable to Professor Mommsen. Rather, he finds that its tendency to obscure the fundamental differences in the structure and political manifestation of Communist and Fascist regimes render it questionable as an analytical tool.

Though the National Socialist regime of coercion was made possible by specific historical circumstances and therefore cannot repeat itself, Professor Mommsen observes similar political movements not necessarily employing the same ideological models of legitimization may well come to the fore in the contemporary world. He concludes that the concept of totalitarianism is as little suited to their analysis as it is to that of past Fascist regimes and that new theoretical approaches are called for.

The concept of totalitarian dictatorship became, over the course of four decades, the key tool in the analysis of Fascist as well as Communist dictatorships. The general acceptance of this concept, which initially had been a theory of political science, beginning in the latter half of the thirties, was not only due to its suitability for purposes of analysis and its capacity to encompass quite varied meanings and incorporate governmental systems quite distinct from each other. Rather, the theory proved to be, at the same time, sufficiently flexible to be adaptable to changing political viewpoints and ideological needs. Scholars of Socialist orientation such as Franz Neumann made use of the concept as much as conservative authors. As it were, the concept provided the common denominator for those who, for most disparate reasons, opposed the elimination of all liberal elements by the dictatorships of Benito Mussolini and Adolf Hitler, later also by that of Stalin.

The fact that this concept carries meanings differing substantially makes virtually impossible the task of defining it comprehensively. Its multifarious aspects, from those sketched in Hannah Arendt's *The Origins of Totalitarianism*, Franz Neumann's *Behemoth*, and Ernst Fraenkel's *Dual State* to Carl Joachim Friedrich's and Zbigniew K. Brzezinski's *Totalitarian Dictatorship and Autocracy* and J. L. Talmon's *Origins of Totalitarian Democracy* make it impossible to delineate validly the relationship to competing concepts such as authoritarianism and fascism.[1]

In a situation such as this it appears meaningful to sketch historically the concept's function by describing its application and thrust. Many authors referring to the theory of totalitarianism in terms of current usage like to forget that the concept originally derived from a specifically conservative authoritarian position. Carl Schmitt's *Die Wendung zum totalen Staat* (1931), Ernst Forsthoff's *Der totale Staat* (1933), and Ulrich Scheuner's *Die nationale Revolution* (1933-34) gave currency to the concept of the total state, a concept evolved earlier and rather casually in Italian fascism, in its specifically antiparliamentarian terms.[2] The term *total*, becoming increasingly fashionable, necessarily reflected Schmitt's decisionist approach, which alone makes its application meaningful. The hopes of Hitler's conservative allies are reflected in their notion of an alternative to the socially and politically amorphous governing structure of a National Socialist regime then in the process of coming into the full possession of political power. This became clear, at the latest, in the wake of the 30th of June 1934. Hitler's coalition partners were eager to develop an authoritarian-statist alternative to the despised parliamentary Weimar regime, an alternative meant to rid itself of the populist admixtures of the National Socialist movement and to create a conservative-paternalistic order secretly modeled after the Prussian state as it was before it received a constitution.[3]

The notion of totalitarian dictatorship, joining the image of the "total state" to the experience of Hitler's personal rule, was picked up by emigrated opponents of the National Socialist regime and utilized as a concept of political combat. It aimed at a Fascist system which, having eliminated all institutional checks and balances, styled itself as a monolithic power structure.[4] Viewed in terms of a comparative study of dictatorship, the evolving concept of "totalitarian rule"—beginning in the mid-thirties—was first applied by Hans Kohn, and then in rapid succession by many leading representatives of American sociology and political science, to the Stalinist system, a system calling for comparison with the National Socialist regime by virtue of its structured terror and the onset of Stalin's purges.[5] The relative popularity of the theory of totalitarian dictatorship in reference to the Third Reich and—analogously—to a Fascist

Italy increasingly ridding itself of restrictions imposed by traditional authoritarianism, is explained by the need to provide for a liberal alternative to the Comintern's theory of fascism. The Comintern's theory of fascism had been elevated at the twelfth plenary session of the ECCI[6] to the position of "official party line" in Dimitrov's vaunted definition of fascism as the openly terroristic manifestation of capitalism. It was to be confronted by a concept free of the explicitly anticapitalist components of the Communist definition of fascism and to proceed from the constitutionalist self-perception of the Western democracies.

Representing specifically the opposite to the self-image of Western democratic systems, the theory of totalitarianism, indeed, could serve as the tool to bring together quite distinct approaches to explain the genesis and describe the structure of Fascist as well as Communist rule. Both of these variants of Democratic regimes appear to correspond in their complete denial of basic civil rights: the denial of the freedom of assembly, the freedom of the press, the separation of powers, the independence of the judiciary, due process in administrative matters, the freedom of expression, the right to the advocacy of social concerns, and free elections. Also, the tools of terrorism employed to attain the monopolization of power, the methods of indoctrination through propaganda, the utilization of rigidly steered party organizations as the springboard for the unlimited exercise of power by the dictator and his closest supporters, as well as the Machiavellian manipulation of national sentiments and emotional needs, appear to be characteristic for the Stalinist as much as the Hitlerian regime. It is, therefore, not surprising that the institutional variant of the theory of totalitarian dictatorship enjoyed increasing popularity even after 1945. It found its most classic expression in the model of totalitarian rule developed by Carl J. Friedrich and Z. K. Brzezinski. They depicted, as the chief comparable characteristic, the role played by the totalitarian mass-membership party as the instrument of domination controlled by the ruling clique.[7]

Characteristic for their analysis was the implication of a comparatively high surface effectiveness and rationality on the part of totalitarian dictatorship, apparently superior to the more complicated processes of decision making in democratic-parliamentarian or presidential-democratic systems. The theory of totalitarianism attributed a high degree of rational efficacy also to the National Socialist regime. The tactic of letting individual power centers such as the SA or SS take the lead in order to present the intentions of the regime as the reflection of the popular mood and thereby legitimize them was too transparent not to be taken as part of a well-planned strategy. The Machiavellian connotation of the totalitarian theory finds a counterpart in the fascism theory of the Comintern, which, by asserting an immediate identity of interests between state-monopolistic capitalism and the Fascist leadership clique, also unacceptably rationalized cause-and-effect relations which really are far more complex.

The historical context of its formulation makes clear that the theory of totalitarianism was derived from the actuality of established dictatorship; therefore, it represents an excessively static model in political theory. This applies as much to the original formulation during the thirties of the theory by Hans Kohn and other authors as to the more broadly conceived theory of Friedrich and Brzezinski. A derivation from considerations of institutional theory is at the base also of the analyses of totalitarianism by Franz L. Neumann and Sigmund Neumann which, in other respects, are significantly more differentiated and more emphatically concerned with throwing light on the constellations of political interest groups. As much as they differed over the economic bases of the Fascist system, these authors accentuated the monolithic ruling structure of the Fascist regime. Ernst Fraenkel's approach ascribing a dialectic relationship to the normative and the decisionist variants of the state and, with the theory of the Dual State, grasping decisive characteristics of the first developmental stage of the National Socialist system up to 1938, does not constitute an exception; this is so insofar as it, too, proceeded from the assumption of unity and cohesiveness in the decision-making process at the top of the dictatorship, implemented by varying strategies. Similar considerations apply to many interpretations of Stalinism, choosing to proceed from the assumption that the dictator himself follows, in all essentials, the pure mandates of power and utilizes ideology only as a manipulatory instrument, adjusting it to fluctuating circumstances.[8]

This variation of the theory of totalitarian dictatorship is marked by a twofold weakness. On the one hand, such an approach encounters the difficulty of having to reconcile the inner frictions, contradictions, and antagonisms of Fascist as well as Communist systems; this usually is done by constructing the political process as the exercise of the *"divide et impera"* tactic on the part of the ruling clique and presuming the general acceptance of a military chain of command from the top to the bottom. But this model does not apply without qualification, and if it does apply, only to varying degrees, to the examples considered as prototypes of totalitarian dictatorship, the Third Reich and Stalin's regime. On the other hand, it is precisely the institutionalist dimension of the theory which does not take into account sufficiently the development and structure of Fascist mass movements—that is to say, the "movement phase" of Fascist regimes.[9] By the same token, the Communist party is envisioned only in the shape of an already institutionalized "party ruling the state," not as a political "movement." A comparable misconception, but based on other premises, became part of the Comintern's theory of fascism, in that it denied the autonomous origin of Fascist mass movements. It linked conceptually national socialism and the preceding authoritarian presidential cabinets, including the political forces on which they were based. The theory of "social fascism" served as the vehicle of linkage. Thus the originally movement-oriented concept of fascism was transformed.[10] The movement's makeup before the seizure of power and that characterizing the regime in power overlap strangely in the Marxist-Leninist conception of fascism; as a result, Marxist-Leninist historiography is quite weak in regard to the analysis of the movement phase of national socialism and Italian fascism and finds it difficult to analyze adequately the roles played by the National Socialist German Workers party and the Partito Fascista within the Fascist power structure. Here too, and running counter to the original intent of stressing the socioeconomic substructure, the tendency prevails to view statically the characteristic power monopoly of new and old elites, and to interpret it as a form of exploitation superimposed upon the masses of society. As in the case of the theory of totalitarian dictatorship, terror and propagandistic indoctrination are presented as the crucial factors in securing power.

Proceeding from the axiom of the comparability in principle of the Communist and National Socialist systems, it followed necessarily for adherents of the theory of totalitarianism that ideological strategies of legitimization be interpreted preeminently in terms of function. This corresponds to the tendency of accentuating, on the one hand, the factor of one-man rule—by interpreting national socialism as Hitlerism[11] – and by progressively viewing the initially ideologically conceived Stalinist system in terms of personal rule. On the other hand, there is correspondence to the tendency of placing extraordinary emphasis on the function of ideology and propaganda, detecting here the chief cause for Fascist mass mobilization. These two tendencies were linked by emphasis on the plebiscitary and charismatic elements and the "leader-cult," which, however, were not fully corresponded to by the characteristics really governing the Stalinist cult of personality.[12]

It is a reflection of the cold war and the resulting aggravation of the ideological conflict of the superpowers that the theory of totalitarianism was variated by many authors in terms of intellectual history and, in like measure, reinterpreted by them into the opposite of the democratic principle, as it is understood in the liberal West.[13] Talmon's differentiation between a liberal and a totalitarian type of democracy was conceived in terms of the messianic and chiliastic elements of Fascist ideology as well as in terms of the exercise of power through terror.[14] At the same time, Talmon indirectly tied into the self-serving claim of neoconservatives depicting national socialism as the consequence of "voting-booth democracy" (Winfried Martini[15])—that is to say of what conservatives considered to be unrestricted mass democracy. A line was drawn by Talmon, leading from Rousseau, Mably, and the Jacobins to Marx, and from him to Lenin and Hitler. Aside from the official position of the Comintern, the Left is on the whole marked by similar efforts to establish historical antecedents; a classical example is found in the theory of Bonapartism, representing the attempt to explain the genesis of fascism on the one hand by going back to Karl Marx's theory of Bonapartism and on the other by dealing more adequately with the dynamic quality of fascism as a movement, not accounted for satisfactorily in the theory of a "state-monopolistic-capitalist conspiracy."[16]

Talmon's approach shares with most other theories of totalitarianism the particular incapacity to categorize historically antiliberal authoritarian regimes not utilizing terror and extreme mass mobilization, though they often may represent the first step of totalitarian dictatorship. These theories do not offer an explanation for the fact that dictatorships with Fascist characteristics may revert to become authoritarian systems, as was the case in Spain. Since mass mobilization in the Communist system at best fulfills a propagandistic legitimizing function—except for its early phase, when political mass radicalization is utilized to seize power—it follows that mass mobilization as a specific criterion of Fascist movements before the seizure of power does not quite fit under the umbrella theory of totalitarianism. Ernst Nolte's fundamental study of *"Fascism during Its Epoch"* (the original title of the German work, rendered in English as *Three Faces of Fascism*), comparing ideological parallelisms of Fascist movements and related integral-nationalist movements[17] constituted, therefore, the break-out from the self-imposed ghetto of the theory of totalitarianism. However, Nolte's work was marked by an overemphasis on the ideological-programmatic content in Fascist propaganda. Issues such as those raised by Fascist propaganda are also reflected in the views of the conservative Right as well as, generally, in imperialist aspirations before the First World War, without causing mass mobilizations comparable to Fascist movements.

Hannah Arendt's work, diverging fundamentally from the established interpretations of totalitarianism and approaching it in terms of its epoch, took a rather different approach by accentuating the social and sociopsychological grounds for the alleged efficacy and decisiveness of what she called the "so-called totalitarian state"; that is to say, she posed the question of what the social and sociopsychological mechanisms were that permitted modern dictatorships to find support in considerable consensus and, above all, explained the rise of Fascist mass movements. In doing so, Arendt took up suggestions made by the Frankfurt school (especially those in the works of Theodor W. Adorno) and developed further the approach to the problems discussed in Erich Fromm's *Escape from Freedom* (1941).[18] More recent studies of fascism carried on in the West return increasingly to these approaches in order to explain the mass support of Fascist parties without, however, always making clear their connection with this earlier work.

In contrast, however, it must be noted that the theory of totalitarianism, though split into innumerable variations, in the main has assumed the features of an ideological syndrome. This was the case in the lesson plans for West German secondary schools during the fifties and sixties.[19] The theory reflected the basic anti-Communist and anti-Stalinist mood, as it also reflected a quite undifferentiated concept of democracy, leaving out of consideration the evident functional shortcomings of classical parliamentarianism under the conditions governing highly industrialized and bureaucratized societies in the process of technological transformation. Here it is clearly evident that the elements critical of capitalism virtually constituting the essence of the original works—as in the case of Franz L. Neumann and others—completely faded into the background, and the positing of totalitarian structures and modes of thought has been largely set apart from socioeconomic spheres of interest and concrete social conditions.[20]

Thus a heuristic model, originally fruitful in terms of the historical insights it yielded, was intellectually impoverished and transformed into an indirectly assertive ideology designed to preserve existing liberal-parliamentary structures.[21] This process will not be halted even by efforts of, above all, West German historians such as Karl Dietrich Bracher, Hans-Adolf Jacobsen, and Klaus Hildebrand to classify together the Bolshevik and the National Socialist revolutions and (especially Bracher) to differentiate between classical bourgeois and "modern" totalitarian "revolutions"—that is to say, "Putschist" strategies in the seizure of power.[22] The permutation of connotations resulting thereby from Bracher's depicting, on the one hand, Lenin as a "successful Putschist," Hitler and Mussolini as victorious "revolutionaries" on the other,[23] is at the least confusing, since both Fascist dictators, unlike Lenin, established their regimes with the consent of the conservative-authoritarian cartels of power. This permutation, at the same time, results in formalizing the theory of totalitarianism to the point of rendering it unyielding in questions of substance. The critique of "The Bane of Totalitarianism Theories,"[24] therefore, proceeds from two directions. For one, the practice of classifying together national socialism and communism, tending to disregard or in fact exclude Italian fascism and Fascist movements in

Southeast-Central Europe and some West-European countries, turns out to be a Procrustean bed for the analysis of the origins of Fascist mass movements.[25] At the same time, the theory of totalitarianism, in many points, adheres too much to the criteria established for themselves by the regimes it is meant to encompass; it is therefore not suited to provide new insights. In particular, the theory does not penetrate the element of partial depoliticization characteristic for such movements and regimes— that is, the tendency of Fascist propaganda to divert attention from concrete social and political concerns and to keep the mass of the population in a state of depoliticized passivity.[26] Above all, however, the theory precludes the question of which institutional, political, and economic mechanisms lead to the overextension of their power and the tendency to virtual self-destruction, evidently characteristic of Fascist regimes in contrast to authoritarian systems. Thus, by postulating an ideological framework based, after all, upon a given concept of political power, fixed in advance in all essential points, and "revolutionary" only by virtue of that conceptual limitation, the theory of totalitarianism obstructs important avenues of research. Above all, societal changes, conflicts between modernization and atavistic tendencies on the part of the ruling clique, are rendered to be but marginal phenomena. The political process appears to be determined from the outset, and thereby Fascist regimes tend to be political systems without history—according to this interpretation—being determined by the ideological resolution of the late dictator. This becomes apparent in the thesis, widely disseminated, that Hitler's program, with the exception of tactical deviations, was fixed in all essentials already during the twenties.[27] As a matter of fact, however, the real concern of modern fascism studies is precisely the examination of the transformation by Fascist regimes of apparently utopian aspirations into actual policies, the road from theory to practice which certainly tends to be extremely contradictory in terms of interest politics.

On the other hand, a temporarily dominant critique of the theory of totalitarianism is due to the growth of neo-Marxist tendencies and the need to bring out the socioeconomic roots of Fascist power seizures *vis-à-vis* explanatory models discussing it in terms of ideology. Scholarship not inclined to or influenced by Marxist-Leninist views, in this process, has dissociated itself from the thesis of a direct correlation between the policies of organized capitalism and the triumph of the Fascist forces. Indeed, Henry A. Turner, Timothy Mason, and Alan Milward have disproven the thesis, still adhered to in modified form by a number of authors in the German Democratic Republic, identifying the National Socialist regime with state-monopolist capitalism and holding that a significant amount of financing of the National Socialist German Labor Party came from corporate business.[28] However, this exculpation cannot relieve capitalist interests of responsibility for the undermining of the liberal-parliamentarian system and the determined interference with the development of the socialist workers' movement. The image, prevalent for many years, of the democratic Weimar Republic as crushed simultaneously by two totalitarian movements mirrors the apologetic character assumed by the theory of totalitarianism during the period of the cold war in regard to the politics of conservative elites. By accentuating too much the Machiavellian and manipulative aspects of the National Socialist movement and regime and its terrorist tactics in seizing power, the political responsibility of the conservative alliance partners of 1933, as well as that of the power elites in industry, administration, and army who continued to fulfill important functions within the regime, is pushed into the background. Characteristic for this attitude is the emotional reaction to the findings of Fritz Tobias, reasonably substantiated and not convincingly disproved to date, that the Reichstag fire of 27 February 1933 was not manipulated by the National Socialists, but was the work of a single man, as was the assassination of Georg Elser.[29] Now as then it is a matter of dogma for many historians, especially in the Federal Republic of Germany, that the National Socialists caused the fire; the actual bearing of the matter on the nature of the regime is limited, at any rate, and does not touch upon its fundamentally criminal character.[30]

In the Federal Republic of Germany, the question whether it is meaningful to incorporate national socialism into a general comparative concept of fascism is met by similarly emotional reactions. These are due to hypersensitivity to neo-Marxist interpretative approaches. Even though, here and there, the inclination to divert attention from the repressive practices of Communist regimes is implicitly evident, the comparative concept of fascism has long established its usefulness in innumerable studies. There is, therefore, no cause to denounce it as the relativization of the democratic-parliamentary system's foundations, as was done especially by Karl Dietrich Bracher.[31] This state of the discussion reveals how much the dialogue over differing methodological approaches and strategies has been transformed into a question of ideology, in which the concept of totalitarianism occupies a key role. Indeed, the theory of totalitarianism is increasingly degenerating into a classificatory tool applicable to universal history, utilized *ex negativo* to legitimize efforts at turning away even reformist critiques of democracy. Meanwhile, in the realm of practical scholarship, a whole series of its basic premises have either shown to be of little use or—for example, in its ascribing of a central role to the "totalitarian" party in a one-party state—do not meet the mark on the basis of the particular hypothesis from which they are drawn.

The weakness of the theory of totalitarianism is most clearly revealed in the analysis of the typology of Fascist movements. They indeed show a number of outward similarities to Communist parties—as a rule imitations of Communist techniques of organization and propaganda—but they also again differ fundamentally from them. This applies first of all to the structure of organization. The National Socialist German Workers' party, indeed, attempted to copy the block and cell system of the German Communist party, but provided it with functions quite different from those prevailing within the Communist cadre party. The promulgation of the "National Socialist Ordinance Governing Business Enterprises" (NSBO) notwithstanding, party cells never were formed within individual business enterprises. Conforming to the principle of "democratic centralism," Communist parties are characterized by a stringent system of hierarchical subordination, finding expression in the exclusion of disobedient members from parliamentary fractions and in clearly delimited competencies of subordinate organizations. Moreover, the system of democratic centralism does not preclude on principle the political discussion of policies and, with that, intra-party integration on all levels of organization; rather, the principle of democratic centralism provides that the decisions of superior party offices, once made, are binding and no longer subject to discussion. Notwithstanding the deterioration and manipulation of intra-party elections and their tendency to turn into mere rites of acclamation, this structure nevertheless does not preclude completely a turnover within the leadership elites.[32]

The National Socialist German Workers' party (NSDAP), representing the purest type of the Fascist party, did not permit intra-party policy formation on any of the organizational levels. Beginning in 1923 and especially after 1925, due to Hitler's influence, any form of intra-party elective procedure was proscribed as a throw-back to parliamentarianism. Leadership appointments came exclusively from the central office of the party. Formally this was the Munich local of the party; in fact, it was a small clique of Hitler's unconditional followers. Initiatives to form a leadership council, comparable to the "Grand Council of Fascism"—an ineffective instrument at any rate—were subverted by any means both during the party's movement phase and after the seizure of power. The Senate chamber of the Munich "Brown House," built specifically to serve as the meeting room for such a council, never fulfilled that function. Repeated efforts by Reichminister of the Interior Wilhelm Frick to create an "electoral senate," intended to become—under the fiction of providing for succession in the leadership after Göring—a kind of intra-party coordinating authority—were on occasion promised by Hitler, but he in turn prevented all concrete steps to realize this project.[33] The high-sounding designation *"Reich* Command of the NSDAP" never stood for a genuine collegial organization; the position of the *Reichsleiter* in charge of this party command remained a mere title.

After the seizure of power Hitler delegated leadership of the party to Rudolph Hess, who was completely devoted to him and, at heart, had the mentality of a subordinate. His staff, at first assigned intermediary functions, after Hess's flight to England reconstituted under Martin Bormann as "Party-Chancellory," did indeed claim—in subterranean competition with the treasurer of the party and chief justice Buch of the Party Court—authority over the organization, but without ever being able to assert that authority unrestrictedly. With that, any kind of oligarchical leadership groups capable of balancing conflicting interests among the lower echelons of the party were lacking. The resolution of such conflicts thus was carried over into the sphere of private life, giving sustained impetus to corruption and leading to notorious rivalries between individuals in leading positions. There was no provision for formalized regular meetings of higher party functionaries; the meeting of the political leadership at the conclusion of the annual party congress served to relieve resentment on the part of the party *vis-à-vis* the organs of the administration; there were no deliberations at these meetings, nor were there any at the irregularily scheduled meetings of the *Reichsstatthalter* and the *Gauleiter* (governors of non-German areas and the provincial party chiefs).[34]

This structural difference from the Communist type of party is a qualitative one. It was rooted in the fact that the party, due to the influence exerted by the Munich leadership clique, was programmed exclusively towards electoral activity; this principle was reflected in the extensive self-sufficiency of the subordinate party organizations, especially the provincial leadership, to the point of influence over programmatic-tactical considerations within the framework of the general propaganda guidelines issued by the Munich party leadership. A significant measure of adaptation to the political and social constellations governing the individual provinces thereby was facilitated. Integration of the party was achieved by means of the *Führer*-principle—imposing itself from without and above—permitting the relatively different regional interests to assert themselves and simultaneously neutralizing them. Efforts to centralize by Gregor Strasser as "Reich Chief of Organizational Matters" *(Reichsorganisationsleiter)* to the contrary, the autonomy of provincial party organizations remained unusually extensive, and the radius of activity permitted to the party functionaries subject to the provincial party organizations depended on the personal attitudes and bureaucratic efficacy of the individual party heads *(Gauleiter)* of the provinces. Even though

Strasser's "Planning Dept. II" (*Organisationsabteilung II*) was devised to serve as a planning apparatus for the coming seizure of power, it, too, served exclusively as an instrument in the electoral struggle.[35] At the time of the seizure of power, therefore, only unclear conceptions regarding the form of the future National Socialist state existed; a number of legislative initiatives drafted by outsiders after January 30, 1933, found no acceptance at all in the ministries which, in the meantime, had been coerced into conformity to the party line.[36]

Unlike the very strict chain of command within Communist parties, expressed in programmatic-tactical directives and permitting of rapid tactical shifts within the briefest possible time limits, the loose National Socialist system of "human guidance" was specifically designed to direct all energies by means of minimal bureaucratic directives, towards propaganda and organizational activity but, on the other hand, to prevent debates over policy. The principle of subordinating party functionaries in two overlapping ways—politically as well as in terms of the functions assigned to specific subordinate organizations, as in the case of local propaganda agencies—served the same purpose. The evident disadvantage of the attendant conflict over competencies on all levels of organization was deliberately relegated to secondary consideration. The intra-party "depoliticization" and coerced conformity (*Gleichschaltung*) does not only run counter to the principles governing the bourgeois parliamentary party, but also to those governing the Communist type of party. This structure explains the extraordinary propagandistic effectiveness of the Nazi party apparatus; by the same token, however, it also explains the capacity to address simultaneously distinct social groups and to bind them—temporarily, at any rate.

The reverse side of this exclusive orientation of the Fascist type of party towards propagandistic mobilization and electoral campaigning is reflected in the characteristic incapacity of the National Socialist German Workers' party to effectively exercise that function of political control ascribed to it in the theory of totalitarianism and to seize the leading positions in the administrative departments. The relative lack of influence, during the regime's phase in power, of the NSDAP as a mass political organization, finds its equivalent in the establishment of independence on the part of the Fascist leadership clique *vis-à-vis* the Partito Fascista in Italy.[37] Similar features do, indeed, also apply to Communist systems; but in the end, the party and its highest collegial supervisory bodies, there, remain essential instruments of legitimization. Deterioration due to the effects of the Stalinist era have facilitated the equating of Fascist and Communist parties. However, developments after Stalin's death showed that a return to collegial leadership was possible, and in the meantime the capacity of Communist leadership oligarchies to remove dictators has become a generally observable development.

These differences might be considered of degree merely, rather than of principle, especially since the example of Mussolini in 1943 bears out the capacity of influential groups within the party, linked to the traditional power elites, to break through the myth of the one-man leadership cult. What matters, however, is the fact that the specific mode of Fascist politics, permitting its designation as a distinctive type alongside imperialism and integral nationalism, and setting it apart from the earlier form of plebiscitary Caesarism, was not capable, as a matter of fact, of rendering the system stable; this may not be said of Communist dictatorships.

It would be an error to assume that the tendency to virtual self-destruction inherent in German national socialism and Italian fascism—though becoming apparent fully in Italy only in the Republic of Salo—is due exclusively to the psychic condition of the Fascist dictators and the inevitable corruption attendant upon the uncontrolled accumulation of power. Rather, this tendency is the result of the *modus operandi* typical for Fascist movements but alien to communism. They exploit traditional structures—coerced into conformity—in the realms of politics, the military, economic life, and the administration, and, by progressively undermining their formal as well as their normative foundations, eliminate them in the end. In order to account for the progressive fragmentation of the system, Robert Koehl has alluded to the concept of feudalism in reference to the internal development of the National Socialist regime. This reference to the elements of feudal society—as in the term *Gefolgschaft* (fealty)—constitutes a perversion of the principle of mutual loyalty—including the right to resist—prevalent in the medieval state system governed by personal bonds.[38] It was especially in the satrapies of the territorial *Kommissar* emerging in the Nazi-occupied Russian territories that atavistic tendencies clearly were revealed, lapsing from the structural integrity of the rational-institutional state. An exception is found in the case of Fascist Spain. But here, characteristically, the Fascist forces came to the fore only secondarily, enabling Generalissimo Franco to bring the Falange under the control of the army and to reshape the partially Fascist system into a genuinely authoritarian one.

It is a characteristic weakness of the theory of totalitarian dictatorship that it ascribes to the National Socialist regime a high degree of "formal rationality"—which, however, prevails in Fascist regimes only in particular segments, always embedded in the cloak of political irrationalism.[39] Of course, one will not wish to ascribe pervasive "formal rationality" to Western political systems either. One may also argue the question whether this term is fully applicable anyway, since the political process in Western industrial societies, too, cannot at all be measured by the standards of the liberal model of rational decision making based on free discussion. Nevertheless, the reversal of the means-ends relation[40] —both in the social and administrative realms—typical of national socialism and partially also of Italian fascism, must be characterized as a tendency on the part of the political system to lose its inner rationality or—in terms of systems —as the surrender of the capacity to regulate the direction of policy.[41]

This is easily demonstrated on the basis of individual programs. The Nazi program of peasant homesteads was faced with a rather extreme measure of rural migration into the cities and, especially in comparison with developments during the Weimar Republic, a decided decrease in the number of newly created homesteads. The explicit favoring of the crafts, trades, and industrial enterprises owned by the middle class took place in the face of an accelerated process of capital accumulation and an increasing domination of the industrial sector by large enterprises. The notion of *Lebensraum* (space to live)—had it not failed because of its inherent *hybris*—would not have led to the German peasant settlements dreamt of by Himmler, but to the development of highly industrialized urban centers in which production would have been carried on by slave labor supervised by groups of German technocrats living in isolation. This list of reversals of programmatic initiatives by the National Socialist German Workers' party into their direct opposites might be continued at will.

Similar discrepancies, however, also appeared within the structure of government on all levels. The system of overlapping *ad hoc* competencies negated any kind of rational division of labor and functions, resulting in the diffusion of the system's energies in a gigantic contretemps of institutions. The conflict between Sauckel as the man responsible for the allocation of labor resources and Speer as the head of the Ministry for Armaments and Production is only a case in point for the political structure of the Fascist party and the corresponding mentality of the Fascist leaders. This mentality is marked by the tendency to short-term and short-sighted mobilization of all available resources to satisfy particular priorities, resulting—in intermediate terms—in mutual obstruction.[42] The much-cited polycracy of the administrative departments was not simply produced by the impotence of the individual officeholders. Rather, the opposite was the case. This polycracy, indeed, to a degree was due to administrative drift permitted by the central leadership clique. Polycratic government was facilitated because areas of competence were demarcated by fluid lines and because departmental potentates could not be assured of enjoying permanently the positions of power they had obtained.

Some of this is found also in Communist systems and must, above all, be attributed to the absence of unhampered public opinion as a corrective to mistakes in policy and the bureaucratic slowness of communications which, if it does so at all, links the decision makers to their local and regional executors of policy. The theory of totalitarian dictatorship—as a rule—implicitly assigns a controlling function to the bureaucratic apparatuses. The reality of the Third Reich rather demonstrates the opposite. The existing bureaucratic institutions were gradually emptied of substance, and the leadership made a habit of frequently approaching political objectives by purposely circumventing the bureaucracies specialized to deal with them. Instead, new "secondary" bureaucracies such as the *Reichssicherheitshauptamt* (Main Office of Reich Security—the notorious SS police control center commanded by Heydrich and later by Kaltenbrunner, among others) or Albert Speer's Armaments Ministry, emerged in the twilight zone between public administration and party apparatus. Their "success" characteristically rested on the utilization of "unbureaucratic" methods which, however, in the intermediate perspective reinforced the same kind of polycratic decentralization that had characterized the political system as a whole from its inception. Centers of resistance were thus enabled to establish themselves within Himmler's S.S. empire. The divergences of interests among the individual agencies assumed grotesque proportions.

The political system of national socialism was characterized by the absence of a center controlling policy decisions routinely and consistently. Bormann, as the Führer's secretary and leader of the party chancellery, expended painstaking bureaucratic efforts to create a substitute, but there remained broad areas he was unable to influence. The dictator and his more narrow circle—a circle often formed haphazardly and, as a rule, not marked by subject matter competency—were unable to handle business routinely, so that important sectors of the political system were allowed to drift aimlessly, particularly since the ministerial bureaucracy was less and less in a position to assert itself against the informal centers of power. It was only in specific areas—during the Second World War in the matter of military command and in dominant questions of foreign policy—that Hitler really made use of his dictatorial powers. In all remaining areas of policy he intervened in an *ad hoc* capacity and frequently only after conflicts of competencies were affecting his own position.[43] The fact that the supposed concentration of all relevant political, military and economic decisions in the hands of the dictator was fictional resulted in an increasing loss of communication between the controlling political and administrative agencies. The isolation of sources of information on the basis of departments and function, surely also a consequence of

Hitler's Social Darwinist principles, led to an almost unbelievable void of communication among those governing the regime, intensified even more by the secrecy requirements of the war. The diffusiveness of decision making was broadened by the increasing loss of procedural detail in the evolution of policy, such as countersignature by concerned departments and the formal issuing of legally binding written commands, the transition to casual "Führer"-directives based exclusively on oral presentations, and the rivalry among intermediary organs—the Reich Chancellery, the Party Chancellery, and a multitude of transient functionaries.

Above all, however, an orderly compromise between diverging interests had to be an exception to the rule in a system such as this, since there were no governmental agencies in which these interests were formally represented. Mediated reconciliation of particularistic interests, therefore, could be attained only partially and in an *ad hoc* fashion. This was not merely the consequence of notorious dilettantism on the part of those holding power within the system, even though the contempt felt for bureaucratic and juridical processes was, indeed, notorious. Rather, this disintegration of the foundations supporting the constitutional state was rooted in a perception of politics exclusively aiming at propagandistic integration and mobilization, capable of mediating diverging interests only within the purview of an ultimate goal conceived chiliastically. The manifold priorities set thus are not a matter of principle but based on tactical consideration; they mean the postponement, not the retraction in principle, of certain measures. Characteristically, therefore, the regime never was able to act on the basis of available resources, which led to constant exaggeration and overlapping of parochial objectives accompanied by a specific tendency to escalate.

It would be going too far to describe in detail a method of governing rooted precisely in the self-perception of the NSDAP during its movement phase, a method which is effective for short-term political mobilization.[44] Important is that the theory of totalitarianism, if it wants to be more than a description of propagandistic manipulatory techniques and of their legitimizing functions, misperceives the political mechanisms underlying Fascist dictatorship, leading to an overestimate of their actual political stability. The argument brought forth by many representing the theory of totalitarianism—namely, that of the two prototypical Fascist regimes (the Third Reich and Fascist Italy) only the former was totalitarian while the latter did not really develop beyond authoritarian structures—that argument is based on standards measuring the extension of power at home and abroad and the utilization of terror. It is undeniable that a comparison of Italian and German fascism reveals concrete differences in the internal distribution of power between Fascist groups and traditional elites.[45] Nevertheless and notwithstanding significant ideological differences, Italian and German fascism are most closely related to each other in terms of their political structure and their sociopolitical foundations. The component destabilizing the system came to the fore much more strongly in the National Socialist system than in Italy. Paradoxically, this was due not least to Hitler's ability to assure himself of the unconditional support by the traditional power elites—a process in which antibolshevism did play a significant role.[46] This support facilitated the placing into the service of Fascist radicalization the political and military apparatus of the state as well as corporate business, but also to corrupt these and permeate them with Fascist ideas so much more thoroughly.

Juan Linz has characterized Fascist systems as in the nature of an "anti-revolt."[47] Indeed, they lack any kind of consistency in social as well as in programmatic terms. As the social composition of Fascist parties by their nature is heterogeneous, mobilizing only existing movements of potential protest whose composition corresponds to national conditions in each case,[48] Fascist ideology serves to mobilize social resentments and adapts to them. Parts of the Fascist program, therefore, are in principle interchangeable except for its antiliberal and anti-Socialist direction called for by the conditions of the interwar period. In terms of substance they differ from the ideological concepts evident in authoritarian-nationalistic tendencies manifested since the onset of imperialism only in the degree of ruthlessness and intensity displayed by their propaganda; there are no political goals here that were not anticipated in integral nationalism.

Characteristic for fascism, however, is the complete absence of any serious concept envisioning the restructuring of social or institutional life. Fascist politics insofar has always been merely simulation, but not in the sense that the Fascist leaders were capable of freeing themselves from the effects of their own propaganda. Rather, this incapacity often results in self-fulfilling prophecies, since it caused many a historian to ascribe to fascism long-term planning and the attainment of goals in stages.[49] As a matter of fact, however, Fascist politics rests on essentially an incredible exaggeration and, with that, perversion of political tendencies in both domestic and foreign policy, so that, in hindsight, policies appear as of striking inner consistency that were merely the consequence of a millenarian pathos produced for the occasion and only partly related to political reality; the fulfillment of promises short of other alternatives could be aspired to precisely because there was no cause for the weighing of rational interests beyond mere tactical considerations.

Fascist systems, therefore, by their inner logic degenerate into government by clique, postponing the realization of originally postulated program points time and again and accelerating, not altering, overall socioeconomic development on the basis of an artificially created and sustained political dynamic. Therefore, only the "negative elements of ideology" not facing up to the veto power of significant social interests assert themselves. In this respect, then, here prevails a specifically parasitic mode of politics, incapable of creating new structures. It consists of the simulation of a political balancing of interests, while real social conflicts are left unresolved—notwithstanding the vaunted notion of *Volksgemein-schaft* (community of the people)—as long as the power of the ruling clique is not affected. Significantly revealing for the manner of Fascist politics is the concept of *Gleichschaltung*—coercing disparate elements to move within the same channels—because it exploits given political and social structures by manipulating them, but not leading up to a total transformation of society. This explains the temporary identity of interests with the traditional elites.

The incapacity to achieve institutional stability and the tendency—developed during the movement phase—to repress crisis symptoms and conflicts over objectives by means of "actionism" necessarily led to a systematically devised process of "cumulative radicalization," which may not by any means be attributed alone to the ideological visions of the dictator and his decisions as leader. In order to compensate for its political sterility, Fascist simulative terminology employs an overblown vocabulary, as clearly demonstrated by the phrase "National Socialist Revolution." It appears to be misleading, therefore, to apply the concept "revolution" to characterize a movement which—though utilizing the entire potential of modern industrial society—essentially is destructive and, as a rule, displays modernizing effects in the context of otherwise reactionary and even atavistic goals.

Concepts like "modern dictatorship" or "new-type revolution"[50] therefore remain formalistic categories, incapable of accounting for the specific structure of Fascist political systems. Moreover, the utilization of technological means to manipulate the masses and to render potential and actual terror effective, on which such attempts at definition focus, cannot be regarded as revolutionary. For it makes a principal difference whether this is done, as in the case of the Nazis in the absence of any substantial social concept or, as in the Communist case, for the sake of a radical egalitarian and anticapitalist concept (failure to reach intended objectives notwithstanding). This difference becomes quite clear if one checks the capacity of system stabilization, which no one will deny to Communist systems.[51] All considerations of political power and bureaucratic deformations notwithstanding, the Communist program retains a rational core serving positive political development and social justice. Here rest the prospects, to be evaluated in relative terms, of what is understood by the slogan "liberalization," a term which has little bearing on the system at any rate. On the basis of experiences up to now, Communist parties and systems do not necessarily preclude convergence with Western constitutional concepts. This can hardly be said of Fascist parties and systems.

A number of authors, indeed, do plead for the elimination of the theory of totalitarian dictatorship as the ideological reflection of the cold war[52] and as an inappropriate model in the analysis of contemporary Communist systems, but they wish to retain the concept "totalitarian" as the opposite of "democracy."[53] If one incorporates into this concept of totalitarianism the inclination to attribute to itself falsely a democratic legitimacy which really is pseudodemocratic and may extend all the way to brainwashing and self-accusations, nearly all post-democratic authoritarian regimes are characterized by it. If one considers by "totalitarian" the pervasion of all aspects of life by an all-encompassing ruling ideology, the term applies to both Communist and Fascist systems. But this correspondence ought not to lead to the assumption of a capacity on the part of Fascist propaganda to effect lasting indoctrination beyond a mere "friend vs. enemy" mentality, without intensifying existing social resentments such as anti-Semitism, antibolshevism, and nationalism. Employed in this fashion in order to obscure the fundamental differences in the structure and political manifestation of Communist and Fascist systems, the concept loses its analytical function—which lies exclusively in the field of the critical theory of ideologies—and it becomes itself an ideological slogan.

In reference to the analysis of the sociopolitical structure of Fascist systems the theory of totalitarianism is obsolete. In the case of national socialism it abstracts from the power structures typical for the Third Reich as they emerged in the course of first the coercive coordination of and then the exclusion of the conservative power elites or their absorption into the Fascist system. At the same time the institutional variant of the theory of totalitarianism obstructs an understanding of the process bringing Fascist movements into power. By setting apart totalitarian rule as that of systems closed off from predecessor regimes, and by thus losing sight of the continuity of socioeconomic and sociopsychological structures, the causes within the whole spectrum of society of the Fascist variant of modern coercive governmental systems are obscured. With that those traditional elites and conservative-nationalist groups are implicitly rehabilitated without whose active participation Fascist potentates would not have attained power. Nor, for that matter, would they have been able to stabilize their regime in relative terms without basing it on an alliance with these conservative-authoritarian forces.

The theory of totalitarianism, regressing—quite contrary to the intentions of Franz Neumann, Ernst Fraenkel, and Hannah Arendt—to its historical point of departure, threatens to obstruct the view of the actual perils to democratically constituted societies. The National Socialist regime of coercion—the result of unique circumstances—will not repeat itself. It was possible because of the deep tension between economic and technological modernization on the one hand and the political backwardness of German society on the other. But the political mechanisms set free by the regime, and populist simulations of the same, may recur anywhere under the conditions of Western industrial societies, without necessary recourse to the ideological models of legitimization utilized in the interwar period.

ERNST NOLTE

– DESPOTISM –
– TOTALITARIANISM –
– FREEDOM-ORIENTED SOCIETY –

This essay is a substantially expanded version of a comment given by Professor Nolte at a session reconsidering totalitarianism at the 1977 annual meeting of the American Historical Association in Dallas.

Though often considered to be the scholar most responsible for breaking the exclusive hold of the concept of "totalitarianism" over contemporary political theory, Professor Nolte here makes clear that he considers the concept by no means superfluous. Postulating four propositions which, to him, are basic to the complex of problems associated with the topic, Professor Nolte locates the dichotomy between the Western liberal political systems and their totalitarian counterparts in the core of the occidental tradition and reality. As old as Western society, the tendency to set apart despotic rule from the freedom-oriented ideal—which is also expressed in the negative use of the term totalitarianism—*will disappear only with the society that gave rise to it. Yet, to Professor Nolte, the criticism leveled against the concept of totalitarianism is symptomatic of profound historical change and consequently somewhat justified; moreover, he observes, the criticism in some ways has led to a reconsideration and deepening of the concept.*

Professor Nolte maintains that in a liberal society various societal forces may call (and did call) each other "despotic," and yet by their mutual restriction can assure liberty. There are societies, however, where nothing of the sort is possible and which, therefore, were called "despotic" and in later times "totalitarian."

Examining the dichotomy of despotism and a "free society" essential for the self-awareness of Western societies, Professor Nolte criticizes

Translated by Annedore Nolte and Ernest A. Menze

those who are propounding the divergent dichotomy of "socialism" on the one hand and "fascism" as a form of monopoly capitalism on the other.

Professor Nolte sees the weakness of the cold-war concept of totalitarianism in the neglect of an essential and unique factor of Western development, namely self-criticism. However, if this factor should come, on its side, to a complete domination of intellectual life, the West would have lost what constitutes the core of the self-awareness of every human group: self-assertion (Selbstbehauptung). Therefore, the concept of totalitarianism should be deepened and differentiated; it may be replaced by another word, but it cannot be repudiated.

In the following essay I endeavor to sketch the historical dimension and social emphasis underlying the concept of totalitarianism and to characterize the significance of criticisms leveled against it from many sides, now and in the past. To this end I advance four theses, to be commented upon subsequently in extreme brevity.

Thesis 1. The tendency finding expression, since about 1930, in the deprecatory use of the term *totalitarianism* is essentially as old as Western society—that is, society European-occidental in origin; this tendency will necessarily prevail as long as the social order giving rise to it continues to be distinct from others and consciously asserts that distinctiveness.

Thesis 2. The criticism advanced beginning in the early sixties against the then-prevailing version of the theory of totalitarianism was rooted in historical changes of a profound nature; therefore it cannot have been entirely unjustified.

Thesis 3. This criticism did not in all its forms imply a general rejection; rather, it entailed in many ways reconsideration and deepening of the concept of totalitarianism, even if partially new or temporarily outmoded terms were used.

Thesis 4. Should the tendency to reject the concept of totalitarianism prevail, it would be an indication of either the impending fall of the social order or a symptom of unprecedented change.

COMMENT ON THESIS 1

It wouldn't take more than a grain of salt to state in good conscience that all of political philosophy governing modern history represents, above all, an analysis of "despotism" and, simultaneously, a struggle, based on Platonic-Aristotelian teaching and on the medieval doctrine of the right to resist tyranny as being lawless, arbitrary rule. Long before Montesquieu, protagonists of the French parliaments such as Pasquier and La Roche Flavin developed the doctrine postulating the need for "counterweights" should the state not take on despotic characteristics; and this doctrine was tied so little to the locale of its origin that it was destined to become, conveyed through many channels, the basis of the Anglo-Saxon constitutional concept of "checks and balances." The last of the great French aristocratic uprisings, the Fronde, produced in its intellectual wake, in the demands of Joly and Le Vassor, the earliest liberal calls on the Continent for personal liberty and the inviolability of property. The Protestant dogmatist Pierre Jurieu and the skeptical founder of historical criticism Pierre Bayle turned, from their exile in the Netherlands, equally against maxims like "Un roi, une foi, une loi"[1] or "La France toute catholique sous Louis le Grand,"[2] maxims employed by French absolutism to promote its otherwise in many ways progressive work. What was Locke's work but the intellectual expression of the fight for preserving the English "liberties" in the face of the Stuart kings' absolutism, an absolutism defended in traditional terms by Filmer, in quite modern terms by Hobbes, both apparently conceiving it as "limited." The term *despotisme oriental*, coming into use in France, served Montesquieu not least in the effort to characterize the struggle of the monarchy against the *pouvoirs intermédiaires* as inimical to liberty. Nicolas Antoine Boulanger, publishing in 1761 his *Recherches sur l'origine du despotisme oriental*, did indeed proudly and explicitly categorize the progressive countries of Europe as nondespotic states; yet by deriving oriental despotism from theocracy, he nevertheless conveyed an unmistakable and polemical reference to the church. A positive application of the concept as in the case of Linguet, but especially in those of the Physiocrats and Diderot, was relatively rare and conditional (*despotisme éclaire*); the main objective of the French Revolution, as that of the Enlightenment's radical thinkers, was above all to overthrow the despotism of kings and priests; yet the revolutionaries in turn soon had to face accusations by their opponents, many of them adherents as recently as 1789, of having turned to a form of despotism by 1793 if not earlier.

When after 1815 everywhere in Europe the forces and interest groups of society shaped their self-image, literally every one of them applied the concept "despotism" to its specific major adversary, often employing it in a quite emotional and ambiguous sense in order to put its own notion of "freedom" into a more favorable light. Liberals of the early nineteenth century like Karl von Rotteck were not by any means alone in referring to their adversaries as representatives of despotism. A conservative like Karl Ludwig von Haller characterized his concept of the patrimonial principality as one promoting liberty, setting it apart from the despotism of those pretending to serve the "common welfare," and in 1832 the *Berliner politisches Wochenblatt* called the despotism of the representative system more inhumane than any other, finding it unyielding to petition and plea.[3] During the second half of the century the Paris Commune had the Vendôme column torn down as a "symbol of despotism"[4] and, for Marx and Engels, Bismarck's empire was as much a "military despotism" as the Second Empire of Napoleon III.[5] Bismarck himself, on the other hand, at the time observed that, in "the socialist penitentiary of the future, the wardens would be the worst of tyrants."[6] Even a nonpartisan element like the Jews did not escape accusation along these lines: Eugen Dühring, long turned from a Socialist into an anti-Semite, characterized Jewish notions of unity as a "despotism of selfishness"[7] thereby tying in to an attitude current among the Enlightenment's "left wing," represented in Baron d'Holbach's attack on the god of the Old Testament as a "despot." By the same token, such peculiar paradoxes as Robespierre's phrase interpreting the revolution as the despotism of liberty *vis-à-vis* tyranny,[8] or Louis Veuillot's claim that despotism is absent wherever the church is free,[9] manifested themselves early on.

And yet in all these struggles against despotism, the opposing party in question apparently never lacked an awareness of other social orders entirely possessed of despotic character. The term *oriental despotism* was not exclusively a political weapon for domestic political consumption, and "Muscovite despotism" possessed, as late as immediately before the outbreak of the First World War, even for German and French Socialists, a quality different from the merely tendential despotism of their domestic political opponents. Examples might easily be added *ad infinitum*, but I break off to formulate a few theses:

a. Only a society characterized by the coexistence and cooperation of various relatively autonomous forces capable of articulating their world views and interests—such as estates and classes, churches and parties, states and academic schools of thought—will experience the extensive use of a concept like "despotism." Here, first of all, a domestic political contest may take place, time and again causing the failure of immanent absolutist claims put forward by the contemporaneously strongest and (usually) most recently risen power within it. Such a society often is referred to by the hardly useful term *pluralistic*; it might better be designated as the "liberal society of the European order"—an order probably founded on the separation of religious and political power within occidental Christendom and today no longer geographically confined to Europe.

b. Within this society lacking a dominant center, a development, tying to each other dialectically revolution and reaction, economics and politics, progress and regression,[10] is taking place, so that the concepts instrumental for society's self-awareness may be detached from the relative circumstances of their origin and thus remain useful.

c. A society permitting the application of the concept "despotism" or a corresponding concept like totalitarianism to a prominent social element, ideological tendency, or even the state itself without calling up destructive sanctions, is a nondespotic or nontotalitarian society. It is bound to develop a concept like despotism or totalitarianism also in order to designate what, on the whole, constitutes its opposite.

COMMENT ON THESIS 2

The need to replace the commonplace concept of despotism with one giving clearer expression to novel and startling social developments was perceived very early: de Tocqueville already observed that "the ancient words *despotism* and *tyranny*" no longer were applicable in view of the coming, strictly regulated mass society, for that was a "novel matter."[11] On the other hand, the fact that the concepts of despotism (respectively tyranny and dictatorship) and totalitarianism remained in concurrent use hardly needs corroboration: as early as 1923 the Soviet Union was called the "terroristic Soviet dictatorship" by Western Marxists,[12] and as late as 1930 a National Socialist *Gauleiter* told Hitler to his face that he was not a Führer in the Germanic sense but an oriental despot.[13] Nor need I go into the early history of the concept of totalitarianism, finding its point of departure in Mussolini's positive self-appraisal by that term (1925) but, in the West, soon assuming a negative connotation and subsequently resulting in the more or less complete identification of the Italian, German, and Soviet regimes. It is self-evident that the shock, particularly of the National Socialist seizure of power and subsequently also that of the Hitler-Stalin pact, had to be great and that it was necessary to subsume under a single concept regimes doubtlessly different in kind, yet so much alike in their contrast to liberal democracy. I will only suggest a few of the reasons for the increasing criticism, beginning about 1960, not infrequently conveying to the "classical" theory of totalitarianism developed in the fifties the stigma of obsoleteness.

a. Soon after Stalin's death in 1953 the Soviet Union entered an early phase of the "Great Thaw," and terror—central to the analysis most of all in Hannah Arendt's work but unmistakably also in the work of Friedrich and Brzezinski—lost its prominent function in Soviet life. Soon terms like *liberalization* and *polycentrism* were used with greater frequency, and the initial stages of the Chinese-Soviet conflict made it definitely clear that "communism as such" was not identical with the monolithic Stalinist system that had for so long been the magnet of Western attention.

b. The complementary development in the West was the gradual waning of the cold war mentality, once most prominently expressed in the publications of people like Borkenau, Burnham, and other former Communists, a mentality generally fostered by an air of Western self-glorification. Tentatively at first, but with growing strength, the conviction gained ground that the West was indeed very much in need of criticism in the West, and that the critique of one's own weakness does represent one of the most characteristic and essential features of Western society.

c. Harmonizing with these tendencies, the conviction gained broad acceptance by the end of the fifties in the circle of academic researchers concerned with the study of communism and Eastern Europe that communism is a changeable system, not to be categorized on the basis of one of its phases, and even less to be identified with the National Socialist regime.

d. Corresponding in time were the beginnings of what I call the "Renaissance of the Left"[14]—the reemergence of a radical criticism of the Western system as such, now discerning no longer merely totalitarian tendencies at home but permeating the very concept of government with a connotation so negative that even National Socialist totalitarianism lost its novel and incomparable character, being considered merely an especially awful example in a long chain of oppression in history. If this point of view initially still found expression in criticism directed equally against East and West, communism and anticommunism, it finally resulted in reviving the original theses of the old pre-Hitlerian and pre-Stalinist Left in extreme form, calling fascism an epiphenomenon of capitalism. This fascism was to be opposed by "real socialism," notwithstanding the latter's temporary deformation due to the pressures exerted on it first by Hitler and subsequently by the Americans. The concept of totalitarianism therefore had to appear as a mere strategem of the capitalistic West in the cold war against the Socialist world system. American intervention in Vietnam facilitated this form of "left-wing Renaissance" at least in western Europe, to the point that the concept of totalitarianism, with the onset of the seventies, had nearly gone out of use even in scholarly literature.

COMMENT ON THESIS 3

Given such profound transformation, the concept of totalitarianism could not remain what it had been for a limited time only to begin with; rather, nothing was more appropriate than the revival in different form of de Tocqueville's postulate. At the very least, a shift in emphasis in the various modes of the concept had to be expected, possibly even resulting in a new term, especially since it appeared desirable to reduce the emotional-polemical connotation of the concept. It seemed appropriate to view the various regimes from more differentiated points of view and to abandon the notion that each totalitarian regime was necessarily always striving for the greatest possible totality, the notion that transitions only from "authoritarianism" to totalitarianism and not reverse "liberalizations" were possible, the notion that there could only be development *toward* authoritarianism. Above all, the differences between the various totalitarian regimes could be stressed without making necessary the abandonment of the concept as such. Thus, terror might be replaced by "mobilization" as the chief characteristic of totalitarianism, and the term itself might be replaced by an expression like "revolutionary mass movement regime"[15] as Robert Tucker had done by 1961. One might also recall that a term like *totality*, originally and in its essential meaning, by no means had a negative connotation or that one of the first books outlining the current conceptual framework was entitled *Le Parti unique.*[16] Why should one not have spoken of "unitarism," "monism," or "party monopolism"? As concepts each could have conveyed a slightly different meaning. The complexity of the phenomenon probably also justified compound terms. Thus in 1964 Ernst Fraenkel contrasted the "autonomous-pluralistic-social-democratic-state-of-laws" of the West to the "heteronomous-monistic-totalitarian-dictatorship" of the East and not *only* of the East.[17] However, since one decided to hold on to the term *totalitarianism* as the one that had, after all, been established, it might nevertheless have been considered advisable to bring out more clearly the substantial differences between Communist and Fascist totalitarianism. Though these differences never were denied by any serious theoretician of totalitarianism, they did not as a rule receive much attention.

To bring out these differences was precisely the intention of my book *Der Faschismus in seiner Epoche*, published in 1963 and translated into English under the title *Three Faces of Fascism*. It may be in order for me to say a few words correcting the widespread misunderstanding of the book as having had a significant share in "overcoming" the concept of totalitarianism by reintroducing the concept of fascism. The misunderstanding is not entirely unfounded, for I had maintained that "in the case, however, that two phenomena reveal significant similarities not due to similar origins, nor to comparable substrata and, moreover, they do not expressly seek similar ends, that similarity either is merely formal, or one of them has adapted itself to the other";[18] also, in the final chapter, I stated unequivocally: "For this very reason the term 'dictatorship in a developing country' is inadequate as applied to the Soviet Union and, despite all structural similarities, the difference to fascism is fundamental."[19] Yet it ought not be overlooked that the concept of "totalitarianism" does find frequent use in the book and that the concept of fascism does not remain undifferentiated. Although, on the one hand, a distinction between "early," "normal," and "radical" fascism is being made, Soviet totalitarianism, on the other hand, is described in contrast to Fascist totalitarianism as a "necessary" system, primarily devoted to the industrial development of a large country without its Telos necessarily being war.[20] However, as little as the evident difference between "radical" and "normal" fascism puts into question the legitimacy of the general concept—a concept based on their similar ideological premises, their parallel historical situations and their comparable social substrata—as little does the "fundamental difference" between the Soviet and the National Socialist system touch on the applicability of the concept of totalitarianism to both, as long as "liberal society—a form of social organization historically exceptional but instrumental in initiating modern developments —clearly remains the point of reference.

It might be said that bolshevism and national socialism are opposites in their relation to the world-historical process as far as overall emancipation is concerned, but that they are alike in their practical relation to the origins of this process. Yet even in their likeness there is a difference. For Fascist totalitarianism came to victory on the soil of this liberal society (although by no means everywhere), so that there is no cause for Western self-glorification; nor is there cause to deny totalitarianism in each case its relative basis of enthusiasm resulting from the credibility or popularity of the ultimate aims. Therefore, *Three Faces of Fascism* was a contribution in deepening and enriching the concept of totalitarianism and not by any means an attempt to "overcome" it. The key phrase is found in the introduction to *Theorien über den Faschismus:* "The concept of totalitarianism already was implicit in the unique juxtaposition of fascism and freedom-oriented *Risorgimento*, and it was bound to attain more general significance with every broadening of the perspective. It remained to be seen how far fascism itself would become totalitarian, thus rendering the material differences irrelevant."[21] I set out to free the concept of totalitarianism, *sit venia verbo*, from its "totalitarian encumbrances," but I did not by any means intend to replace it with the concept of fascism. If books were not always so readily stereotyped as belonging in specified topical boxes it would have long ago become clear that *Deutschland und der Kalte Krieg*, too, is a continuation of this effort, though the emphasis again has been changed.

COMMENT ON THESIS 4

However, if one is convinced that historical thinking must be governed by *ex post facto* logic and aim at a "clean sweep," all of this may be considered as a half-way measure leading sooner or later, in more rigid minds, to the insight that the concept of totalitarianism was a cold war weapon and that the real conflict in the contemporary world was between capitalism and socialism, a conflict only aggravated by the exceptional configuration of the Fascist state into which capitalism developed (at least potentially) to defend itself with the utmost determination.[22] Socialism and fascism, far from being species of a generic concept, relate to each other like fire and water, the one standing in the humanistic tradition of the Enlightenment, sustained by the working class, and devoted to the elimination of all oppression, the other growing precisely out of the antihumanitarianism of the Enlightenment's opponents, finding its social base in the declassé middle class, and escalating capitalist exploitation into a potentially worldwide system of oppression.[23] It is obvious that this view, with only minor modification, signifies the return to a conception self-evident to all European Socialists before the First World War but given up soon after the war's end under the impact of the Russian Revolution and its unexpected (or even expected) consequences and replaced, to begin with, by the opposites of democracy and dictatorship. Its reappearance, first of all, is a symptom of the radically changed situation after Stalin's death and the waning of the cold war. In conclusion, I do not ask whether this conception might not be correct, though it evidently represents a regression, a denial of most profound historical experiences. I merely ask what would result if this conception, undeniably gaining ground for nearly fifteen years and sustained by numerous similarly inclined tendencies, were to triumph universally. It will become clear that this line of questioning does not preclude an answer to the question of merit. But first it remains to be established that this tendency, from the outset, is divided into two major and mutually antagonistic currents with consequences to be considered separately. For the one sees socialism realized in the Soviet Union and/or in Cuba, in Cambodia, and/or in Angola; the other considers "real socialism," either an awful deformation of socialism as such, nowhere realized yet, or even opposes it with as much determination as it does capitalism.

Of the adherents of "real socialism" only those considering the Soviet Union and the German Democratic Republic as the model are of practical interest for the foreseeable future. Though they have not made progress in the larger public arena, they have done so, extraordinarily, in the smaller arena of academic life. A professor who fifteen years ago left Berlin or Marburg, Frankfurt or Hamburg for Cambridge or Sidney, returning now, would stand completely flabbergasted before the book displays stocked with party literature from the Soviet Union and the German Democratic Republic; he would read the wall posters present everywhere, and he would rub his eyes. It is not my intention to denounce this development; rather, what matters is an awareness of its significance gained from the vantage of detachment. Not much less than half the active academic youth of the Federal Republic of Germany feels by far closer ties to the Soviet Union and the German Democratic Republic than to their own state or the "West"—even if its production figures should grow further to dizzying heights and all workers were largely satisfied with their situation. But even the supporters of the Soviet Union and the German Democratic Republic cannot deny that socialism, according to Marx and Engels, had to proceed from the highest stage of capitalism and that the history of the Federal Republic and the West would have been without meaning and unreal if the direction of their future were to be modeled after the present of the Soviet Union and the German Federal Republic. But that is precisely the thesis. It is mainly sustained by the negation of all similarities to fascism not only in the structural but also in all other aspects of Leninism-Stalinism. The thesis thus represents the reversal of that simplism responsible, in good part, for every setback the theory of totalitarianism has suffered in its most widely accepted form; the inherent weakness of this intellectual effort at submission is so striking that one may be allowed to trust in the imperativeness and insurmountability of the resistance to it.

There is a high degree of probability that the part of the Left refusing to consider "real socialism" a paradigm, too, must be viewed as a form of this resistance. Nevertheless, only fringe groups display a tendency to make use of the concept of totalitarianism or an analogous one. What principally matters to them is fascism as a phase in the history of mankind. However, it is in terms of capitalist societies that a discussion of class struggle, class structure, and unacceptable compromises between classes is most appropriate; in effect, these may be the only terms in which it may be carried on. Here, indeed, such struggles take place in the full light of day, though on closer inspection it ought to readily become clear that (except for the case of nationwide wage negotiations and large strikes) the participating constituencies are not classes, and that classes as such and as entities never struggle against each other. To be sure, now and then one also speaks of "class-struggles in the Soviet Union," but in view of the scarcity of sources and concrete data, the phrase sounds strangely hollow, and it is not probable that the researcher was present when the traffic lights were held on red to enable a functionary of the highest leadership to reach an important meeting without delay. That "class structures determined by economic factors" are as little a matter of course as "class struggles," that they are rather made possible by a certain minimum of social mobility on the part of individuals and groups as well as an un-constrained public life—that all of this to date exists only in capitalist society, a society today the only one manifestly free—all of this the Left does not wish to acknowledge even though, in its better moments, it may not be far from the insight that "socialism" is a borderline concept and that nothing is more dangerous than the effort to realize integrally a concept of this sort. Nevertheless, the possibility must not be excluded that a Left such as this, with its exclusive interest in class struggles and class structures, oppressions and revolutions, dissolution of governing structures and "emancipation of anything and everything," one day may totally govern intellectual life in the Federal Republic of Germany, if not the Western world. This would represent the manifestation of a phenomenon without precedent.

All states and cultures known to us have been possessed by self-awareness essentially based on self-praise. In this respect, royal Babylonian inscriptions and papal encyclicals, Ciceronian addresses and decrees of the first French national assembly fully correspond to one another. Only among the states of the liberal system has there been a self-criticism publicly effective, representing more than the establishment of new faith soon to be suppressed or, in turn, to become a new orthodoxy. This self-criticism has been an essential element in the development of a liberal social system such as this; however, never and nowhere to date has it reigned the field alone. It was always dissent and nonconformism and attained its acuteness and also its dignity through awareness of a prevailing and positive self-perception. Indeed, all of German historical literature of the period after 1870 is dominated and inspired by the pride in the foundation of the Second Empire, but the same also goes, *mutatis mutandis*, for English and French historical writing. Yet precisely, for the same reason was it possible for men like Ludwig Quidde, W. H. Dawson, and Gabriel Monad to oppose the prevailing nationalist tendencies, and posterity has vindicated them in important respects. Ever since the "Western world" has become possessed of an awareness of its unity and its seminal function in the process of industrialization, it has developed, above all, one major feature of positive self-awareness: the liberal optimism about progress. But there were always thinkers criticizing it: Schopenhauer, Nietzsche, Renan, and (to a certain extent) Herbert Spencer. In the case of Marxism, self-criticism became a movement, but a movement containing impulses to a deepened sense of Western self-awareness. Nevertheless, Marxism still did not become the main current of intellectual life anywhere. As a result of the war and under the impact of the Russian Revolution, fascism, as the most extreme countercurrent, came to the fore, orienting itself especially in its radical German manifestation both in a Western and anti-Western sense. The concept of totalitarianism was developed, first of all, to confront fascism; in the course of the cold war, it became the basis of Western self-awareness, above all *vis-à-vis* the Soviet Union. However, the concept never was uncontroversial and the revisionism gaining ground, beginning in 1960, was sustained by ties to the "anti-Fascist" or "democratic" tendency associated with Roosevelt (or at any rate with Rooseveltians). The Soviet Union, on the other hand, notwithstanding all efforts at liberalization, remained even after Krushchev's secret indictment of Stalin a state of unconditional self-praise. However, in the West self-criticism seems in the process to pervade, like a cancer, the entire realm of society's self-awareness, so that even the addresses of statesmen on festive occasions affirm the system only reluctantly. A civilization drawing its self-awareness at last *only* from the critique of itself and its history, a civilization whose rulers are devoid of ideas or governed by ideas hostile to any form of rule, a civilization where the Left has surrendered its claim to nonconformism and now represents conformism—a civilization such as this would be something entirely new in the history of the world. But it would also be an untruth. *It* would represent by no means a real negation of capitalism but something like a flower of the morass.

This state of affairs has not been reached yet, and it will possibly never be reached. But the existence of an extensive edifice of empirical science is in itself not a sufficient counterweight. Only if a deepened and differentiated concept of totalitarianism, unburdened of emotionalism and yet not neutral, will be developed and will gain broadly based acceptance—be it even under a new term and within a new context—the West as a liberal society oriented toward freedom will continue to exist, and truth will be given a chance: that is, the struggle for truth and with that the denial of the illusion—so conducive to action—of being in its undisputed possession.

ROBERT SOUCY

TOTALITARIANISM OF THE CENTER

Professor Soucy's contribution is based on comments made by him on a paper reconsidering totalitarianism, given by Professor Michael Curtis of Rutgers University at the 1977 annual meeting of the American Historical Association in Dallas. Proceeding from an account of personal experiences with the "cult of consensus"—which he finds at the base of the totalitarian mentality—in the unlikely setting of an elite liberal arts college, Professor Soucy ventures to locate the totalitarian mind in the mainstream of life. As an historian Professor Soucy is more concerned with the genesis of various forms of totalitarianism than with their taxonomy. His allusion to the "cult of consensus" on a predominantly liberal college campus in the context of a paper on French Fascist movements arose from his conviction that totalitarianism will take root in the center as well as at the right and left extremes of the political spectrum.

By concentrating on France and emphasizing the roots of totalitarianism in the center, Professor Soucy broadens the canvas on which this reappraisal of the concept is laid out. His contention that the lack of mass support of French Fascist movements is explained by the co-option—in part—of their ideas by the French Radical party may goad researchers to look at parallel situations in other settings. Addressing the question of why masses of people accept totalitarian doctrines before the regimes attain power, Professor Soucy reexamines the problem of "totalitarian democracy" discussed also by other contributors to this volume. In the case of France, Soucy finds broad agreement on seven major propositions not only between the Centrists of the French Radical party and French Fascists, but also between the latter and the French population as a whole.

Professor Soucy's linking of broadly based anti-Marxist, anti-Modernist, passionately nationalist, imperialist, sexist, and benignly anti-Semitic traits in a Centrist totalitarian syndrome calls for comparative analysis.

Totalitarianism comes in a variety of forms, some being more subtle than others. It is a mistake to see totalitarianism as an expression of the extreme Right or the extreme Left only: it can also be an expression of the political and cultural Center. Banal examples of this abound, even in "democratic" societies, though we may not pay sufficient attention to them, habituated as we are to more familiar categorizations. To begin with a most banal and far-fetched example (but is it so banal and far-fetched?), I teach courses in European intellectual history at a small liberal arts college in Ohio, Oberlin, whose students are largely Left-Center. It is a painful event for me every year when I give a series of lectures on Freud. Instead of debunking Freud (the path to easy popularity), I defend him, or at least argue that not all his ideas are necessarily reactionary, sexist, or obsolete, whereupon the wrath of the democratic majority descends upon me. For awhile I am no longer considered to be a desirable teacher, no longer a comrade—i.e., no longer someone who *agrees* with the majority. I am *dis*agreeable. I am told that I have offended people's sensitivities (in my more megalomaniacal moments I compare myself to Calvin offending the sensitivities of French Catholics, to Stefan Zweig offending the sensitivities of German Nationalists, or to George Bernard Shaw offending the sensitivities of everybody). I have even wondered whether it was prudent, in terms of next year's salary increase, to play the devil's advocate in class discussions, or even to employ the Socratic method, for I sometimes bruise student egos in doing so, and, as a student of Freud, I am all too aware how such bruises can return to haunt me on student course evaluation forms, which have come to play an increasingly powerful role at my institution. Although I have not become a completely cringing lackey of the Center (at least not consciously), the temptation is there—even with tenure (I imagine it is even greater among untenured professors these days). Academic freedom, after all, is a liberal, not a democratic principle. Certain forms of intimidation, particularly the more subtle forms, may be very democratic, very majority-oriented. A cult of "consensus" can seriously erode intellectual pluralism and ideological diversity if unrestrained by a commitment to liberal values, especially in small private colleges under increasing economic pressure to cater ideologically as well as academically to their "customers" (indeed, the "I pay, you obey" formula seems to crop up repeatedly and unashamedly in American "student power" rhetoric today, even among ostensibly left-wing students).

Granted, there is an enormous difference between this kind of intimidation and the more blatant and extensive kinds employed by fascism in power (even though the success of Nazi ideas in many German universities before 1933 is not insignificant). I hasten to add that neither students nor administrators at Oberlin College are Fascists: the Center they represent in their institutional context is not the Center Fascists defended in their much different and much larger context. If anything, most student values at Oberlin are diametrically opposed to fascism. Nor does Oberlin impose total ideological conformity on its teachers: I have not been fired despite my taste for giving free reign to heretical ideas. There are, after all, *degrees* of authoritarianism (even "totalitarian" regimes rely on *some* popular consent), ahd the gap between Oberlin and Buchenwald is so wide as to make any comparison between the two intellectually ridiculous at best and morally frivolous at worst. Still, degrees—even lesser degrees—can be important, especially if one is more concerned with the genesis of totalitarianisms than with their taxonomy, particularly with the way predominantly liberal societies may become totalitarian under stress or contain mild forms of totalitarianism within them already. Especially important are those points on the scale where the liberal Right gives way to the authoritarian Right and where the liberal Left gives way to the authoritarian Left.

If one looks at French politics in the 1920s and 1930s, however, such a formulation of the problem may be askew, for what was most crucial during this period was not whether the liberal Right or the liberal Left would go authoritarian but whether the liberal Center would—for this was where the decisive power lay. What is so striking about the major French Fascist movements of the era—the Légion, the Faisceau, the Action Française, the Jeunesses Patriotes, the Solidarité Française, the Croix de Feu, the Francistes, the Parti Populaire Francais, and (after 1942) the Rassemblement Nationale Populaire—is the Centrist nature of much of their ideology. Obviously French Fascists were not Centrists in all respects, or their numbers would have been much larger. But in a number of important areas, they were Centrists, and their main competitor, therefore, was not a party of the Right or a party of the Left but France's major Centrist party of the period, the French Radical party. Such a formula may help explain why fascism failed in France in the interwar period: it failed not because many of its doctrines were rejected by a majority of French citizens but because they were co-opted by the French Radical party—and also because the major domestic enemy of both French fascism and French radicalism, the Socialist threat, could be tamed by liberal methods, by the methods of the French Radical party, and therefore harsher methods, Fascist methods, became unnecessary.

Radicals, it is true, were not Fascists, and indeed joined the Popular

Front in 1936 in part to *resist* fascism. But they were not Socialists, either, and they joined with the Right in 1937 and 1938 to destroy the Popular Front. Edouard Daladier, the leader of the French Radical party, marched arm in arm with the Socialist Blum and the Communist Thorez in 1936, but he also undermined the Socialists in 1937 and suppressed the Communists in 1939. Nor should one overlook the image presented by an annual congress of the French Radical party during the Popular Front era when one section of the delegates burst into singing the "Internationale" with arms outstretched into the Socialist clenched fist and another section of the delegates replied with the "Marseillaise" and the Fascist salute. Within the Radical "consensus," there was a Left and a Right, and in the end it was the Right, not the Left, that triumphed. And in winning, it deprived French Fascists of the potential constituency they needed—a constituency that had little difficulty accepting Marshal Pétain and Vichy centrism in 1940. Anyone who sees the collapse of the Third Republic and the launching of the Vichy regime, in terms of popular support, as more of a break than a continuity should read Robert Paxton's work on Vichy France in tandem with Joel Colton's study of Léon Blum and the Popular Front.[1] (That numerous continuities also existed between Wilhelminian, Weimar, and Nazi Germany, especially at the level of popular culture, has already been documented in George Mosse's seminal work, *The Nationalization of the Masses.*[2])

If French fascism failed, in part, because it was co-opted by French radicalism, what exactly were the doctrines, attitudes, and values that were co-opted? And to what extent were they Centrist—that is, reflective of a large portion of the French population? And if they were Centrist, and therefore not so much a matter of *imposed* totalitarianism than *willing* totalitarianism, then what was the nature of their appeal? For it is important to know not only how totalitarianisms impose their doctrines on masses of people *after* they come to power, but why masses of people accept these doctrines willingly and even enthusiastically *before* they come to power. Where fascism in the 1920s and 1930s is concerned, the issue of totalitarian democracy is just as important as that of totalitarian autocracy.

Space limitations do not permit me to make a full case for the often democratic or Centrist nature of French fascism during the period, or to qualify that case by dwelling on the un-Centrist and undemocratic aspects of French fascism that allowed it to be outcompeted by the French Radical party (I have commented on the latter elsewhere[3]). I simply want to suggest a few areas of compatibility, a few things that Radical centrism and Fascist centrism had in common—and perhaps by implication the nature of their appeal. It is my contention that Centrists of the French

Radical party in the interwar period and a majority of the French population as a whole agreed with French Fascists on the following propositions:

Proposition One. That Marxism in general was bad, and that communism in particular was pernicious. As Jacques Doriot, the leader of the
Fascist Parti Populaire Français, declared in 1938: "Our policy is simple:
we seek the union of Frenchmen against Marxism. We want to clear France
of agents of Moscow." Or as one of Doriot's lieutenants emphasized:
"*Communisme voilà l'ennemi!*" (Communism—there is the enemy!).

Proposition Two. That Marxist doctrines of class conflict were bad
and liberal and conservative doctrines of class conciliation were good.
For Marcel Déat, head of the Fascist Rassemblement Nationale Populaire
in 1942, this was the very meaning of totalitarianism. "Totalitarianism,"
he wrote, "is conciliation, a reconciliation." Pierre Taittinger of the
Jeunesses Patriotes concurred, although he made it clear that such conciliation excluded the Communists. In 1926 he announced: "The task we
have undertaken is above all one of National Reconciliation. In our eyes,
all classes are mixed: management and labor, rich and poor, manual
laborers and intellectuals, are grouped in the same phalanx. But we detest
those who make a profession of detesting France. We will never deal with
those artisans of revolution, those profiteers of hatred, I mean the Communists." Conciliation, in other words, was to be on *his* terms. Such
French Fascist leaders as Taittinger, Redier, Valois, Maurras, la Rocque,
Renaud, Doriot, and Déat all wanted to destroy Marxism, either euphemistically in behalf of "syndicalism" or less euphemistically in behalf of
corporatism—in either case depriving trade unions of any real bargaining
power *vis-à-vis* management. The rhetoric of Fascist "socialism" was often
revolutionary, but the reality was usually reactionary. The Centrist backlash to the Matignon accords of 1936,[4] a backlash even more intense
among small business than big business, suggests that here especially
French fascism was very much in the mainstream. Equally mainstream
was the alternative to class conflict preached by French Fascist ideologues:
upward social mobility for the more dynamic. Georges Valois of the
Faisceau echoed other French Fascists, as well as the Jacobin and
Napoleonic traditions, when he declaimed: "Careers open to talent!"

Proposition Three. That big business and economic modernism were
bad and small business and economic traditionalism were good. Thus,
so-called Fascist "socialism" attacked big business—or "capitalism" as they
sometimes called it—while defending small business and the middle classes
at large, as well as the property-holding peasantry. In 1938 Doriot
lamented what he called the "ruin" of the middle classes as a result of
the "frightful" tax burdens they had to bear, and in 1942 Dèat declared

that "the necessary rescue of our middle classes will be one of the happiest effects, one of the essential objectives, of the National Revolution. And that is what socialism should mean to them. At this point we are a long way from any Marxist nonsense about the automatic concentration of our large enterprises and about the inevitable elimination of our small producers, people whom the Marxists would discard, throwing them into the wage-earning class." Earlier Fascist Socialists like Georges Valois and Pierre Taittinger railed in the 1920s against inflation and excessive government spending and called for lower taxes, a balanced budget, and a sound franc (how Centrist can you get!). As noted in the platform of the Parti Populaire Français in 1936, "The PPF will defend the interests of all those whose activity constitute a traditional element of social equilibrium in France"—a very Centrist proposition indeed.

Proposition Four. That nationalism was good and internationalism—even Fascist internationalism—was bad. The doctrine of the PPF, said Doriot in 1936, was one of "intransigent nationalism." He added: "Our credo is *la patrie.*" One of the party's intellectuals, Pierre Drieu La Rochelle, emphasized in 1937 that a Fascist takeover in France, by *French* Fascists, was needed to strengthen France against Germany, against *German* Fascists. Drieu vehemently condemned any notion of allowing France to be invaded by foreign troops, including Fascist troops. "It is all very nice," he wrote, "to shout 'Long live the Soviets' or 'Bravo Hitler' when one is tranquilly at home among Frenchmen, comfortably settled. But it might not be so pretty when there are thousands of Stalinist or Hitlerian mercenaries tramping their boots across our soil, singing their own songs, swearing in their own language, and looking at our women." No doubt most Frenchmen agreed, just as they would have agreed with the slogan of the Croix de Feu (and later of Vichy): 'Fatherland, Family, Work."

Proposition Five. That colonialism in North Africa and Indo-China was good, another Centrist proposition.

Proposition Six. That traditional sex roles were good and that the emancipated woman posed a serious threat to French morality. Drieu La Rochelle's cult of male virility and his remark that "feminism was the most unfortunate of modern pretensions" may have overstated common feelings; but, as Theodor Zeldin has shown in his social history of France between 1848 and 1945, they were very much common feelings.[5]

Proposition Seven. That French Jews were not as French as other Frenchmen. In this connection, it is significant that as late as 1967, according to one poll, nearly half of all Frenchmen agreed with General De Gaulle's characterization of the Jews as being "an elite people, sure of itself and domineering" who had "provoked, or more exactly, aroused ill-will in certain countries at certain times." Another poll indicated that

22 percent of Frenchmen believed that all French Jews should "go back" to Israel. An earlier poll concluded that one out of three Frenchmen opposed having a Jew for president. This same poll showed that 17 percent of those questioned thought French Jews were not really French, an improvement over the 46 percent who thought so in 1946.[6]

In light of all this, it is not surprising that Drieu La Rochelle would insist that Jacques Doriot was very much a Centrist—but, as Drieu added, a "violent Centrist," that is, a Centrist who sought to achieve through authoritarian political methods what the French Radical party tried to achieve through liberal political methods. For Drieu, French radicalism was also a fascism, a *kind* of fascism, but one which had grown too old and parliamentary. Thus he wrote:

It is necessary to replace this old fascism with another. And fascism will be nothing more than a new radicalism, a new movement of the petite bourgeoisie, disciplined and organized into a party which will insert itself between big capitalism, the peasantry, and the proletariat, and which, through terror and authority, will impose on their diverse interests an old charter in a renovated form.

One has to admire the old Radical party for its ability to defuse this competitor. After 1940, under the Vichy Regime, Pierre Laval, an ex-Radical party politician, would continue to do so—although it was not always clear who was co-opting whom. French Fascist ideology in the 1920s and 1930s, it is true, was more totalitarian; but, in some areas at least, it was no less democratic.

PART THREE

BEHAVIORAL DIMENSIONS

STANLEY MILGRAM

BEHAVIORAL STUDY OF OBEDIENCE

Upon publication in 1963 in the Journal of Abnormal and Social Psychology, *Professor Milgram's paper received considerable attention in the field of psychology.*[1] *Subsequently, critically examined and discussed by his peers, Professor Milgram's findings had an impact going far beyond the laboratories of social psychologists, affecting decisively the prevailing notions of obedience to authority in human life.*[2] *Some of Professor Milgram's responses to his critics are included in a volume of essays which reflects the scope of his research interests over the years.*[3] *Whereas much attention has been given to obedience induced by coercion, Professor Milgram's research concentrated on the willing obedience of men to properly constituted and legitimized authority.*[4] *In devising a set of experiments calling on naive subjects to inflict increasingly severe and painful electric shocks—in the name of science—on innocent and eventually loudly protesting learners, Professor Milgram was motivated by his own questions over the massive evidence of such conduct in the course of history. Troubled particularly by the broadly based and even enthusiastic support given to totalitarian regimes and the willing obedience there to the most atrocious commands, he wondered whether such conduct could be approximated, probed, and measured in a laboratory setting.*[5]

In a volume reexamining the appropriateness of the concept of totalitarianism in the terminology and classificatory repertoire of history and the social sciences, Professor Milgram's revelations pertaining to man's inclination to obey willingly clearly antisocial and inhumane commands undoubtedly deserve to be included. Together with Dr. Lifton's observations regarding the human disposition to transcend death through psychological totalism, they serve as a reminder to the urgent need for the further

189

study of obedience. In the process the noncoercive situational factors of totalitarian societies deserve particular attention because they are, notwithstanding the role played by terror and the differential of personality dynamics, the key to an understanding of the functioning of totalitarian regimes. Prefacing the pioneering essay reprinted in this volume, a brief overview of Professor Milgram's work and its critical reception are in order.[6]

Central to Professor Milgram's work over more than two decades has been a concern with the influence of social forces on the individual, who often perceives the self to be independent of them.[7] *Balancing the curiosity of challenging the expected with a healthy regard for skepticism and subjecting all his work to the most rigorous mandate of scientific objectivity, Professor Milgram experimentally measured the individual's reactions to a variety of social forces. Though his studies of "the individual in the city," "the individual and the group," and "the individual in a communicative web" all have bearing on some of the questions raised in this volume, it is his work on "the individual and authority" that is of central interest here.*[8]

Professor Milgram's experiments in obedience to authority were conducted during the early sixties at Yale University and in an inconspicuous setting in Bridgeport apart from the university. Building on other work done on the impact of group pressure in the conflict between truth and continuity, altruism and self-interest, Professor Milgram shaped his own experiment so as to truly test the individual conscience in a conflict with legitimized authority.[9] *Contrary to his expectations, he found that, "with numbing regularity, good people were seen to knuckle under to demands of authority and to perform actions that were callous and severe."*[10] *Carefully safeguarding the scientific integrity of the experiments by changing the locale and introducing variables such as peer pressure, role permutations, etc., Professor Milgram found that the high percentage of subjects willingly obeying commands to inflict—in the name of science—painful shocks upon innocent victims experienced in the original experiments did not decline significantly.*

The experiments and the pessimistic conclusions concerning the nature of man necessarily flowing from them became the subject of challenges.[11] *The efforts to explain the phenomenon of totalitarianism in terms of social psychology, of course, go back many years. Ever since the inception of Fascist regimes in Italy and Germany, observers have wondered about the willing submission of so many to them, and numerous explanations have been advanced.*[12] *But Professor Milgram's empirical verification of the general inclination of man to obey properly legitimized authority— even if it is exercised with malevolent intent—suggest that previous inter-*

pretations have fallen short of the mark. Though Professor Milgram's findings are not considered conclusive by all, they certainly merit to serve as the basis of additional studies. They deserve particular attention on the part of historians and social scientists inclined to resist the recognition of a totalitarian syndrome in human affairs in the center as well as at the extremes of the political spectrum.

This article describes a procedure for the study of destructive obedience in the laboratory.[1] It consists of ordering a naive subject to administer increasingly more severe punishment to a victim in the context of a learning experiment. Punishment is administered by means of a shock generator with 30 graded switches ranging from Slight Shock to Danger: Severe Shock. The victim is a confederate of the experimenter. The primary dependent variable is the maximum shock the subject is willing to administer before he refuses to continue further. Twenty-six subjects obeyed the experimental commands fully, and administered the highest shock on the generator. Fourteen subjects broke off the experiment at some point after the victim protested and refused to provide further answers. The procedure created extreme levels of nervous tension in some subjects. Profuse sweating, trembling, and stuttering were typical expressions of this emotional disturbance. One unexpected sign of tension—yet to be explained—was the regular occurrence of nervous laughter, which in some subjects developed into uncontrollable seizures. The variety of interesting behavioral dynamics observed in the experiment, the reality of the situation for the subject, and the possibility of parametric variation within the framework of the procedure, point to the fruitfulness of further study.

Obedience is as basic an element in the structure of social life as one can point to. Some system of authority is a requirement of all communal living, and it is only the man dwelling in isolation who is not forced to respond, through defiance or submission, to the commands of others. Obedience, as a determinant of behavior, is of particular relevance to our time. It has been reliably established that from 1933 to 1945 millions of innocent persons were systematically slaughtered on command. Gas chambers were built, death camps were guarded, daily quotas of corpses were produced with the same efficiency as the manufacture of appliances. These inhumane policies may have originated in the mind of a single person, but they could only be carried out on a massive scale if a very large number of persons obeyed orders.

Obedience is the psychological mechanism that links individual action to political purpose. It is the dispositional cement that binds men to systems of authority. Facts of recent history and observation in daily life suggest that for many persons obedience may be a deeply ingrained behavior tendency, indeed, a prepotent impulse overriding training in ethics, sympathy, and moral conduct. C. P. Snow (1961) points to its importance when he writes:

When you think of the long and gloomy history of man, you will find more hideous crimes have been committed in the name of obedience than have ever been committed in the name of rebellion. If you doubt that, read William Shirer's *Rise and Fall of the Third Reich*. The German Officer Corps were brought up in the most rigorous code of obedience ... in the name of obedience they were party to, and assisted in, the most wicked large scale actions in the history of the world.

(p. 24)

While the particular form of obedience dealt with in the present study has its antecedents in these episodes, it must not be thought all obedience entails acts of aggression against others. Obedience serves numerous productive functions. Indeed, the very life of society is predicated on its existence. Obedience may be ennobling and educative and refer to acts of charity and kindness, as well as to destruction.

GENERAL PROCEDURE

A procedure was devised which seems useful as a tool for studying obedience (Milgram, 1961). It consists of ordering a naive subject to administer electric shock to a victim. A simulated shock generator is used, with 30 clearly marked voltage levels that range from 15 to 450 volts. The instrument bears verbal designations that range from Slight Shock to Danger: Severe Shock. The responses of the victim, who is a trained confederate of the experimenter, are standardized. The orders to administer shocks are given to the naive subject in the context of a "learning experiment" ostensibly set up to study the effects of punishment on memory. As the experiment proceeds the naive subject is commanded to administer increasingly more intense shocks to the victim, even to the point of reaching the level marked Danger: Severe Shock. Internal resistances become stronger, and at a certain point the subject refuses to go on with the experiment. Behavior prior to this rupture is considered "obedience," in that the subject complies with the commands of the experimenter. The point of rupture is the act of disobedience. A quantitative value is assigned to the subject's performance based on the maximum intensity shock he is willing to administer before he refuses to participate further. Thus for any particular subject and for any particular experimental condition the degree of obedience may be specified with a numerical value. The crux of the study is to systematically vary the factors believed to alter the degree of obedience to the experimental commands.

The technique allows important variables to be manipulated at several points in the experiment. One may vary aspects of the source of command, content and form of command, instrumentalities for its execution, target object, general social setting, etc. The problem, therefore, is not one of designing increasingly more numerous experimental conditions, but of selecting those that best illuminate the *process* of obedience from the sociopsychological standpoint.

RELATED STUDIES

The inquiry bears an important relation to philosophic analyses of obedience and authority (Arendt, 1958; Friedrich, 1958; Weber, 1947), an early experimental study of obedience by Frank (1944), studies in "authoritarianism" (Adorno, Frenkel-Brunswik, Levinson, and Sanford, 1950; Rokeach, 1961), and a recent series of analytic and empirical studies in social power (Cartwright, 1959). It owes much to the long concern with *suggestion* in social psychology, both in its normal forms (e.g., Binet, 1900) and in its clinical manifestations (Charcot, 1881). But it derives, in the first instance, from direct observation of a social fact; the individual who is commanded by a legitimate authority ordinarily obeys. Obedience comes easily and often. It is a ubiquitous and indispensable feature of social life.

METHOD

Subjects. The subjects were 40 males between the ages of 20 and 50, drawn from New Haven and the surrounding communities. Subjects were obtained by a newspaper advertisement and direct mail solicitation. Those who responded to the appeal believed they were to participate in a study of memory and learning at Yale University. A wide range of occupations is represented in the sample. Typical subjects were postal clerks, high school teachers, salesmen, engineers, and laborers. Subjects ranged in educational level from one who had not finished elementary school, to those who had doctorate and other professional degrees. They were paid

$4.50 for their participation in the experiment. However, subjects were told that payment was simply for coming to the laboratory, and that money was theirs no matter what happened after they arrived. Table 1 shows the proportion of age and occupational types assigned to the experimental condition.

TABLE 1

Distribution of Age and Occupational Types in the Experiment

Occupations	20-29 years n	30-39 years n	40-50 years n	Percentage of total (Occupations)
Workers, skilled and unskilled	4	5	6	37.5
Sales, business, and white-collar	3	6	7	40.0
Professional	1	5	3	22.5
Percentage of total (Age)	20	40	40	

Note: Total N = 40.

Personnel and Locale. The experiment was conducted on the grounds of Yale University in the elegant interaction laboratory. (This detail is relevant to the perceived legitimacy of the experiment. In further variations, the experiment was dissociated from the university, with consequences for performance.) The role of experimenter was played by a 31-year-old high school teacher of biology. His manner was impassive, and his appearance somewhat stern throughout the experiment. He was dressed in a gray technician's coat. The victim was played by a 47-year-old accountant, trained for the role; he was of Irish-American stock, whom most observers found mild-mannered and likable.

Procedure. One naive subject and one victim (an accomplice) performed in each experiment. A pretext had to be devised that would justify the administration of electric shock by the naive subject. This was effectively accomplished by the cover story. After a general introduction on the presumed relation between punishment and learning, subjects were told:

But actually, we know *very little* about the effect of punishment on learning, because almost no truly scientific studies have been made of it in human beings.

For instance, we don't know how *much* punishment is best for learning —and we don't know how much difference it makes as to who is giving the punishment, whether an adult learns best from a younger or an older person than himself—or many things of that sort.

So in this study we are bringing together a number of adults of different occupations and ages. And we're asking some of them to be teachers and some of them to be learners.

We want to find out just what effect different people have on each other as teachers and learners, and also what effect *punishment* will have on learning in this situation.

Therefore, I'm going to ask one of you to be the teacher here tonight and the other one to be the learner.

Does either of you have a preference?

Subjects then drew slips of paper from a hat to determine who would be the teacher and who would be the learner in the experiment. The drawing was rigged so that the naive subject was always the teacher and the accomplice always the learner. (Both slips contained the word "Teacher.") Immediately after the drawing, the teacher and learner were taken to an adjacent room and the learner was strapped into an "electric chair" apparatus.

The experimenter explained that the straps were to prevent excessive movement while the learner was being shocked. The effect was to make it impossible for him to escape from the situation. An electrode was attached to the learner's wrist, and electrode paste was applied "to avoid blisters and burns." Subjects were told that the electrode was attached to the shock generator in the adjoining room.

In order to improve credibility the experimenter declared, in response to a question by the learner: "Although the shocks can be extremely painful, they cause no permanent tissue damage."

Learning task. The lesson administered by the subject was a paired-associate learning task. The subject read a series of word pairs to the learner, and then read the first word of the pair along with four terms. The learner was to indicate which of the four terms had orginally been paired with the first word. He communicated his answer by pressing one of four switches in front of him, which in turn lit up one of four numbered quadrants in an answer-box located atop the shock generator.

Shock generator. The instrument panel consists of 30 level switches set in a horizontal line. Each switch is clearly labeled with a voltage designation that ranges from 15 to 450 volts. There is a 15-volt increment from one switch to the next going from left to right. In addition, the following verbal designations are clearly indicated for groups of four switches going from left to right: Slight Shock, Moderate Shock, Strong Shock, Very Strong Shock, Intense Shock, Extreme Intensity Shock, Danger: Severe Shock. (Two switches after this last designation are simply marked XXX.)

Upon depressing a switch: a pilot light corresponding to each switch is illuminated in bright red; an electric buzzing is heard; an electric blue light, labeled "voltage energizer," flashes; the dial on the voltage meter swings to the right; various relay clicks are sounded.

The upper left-hand corner of the generator is labeled Shock Generator, Type ZLB, Dyson Instrument Company, Waltham, Mass. Output 15 Volts–450 Volts.

Details of the instrument were carefully handled to insure an appearance of authenticity. The panel was engraved by precision industrial engravers, and all components were of high quality. No subject in the experiment suspected that the instrument was merely a simulated shock generator.[2]

Sample shock. Each naive subject is given a sample shock on the shock generator, prior to beginning his run as teacher. This shock is always 45 volts, and is applied by pressing the third switch of the generator. The shock is applied to the wrist of the naive subject, and has its source in a 45-volt battery wired into the generator. This further convinces the subject of the authenticity of the generator.

Shock instructions. The subject is told to administer a shock to the learner each time he gives a wrong response. Moreover—and this is the key command—the subject is instructed to "move one level higher on the shock generator each time the learner flashes a wrong answer." He is also instructed to announce the voltage level before administering a shock. This serves to continually remind subjects of the increasing intensity of shocks administered to the learner.

Preliminary and regular run. Pretests revealed that the procedure of reading words and administering shocks requires some practice before it can be handled smoothly. Therefore, immediately preceding the regular run, the teacher is given a preliminary series of 10 words to read to the learner. There are 3 neutral words in the practice series (i.e., words that the learner answers correctly), so that shocks are administered for 7 of the words, with the maximum shock at 105 volts (moderate shock). Almost all subjects master the procedure by the time the preliminary run is over.

Subjects are then presented with a second list, and are told that the procedure is the same as for the first list; the experimenter adds, however:

When you get to the bottom of the list, repeat it over again, and continue giving shocks, until the learner has learned all the pairs correctly.

The experimenter instructs the subject to,

start from 15 volts and increase the shock level one step each time the learner gives a wrong answer.

Feedback from the victim. In all conditions the learner gives a predetermined set of responses to the word pair test, based on a schedule of approximately three wrong answers to one correct answer. In the present experimental condition no vocal response or other sign of protest is heard from the learner until Shock Level 300 is reached. When the 300-volt shock is administered, the learner pounds on the wall of the room in which he is bound to the electric chair. The pounding can be heard by the subject. From this point on, the learner's answers no longer appear on the four-way panel.

At this juncture, subjects ordinarily turn to the experimenter for guidance. The experimenter instructs the subject to treat the absence of a response as a wrong answer, and to shock the subject according to the usual schedule. He advises the subjects to allow 5-10 seconds before considering no response as a wrong answer, and to increase the shock level one step each time the learner fails to respond correctly. The learner's pounding is repeated after the 315-volt shock is administered; afterwards he is not heard from, nor do his answers reappear on the four-way signal box.

Experimenter feedback. At various points in the experiment the subject may turn to the experimenter for advice on whether he should continue to administer shocks. Or he may indicate that he does not wish to go on. It was important to standardize the experimenter's responses to these inquiries and reactions.

If the subject indicated his unwillingness to go on the experimenter responded with a sequence of "prods," using as many as necessary to bring the subject into line.

Prod 1: Please continue. *or* Please go on.
Prod 2: The experiment requires that you continue.
Prod 3: It is absolutely essential that you continue.
Prod 4: You have no other choice, you *must* go on.

The prods were always made in sequence: Only if Prod 1 had been unsuccessful, could Prod 2 be used. If the subject refused to obey the experimenter after Prod 4, the experiment was terminated. The experimenter's tone of voice was at all times firm, but not impolite. The sequence was begun anew on each occasion that the subject balked or showed reluctance to follow orders.

Special prods. If the subject asked if the learner was liable to suffer permanent physical injury, the experimenter said:

Although the shocks may be painful, there is no permanent tissue damage, so please go on. [Followed by Prods 2, 3, and 4 if necessary.]

If the subject said that the learner did not want to go on, the experimenter replied:

Whether the learner likes it or not, you must go on until he has learned all the word pairs correctly. So please go on. [Followed by Prods 2, 3, and 4 if necessary.]

Dependent Measures. The primary dependent measure for any subject is the maximum shock he administers before he refuses to go any further. In principle this may vary from 0 (for a subject who refuses to administer even the first shock) to 30 (for a subject who administers the highest shock on the generator). A subject who breaks off the experiment at any point prior to administering the thirtieth shock level is termed a *defiant* subject. One who complies with experimental commands fully, and proceeds to administer all shock levels commanded, is termed an *obedient* subject.

Further records. With few exceptions, experimental sessions were recorded on magnetic tape. Occasional photographs were taken through one-way mirrors. Notes were kept on any unusual behavior occurring during the course of the experiments. On occasion, additional observers were directed to write objective descriptions of the subjects' behavior. The latency and duration of shocks were measured by accurate timing devices.

Interview and dehoax. Following the experiment, subjects were interviewed; open-ended questions, projective measures, and attitude scales were employed. After the interview, procedures were undertaken to assure that the subject would leave the laboratory in a state of well being. A friendly reconciliation was arranged between the subject and the victim, and an effort was made to reduce any tensions that arose as a result of the experiment.

RESULTS

Preliminary Notions. Before giving an account of the experimental results, it is instructive to consider how persons predict others will perform when commanded to administer powerful shocks to another person. Fourteen Yale seniors, all psychology majors, were provided with a detailed description of the experimental situation. They were asked to reflect carefully on it, and to predict the behavior of 100 hypothetical subjects. More specifically, they were instructed to plot the distribution of obedience of "100 Americans of diverse occupations, and ranging in age from 20 to 50 years," who were placed in the experimental situation.

There was considerable agreement among the respondents on the expected behavior of hypothetical subjects. All respondents predicted that only an insignificant minority would go through to the end of the shock series. (The estimates ranged from 0 to 3%; i.e., the most "pessimistic" member of the class predicted that of 100 persons, 3 would continue through to the most potent shock available on the shock generator—450 volts.) The class mean was 1.2%. The question was also posed informally to colleagues of the author, and the most general feeling was that few if any subjects would go beyond the designation Very Strong Shock.

Result of Experiment I: Subjects accept situation. With few exceptions subjects were convinced of the reality of the experimental situation, that they were administering shocks to another person, and the most potent shocks were extremely painful. In the post-experimental interview subjects were asked: "How painful to the learner were the last few shocks that you administered to him?" Subjects were instructed to indicate their answers on a printed 14-point scale ranging from "Not at all painful" to "Extremely painful." The model response was 14 (Extremely painful) with the mean at 13.42.

Signs of extreme tension. Many subjects showed signs of nervousness in the experimental situation, and especially upon administering the more powerful shocks. In a large number of cases the degree of tension reached extremes that are rarely seen in sociopsychological laboratory studies. Subjects were observed to sweat, tremble, stutter, bite their lips, groan, and dig their fingernails into their flesh. These were characteristic rather than exceptional responses to the experiment.

One sign of tension was the regular occurrence of nervous laughing fits. Fourteen of the 40 subjects showed definite signs of nervous laughter and smiling. The laughter seemed entirely out of place, even bizarre. Full-blown, uncontrollable seizures were observed for 3 subjects. On one occasion we observed a seizure so violently convulsive that it was necessary to call a halt to the experiment. The subject, a 46-year-old encyclopedia salesman, was seriously embarrassed by his untoward and uncontrollable behavior. In the post-experimental interviews subjects took pains to point out that they were not sadistic types, and that the laughter did not mean they enjoyed shocking the victim.

Distribution of scores. It had been conjectured that persons would not, in general, agree to administer shocks beyond the level designated as Very Strong Shock. The distribution of maximum shocks for this experiment is shown in Table 2. The obtained distribution of scores deviates radically from the prediction.

TABLE 2

Distribution of Breakoff Points

Verbal designation and voltage indication	Number of subjects for whom this was maximum shock
Slight Shock	
15	0
30	0
45	0
60	0
Moderate Shock	
75	0
90	0
105	0
120	0
Strong Shock	
135	0
150	0
165	0
180	0
Very Strong Shock	
195	0
210	0
225	0
240	0
Intense Shock	
255	0
270	0
285	0
300	5
Extreme Intensity Shock	
315	4
330	2
345	1
360	1
Danger: Severe Shock	
375	1
390	0
405	0
420	0
XXX	
435	0
450	26

Upon command of the experimenter, each of the 40 subjects went beyond the expected breakoff point. No subject stopped prior to administering Shock Level 20. (At this level—300 volts—the victim kicks on the wall and no longer provides answers to the teacher's multiple-choice questions.)

Of the 40 subjects, 5 refused to obey the experimental commands beyond the 300-volt level. Four more subjects administered one further shock, and then refused to go on. Two broke off at the 330-volt level, and 1 each at 345, 360, and 375 volts. Thus a total of 14 subjects defied the experimenter. It is instructive to reprint their remarks at the point of defiance, as transcribed from the tape recordings:

[0124] I think he's trying to communicate, he's knocking. . . . Well it's not fair to shock the guy . . . these are terrific volts. I don't think this is very humane. . . . Oh, I can't go on with this; no, this isn't right. It's a hell of an experiment. The guy is suffering in there. No, I don't want to go on. This is crazy. [Subject refused to administer more shocks.]

[0123] He's banging in there. I'm gonna chicken out. I'd like to continue, but I can't do that to a man. . . . I'm sorry I can't do that to a man. I'll hurt his heart. You take your check. . . . No really, I couldn't do it.

These subjects were frequently in a highly agitated and even angered state. Sometimes, verbal protest was at a minimum, and the subject simply got up from his chair in front of the shock generator, and indicated that he wished to leave the laboratory.

Of the 40 subjects, 26 obeyed the orders of the experimenter to the end, proceeding to punish the victim until they reached the most potent shock available on the shock generator. At that point, the experimenter called a halt to the session. (The maximum shock is labeled 450 volts, and is two steps beyond the designation: Danger: Severe Shock.) Although obedient subjects continued to administer shocks, they often did so under extreme stress. Some expressed reluctance to administer shocks beyond the 300-volt level, and displayed fears similar to those who defied the experimenter; yet they obeyed.

After the maximum shocks had been delivered, and the experimenter called a halt to the proceedings, many obedient subjects heaved sighs of relief, mopped their brows, rubbed their fingers over their eyes, or nervously fumbled cigarettes. Some shook their heads, apparently in regret. Some subjects had remained calm throughout the experiment, and displayed only minimal signs of tension from beginning to end.

DISCUSSION

The experiment yielded two findings that were surprising. The first finding concerns the sheer strength of obedient tendencies manifested in this situation. Subjects have learned from childhood that it is a fundamental breach of moral conduct to hurt another person against his will. Yet, 26 subjects abandon this tenet in following the instructions of an authority who has no special powers to enforce his commands. To disobey would bring no material loss to the subject; no punishment would ensue. It is clear from the remarks and outward behavior of many participants that in punishing the victim they are often acting against their own values. Subjects often expressed deep disapproval of shocking a man in the face of his objections, and others denounced it as stupid and senseless. Yet the majority complied with the experimental commands. This outcome was surprising from two perspectives: first, from the standpoint of predictions made in the questionnaire described earlier. (Here, however, it is possible that the remoteness of the respondents from the actual situation, and the difficulty of conveying to them the concrete details of the experiment, could account for the serious underestimation of obedience.)

But the results were also unexpected to persons who observed the experiment in progress, through one-way mirrors. Observers often uttered expressions of disbelief upon seeing a subject administer more powerful shocks to the victim. These persons had a full acquaintance with the details of the situation, and yet systematically underestimated the amount of obedience that subjects would display.

The second unanticipated effect was the extraordinary tension generated by the procedures. One might suppose that a subject would simply break off or continue as his conscience dictated. Yet, this is very far from what happened. There were striking reactions of tension and emotional strain. One observer related:

I observed a mature and initially poised businessman enter the laboratory smiling and confident. Within 20 minutes he was reduced to a twitching, stuttering wreck, who was rapidly approaching a point of nervous collapse. He constantly pulled on his earlobe, and twisted his hands. At one point he pushed his fist into his forehead and muttered: "Oh God, let's stop it." And yet he continued to respond to every word of the experimenter, and obeyed to the end.

Any understanding of the phenomenon of obedience must rest on an analysis of the particular conditions in which it occurs. The following features of the experiment go some distance in explaining the high amount of obedience observed in the situation.

The experiment is sponsored by and takes place on the grounds of an institution of unimpeachable reputation, Yale University. It may be reasonably presumed that the personnel are competent and reputable. The importance of this background authority is now being studied by conducting a series of experiments outside of New Haven, and without any visible ties to the university.

The experiment is, on the face of it, designed to attain a worthy purpose—advancement of knowledge about learning and memory. Obedience occurs not as an end in itself, but as an instrumental element in a situation that the subject construes as significant, and meaningful. He may not be able to see its full significance, but he may properly assume that the experimenter does.

The subject perceives that the victim has voluntarily submitted to the authority system of the experimenter. He is not (at first) an unwilling captive impressed for involuntary service. He has taken the trouble to come to the laboratory presumably to aid the experimental research. That he later becomes an involuntary subject does not alter the fact that, initially, he consented to participate without qualification. Thus he has in some degree incurred an obligation toward the experimenter.

The subject, too, has entered the experiment voluntarily, and perceives himself under obligation to aid the experimenter. He has made a commitment, and to disrupt the experiment is a repudiation of this initial promise of aid.

Certain features of the procedure strengthen the subject's sense of obligation to the experimenter. For one, he has been paid for coming to the laboratory. In part this is canceled out by the experimenter's statement that:

Of course, as in all experiments, the money is yours simply for coming to the laboratory. From this point on, no matter what happens, the money is yours.[3]

From the subject's standpoint, the fact that he is the teacher and the other man the learner is purely a chance consequence (it is determined by drawing lots) and he, the subject, ran the same risk as the other man in being assigned the role of learner. Since the assignment of positions in the experiment was achieved by fair means, the learner is deprived of any basis of complaint on this account. (A similar situation obtains in Army units, in which—in the absence of volunteers—a particularly dangerous mission may be assigned by drawing lots, and the unlucky soldier is expected to bear his misfortune with sportsmanship.)

There is, at best, ambiguity with regard to the prerogatives of a psychologist and the corresponding rights of his subject. There is a vagueness of expectation concerning what a psychologist may require of his subject, and when he is overstepping acceptable limits. Moreover, the experiment occurs in a closed setting, and thus provides no opportunity for the subject to remove these ambiguities by discussion with others. There are few standards that seem directly applicable to the situation, which is a novel one for most subjects.

The subjects are assured that the shocks administered to the subject are "painful but not dangerous." Thus they assume that the discomfort caused the victim is momentary, while the scientific gains resulting from the experiment are enduring.

Through Shock Level 20 the victim continues to provide answers on the signal box. The subject may construe this as a sign that the victim is still willing to "play the game." It is only after Shock Level 20 that the victim repudiates the rules completely, refusing to answer further.

These features help to explain the high amount of obedience obtained in this experiment. Many of the arguments raised need not remain matters of speculation, but can be reduced to testable propositions to be confirmed or disproved by further experiments.[4]

The following features of the experiment concern the nature of the conflict which the subject faces.

The subject is placed in a position in which he must respond to the competing demands of two persons: the experimenter and the victim. The conflict must be resolved by meeting the demands of one or the other; satisfaction of the victim and the experimenter are mutually exclusive. Moreover, the resolution must take the form of a highly visible action, that of continuing to shock the victim or breaking off the experiment. Thus the subject is forced into a public conflict that does not permit any completely satisfactory solution.

While the demands of the experimenter carry the weight of scientific authority, the demands of the victim spring from his personal experience of pain and suffering. The two claims need not be regarded as equally pressing and legitimate. The experimenter seeks an abstract scientific datum; the victim cries out for relief from physical suffering caused by the subject's actions.

The experiment gives the subject little time for reflection. The conflict comes on rapidly. It is only minutes after the subject has been seated before the shock generator that the victim begins his protests. Moreover, the subject perceives that he has gone through but two-thirds of the shock levels at the time the subject's first protests are heard. Thus he understands that the conflict will have a persistent aspect to it, and may well become more intense as increasingly more powerful shocks are required. The rapidity with which the conflict descends on the subject, and his realization that it is predictably recurrent may well be sources of tension to him.

At a more general level, the conflict stems from the opposition of two deeply ingrained behavior dispositions: first, the disposition not to harm other people, and second, the tendency to obey those whom we perceive to be legitimate authorities.

ROBERT JAY LIFTON

DEATH AND HISTORY
Ideological Totalism, Victimization, and Violence

Professor Robert Jay Lifton proceeds from the basic premise that psychologists endeavor to understand man by creating paradigms or models. Though fully aware of the great debt owed to the pioneers in his field, he has long been convinced that the established paradigms of psychological science are insufficient to illuminate the fullness of contemporary human experience and that the ailments of modern man call for a new psychology. A psychiatrist and member of the medical profession, Dr. Lifton has devoted much of his professional life to probing for the roots of dislocation that have marked contemporary society and, in so doing, he has time and again reached across the frontiers of individual disciplines to share with colleagues in the fields of history and the social sciences some of the insights his research gave him.

Not limiting himself to the manifestations of totalitarianism discussed in this volume, but ranging widely over experiences of holocaust and ideological totalism around the globe and through the ages, Dr. Lifton has come to put forward a new paradigm of the human encounter with death and the question of transcendence in the continuity of life. Deeply concerned with historical change, especially in terms of the extreme situational factors that have governed the contemporary world, he has labored unceasingly to shape a psychological instrument of liberation, facilitating the escape from totalism and the attainment of autonomous human existence. The Broken Connection, *from which the following excerpts are taken, (New York, 1979, pp. 283, 292-306, 308-309, 309-310, 314-315, 316-318, 321-325) makes the exploration of the extremity of holocaust the bridge to overcome suppressed fear in order to achieve liberation.*

In the excerpts reprinted here Dr. Lifton charts the four-step sequence from historical dislocation to ideological totalism and from there to the victimization and violence characteristic of totalitarian regimes, but not only of them. Examining the situation of China between the two world wars and of the United States in the sixties and seventies in terms of evident psychohistorical dislocation, Dr. Lifton finds the explanations advanced too immediate and logical to account for the deeper causes and the patterns of desymbolization at the root. Turning to Germany, Dr. Lifton observed that there some progress has been made by perceptive researchers in their probing of the collective psychological dislocation caused by the Nazi experience. Discussing the German "inability to mourn" their lost Führer, Dr. Lifton relates the resulting psychic numbing and stasis to similar instances of painful desymbolization elsewhere, both in terms of short-term cataclysmic change and long-range development. Struck by the generally destructive consequences of such collective dislocation–ideological totalism, victimization, and violence–Dr. Lifton suggests modes of survivor illumination to break this vicious cycle.

However, Dr. Lifton observes, more often than not, man adapts to rather than escaping the condition of psychological dislocation. Collectively restless and unhappy, deprived of his shared sense of immortality, man seeks solace in what Dr. Lifton came to term, in his study of Chinese Communist thought reform, "ideological totalism." Ideological totalism utilizes common guilt feelings to monopolize the claim to absolute virtue. Thus fortified, Dr. Lifton observes, ideology negates individual experience and history; representing immortality, it in turn becomes the arbiter of life and death. Concentrating on man's eternal longing to overcome the terror of death and nothingness, Dr. Lifton finds that ideological totalism time and again has been man's tool to free himself from fear. The collective reassertion of eternal life expressed in ideological totalism–such as in the brutal fraternities of totalitarian paramilitary organizations–fulfills itself in victimization and violence.

Dr. Lifton prefers the term victimization to prejudice, because it more fittingly conveys the inherent life-death, good-evil dichotomy on which ideological totalism thrives. Addressing the problem of scapegoating in terms of spiritual cleansing and the reconstruction of moral order without the need of collective self-confrontation, Dr. Lifton surveys the historical evidence of its devastating effects. Climaxing in National Socialist anti-Semitism, Dr. Lifton observes, victimization and violence there became a metahistorical necessity based on a craving for transcendence. Seeing in totalitarianism the "deification of a power system," Dr. Lifton suggests that the god-devil vision entailed by victimization and violence via psychological dislocation nevertheless may be overcome

*by a new psychology of survivor illumination and the development of
other dimensions of awareness, discussed in the concluding parts of*
The Broken Connection.

We must approach history with a sense of man's eternally inadequate,
yet impressively imaginative, efforts to absorb the idea of death and create
lasting images of the continuity of life. *We can understand much of human
history as the struggle to achieve, maintain, and reaffirm a collective sense
of immortality under constantly changing psychic and material conditions.*
For modes of immortality to be symbolically viable—for people to experience their power—they must connect with direct, proximate experience as well as provide ultimate patterns of continuity. A viable
biological (or biosocial) mode, for instance, includes intense, direct (or
proximate) emotions as well as a more unspoken sense of unending continuity. A religious mode around Christian imagery must include direct
involvement in prayer, service, or other forms of ritual, as well as ultimate
imagery of transcendence or rebirth.

Over the course of history, imagery of immortality has moved from the
magical and the supernatural, to the natural and man-centered—and from
literal (the concrete belief in eternal life) to symbolic image-feelings
around rebirth, renewal, and continuing life . . .

. . . In studies involving long-term adaptations and innovations[1] rather
than sudden disaster or direct death encounter, I found that ultimate
questions were crucial to everyday experience. And more important for
our argument here, they are crucial to our sense of shared history and to
shifts in the historical imagery.

The capacity for these shifts seems limitless. For as Susanne Langer
tells us,

The great dreams of mankind, like the dreams of every individual man,
are protean, vague, inconsistent, and so embarrassed with the riches
of symbolic conception that every fantasy is apt to have a hundred
versions.[2]

And Loren Eiseley, more bitterly, speaks of man as a "fickle, erratic,
dangerous creature whose restless mind would try all paths, all horrors,
all betrayals . . . believe all things and believe nothing . . . kill for shadowy
ideas more ferociously than other creatures kill for food, then, in a generation or less, forget what bloody dream had so oppressed him."[3] There is
more to say about man's propensity for collective violence. But the
point here is that, in the face of his potentially endless flow of images,
man seeks lasting symbolic structure. Man may seem, as Eiseley claims, to

quickly forget his own oppressive "bloody dreams," but he does not so much forget them as continue to struggle with their fragments. He is ever in quest for the mental form that can contain those fragments and balance his death terror with a life-giving vision that connects him with past and future. When one seeks to understand historical choices, all paths lead to the ultimate.

DISLOCATION AND TOTALISM

We have associated historical aberration with collective forms of destruction and self-destruction. Our focus here is on ways in which historical struggles with death imagery contribute to these expressions of physical and spiritual destruction. Nuclear threats loom so large that one might well begin any discussion with something on the order of the atomic aberration. But collective assaults on human beings hardly began with the nuclear age. We require more general theory on our historical aberrations that can include both pre-nuclear and nuclear forms and at the same time speak to the quantum *mental* leap from one to the other. For our assumption is that we are dealing with breakdowns in man's sense of symbolic unity and impairment of his sense of immortality. We shall chart a dangerous four-step sequence from dislocation to totalism to victimization to violence, the first two steps of which we shall examine in this chapter.

Psychohistorical Dislocations. During certain historical periods, man has special difficulty in finding symbolic forms within which to locate himself. One could argue that this is man's 'natural' state. When, after all, has he been comfortable within his own symbolizing skin—that is, his sense of self? Our assumptions of such premodern comfort—of historical 'fit' between individuals and prescribed cosmologies—tend to be colored by a kind of retrospective romanticism. But there are surely degrees in our sense that the particular time we live in is discordant and "out of joint."

From our standpoint, such dislocations have to do with what might be called general or historical desymbolization. This is characterized by an inability to believe in larger connections, by pervasive expressions of psychic numbing. These states can be directly manifested in various kinds of apathy, unrelatedness, and general absence of trust or faith; or more indirectly in social, artistic, and political struggles to break out of that numbing.

As an example of psychohistorical dislocation, one thinks of China between the two world wars, referred to then as "the sick man of Asia." One might also consider, though the situation is much less extreme, the

United States in the 1960s and 1970s. In both cases dislocations have been widely felt, but explanations for them have been too immediate and too logical. It is not wrong to emphasize Vietnam and Watergate in accounting for various versions of American numbing and struggles against that numbing. But Vietnam and Watergate are themselves expressions of much more fundamental and longstanding patterns of American desymbolization around political, social, and religious belief-systems and institutions.[4]

There has, in fact, been very little psychological, and still less psychohistorical, theorizing about collective forms of dislocation and malaise. Two gifted German psychoanalysts, Alexander and Margarete Mitscherlich, have provided an interesting exception in their exploration of psychological patterns in post-World War II Germany.

The Mitscherlichs argue that a general "inability to mourn"[5] for their lost Führer had widespread collective consequences for Germans during the first few decades after World War II. Hitler had served as a "collective ego-ideal." His death, therefore "was not the loss of an ordinary person," but of a love object who had "filled a central function in the lives of his followers." That plus his exposure as "a criminal of truly monstrous proportion" resulted in "a central devaluation and impoverishment" in each individual German ego. In terms of our earlier discussion of the myth of the hero, we may say that the Mitscherlichs address the psychological consequences around a hero whose transcendence, and mastery over death, previously embraced, suddenly becomes radically tainted. In that way "the prerequisites for a melancholic reaction were created (following Freud's arguments in "Mourning and Melancholia")." Instead of succumbing to melancholia, Germans invoked defense mechanisms, mostly denial and some repression, through which they could "avoid self-devaluation by breaking all affective bridges linking them to the immediate past." But that same defensive process resulted in widespread apathy and indifference concerning immediate social experience. Lively interest was more or less confined to economic and technological matters, and about virtually everything else Germans remained "chained to our psychosocial immobilism as to an illness involving symptoms of severe paralysis." The society deeply feared trying anything new—as if living under a powerful, unspoken "watchword" of "no experiments!" This contrasted strikingly with pre-Nazi German social history of the nineteenth and twentieth centuries.

Germans (at least of the wartime generation) remained stuck in that psychological stance, the argument goes, because a mourning process for their Führer would have required experiencing precisely the emotions they felt the need to ward off—guilt, shame, and other forms of anxiety. The resulting psychic immobilism for that generation took on a lasting quality, a kind of autonomy that required continuous reinforcement of defense mechanisms of denial, repression, and isolation, in a vicious circle of un-mastered history.

The Mitscherlichs, in effect, offer a theory of historical dislocation taking the form of collective stasis. There are difficulties with their theory —they seem to hold too literally to Freud's clinical observations around mourning and melancholia, and they are obscure about the theoretical links between their own clinical observations and larger historical behavior. But, as was frequently the case with Freud himself, their sensibilities outdistanced their theory: they draw creatively from a libido-theory model in ways that suggest the limitations of that model in approaching historical experience.

What the Mitscherlichs describe as the inability to mourn is part of a general breakdown in the symbolizing process, a form of dislocation that may accompany any period of confusing historical change but especially one in which existing image-feelings and modes of immortality have been radically dishonored. The result is not only blocked or re-pressed mourning but more general survivor conflict. Germans survived the death and loss of not only their Führer but also their visions of personal and national virtue, cleansing, revitalization, and triumph around the larger Nazi experience. They did use the kind of defenses the Mitscher-lichs describe—we would place them in the general category of numbing— to avoid anything resembling confrontation of the death encounter, the overall historical project. The specter of guilt is at the center here, as the Mitscherlichs suggest, and is probably of much greater importance than generally realized in the survival of more ordinary—less evil—historical periods. But this pattern of numbed guilt may not be so much the cause of the collective stasis described by the Mitscherlichs as a component of the general inability of this group of survivors to find significance in—give inner form to—their death immersion. For in speaking of the survivor we invoke a theory of imagery and meaning. Numbed guilt is part of formula-tive impairment: it can neither be acknowledged nor avoided because one finds no available images and symbolizations within which to master and transcend it. Equally, one cannot find any such "formulation" or meaning because, to be authentic, it would entail confronting potential dimensions of guilt one is unable to handle psychically. Confronting guilt and taking the path of survivor illumination involves the difficult psychic work of examining ultimate questions and altering modes of immortality. The opposite survivor tendency involves a simultaneous combination of numbed guilt and retained ultimate imagery that is neither functional nor alterable.

From this standpoint, during any period of upheaval and change the overall problem is not mourning as such but the capacity to construct the kinds of immediate and ultimate image-feelings that give form to experience—that is, the problem of formulation. Collective formulation can be suddenly and radically undermined (as in the case of extreme historical experience such as that of the Nazi era); or it can be more gradually subverted over decades and even centuries, as in the case of the European and American historical experience more or less from the time of the Renaissance. In either case we may speak of psychohistorical dislocation, and of the breakdown of symbolizations around family, religion, authority in general, and the *rite de passage* of the life cycle. The old symbolizations remain, as do the institutional arrangements for promulgating them, but both image and institution are experienced as psychic burdens rather than as sources of vitality. That was the message of student protesters in various parts of the world during the late 1960s.

Survivor theory also sheds some light on the emergence of pockets of startling creativity in the midst of dislocation. While so many Germans were undergoing the post-World War II stagnation Mitscherlich described, Günther Grass was writing *The Tin Drum*, one of the greatest novels written anywhere since World War II; Heinrich Böll was producing his exquisitely sensitive fiction; and Jakov Lind his stark and brutal stories and autobiographical writings. All three probed questions of death and their relationship to life in the context of Nazism and after. All wrote as survivors directly confronting their death immersion, within a literature of survival.[6]

We cannot be surprised that this genre found such powerful expression in post-World War II Germany. But it hardly originated there. One could say that Homer and Dostoyevsky were preoccupied with similar questions. They too described dislocated man—man as survivor—his death immersion culminating in a search for immortalizing connections in the face of vast and threatening desymbolization.

This model of the creative survivor is not confined to literature or art, but extends to all areas of human expression including social thought and political action. When collectively experienced, the model suggests an alternative to the destructive sequence from dislocation to totalism, victimization, and violence. The alternative, historical as well as individual, is that of survivor illumination. It requires a degree of collective confrontation of death and loss all too rarely achieved. But the ideal persists, and even the most limited approximation inspired by it can have considerable human value.

Dislocation creates a special kind of uneasy duality around symbolization: a general sense of numbing, devitalization, and absence of larger meaning on the one hand; and on the other, a form of image-release, an explosion of symbolizing forays in the struggle to overcome collective deadness and reassert larger connection. This "protean style" of individuals —the capacity for psychological shape-shifting (involving belief-systems, relationships, and styles of living) as well as for acting on multiple, seemingly divergent images that are simultaneously held—can apply to large groups of people, even to societies. We can thus speak of a protean historical situation in which, in terms of imagery and sometimes behavior, everything becomes possible.[7]

That very protean capacity can be lethal, as Loren Eiseley suggests:

If one were to attempt to spell out in a sentence the single lethal factor at the root of declining or lost civilizations up to the present, I would be forced to say, "adaptability." I would have to remark, paradoxically, that the magnificent specialization of gray matter which has opened to us all the climates of the earth, which has given us music, surrounded us with luxury, entranced us with great poetry, has this one flaw: it is too adaptable. In breaking free of instinct and venturing naked into a universe which demanded constant trial and experiment, a world whose possibilities were unexplored and unlimited, man's hunger for experience became unlimited also. He has the capacity to veer with every wind, or, stubbornly, to insert himself into some fantastically elaborated and irrational social institution only to perish with it.[8]

What Eiseley is suggesting is that the evolutionary emergence of man the symbolizer creates a terrible danger to the species in the form of indiscriminate image-hunger. Eiseley goes on, despairingly, to associate this image-hunger with an ultimate species emptiness: "It is almost as though man had at heart no image, but only images, that his soul was truly . . . vacant . . ." The conceptual issue raised by Eiseley's metaphor is that of the relationship between human evolution and the ever-varying waves of individual and historical imagery. Eiseley tells us, in effect, that the first releases the second but that beyond that there is no relationship. But we have been viewing the quest for ultimate imagery as itself expressing evolutionary correction—as a way of mentalizing—our involvement in living processes larger than ourselves (whether we refer to them as evolution or God's creation). Our images, then, though wildly varied, are nonetheless bound by the nature of that collective quest. And that is true of even the most demonic of images and their associated feelings and adaptations. We draw not from vacancy, as Eiseley claims, in constructing our version of collective life—in making history—but from our own version of an evolutionary heritage. This does not lessen the danger of our images, but, if anything, deepens the paradox. When we feel ourselves dislocated and experience threats to physical or symbolic existence, we open the floodgates of our minds, call forth a gamut of images from the most fragmented to the most enveloping, and become newly vulnerable to precisely the images we have called forth. Historically speaking we move from dislocation to partial "relocation" to new dislocation—or worse.

Ideological Totalism. Dislocation breeds collective forms of restlessness and unhappiness. That loss of a shared sense of immortality leads men to seek radical measures for its recovery. Those measures can take the form of ideological totalism—an extremist meeting ground between people and ideas that involves an all-or-none subjugation of the self to an idea-system.

I developed critieria for ideological totalism from a study of Chinese Communist "thought reform" (or "brainwashing"), but then attempted to generalize their applicability to a wide variety of practices—political, religious, educational, and scientific—in various cultures, including my own. In doing so I raised questions about such divergent enterprises as the German Nazi movement, American "McCarthyism" during the 1950s, and (in much milder, more indirect ways) about training procedures conducted by Jesuits and psychoanalysts.[9] Similar questions have been raised concerning extremist cults, such as Scientology and the Unification Church, in America and elsewhere.

Eight psychohistorical themes characterize a totalistic environment. Each theme is based on an absolute philosophical assumption—an extreme image—that is in turn an expression of an exclusive and incontestible claim to the symbolization of immortality. Thus, on the basis of an assumption of omniscience and of exclusive possession of truth, the totalistic environment attempts to control all communication within a given environment ("milieu control"). On the basis of its alleged "higher purpose" it engages in "mystical manipulation" or a no-holds-barred policy of molding human behavior. On the assumption that it contains the key to absolute virtue, it mobilizes the vast human potential for guilt and shame in its imperative of eliminating all "taints" and "poisons" or its "demand for purity." Around the claim to total ownership of the individual self—including psychic components of imagination and memory—it imposes an ethos of total exposure or a "cult of confession." Around its imposed monopoly on immortalizing ideas and images, it makes of them a "sacred science," one combining deification of the Word with the equally absolute secular authority of scientific method. On the basis of that "sacred science," it institutes "loading of the language" in ways that eliminate ambiguity about even the most complex human problems and reduces them to definitive-sounding, thought-terminating images. The insistence on ultimate primacy of the idea-system automatically imposes a principle of "doctrine over person," so that direct experience and past history are subsumed to (or negated by) ideology and the individual pressed to remake himself to fit the doctrinal mold.

Finally, there is the overall assumption that there is just one valid mode of being—just one authentic avenue of immortality—so that an arbitrary line is drawn between those who possess no such right. This impulse toward "the dispensing of existence" is the ultimate and inevitable outcome of ideological totalism, whether expressed in merely metaphorical or in murderous ways.[10]

When I first wrote about these themes I had not yet thought out the paradigm of death and continuity or the concept of symbolic immortality. I was groping toward that perspective in attributing the appeal of ideological totalism to "the ever-present human quest for the omnipotent guide—for the supernatural force, political party, philosophical ideas, great leader, or precise science—that will bring ultimate solidarity to all men and eliminate the terror of death and nothingness." Mostly, I focused on what I would now call *proximate* psychological issues in discussing variations in susceptibility to totalism—issues around early lack of basic trust, experience of unusual parental domination, degree of inclination toward guilt feelings, and conflict or crisis around identity. I was aware that all of these were a matter of degree, part of every individual background. I looked on the capacity for totalism as a consequence of the nature of human childhood—its prolonged period of helplessness and dependency readily creating in the child a need to form imagery of omnipotence around those who first nurture and "control" him, imagery that can contribute greatly to a later embrace of totalism. These vulnerabilities can intensify through rapid historical change, leading to a desire to sweep aside the confusions of existing emotions and institutions in favor of total simplicity and absolute coherence.

Totalistic programs seek a once-and-for-all resolution of dilemmas around death imagery and human continuity. Their impulse is not merely to "stop time" (on the order of obsessive-compulsive behavior) but to "stop history." The immortalizing system insists upon its own permanence and immutability. What is prescribed is the very flow and change in collective symbolization that makes man the historical animal he is. His sense of underlying threat—the overwhelming intrusion of various forms of death anxiety—is so great that the symbolizing process itself—the faculty that makes man man—either must be shut down, or radically contained. The "living machine" of individual neurosis is extended to something on the order of a "history machine."

And the totalistic milieu embodies the self-contradiction of that phrase. History as a grand concept is embellished, laid claim to, but in immediate operation it is looked on as a large mechanism whose parts must be totally meshed and controlled. As in individual obsessiveness, the collective rituals ward off the "horrific" temptation toward exactly what is most forbidden—

alternative images and feelings, especially around ultimate matters. And underlying the totalistic system is parallel imagery of annihilation, but on a collective rather than individual scale—annihilation of one's nation, culture, religion, or even scientific or intellectual belief-system. Should there be a significant opening out of the self-closed totalistic system, so the image goes, that which is most precious—the immortalizing vehicle—will disintegrate.

That absolutist image-feeling is a further manifestation of collective survivor experience. Because imagery death and loss are now tolerable, there is a need for some kind of reversal, for dramatic or even instant revitalization, and above all for an air-tight guarantee of immortality. In its most primitive expression, the survivor reaction can take the form of glorification of death, blood, and killing. Here we may speak of survivor paranoia (and addiction to survival), a continuous struggle to master the death immersion—the "traumatic situation"—by having it in some way reenacted (on the order of the "repetition compulsion"), changing or rearranging the participants, but always with an onrush of survival on the part of oneself or one's group. The repetition is not so much that of the original event (as Freud emphasized) as its death-component, whether the latter is understood as actual physical annihilation or such psychic counterparts as extreme humiliation and deprivation. The addiction can be to images of death (various forms of carnage) rather than actual killing and dying. In either case this survivor addiction has the psychological significance of struggling to reclaim control of death and symbolization of immortality. Modern Fascist movements epitomize this success. One can point, for instance, to the swashbuckling "Free Corps" in post-World War I Germany, with their imagery of revenge against German humiliation in World War I and at Versailles, of lust for blood and death, of specific enemies (a loose category) and of others on principle. Above all the Free Corps (or "Freebooters") had the need to remain in military formations, in something approximating combat, and "were simply not suited for the work of peace."[11] They were "the men who lived national socialism before it was organized," as one of them aptly put it. And they became much of the nucleus for that movement, as well as object of some of its purges. Hitler further developed this kind of imagery, and was personally preoccupied with death and blood ("one creature drinks the blood of another. The death of one nourishes the other").[12]

Hitler also mediated individual and collective patterns of machinelike repetition and obsessiveness—in his daily schedule, film-viewing, and above all in his perpetual completely repetitious monologues. Hitler seemed to want Germany to "stop time," so that he could install his "historical machine," ever viewing time as the enemy ("Time always . . . works against us") and seeking self-immortalizing imagery that could break out of this disturbing restriction. ("The greatest field commander [or some such related designation] of all time"—the "of all time" the operative psychological requirement).[13] And there is the famous Falangist slogan, "Hail to death!" One worships the source of one's terror and imposes the worship, and aversion of the terror, on everyone else. The process, moreover, works—at least to a degree. The death-worship is accompanied by revitalizing imagery—the vision of the "New Germany"—in ways that evoke and maintain powerful enthusiasms.

At least for a time there can be a collective sense of survivor redemption —shared image-feelings of the recovery and reassertion of the eternal life of the group.

These feelings can also be evoked by totalistic groups without focus on death-worship *per se*. The Chinese Communist movement has had its share of violence and death imagery. But it has concentrated heavily on the revitalization side—on the "New China" rather than the taste of blood. In the Cultural Revolution of 1966-68, there was a dawn rally in the Great Square of Peking, at which Mao Tse-tung appeared before one million screaming and chanting young followers in a scene reminiscent to many of the celebrated Leni Riefenstahl film of the Nazis' Nuremberg rally, "The Triumph of the Will." This symbolism is not only of a "new community" but also of a "community of immortals—of men, women, and children entering into a new relationship with the revolutionary process." The event conveyed "a blending of the immortal cultural and racial substance of the Chinese as a people with the equally immortal Communist revolution."[14]

Ideological totalism, then, provides a kind of cutting-edge of survivor possibility—a form of alchemy in which collective imagery of disintegration is transmitted into shared reassertion of eternal life—but alchemy with its own cost.

VICTIMIZATION AND MASS VIOLENCE

The step from totalism to victimization is easy; in fact totalism *requires* victimization, the claim to ultimate virtue requires a contrasting image— and all too often an embodiment—of absolute evil. *Victimization* is a more accurate word than *prejudice* for the phenomenon at hand because it better suggests its life/death connections. To be sure, within the phenomenon there is a continuum from mild "discrimination" to slavery and other forms of brutalization and violence. But along the full continuum one can find what Edgar Gardner Murphy, commenting on American race relations in 1911, called an "animus of aggrandizement."[15] The two words are especially apt. *Animus* suggests not only enmity but the soul—or life—principle sought by the victimizers in their aggrandizement, that is their expansion of their own power at the cost of the victim's.

Victimization involves the creation of a death-tainted group (of victims) against which others (victimizers) can contrast their claim to immortality. Victimizers actually experience a threat to the life of their own group, around which they justify their actions. There are innumerable ways in which that sense of threat can be displaced onto those selected as victims. But once that has been done, a lasting target has been found for the victimizing imperative. The Nazis (and the "Freebooters" who preceded them), in seeking their scapegoat for "the death of Germany" in World War I, included such groups as Communists, leftists, politicians, and the bourgeoisie, before settling more or less exclusively on the Jews. The advantage of creating a scapegoat is that it allows the survivor group to avoid confronting its own death anxiety and death guilt, to find an absolute resolution to the struggle between internal and external blaming, and to move from victimized to victimizer. A victimizer's image of himself as a victim is crucial. He is likely to feel himself continually vulnerable to the deadly assaults of gods, devils, and enemies, and finds that he can best reassert his life-power by victimizing others. In contrast, those groups of survivors who become genuinely autonomous tend to transcend both the victims' identity and the need to be victimizers. That autonomy accompanies the construction of meaning—an alternative formulation—in some degree collectively experienced. But for those who can derive meaning only from a scapegoating formulation, a perpetual victim-victimizer ethos takes hold and every act of aggression against the target group is understood as anticipatory "defense," appropriate revenge, or a combination of both.[16]

This scapegoating formulation has only partial relationship to actual scapegoating ritual. That ritual (the name derives from ancient Hebrew practice, but is applied to related practices, especially in primitive cultures) involves the transfer of a community's sin or evil to a person or an animal in order to restore the general moral order. The ritual seeks to cleanse the community of its taint of guilt in order to bring about a "rehabilitation of impaired holiness. . . . [For] where holiness is sullied, there too, is life itself impaired, and . . . no continuance can be expected unless and until the taint is removed."[17] Unacknowledged (we would say numbed) guilt, by contrast, could cause the death or disintegration of the community, or even (with the Hebrew development of the ritual) inflict "injury upon God." Failure to confront communal guilt (render it animating) was "a crime against the Kingdom of God" which threatened the entire "divine plan."[18] What we are calling a scapegoating survivor formulation lays claim to the primal purposes of the original ritual: the designation of a bearer of collective taint (of guilt and death) in order to bring about a general spiritual cleansing, a reconstruction of moral order, and renewed life-power. But the original ritual is also perverted in such survivor formulation, and in victimization in general. What is avoided is the collective self-confrontation at the heart of the ritual— "The essential point about the scapegoat is that it removes from the community the taint and impurity of sins *which have first to be openly and fully confessed*"[19] —by evolving imagery around a special group of victims who become, among other things, surrogates for the unperformed psychological work. The victims become psychologically necessary, and must be spuriously admitted to the victimizers' community as substitute-bearers of the death-taint. They cannot be permitted to stray too far from it, physically or psychologically, if the victimizing process is to be maintained. On that availability rests, psychologically speaking, the life of the victimizers.

But we must look beyond the scapegoating theme for additional cultural and historical evidence for a concept of victimization in which, by an imagined symbolic balance, the collective relationship to immortality depends upon its collective denial to others. Mircea Eliade, for instance, stresses the distinction made in early cultures between what he calls the "sacred space" of their inhabited territory and the "unknown and indeterminant space" surrounding it. There is "our world, the cosmos" and the " 'other world,' a foreign, chaotic space, peopled by ghosts, demons, [and] 'foreigners.' "[20] In the virtually universal process of what Eliade calls "making the world sacred," there tends to develop a spatial polarization between "life area" and "death area," between those who (according to later terminology) were within or "beyond the pale." We would associate this sacralization of space with early expressions of biological and religious symbolizations of immortality; and its regular accompaniment by a designated and peopled "death space" suggests the beginnings of victimization. Related imagery persists to the present, as suggested by the widespread tendency to equate exile with death. Indeed the Japanese term *bōmei suru*, "to be exiled," can also be read, more literally, as "to lose life," containing as it does the same Chinese character as the verb *nakunaru*, "to die."

Still more specific are distinctions made in the Pyramid Texts: The eternal life of the pharaoh is repeatedly proclaimed, and "the word *death* never occurs . . . except in the negative or applied to a foe." The texts repeatedly insist that the dead kings live: "King Peti has not died the

death, he has become a glorious one in the horizon"; "Ho! King Unis!
Thou didst not depart dead, thou didst depart living . . ."[21] The immortali-
zation of even a king depended upon the concept of an enemy deprived
of that status. Indeed, these forty-five-hundred-year-old texts suggest
what may be the most fundamental of all definitions of *an enemy: a
person who must die, so that one may oneself transcend death*. They also
provide important early clues to the significance of the enduring association of kings with divinity. The king is divine because he is the embodiment of the immortality principle, a representative of the gods if not a
god himself. By identifying with their king and his relationship to divinity,
ordinary people can share that immortality. For early Egyptians both
their pharaohs and the god of Osiris were "guarantors of immortality."[22]
At times the texts suggest a merging of kings with Osiris, who is both
fertility god and god of the dead. And the ordinary man can connect with
the immortality of god or king or god-king, as the Coffin Texts also
suggest:

> I live, I die, I am Osiris.
> I have entered you, and have reappeared through you.
> I have waxed fat in you.
> I have grown in you.
> I have fallen upon my side [the expression for the death of Osiris].
> The gods are living from me.
> I live and I grow as Neper [the corn-god] who takes out the
>   Honored Ones.
> Geb [the earth-god] has hidden me.
> I live, I die, I am barley, I do not perish![23]

Nonetheless there apparently were class distinctions in regard to
immortality—some were more immortal than others. Breasted speaks of
the "royal hereafter," as "democratised" in historical sequence from royal
prerogative, to "mortuary *largesses* of the royal treasury" for nobles to
build their tombs, to more general prayers for what the tombs record as
"an offering which the king gives," which referred literally to money
provided for tombs but probably had the additional symbolic meaning
of royal dispensation for proper burial and access to immortality.[24]
That democratization of eternal life developed with the cult of Osiris
and the evolution of moral criteria influencing one's destiny in ways
that prefigured Judaism and Christianity, so that "for the first time
immortality dawned upon the mind of man as a thing achieved in a man's
soul."[25]

Early Egyptian class distinctions (kings and nobles "might dwell at will
with the Sun-god in his glorious celestial kingdom," while common people
thought of their dead as "dwelling in the tomb, or at best inhabiting the

gloomy realm of the West, the subterranean kingdom ruled by the old mortuary gods") never ceased to operate in this ultimate form of human "power-struggle." The immortality-centered class structure may be based upon hereditary ties to royalty and nobility, ownership of land, wealth, special knowledge, technical skill, or political or religious standing. No matter how egalitarian its claim, virtually no social movement has eliminated distinctions between its "faithful" and "heathen," its "elect" and its "doomed." Discrimination and victimization, moreover, may take two forms: either denial of *any* access to continuing life; or more subtle gradations in levels of immortality offered. Just as Egyptian servants might expect their hereafter to involve the same kind of menial life, so may religious or political sinners be afforded low places on the hierarchy of collective spirituality or of enduring revolution. In all cases the dispensed denial or restriction is in the service of the dominant group's psychic economy around death anxiety and a sense of continuing life.

These principles take on nasty clarity as we observe their operation in four kinds of victimization—class-caste, color, religious, and political.

When living in Japan in the early 1950s, I was struck by the extreme discomfort most people showed—even progressive students—when the subject of outcasts arose. The Japanese term for that group, *Eta*, has the literal meaning of "abundant defilement," "full of pollution," or "full of filth." The word itself is taboo because it is so pejorative—but I gained the distinct impression that people did not like to say the word because it carried some of the disturbing taint of the outcast group itself. Those early impressions took on new meaning for me a decade later in my Hiroshima study. Hiroshima and Nagasaki survivors or *hibakusha* were often compared to outcast groups because of a discrimination they encountered in both marriage arrangements and work and because of their generally low socioeconomic standing. In exploring the extensive death taint of atomic-bomb survivors (in others' imagery about them as well as their self-imagery) and then reading more about outcast groups in Japan and India, I came to realize that the comparison had profound conceptual implications for the relationship of victimization to death imagery and struggles around immortality . . .

. . . With Indian "Untouchables," the situation has been even more extreme. They have been forbidden from entering certain streets or lanes, or else required to carry brooms to brush away their footprints as they passed; or to carry little pots around their necks into which they could spit without contaminating the ground; or to keep specific distances from people of higher castes or shout a warning before entering particular streets (though in other situations they might be prohibited from raising their voices "because the sound of . . . [their] voice [s] falling on a caste

Hindu's ear was deemed to be as polluting as . . . [their] touch." As in the case of *Eta*, they could not enter Hindu temples, homes, or public establishments, or drink from a common village well. They have served as "scavengers and sweepers, the handlers of the carcasses of . . . dead animals whose flesh they eat and whose skins they tan, the carriers of waste and night soil, the beggars and the scrapers, living in and off the dregs and carrion of the society."[26] We again encounter the association of filth and defilement with death anxiety. But the victimizing process is even more compulsive than in the case of *Eta* because it is theologically prescribed within an institutionally hardened caste system . . .

. . . We have emphasized the origins of *Eta* and Untouchables in low-caste assignment to death-tainted occupations. Untouchables, in addition, are thought to be remnants of the indigenous population conquered four or five thousand years ago by Aryan invaders (it is possible that *Eta* had similar origins in conquest, as that has frequently been the case with slave castes). But in this process, imagery around color has been highly significant. The Sanskrit word *varna*, used for caste or class—and as a category including the four Hindu castes mentioned—literally means color. The Aryan (Sanskrit for noble) invaders (1500 B.C.) who came to form the higher Hindu castes, were an Indo-European people who were said to be fair, in contrast to the aboriginal "dark people" they conquered. And even in the case of *Eta*, an "invisible race" in that they are not racially separable from their countrymen, they are frequently thought of as darker than ordinary Japanese—and that association very likely predates Western influence.

All this raises the possibility, in connection with victimization by color, that anxieties around darkness and blackness extend beyond questions of which racial shade is immediately dominant. In the white West, there is certainly no doubt about the association of blackness with impurity, evil, and death; and whiteness with purity and immortality. Certainly in the white West, those associations are old and deep. There is even an etymological connection between the Latin *niger* (black), (which also had the figurative meaning of wicked) and *nigromantia, necromantia*, and *necromancy*, the art of conjuring up the spirits of the dead or "black magic."[27]

This early association of black with death-linked sorcery gave rise to a vast popular vocabulary, starting with "black magic" and extending to the related idea of "black arts" and its extension into a theological "black mass"—and then into a secular idiom, with blackmail, blackball, black-guards, blacklist, black market, black book, and many more . . .

. . . We have already begun to suggest the special significance of religious imagery for all forms of victimization. Religion has been the primary source of man's overt symbolization of immortality. Threats to that immortality are posed by antireligious groups (heathen, heretics, antichrists, and other "sinful" collectivities). Here it is particularly useful to look directly at what Freud said about persecution of the Jews.

Freud suggests a number of psychological causes for the extraordinary historical persistence and intensity of anti-Semitism. One of them was meant to have special reference for the Nazi movement, whose venom toward the Jews was clearly apparent in the mid-1930s, when Freud wrote *Moses and Monotheism*. "We must not forget," Freud cautioned,

that all those people who excel today in their hatred of Jews became Christians only in late historic times, often driven to it by bloody coercion. It might be said that they are all "misbaptized." They have been left, under a thin veneer of Christianity, what their ancestors were, who worshipped a barbarous polytheism. They have not got over a grudge against the new religion which was imposed on them; but they have displaced the grudge onto the source from which Christianity reached them. The fact that the Gospels tell a story which is set among Jews, and in fact deals only with Jews, has made this misplacement easy for them. Their hatred of Jews is at bottom a hatred of Christians, and we need not be surprised that in the German National-Socialist revolution this intimate relation between the two monotheist religions finds such a clear expression in the hostile treatment of both of them.[28]

In other translations the "misbaptized" is rendered as "badly christened." And this concept of "badly christened" Christians is consistent with our own emphasis on the enormous psychological difficulty faced by any people in making a transition in modes (or elements of modes) of immortality. Freud also brought in his theories around primeval parricide in connection with Christ's death, so that the Christian accusation toward Jews, "You killed our God!" refers back to the much earlier murder of Moses and ultimately to the *Totem and Taboo* thesis of the primal horde and the first parricide. Freud's suggestion here is that the sacrifice of a "son" (Jesus) represents the atonement for that earlier sequence. And by making that son the son of God, Christianity becomes a "son religion" in contrast with the Judaic "father religion" and "has not escaped the fate of having to get rid of the father."[29]

Here the reasoning is convoluted, but again consistent with the idea of an intra-monotheistic struggle over claims to immortalizing power. We would claim that this generational clash has much less to do with possessing the mother than possessing the power of life-continuity. In addition, Freud suggested that the very existence of a Jewish remnant, a group that persists as a people separate and different from their "hosts"—despite centuries of "the most cruel persecutions"—is a nagging reminder to

Christians of the incomplete triumph of the newer claim to immortality. The situation is all the more painful to Christians, Freud felt, because the Jews had been the "first-born, favourite child of God the Father." We would shift the emphasis from that of "family dynamics" to a suggestion of "intimate rivalry" for ultimate power between the two religions closest to one another in their origins and their monotheistic visions. This is consistent with Freud's principle of what he calls "the narcissism of minor differences." As in other situations the "narcissism" involved turns out to be the most fundamental struggle with disintegration and renewal . . .

. . . Some recent historical and linguistic observations[30] suggest the central significance for the Nazi movement of the Jew as psychological victim. " 'The Final Solution of the Jewish Question' in the National Socialist conception was not just another anti-Semitic undertaking, but a meta-historical program devised with an eschatological perspective. It was part of a salvational ideology that envisaged the attainment of Heaven by bringing Hell on earth."[31] More specifically, the Nazi movement became a pseudo-religion which drew heavily upon Judeo-Christian metaphysics, albeit in perverted and reversed form. One of Hitler's greatest rhetorical talents was to evoke in the German people a sense of perpetual life-or-death crisis. Always at stake was the spirit, essence, vitality, and purity—that is the life-power—of the German people. And the threatening force was the Jew, by his very existence.

The Jew was the embodiment of moral decay—of physical and sexual perversion, spiritual petrifaction, and cultural degeneracy. The images are closely linked to death and deterioration—the Jews as carriers of filth and disease, of plague and syphilis and "racial tuberculosis," as spreaders of every kind of "poison," and as parasites, vampires, bloodsuckers, and racial contaminators. The Aryan becomes, importantly, the counter-Jew or anti-Jew. He is the embodiment of German racial revitalization, renaissance, and renewal. His is the special charisma of world leadership, the possession of life-power. He is, that is, the ultimate anti-Antichrist. For in this victim-centered cosmology, the Antichrist (the Jew) comes first and creates the Aryan or anti-Antichrist.

No wonder, then, that the Nazi victimizing impulse preceded and took priority over everything else—even when technological and transportation requirements of the death camps interfered with a failing war effort. For Hitler meant it when he wrote in *Mein Kampf*: "I believe that I am acting in accordance with the will of the Almighty Creator: *by defending myself against the Jew, I am fighting for the work of the Lord*." He similarly pitted the Aryan "men of God" against the Jewish "men of Satan," and spoke of the Jew as "the anti-man, the creature of another god . . . [who] must have come from another root of the human race."[32] In the final words of his political testament, which he dictated on the last day of his life—his "suicide note" to the German people—he reaffirmed his "highest" aim: "Above all I charge the leaders of the nation and those under them to scrupulous observance of the laws of race and to merciless opposition to the universal poisoner of all peoples, international Jewry."[33]

We sense the emptiness at the heart of the victimizing process. The victim himself must become the source of "religious inspiration"—of animating visions of the spiritual purity and eternal life of one's "sacred community." One implication of this argument is that these collective patterns of victimization cannot be understood as secondary to Hitler's individual psychopathology. His and his ideologues' depiction of Jews made use of relatively conventional victimizing imagery (victim as death-linked, defiled, degenerate, "poisoner"). That imagery, centering on the Jew, has long been available in Germany and elsewhere in Europe. What needs to be explained in psychobiographical approaches to Hitler is the way in which his psychopathology combined with his extraordinary capacity to articulate these victimizing impules along with their revitalizing components so effectively for a large segment of the German people. Thus, Rudolf Binion[34] is right in his focus upon Hitler's capacity to articulate Germany's collective trauma following World War I, but in my judgment misleading when he sees so much of the source of Hitler's rabid anti-Semitism in his traumatic experiences during World War I and his feelings toward the Jewish physician who attended his mother during her fatal disease. Nor does the poison-centered imagery of that victimization derive from the gaseous poison Hitler inhaled during World War I or the iodoform treatment the physician employed. We see again the truth—even prophecy—in Freud's characterization of the Nazis as "badly-christened Christians." Theirs was the most malignant of all outcomes of the two-thousand-year-old struggle with the demanding images of monotheism—with man's efforts to spiritualize his relationship to the evolutionary process . . .

. . . Twentieth-century totalitarianism recreates in its own image the processes of religious victimization. The resulting political victimization becomes even more central to the project than in the original religious model. For the political totalizers may well be more vulnerable to anxieties around collective vitality and therefore more in need of a constant flow of victims around whom those anxieties can be expressed, if not overcome. What Kenneth Burke calls the "curative role of victimage" stems from "the rhetoric of religion."[35] But certain aspects of it may be especially clear in its political forms. Indeed the process of victimization—of locating and abusing enemies of the State, Party, working class, or the People—becomes crucial to maintaining the structure and function of the regime.

For in addition to imposing external controls, totalitarian governments seek total mobilization of spiritual power. But they (in Camus's terms) confuse totality with unity, and a psychological mechanism is needed to help deny that confusion—which is where victims come in.

The victim can be held responsible for what is, in essence, an impossible project. Lenin is reputed to have said, "We must be engineers of the human soul,"[36] which may well be the most ambitious and illusory process ever embarked upon, for it suggests mobilizing spirit and technique on behalf of political salvation. This process requires internal "enemies and betrayers" who "try to prevent [that salvation] in the same way . . . the devil tries to undermine and destroy the work of those who are in the service of the City of God."[37] But the language becomes contemporary, political, and potentially genocidal—with the call to "liquidate," "exterminate," or "destroy" all such enemies and betrayers. The victims come to be viewed as deadly contaminants, agents of a disease or a diabolical force that threatens to destroy the entire project. They are seen as subverters of the powerful psychological satisfactions totalitarianism can provide— of shared feelings of vitality and purpose and of visions of national and revolutionary immortality. They become associated, for totalitarian manipulators and many ordinary people as well, with disturbing images of chaos and disintegration. A scapegoating principle also prevails, in that the victims become repositories for everyone's sense of guilt over inability to achieve prescribed levels of purity in belief and behavior. Kenneth Burke has stated the sequence with cryptic poetic brilliance:

> Here are the steps
> In the Iron Law of History
> That welds Order and Sacrifice:
>
> Order leads to guilt
> (for who can keep commandments!)
> Guilt needs Redemption
> (for who would not be cleansed!)
> Redemption needs Redeemer
> (which is to say, a Victim!)
>
> Order
> Through Guilt
> To Victimage
> (hence: Cult of the Kill). . . .[38]

Ultimately, as the symbolizing force of the whole project wanes (as in the Soviet Union today, for instance) totalitarianism can be defined as "deification of a power system."[39] At that point anyone who tries to think for himself may become a victim: "The heretic is one who has personal ideas."[40] The totalitarian regime, moreover "insists on holding every man, even the most servile, responsible for the fact that rebellion ever existed and still exists under the sun."[41] That is, there is a shared sense that totalitarian victimization may strike anyone, and that anyone may "deserve" it.

In political victimization, then, there is a linguistic polarization of "ultimate terms": "god terms" for the embodiment of one's group vision, and "devil terms" for one's designated victims, or political enemies. Thus in Chinese revolutionary practice, as expressed in the throught-reform procedure, devil-victims were "capitalists," "imperialists," "members of the exploiting classes," "bourgeoisie," "lackeys," or "running dogs" of any of these groups; and later on, "revisionists" (meaning those who followed the Soviet path). And each of these nouns could be readily turned into an adjective to describe one's tainted mentality ("harboring revisionist ideas") in a kind of pre-victim designation. These are sharply contrasted with the "god categories"—"Communists," "the People," "the Party," etc.

The devil-victims, as contaminators, are associated with "filth," "evil," and various Machiavellian schemes; they are "decadent," "dying," in the midst of their "last gasps," or relegated to the "ash can of history." During the Chinese Cultural Revolution, the terms were folkloric and colorful: "demons," "devils," "monsters," "ogres," "ghosts," and "freaks." These words suggest the death-tainted and nonviable, those severed from human continuity. In contrast, the "god categories" are "the way of the future," "on the side of history," energized by knowledge and virtue and an aura of progress and permanence—in other words, on a direct path to immortality. We then see the "logic" of the totalist theme of "dispensing of existence"—and of acting upon that theme by persecuting, in whatever form, members of the "devil group." We can also understand the special emotion behind the term *deviationist* or *revisionist*. For these suggest a person who originally embraced the true path to immortality but then, while claiming to maintain it, created a subversive alternative that threatened to undermine the entire immortalizing structure.[42]

Rightist political rhetoric calls forth similar principles in more or less reverse fashion. In America, for instance, the "devil term" has been "Communist" (whether as noun or adjective). Variations have included "atheistic communism," "Communist dupe," being "soft on communism"— as well as "collectivism," "socialism," or even "liberalism" or "liberal." These tend to be equated with "un-American" or with "destroying our American way of life," "threatening the fabric of American life," or "subverting American values." Though the categories can become stereotyped, and the terms applied almost automatically, they nonetheless connect with deep anxieties around desymbolization and imagery of death taint. (The same can be said of former Vice-President Agnew's more colorful invocation of "rotten apples," to characterize people in some of these devil categories.) In contrast, the "god category" has included traits and groups that suggest the pure and the eternal: in the form of hallowed principles of "individualism," "individual initiative," and "private property"; of the theological mandate of the "God-fearing"; or of the immortal cultural substance of being "part of the American way of life" or simply "American."

The first of these two forms of political victimization (mostly in the idiom of Marxism, Leninism, or Stalinism) can be called transformationist. It is carried out around a vision of remaking the individual, together with social existence in general, into something totally new. The second is restorationist, in the sense of drawing upon an equally utopian past—a golden age that never was—as the absolute human goal. These visions of Ultimate Future and Ultimate Past psychically resemble one another, based as they both are upon image-feelings of perfect harmony and total absence of conflict or strife. Those image-feelings connect at the individual-psychological level with the perceived "oneness" of the early mother-child relationship, and at the collective level with religious and philosophical visions (both Eastern and Western) of absolute spiritual harmony. Thus, whether a member of the Chinese Communist "Red Guard" (during the Cultural Revolution of the late 1960s) persecutes alleged "reactionaries" or "revisionists," or an American Minute Man (or member of the John Birch Society) seeks to suppress or deal violently with alleged "Communists," the victimizing imagery is part of a quest for that oneness. If only we could eliminate those disturbers of the cosmic peace, the imagery implies, we could achieve total brotherhood of our own (biosocial immortality) and a psychic state of absolute purity (experiential transcendence). In victimizing others, then, one seeks not only to master ongoing history but to enter into a state outside of historical time.

Not all expressions of transformation and restoration are associated with victimization—there are endless varieties of both in historical experience in general. But they can be extremely dangerous when they enter a totalizing, and victimizing, phase. The classical sequence is from transformation (revolution) to restoration (counterrevolution). Jean-Paul Sartre, in his classical essay on anti-Semitism, brilliantly suggests some of these principles, in ways that apply to German Nazis and their American imitators no less than French anti-Semites. Sartre first identifies anti-Semitism as a "total choice of oneself, a comprehensive attitude that one adopts not only toward Jews but toward men in general, toward history

and society . . . a conception of the world . . . [a] syncretic totality."[43]
It is, in other words, an involvement of the entire symbolic life. He goes on
to stress the importance for the anti-Semite of the experiential element:
"[Having] chosen hate . . . it is the *state* of passion that he loves." Sartre
speaks of what we could call restorationist nostalgia for perfect harmony,
a vision in which "the primitive community will suddenly reappear and
attain its temperature of fusion"—hence the slogan, "reunion of all
Frenchmen!" History is seen as a Manichean "struggle of the principle of
Good with the principle of Evil" in which "one . . . must triumph and
the other be annihilated"—the quest for immortalizing purity behind all
victimizing totalism:

Underneath the bitterness of the anti-Semite is concealed the optimistic
belief that harmony will be re-established of itself, once Evil is eliminated
. . . Knight-errant of the Good, the anti-Semite is a holy man. The Jew
also is holy in his manner—holy like the untouchables, like savages under
the interdict of a taboo. Thus the conflict is raised to a religious plane,
and the end of the combat can be nothing other than a holy destruction.[44]

Finally, Sartre emphasizes the pervasive death anxiety so central to the
whole process:

[The anti-Semite] is a man who is afraid. Not of the Jews, to be sure, but
of himself, of his consciousness, of his liberty, of his instincts, of his
responsibilities, of solitariness, of change, of society, and of the world—of
everything except the Jews. He is a coward who does not want to admit
his cowardice to himself; a murderer who represses and censures his
tendency to murder without being able to hold it back, yet who dares to
kill only in effigy or protected by the anonymity of the mob; a malcon-
tent who dares not revolt from fear of the consequences of his rebellion.
. . . Anti-Semitism, in short, is fear of the human condition.[45]

This fear of the human condition is bound up with primal anxieties
around separation, annihilation, and stasis, with the death imagery
associated with radically impaired symbolization of immortality. The
victimizer seeks public confirmation of the absolute distinction between
his own immortality and the victim's death taint—when an Albigensian
recanted his heresy before the Papal Inquisition, when a Jew renounced
his religion and asserted his conversion to Christianity before the Spanish
Inquisition, when a Chinese intellectual condemned his bourgeois past
and affirmed his embrace of communism, when an American ex-radical
renounced his evil associations before a congressional committee and
affirmed his Americanism—all these provided public theater for the reassertion of the "true path" to immortality, always set off against the "deadly
error" of the wrong path. When the process becomes extensive or violent—

the public autos-da-fé of the Spanish Inquisition, the Red Guard denunciations and physical abuse of old party members, and the McCarthyite vilification of distinguished American statesmen—it reflects the resurgence of death anxiety within the victimizing group. And since the state of transcendent unity sought is never attainable, the hunger for victims may be unassuageable.

ERNEST A. MENZE

OBEDIENCE AND HUMAN AUTONOMY

Though a consensus of scholars concerning the merits of a concept incorporating regimes of the Left as well as of the Right, in terms of their governing features, may never be reached, the demand to account for the dynamics of twentieth-century mass-movement regimes continues unabated. The contributors to this volume appear to agree on the need for further exploration of the various questions raised in connection with the topic of totalitarianism, whether they approve of the concept or not. The question of the often-enthusiastic support given to totalitarian regimes appears to be incompletely understood. The contributions of Professor Milgram and Dr. Lifton provide some answers and suggest avenues of further research. This epilogue reflects on their work.

Dr. Lifton's efforts are directed to help us grasp better the psychological universe created by holocaust. As he says: "For only by understanding more of what happens to victims and survivors, and of what motivates victimizers, can we begin to imagine the future holocausts that threaten us, and thereby take steps to avoid them."[1]

In this context, Professor Milgram's work, with its apparently hopeless prognosis regarding the future of humanity, is of particular interest. If ordinary Americans, given proper legitimization of authority, are capable of inflicting pain on innocent victims, so it seems, what hope is there for the rest of humanity, less blessed—on the whole—with the freedom of information and movement Americans enjoy? Man's inclination to obey authority appears too deeply rooted to allow for transcendence of these anthropological shackles. Are the victimizers, then, in turn merely "victims" of evolutionary forces? Is a general pardon for them thus suggested? This is not how Professor Milgram's work is to be interpreted. Rather, a connection between Dr. Lifton's concern with the obstacles in the way of "protean man" and Professor Milgram's definition of these obstacles appears to be in order. By defining these obstacles, that is, by making clear their ancient roots and enormous extent, but by simultaneously rendering finite their power to obstruct, Professor Milgram enables us to forge the weapons to overcome not only the extremes of man's cruelty to man, but also to cut down the numbness and indifference of the bystander. In this context, Professor Milgram's introduction into his experiments of variables such as adjustments in the physical proximity of subject and victim, variations in the utilization of peer pressure, etc., have been instrumental.[2]

Dr. Lifton's work makes clear that the holocaust teaches us something about our more ordinary confrontations with death and violence.

The Milgram experiments, in their extreme demonstration of man's capacity to inflict pain, given proper legitimization, teach us something about "more ordinary confrontations" with obedience, conformity, and their dismal consequences.

Dr. Lifton convinces us of the *necessity* to find connections between the extreme and the ordinary in our experience. This epilogue focuses on the need to find the connection between the extreme and the ordinary in the experience of Nazi Germany. Dr. Lifton's conception of the nature of the investigator's own involvement, "that combination Buber called distance and relation"[3] serves as a reminder of the Scylla of too much distance and the Charybdis of romanticizing and glorifying the personal experience, of "spurious neutrality and compensatory glorification," as a path is charted across the universe shaped by holocaust. In the process it became necessary to challenge the notion that terror is ". . . the essence of totalitarian domination",[4] that it is the principal tool of population control.[5] The evidence of the terror applied by totalitarian regimes is, of course, indisputable. Nevertheless, it appears that in the case of Germany, what to the victims was terror, to most Germans appeared to be justice overdue those who broke the bonds of order. Of course, most of those stressing the role of terror are not unaware of the "voluntary aspects" of totalitarianism.[6] Theodor Adorno and his associates convincingly indicated the conditions apt to shape a "political philosophy and social outlook which has no room for anything but a desperate clinging to what appears to be strong and a disdainful rejection of whatever is relegated to the bottom," and Bruno Bettelheim pointed out that "Kadavergehorsam"—corpselike obedience, traditionally expected of German soldiers and exemplified by Eichmann—was not too long ago considered to be the most desirable attitude of the American slave.[7] The devotion to and enthusiastic support of totalitarian regimes by the multitudes speak to us out of the record unambiguously. Yet the tenor of the textbook interpretations remains one emphasizing terror and clever manipulation; the question of the basic disposition, the readiness to accept and to submit to authority, though fully explored and elucidated by perceptive researchers, does not seem to penetrate the presentations in classrooms and the media. For example, a Brooklyn College political scientist, examining "The Murderous Mind" of Adolf Eichmann in the pages of *The New York Times Magazine* (via an analysis of six psychologists who were not apprised of the subject's identity when asked to examine his psychological test drawings), attributed the "enormities perpetrated by the Third Reich" to a "handful of psychopaths" who rallied "to their banner a large proportion of the psychopathic population of Germany" and "kept the rest of the German population in check by a reign of real (and, even more effective, imagined) terror."[8]

When an astounding set of experiments such as those of Stanley Milgram reveals the universality of man's disposition to obedience which, conditioned by evolution, under given circumstances defies even the most elementary commands of human decency, such findings are applied to relevant historical situations only reluctantly. How can the setting of an American laboratory in which a carefully selected number of volunteers is deceived into believing that each of them is administering electric shocks—in the name of science—to an imaginative actor-subject, writhing in pain, be compared to the gruesomely real practices of the totalitarian regimes? Evidently, a careful distinction between today's labs and Hitler's horror chambers must be made. Particularly, the traditional German emphasis on obedience as a prime virtue must not be lost sight of.

Hermann Glaser shocked his countrymen in 1964 when his *Spiesser Ideologie*, published here under the title *The Cultural Roots of National Socialism*, pinpointed their longstanding propensity to submit joyfully to the most banal and awful of authorities.[9]

His samples of the "poetry of security"—*Sekuritätsdichtung*, so closely tied to obedience and authority, submissiveness and power—ranging from trashy popular songs to the artistic niveau of Stefan George, indicate what nurtured the minds and spirits of generations of Germans in the last century and a half and helped ready them for the things to come.[10] A perusal of the "Gartenlaube"-type "family" periodical literature of the nineteenth century confirms Glasser's samples as representative: Page after page one runs into German loyalty, German duty, German discipline, German virtue, German honor, but more than anything else, German loyalty as the expression of German being. Not only were the anti-Napoleonic "Wars of Liberation" "holy wars"; even Bismarck's war (with Austria) against little Denmark was a "holy war," and the popular taste ran to "Hingabe," devotion and submission.[11] To be sure, there was other fare. But it was more often than not left untouched or misread. Even a "sob story" such as Louise Mühlbach's "Der Kurfürst und der Geldfürst" ("The Prince Elector and the Money Prince"), supposedly depicting Meyer Amschel Rothschild's life in terms of his relations to the Hessian elector, though caricaturing ghetto life, contained constructive thoughts. But in the end it was Rothschild's loyalty to the Hessian Kurfürst that was served to the journal's readers as the lesson to be learned from this tale.[12] It was the Jew's *German* loyalty and reliability, based on his obedience to an authority he had defined himself to be subject to, that was his saving grace.

The dangerous confusion of loyalty and obedience eventually became a national obsession. When the belt buckles of Himmler's SS read "Meine Ehre heisst Treue" ("My honor is loyalty"), this really meant "My honor is obedience."[13] In the case of Germany, then, obedience to authority was not so much induced by fear; it represented the satisfaction of a "longing to please," bred into people in Milgram's terms of prehistorical evolution as well as in the terms of concretely definable historical circumstances spanning many centuries.

An explanation of the German embrace of totalitarian rule in the absence of outright terror against those who embraced it may be found in Jürgen Habermas's critique of Hannah Arendt's "Communications Concept of Power."[14] To Arendt, Habermas observed, it was the police state which isolated men from one another and brought them to act politically—but to be sure, not in terms of genuine political action—as accomplices of the totalitarian regime.[15] Habermas does not see Arendt's claim—he calls it her "credo"—of the "impotence of the powerful," who have "to borrow their power from the producers of power," verified in the pages of history. He does not deny that "political rule can last only so long as it is recognized as legitimate." But he feels that such recognition is induced by means of "unperceived structural violence" which shapes ideologies through "inconspicuously working communication blocks."[16] Thus Habermas asserts,

one can give a plausible account of how convictions are formed in which subjects deceive themselves about themselves and their situation. Ideologies are, after all, illusions that are outfitted with the power of common convictions. This proposal is an attempt to render the communicative production of power in a more realistic version. In systematically restricted communications, those involved form convictions subjectively free from constraint, convictions which are, however, illusionary. They thereby communicatively generate a power which, as soon as it is institutionalized, can also be used against them.[17]

Coined by the Norwegian political scientist Johan Galtung, in reference to the coercive force exerted on developing nations—not by the political influence of the industrial states, but by the structures of the world market—the term *structural violence* was adapted by Habermas and others to depict the impact of unperceived communication blocks in the shaping of values and dependencies.[18] Characterizing "conditions of dependence rooted in social structures which facilitate the latent application of force not necessarily apparent as the oppression of persons by persons," structural violence, in Habermas's view, may also characterize relations within a family. Pointing to empirical studies in "pathogenic," that is to say, illness causing families, Habermas observed that "an unresolved family conflict frequently is settled at the expense of the weakest family member: in such cases the family system may be described by reference to the expression 'structural violence.'"[19]

Transferred to the larger unit of the nation, the unresolved conflicts in the case of nineteenth-century Germany were settled at the expense of society's weakest members, the masses lacking antonomy. An allusion to the dependencies caused by "pathogenic" society may be seen in Freud's explication of "the mass and the primeval horde":

The awesome, coercive character of mass formation, revealed in its suggestive manifestations, therefore, may well be traced to its descent from the primeval horde. The leader of the mass still is the feared primeval father, the mass still wants to be dominated by unlimited power, it still is addicted—in the highest degree—to authority, in Le Bon's term, it thirsts for submission.[20]

Helmut Schelsky views structural violence in terms of conscious manipulation of society by the "producers of meaning" through language and professional strictures, thereby lending weight to conspiratorial theories.[21] Habermas, on the other hand, insists on the deeply rooted structural causes in the shifts of meaning that have affected crucial theoretical terms and refuses to accept the notion of effective domination by means of ideologically steered political language.[22]

There is no doubt that the regimes commonly designated as totalitarian manipulated language to exercise effective control. But this ideological steering of terminology was rooted in structures and values generated over eons, automatically satisfying primeval needs in the agents as well as in the victims of structural violence.

Habermas's notion of "unperceived structural violence" and its consequences in the generation and application of political power still allows a measure of optimism regarding the "nature of man" because, once the historical conditions of distorted communication are made clear, emancipation becomes possible. In the case of Germany this "structural violence" can be detected retrospectively in many areas and over a long period of time. More than others, Germans were conditioned to obedience by deeply rooted values. Viewed together, however, with Milgram's findings of the general readiness of man to submit to authority legitimized by ideological justification, the German model makes the nature and prospects of mankind appear in a dimmer light. Milgram's laboratory, though "manipulative," may be seen as an example of structural violence. His references to the Trobriander's witchcraft or the Jesuit's fanatical faith and inquisitory practices suggest other modes of "structural violence." Whether based on genuine consensus or "structural violence," Milgram leaves no doubt that in all cases

Ideological justification is vital in obtaining willing obedience, for it permits the person to see his behavior as serving a desirable end. Only when viewed in this light is compliance easily exacted.[23]

Though the ideological justification required for the shift to the "agentic state" is more readily at hand in some situations than in others, Milgram leaves no doubt about the general disposition of all men to submit to authority, and that *it*, rather than aggression, rage and anger enables his subjects to act cruelly toward others:

. . .Something far more dangerous [than anger and rage against others] is revealed: the capacity for man to abandon his humanity, indeed the inevitability that he does so, as he merges his unique personality into larger institutional structures.
This is a fatal flaw nature has designed into us, and which in the long run gives our species only a modest chance of survival.
It is ironic that the virtues of loyalty, discipline, and self-sacrifice that we value so highly in the individual are the very properties that create destructive organizational engines of war and bind men to malevolent systems of authority.[24]

To the National Socialists "an honorable self-subordination by mutual contract was the genius of the Germanic *Reich* idea," observed Robert Koehl. "Loyalty *(Treue)* and honor *(Ehre)* were made the ultimate values in life for upholders of the contract, whether lords or vassals."[25] But in thus, in Koehl's words, "oversimplifying the scholarly theories of the Germanic origins of feudalism" without trepidation and rather effectively, the National Socialists only demonstrated the effectiveness of the "structural violence" that, unperceived, had been done to them and to generations before them and that had destroyed whatever there had been built up of human autonomy. The ultimate tragedy, to this observer, lies in the fact that this structural violence was not caused by correctible socioeconomic structures and institutions, as the Marxists might have it, but apparently was rooted more deeply in a disposition to activate Milgram's "agentic state." This disposition in part grows out of the cumulative factors of German history, factors which help explain why Germans more readily than others find ideological justifications to inflict this "agentic state" upon themselves. Comparative studies might provide us with answers to the many questions that arise from these observations.

Stephen F. Cohen, examining the relationship of bolshevism and Stalinism, observed that "there is, in particular, the important question of Stalinism's popular support in Soviet society, a problem largely ignored and inconsistent with the imagery of a 'totalitarian' regime dominating a hapless, 'atomized' population through power techniques alone. Though the coercive aspects of the Stalinist system can scarcely be exaggerated, this seems no more adequate as a full explanation than would a similar interpretation of Hitler's Germany." And, further on, perhaps unwittingly echoing Habermas's concept of "unperceived structural violence," Cohen concluded: "Neither Bolshevik tradition, the once-modest Lenin cult, nor Stalin's personal gratification can explain the popular dimensions it acquired. For this we doubtless must return to older values and customs, to 'unwritten mandates borne by the wind.' Not surprisingly, these popular sentiments have outlived Stalin himself."[26]

Whether we look at Professor Cohen's "older values and customs" as the source of Stalin's popular social base, whether we look at the German disposition to loyalty and obedience perhaps revealed in the meaning of the word *brav* (differing from the connotation of courage and daring prevalent in French and English by clearly depicting the quality of being *folgsam* and *artig*—i.e., "obedient" in German), whether we turn to Dr. Lifton's *Thought Reform and the Psychology of Totalism in China*, we find everywhere what he called the "mystical imperative" to obey linked to sufficient legitimization, legitimization based on "milieu control."[27] Whereas Habermas perceives "structural violence" to be non-manipulative as well as unperceived by the victim, Lifton sees the manipulative behavior of those exercising "milieu control" impelled by a "special kind of mystique."[28] Though it has been many years since Dr. Lifton described "the capacity for totalism" as perhaps "most fundamentally a product of human childhood itself, of the prolonged period of helplessness and dependency through which each of us must pass,"[29] his recognition has not yet been sufficiently utilized by historians in their interpretation of the past and by social scientists in their charting of a better future. Yet without broadest recognition of this built-in human handicap, efforts to create more favorable circumstances will not be made, and individuation will not take the place of conformity.

The lesson of what Hannah Arendt called "the fearsome, word-and-thought-defying *banality of evil*" will not have been learned until contemporary consciousness comes to terms with the holocaust and its implications for all of humanity.[30] No longer will any man then be able to feel what Arendt recorded as Eichmann's reaction to the guilty verdict, that "his virtue had been abused by Nazi leaders. But he was not one of the ruling clique, he was a victim, and only the leaders deserved punishment."[31]

Although the historian is compelled to dwell in the past, and the task of the social and healing sciences is, among other things, to render contemporary man fit to dwell in peace with one another in the present and the future, cooperation between the disciplines appears possible, facilitating the building of bridges between past and present. It is unfortunate that the term psychohistory has assumed meanings in general usage not corresponding to the merits of the enterprise. Perhaps another term can be found to convey the convergence of historical forces and psychological dynamics so central to Dr. Lifton's analysis of the past and his prognosis of the "protean" future of contemporary consciousness. If historians and psychologists are to work together, in cooperation with other academic disciplines, in the shaping of a consciousness mastering the effects of holocaust and the oppressive presence of death in the twentieth century, they must begin by jointly defining terminology. This applies not only to the coordination of nomenclature in cooperative ventures in psychohistory, but also to the clarification of terms used preeminently within the disciplines, but read by the public at large, such as *totalism* in psychology and *totalitarianism* in the social sciences. As some historians and political scientists are getting ready, perhaps prematurely, to abandon the label "totalitarianism" as an insufficient classificatory tool, they ought to consult their colleagues in the behavioral sciences as to the justification of such a step.

It is highly significant that Dr. Lifton concluded his recent study of *The Life of the Self: Toward a New Psychology* with a pointed reference to Stanley Milgram, citing his warning that "Men are doomed if they act only within the alternatives handed down to them."[32] For the realization that "terror" was much less central to totalitarian rule than generally assumed, that it served varying purposes and was applied selectively, does not mean that the regimes were any less totalitarian. Rather, the disposition to total submission, so strikingly demonstrated by Milgram even in societies operating under the best of possible circumstances, calls for a redefinition of the totalitarian model, not the denial of its existence. And I suspect it will be only with the assistance of behavioral scientists that historians and social scientists will come to terms with their obligation to rethink their classificatory systems. And in Dr. Lifton's affirmation of the life of the self through confrontation, enhanced sensitivity and renewal confirmation is found that avoidance (Milgram's bystander), numbing, and stasis can be overcome—providing we admit to their existence—actually and in full flower in totalitarian regimes of the past and present, and potentially, and even more than potentially when the occasion arises, in our insufficiently liberated free societies.

NOTES

Introduction. Totalitarianism: An Outmoded Paradigm?

1. Allan Mitchell, "Bonapartism as a Model for Bismarckian Politics," *Journal of Modern History*, vol. 49, no. 2, June 1977, pp. 181-209.

2. Friedrich Gottlieb Klopstock, "Die deutsche Gelehrtenrepublik, Ihre Einrichtung, Ihre Gesetze. Geschichte des letzten Landtags," *Ausgewählte Werke* (Munich, 1962), pp. 875-929.

3. Leonard Shapiro, *Totalitarianism* (New York, Washington, London, 1972), p. 17.

4. Ibid., p. 99.

5. Wolfgang Wippermann, *Faschismustheorien: Zum Stand der gegenwärtigen Diskussion* (Darmstadt, 1975), p. 64.

6. Walter Schlangen, "Der Totalitarismusbegriff. Grundzüge seiner Entstehung, Wandlung und Kritik," *Politik und Zeitgeschichte. Beilage zur Wochenschrift Das Parlament*, vol. 20, 1970, B 44, Oct. 1970, p. 3, cited in Wippermann, *Faschismustheorien*, p. 66.

7. Reinhard Kühnl, " 'Linke' Totalitarismusversionen," in M. Greiffenhagen, R. Kühnl, J. B. Müller, *Totalitarismus: Zur Problematik eines politischen Begriffs* (Munich, 1972), p. 107. However, Neumann was by no means unaware of the structural similarities of the National Socialist and the Soviet regimes. Examining the relationship of the party to the totalitarian state he says:"One-party states reveal three types of relations between party and state. In Italy, the party is 'incorporated' in the state; the party is an organ of the state, a 'state party.' Soviet Russia gives the party full command over the state, and the periodic purges are to a considerable extent aimed at preventing the accumulation of autonomous political power in the hands of the state bureaucracy. The German type stands somewhere between the two and is difficult to analyze." Franz Neumann, *Behemoth: The Structure and Practice of National Socialism*, 1933-1944 (New York, 1942; rev. ed. 1944), p. 67.

8. Sigmund Neumann, *Permanent Revolution: Totalitarianism in the Age of International Civil War* (London, 1965; originally published under the title *The Total State in a World at War*); Ernst Fraenkel, *The Dual State: A Contribution to the Theory of Dictatorship* (New York, 1941); Hannah Arendt, *The Origins of Totalitarianism* (New York, 1951); Carl Joachim Friedrich and Zbigniew Brzezinski, *Totalitarian Dictatorship and Autocracy* (Cambridge, Mass., 1957).

9. Ernst Nolte, "Konservativismus und Nationalsozialismus," *Zeitschrift für Politik*, NF 11, 1964, pp. 5-20, reprinted in Ernst Nolte, *Marxismus, Faschismus, Kalter Krieg: Vorträge und Aufsätze, 1964-1976* (Stuttgart, 1977), pp. 117-35, 118.

10. Klaus Jürgen Müller feels that it was Ernst Nolte who "freed fascism from the context of comparative theories of totalitarianism and reinstated it as a phenomenon in its own right." Klaus Jürgen Müller, "French Fascism and Modernization," *Journal of Contemporary History*, vol. 11, no. 4, Oct. 1976, pp. 75-107. Wolfgang Wippermann credits Nolte with having "overcome the heteronomous theory of totalitarianism" (op. cit., p. 77). Professor Nolte, however, seems not inclined to accept such credit, since he does not consider the concept of totalitarianism as generally superfluous; he sees it transcending the chronological confinement of the cold war period, as operative in the development of recent theoretical constructs like that of A. James Gregor (Nolte, *Marxismus, Faschismus, Kalter Krieg*, pp. 8, 194; A. James Gregor, *The Fascist Persuasion in Radical Politics*, Princeton, N.J., 1974). See also Professor Nolte's contribution to this volume.

11. For Nolte's latest work see note 9 above. For Tucker see (in addition to his standard works on the Soviet political mind and Stalin) Robert C. Tucker, ed., *Stalinism: Essays in Historical Interpretation* (New York, 1977), esp. "Introduction: Stalinism and Comparative Communism," pp. xi-xx, xiii.

12. For an example of the New Left assault on the totalitarian concept see Bernard Blanke, "Rot gleicht Braun," *Das Argument*, 33, vol. 7, no. 2, May 1965, pp. 27-34. See also Reinhard Westphal, "Psychologische Theorien über den Faschismus," *Das Argument*, 32, vol. 7, no. 1, 1965, pp. 30-39; Wolfgang Fritz Haug et al., "Ideologische Komponenten in den Theorien über den Faschismus" (Blanke, op. cit., constitutes part of this collective effort), *Das Argument*, 33, vol. 7, no. 2, 1965, pp. 1-34; Bernhard Blanke et al., "Die Faschismus Theorie der DDR," ibid., pp. 35-48; Tim Mason, "Der Primat der Politik: Politik und Wirtschaft im Nationalsozialismus," *Das Argument*, 41, vol. 8, no. 6, 1966, pp. 473-94; Eberhard Czichon, "Der Primat der Industrie im Kartell der nationalsozialistischen Macht," *Das Argument*, 47, vol. 10, no. 3, 1968, pp. 168-92; and Mason's response, "Primat der Industrie? Eine Erwiderung," pp. 193-209, followed by Dietrich Eichholtz and Kurt Gessweiler, "Noch einmal: Politik und Wirtschaft, 1933-1945," pp. 210-27.

13. For examples of this scholarship in fascism studies see (in addition to the tenth anniversary issue of the *Journal of Contemporary History* cited in note 10 above, which was entirely devoted to fascism studies) Wolfgang Schieder, ed., *Faschismus als soziale Bewegung: Deutschland und Italien im Vergleich* (Hamburg, 1976); Hans-Ulrich Thamer and Wolfgang Wippermann, eds., *Faschistische und Neofaschistische Bewegungen: Probleme empirischer Faschismusforschung* (Darmstadt, 1977); Reinhard Kühnl, ed., *Texte zur Faschismusdiskussion: Positionen und Kontroversen* (Hamburg, 1974); Henry A. Turner, Jr., ed., *Nazism and the Third Reich* (New York, 1972) and *Reappraisals of Fascism* (New York, 1975); Renzo DeFelice, *Interpretations of Fascism* (Cambridge, Mass., and London, 1977); Walter Laqueur, ed., *Fascism: A Reader's Guide* (Berkeley and Los Angeles, 1976).

14. Karl Dietrich Bracher, *Zeitgeschichtliche Kontroversen um Faschismus, Totalitarismus, Demokratie* (Munich, 1976). Part of this work was translated for inclusion in the present volume.

2. The Concept of Totalitarianism in Political Theory

1. "The coming-to-grips with totalitarianism is one of the essential tasks in the political education of our youth. Teachers on all levels of education, therefore, are obliged to familiarize students with the characteristics of totalitarianism and the major features of bolshevism and national socialism as the most important totalitarian systems of the twentieth century." Decision of the Permanent Conference of the Ministers of Cultural Affairs, 5 July 1962, in *Laufende Mitteilungen zum Stand der politischen Bildung in der Bundesrepublik Deutschland*, ed. Friedrich Minssen (Frankfurt a.M., 1964), p. 5.

2. Otto Stammer, "Aspekte der Totalitarismusforschung," *Soziale Welt*, 12 (1961), p. 107.

3. Peter Christian Ludz, "Entwurf einer soziologischen Theorie totalitär verfasster Gesellschaft," in Peter Christian Ludz, ed., "Studien und Materialien zur Soziologie der DDR," *Kölner Zeitschrift für Soziologie und Sozialpsychologie*, Sonderheft 8 (1964), pp. 12f.

4. Martin Drath, "Totalitarismus in der Volksdemokratie," introduction to Ernst Richert, *Macht ohne Mandat* (2d ed., Cologne and Opladen, 1963), p. xiv (Schriften des Instituts für politische Wissenschaft, vol. 11).

5. Peter Christian Ludz, "Totalitarismus oder Totalität? Zur Erforschung bolschewistischer Gesellschafts- und Herrschaftssysteme," *Soziale Welt*, 12 (1961), p. 129.

6. Compare Stammer, "Totalitarismusforschung," p. 107 (see note 2 above).

7. Max G. Lange, *Politische Soziologie: Eine Einführung* (Berlin and Frankfurt a.M., 1961), p. 197.

8. Ludz, "Totalitarismus," p. 130 (see note 5 above).

9. Karl Loewenstein, *Verfassungslehre* (Tübingen, 1959), p. 57 (American ed., *Political Power and the Governmental Process*, Chicago, 1957).

10. Drath, "Totalitarismus," p. xxvi (see note 4 above).

11. Alexander Rüstow, *Ortsbestimmung der Gegenwart: Eine universalgeschichtliche Kulturkritik*, vol. 1 (Zurich, 1950), p. 19.

12. Ibid., vol. 3 (1957), p. 266.

13. Ibid., pp. 489ff.

14. Pitirim Sorokin, *Social and Cultural Dynamics* (New York, 1937; new ed., New York, 1962); compare Jules Monnerot, *Soziologie des Kommunismus* (Cologne, Berlin, 1952), pp. 301, 323, 334.

15. Franz Neumann, *Demokratischer und autoritärer Staat* (Studien zur politischen Theorie, Frankfurt a.M., Vienna, 1967), p. 236 (American ed. *The Democratic and the Authoritarian State: Essays in Legal and Political Theory*, Glencoe, Ill., 1957).

16. Robert Morrison MacIver, *Macht und Autorität* (Frankfurt a.M., 1953). pp. 181ff. (American ed., *The Web of Government*, New York, 1947); Guglièlmo Ferrero, *The Principles of Power: The Great Political Crisis of History* (New York, 1942).

17. "Totalitarismus," *Fischer-Lexikon*, vol. 2, *Staat und Politik*, ed. Ernst Fraenkel and Karl Dietrich Bracher (new ed., Frankfurt a.M., 1964), p. 328.

18. "Totalitarismus," *Staatslexikon*, vol. 7 (Freiburg, 1962), column 1018.

19. Wilhelm Hennis, *Politik und praktische Philosophie* (Neuwied and Berlin, 1963), pp. 70f.

20. Karl Popper, *Der Zauber Platons* (Bern, 1957), pp. 126ff. (English ed., *The Spell of Plato*, 3d rev. ed., London, 1957).

21. Karl Wittfogel, *Die orientalische Despotie: Eine vergleichende Untersuchung totaler Macht* (Cologne, Berlin, 1962; American ed., *Oriental Despotism: A Comparative Study of Total Power*, New Haven, Ct., 1957).

22. Eric Voegelin, *Wissenschaft, Politik und Gnosis* (Munich, 1959); idem, *Die neue Wissenschaft der Politik* (Munich, 1959).

23. Voegelin, *Wissenschaft, Politik und Gnosis*, pp. 56f, 16, 19.

24. This difficulty is encountered in the works of many of the authors addressing the phenomenon of totalitarianism in ideological terms. Compare Waldemar Gurian, "Totalitarianism as Political Religion," in Carl J. Friedrich, ed., *Totalitarianism: Proceedings of a Conference Held at the American Academy of Arts and Sciences, March 1953* (Cambridge, Mass., 1954), pp. 119ff. Expressions like "secularized religion," "substitute religion," and "*Ersatzreligion*" say little about the role played by ideology in each case. A (probably not sufficiently refined) schema was sketched by Martin Greiffenhagen, " 'Politische Theologie' und Politik Wissenschaft," *Gesellschaft—Staat—Erziehung*, 8 (1963), pp. 142ff.

25. Erwin Faul, *Der moderne Machiavellismus* (Cologne, Berlin, 1961), pp. 13, 163.

26. Hermann Rauschning, *Gespräche mit Hitler*, "Preface," cited after Faul, *Machiavellismus*, p. 302 (English ed., *Hitler Speaks: A Series of Political Conversations on His Real Aims*, London, 1939).

27. Faul, *Machiavellismus*, p. 304.

28. Ibid., pp. 338, 339, 340, 341, 344f.

29. Jacob L. Talmon, *Die Ursprünge der totalitären Demokratie* (Cologne, Opladen, 1961; English ed., *The Origins of Totalitarian Democracy*, London, 1952).

30. Compare, among many others, Kurt Schilling, *Geschichte der sozialen Ideen* (Stuttgart, 1957), pp. 293ff.; Herbert Krüger, *Allegemeine Staatslehre* (Stuttgart, 1964), pp. 762f.; John W. Chapman, *Rousseau: Totalitarian or Liberal?* (New York, 1956). Chapman speaks of "totalitarian implications" (pp. 74ff.).

31. Richard Löwenthal, "Totalitäre und demokratische Revolution," *Der Monat*, vol. 13, no. 146 (1960), p. 33.

32. Talmon, *Ursprünge*, pp. 6ff. (see note 29 above).

33. Gerhard Leibholz, *Strukturprobleme der modernen Demokratie* (Karlsruhe, 1958), p. 225.

34. Otto Stammer, "Politische Soziologie," in Arnold Gehlen and Helmut Schelsky, *Soziologie: Ein Lehr- und Handbuch zur modernen Gesellschaftskunde* (6th ed., Düsseldorf, Cologne, 1966), p. 292.

35. Löwenthal, "Totalitäre und demokratische Revolution," p. 32 (see note 31 above); Lange, *Politische Soziologie*, p. 192 (see note 7 above).

36. Sigmund Neumann, *Permanent Revolution: Totalitarianism in the Age of International War* (London, 1965); Zbigniew K. Brzezinski, *The Permanent Purge: Politics in Soviet Totalitarianism* (Cambridge, Mass., 1956); see also Löwenthal, "Totalitäre und demokratische Revolution," pp. 31ff., (see note 31 above).

37. Hannah Arendt, *Elemente und Ursprünge totaler Herrschaft* (Frankfurt a.M., 1955), p. 659 (American ed., *The Origins of Totalitarianism*, new ed., with added prefaces, New York, 1973, pp. 417-418).

38. Monnerot, *Soziologie*, p. 315 (see note 14 above).

39. Karl Mannheim, *Mensch und Gesellschaft im Zeitalter des Umbaus* (Darmstadt, 1958), pp. 129 f. (English and American eds., *Man and Society in an Age of Reconstruction: Studies in Modern Social Structures*, London, 1960; New York, 1967). The technological argument is advanced also by George F. W. Hallgarten, *Dämonen oder Retter?* (Frankfurt a.M., 1957, p. 181). Compare also Emil Lederer, *The State of the Masses* (New York, 1940), p. 45.

40. Dietrich Goldschmidt, in his introduction to Reinhard Henskys, *Die national-sozialistischen Gewaltverbrechen* (Stuttgart, Berlin, 1964), p. 13.

41. Arendt, *Elemente*, p. 750f. (English trans., pp. 476f.); see note 37 above.

42. Carl Joachim Friedrich, *Totalitäre Diktatur* (Stuttgart, 1957).

43. Ibid., p. 13.

44. I have avoided citing examples of definitions of totalitarianism based on the studies employing quantitative methods; interesting as they are *per se*, they have not yet done much to advance political theory. For examples of such efforts, see N. S. Timasheff, "Totalitarianism, Despotism, Dictatorship," in *Totalitarianism*, p. 40ff. (see note 24 above); Robert A. Dahl, "Politische Systeme: Ahnlichkeiten und Unterschiede," in Ekkehart Krippendorf, ed., *Political Science: Amerikanische Beiträge zur Politikwissenschaft* (Tübingen, 1966), p. 149ff.

45. In the following it cannot be my purpose to develop a comprehensive theory of the total state. I only raise points that appear to me to be particularly significant to a theory of totalitarianism and base my comments mainly on the study of Ernst Forsthoff, *Der totale Staat* (Hamburg, 1931). This study offers a wealth of pertinent material. For a useful overview of the literature, see Gerhard Schulz, "Der Begriff des Totalitarismus und der Nationalsozialismus," *Soziale Welt*, 12 (1961), pp. 112ff.

46. Adam H. Müller, *Die Elemente der Staatskunst*, Jakob Baxa, ed., vol. 1, (Jena, 1922), p. 48; *Die Herdflamme* (Othmar Spann, ed., 1, 1).

47. Compare Martin Greiffenhagen, *Das Dilemma des Konservativismus* in *Deutschland* (Munich, 1971).

48.   Ernst Forsthoff, *Der totale Staat* (Hamburg, 1933), p. 29.
49.   Ibid., p. 30; compare also pp. 33, 34, 41, 42, 42.
50.   Forsthoff, *Der totale Staat*, pp. 33, 34 (see note 48 above).
51.   Compare Ibid., pp. 29, 30, 31, 33, 34, 37, 38, 43. The differentiation of the authoritarian and the total state was introduced by Heinz O. Ziegler, *Autoritärer oder totaler Staat* (Tübingen, 1932; vol. 90 of *Recht und Geschichte in Staat und Gegenwart*).
52.   Compare ibid., pp. 39f.; in this respect Forsthoff follows the "friend-foe" thesis of Carl Schmitt. For the orientation of the National Socialist concept of the people toward "origins," see Hans Freyer, *Der politische Begriff des Volkes* (Neumünster, 1933); Ernst Wilhelm Eschmann, *Vom Sinn der Revolution* (Jena, 1933).
53.   Ibid., p. 41. These sentences reveal clearly that the National Socialist state did not, strictly speaking, call for or even permit democratic legitimization–a point to be discussed further in the following.
54.   Adolf Hitler, *Mein Kampf* (Munich, 1937), p. 420.
55.   Compare Forsthoff, *Der totale Staat*, pp. 43ff.
56.   Ralf Dahrendorf, *Gesellschaft und Demokratie in Deutschland* (Munich, 1965), p. 434 (American ed., *Society and Democracy in Germany*, New York, 1967, p. 404).
57.   Ibid., p. 437 (American ed., pp. 407-8).
58.   David Schoenbaum, *Hitler's Social Revolution: Class and Stature in Nazi Germany, 1933-1939* (New York, 1966), p. xxii.
59.   Dahrendorf, *Gesellschaft*, p. 448 (see note 56 above).
60.   Compare Paul Sering (pseudonym of Richard Löwenthal), *Jenseits des Kapitalismus* (Lauf bei Nürnberg, 1946), pp. 118ff.; *Revolution*, pp. 29ff. (see note 31 above).
61.   Drath, "Totalitarismus," pp. xxvi, xxvii, (see note 4 above).
62.   Loewenstein, *Verfassungslehre*, pp. 53, 55 (see note 9 above).
63.   This widely accepted thesis was expressed in this form by von der Gablentz: "Authoritarian states differ from total states fundamentally in that they are not ideological and therefore permit areas of freedom outside the political realm." Otto Heinrich von der Gablentz, *Einführung in die Politische Wissenschaft* (Cologne, Opladen, 1965), p. 272.
64.   Loewenstein, *Verfassungslehre*, p. 53 (see note 9 above).
65.   Theo Stammen, *Regierungssysteme der Gegenwart* (Stuttgart, Berlin, Cologne, Mainz, 1967), pp. 124ff.
66.   Maurice Duverger, *Die politischen Regime* (Hamburg, 1960).
67.   Eleonore Sterling, *Der unvollkommene Staat: Studien über Diktatur und Demokratie* (Frankfurt, a.M., 1965).
68.   Drath, "Totalitarismus," p. xxxi, (see note 4 above).
69.   Loewenstein, *Verfassungslehre*, p. 56 (see note 9 above).
70.   Drath, "Totalitarismus," p. xvii (see note 4 above).
71.   Stammer, "Totalitarismusforschung," pp. 100, 102 (see note 2 above).
72.   Ludz, "Soziologische Theorie," pp. 18, 19, 21 (see note 3 above).
73.   Drath, "Totalitarismus," p. xvii (see note 4 above). Loewenstein, too, considers the establishment of an integral totalitarian system a difficult task (see Loewenstein, *Verfassungslehre*, p. 57, see note 9 above); compare also Otto Stammer, "Gesellschaft and Politik," in Werner Ziegenfuss, ed., *Handbuch der Soziologie* (Stuttgart, 1956), p. 580.
74.   Compare George F. Kennan, "Totalitarianism in the Modern World," in *Totalitarianism*, p. 19 (see note 24 above); Leo Löwenthal, "Discussion," ibid., p. 222; Karl Dietrich Bracher, *Die Auflösung der Weimarer Republik: Eine Studie zum Problem des Machtverfalls in der Demokratie* (3d ed., Villingen, 1960), pp. 97f.; Maurice Duverger, *Die politischen Regime* (Hamburg, 1960), pp. 117ff.; Hartmut Zimmermann, "Probleme der Analyse bolschwistischer Gesellschafts-

systeme: Ein Diskussionsbeitrag zur Frage der Anwendbarkeit des Totalitarismusbegriffs," *Gewerkschaftliche Monatshefte*, 12 (1961), p. 198; Arnold Künzli, "Rot ist nicht braun," ibid., pp. 207ff.; Stammer, "Totalitarismusforschung," p. 105 (see note 2 above); Lange, *Politische Soziologie*, p. 197 (see note 7 above); Ernst Nolte, *Der Faschismus in seiner Epoche* (Munich, 1963), p. 34 (American ed., *The Three Faces of Fascism*, New York, Chicago, San Francisco, 1965); Oskar Anweiler, "Totalitäre Erziehung: Eine vergleichende Untersuchung zum Problem des Totalitarismus," *Gesellschaft–Staat–Erziehung*, 9 (1964), pp. 179ff.; Greiffenhagen, "Totalitarismus rechts and links: Ein Vergleich von Nationalsozialismus and Kommunismus," *Gesellschaft–Staat–Erziehung*, 12 (1967), pp. 285ff.

75. Dahrendorf, *Gesellschaft*, p. 445 (see note 56 above).

76. Zimmermann, "Bolschewistische Gesellschaftssysteme," p. 196 (see note 74 above); George F. W. Hallgarten, for that reason, calls the National Socialist movement pseudorevolutionary (*Why Dictators? The Causes and Forms of Tyrranical Rule Since 600 B.C.*, New York, 1954).

77. Compare Christian Graf von Krochow, "Nationalstaat und Demokratie: Zur Geschichte und Gegenwart eines deutschen Strukturproblems," *Gesellschaft–Staat–Erziehung*, 12 (1967), pp. 98ff.

78. von der Gablentz, "Einfürung," p. 267 (see note 63 above).

79. Dahrendorf, *Gesellschaft*, p. 441 (see note 56 above).

80. Hans Buchheim, *Totalitäre Herrschaft: Wesen und Merkmale* (Munich, 1962), p. 33 (American ed., *Totalitarian Rule: Its Nature and Characteristics*, Middletown, Ct., 1968). Also in the same vein: Klaus Hornung, *Totalitäre Herrschaft* (Schriftenreihe der Landesanstalt für Erziehung und Unterricht: Politik und Soziologie, vols. 1-3, Stuttgart, 1966).

81. Compare Helmut Gollwitzer, for example, ... *und führen, wohin du nicht willst: Bericht einer Gefangenschaft* (Munich, 1951).

82. T. W. Adorno, Else Frenkel-Brunswick, Daniel J. Levinson, and R. Nevitt Sandford, *The Authoritarian Personality* (New York, 1950, 1969), p. 632.

83. Schulz, "Totalitarismus," p. 114 (see note 45 above).

84. Ibid., p. 114.

85. S. S. Jenkner, "Zur Anwendung von Integrations- und Konfliktmodellen bei der Erforschung bolschewistischer Gesellschafts- und Herrschaftssysteme," *Moderne Welt*, 3 (1961/62), p. 381.

86. Compare Heinz Höhne, *Der Orden unter dem Totenkopf: Die Geschichte der SS* (Güterslohe, 1967).

87. von der Gablentz, "Einführung," p. 271 (see note 63 above).

88. Herbert Marcuse, *Kultur und Gesellschaft* (vol. 1, Frankfurt, 1967), p. 37.

89. Compare Seymour Martin Lipset, *Political Man: The Social Bases of Politics* (London, Melbourne, Toronto, 1960), pp. 140ff.; Otto Sauer, Herbert Marcuse, Arthur Rosenberg et al., *Faschismus und Kapitalismus: Theorien über die sozialen Ursachen und die Funktion des Faschismus* (Frankfurt, Vienna, 1967).

90. Karl Marx and Friedrick Engels, *Manifest der kommunistischen Partei* (Berlin, 1967), p. 28 (italics mine).

91. Loewenstein, *Verfassungslehre*, p. 57 (see note 9 above).

92. Ludz, "Totalitarismus," p. 132 (see note 5 above).

93. Ludz, "Soziologische Theorie," pp. 18f. (see note 3 above); idem, "Totalitarismus," pp. 133ff. (see note 5 above); Stammer, "Totalitarismusforschung," p. 106 (see note 2 above); Zimmermann, "Bolschewistische Gesellschaftssysteme," pp. 198ff. (see note 74 above).

94. Werner Hofmann, *Stalinismus und Antikommunismus: Zur Soziologie des Ost-West-Konflikts* (Frankfurt a.M., 1967), pp. 40, 13, 93f.

95. Ibid., p. 18.

96. Compare Schulz, "Totalitarismus," p. 125 (see note 45 above). See also Zimmermann, "Bolschewistische Gesellschaftssysteme," p. 196 (see note 74 above).

97. Hofmann, *Stalinismus*, p. 19 (see note 94 above).

98. Ernst Nolte, *Der Faschismus in seiner Epoche*, p. 34f. (see note 74 above).

99. John H. Herz and Gwendolen M. Carter, *Regierungsformen des zwanzigsten Jahrhunderts* (Stuttgart, 1962), p. 15; von der Gablentz, "Einführung," p. 262 (see note 63 above).
100. Compare Hans-Joachim Lieber, "Ideologie und Wissenschaft im totalitären System," in Walter Hofer, ed., *Wissenschaft im totalen Staat* (Munich, 1964), pp. 14ff.; Mannheim, *Mensch und Gesellschaft*, pp. 129ff. (see note 39 above).

3. Bolshevism and Stalinism

1. I base this judgment on a survey of the literature published from the late 1940s onward. Other writers have commented, approvingly or disapprovingly, on this consensus. See Hannah Arendt, "Understanding Bolshevism," *Dissent*, January-February, 1953, pp. 580–83; Isaac Deutscher, *Russia in Transition* (New York, 1960), p. 217; and H. T. Willets, "Death and Damnation of a Hero," *Survey*, April, 1963, p. 9. A major exception over the years has been Robert C. Tucker, who sees major discontinuities, even a "gulf," between bolshevism and Stalinism. See the essays collected in his *Soviet Political Mind* (rev. ed., New York, 1971). Barrington Moore's *Soviet Politics: The Dilemma of Power* (rev. ed., New York, 1965) differs from the consensus interpretation in important respects but generally falls into the continuity school.
2. This essay grows out of a larger study which includes a more general critique of Western literature on Soviet history and politics.
3. For a similar point, see Robert M. Slusser, "A Soviet Historian Evaluates Stalin's Role in History," *American Historical Review*, vol. 77, no. 5 (December, 1972), p. 1393. Until recently there were few academic studies of Soviet Stalinism as a specific phenomenon. For an early and interesting attempt to define and analyze Stalinism as a political movement in Western Communist parties, see Irving Howe and Lewis Coser, *The American Communist Party: A Critical History* (Boston, 1957), chap. 11.
4. Abraham Rothberg, *The Heirs of Stalin; Dissidence and the Soviet Regime* (Ithaca, N.Y., 1972), pp. 377–78. For a similar critical point, see Tucker, *Soviet Political Mind*, p. 19.
5. Perhaps the first writer to argue that Stalin's policies should be termed "Stalinism" and "not Marxism or even Leninism" was Walter Duranty. See his series of dispatches to the *New York Times* in June 1931, collected in *Duranty Reports Russia* (New York, 1934), pp. 186–219. They were answered, and the term *Stalinism* rejected, by the leader of the Communist Opposition in the United States. Jay Lovestone, "The Soviet Union and Its Bourgeois Critics," *Revolutionary Age*, August 8, 22, and September 15, 1931.
6. Leon Trotsky, *Stalinism and Bolshevism* (New York, 1972), pp. 15, 17, and his *Revolution Betrayed* (New York, 1945). See also "Does the Soviet Government Still Follow the Principles Adopted Twenty Years Ago" *Writings of Leon Trotsky, 1937-38* (New York, 1970), pp. 169–72; and *Their Morals and Ours* (New York, 1937).
7. Many Soviet and non-Soviet Communists later said that their critical attitude toward Stalinism was diminished in the 1930s by their perceived choice between Soviet Russia and Hitler's Germany. This explanation is often dismissed unfairly. Such an outlook also influenced the thinking of non-Communists, including some anti-Communist Russian émigrés. See, for example, Nicholas Berdyaev, *The Origins of Russian Communism* (Ann Arbor, Mich., 1960), p. 147.
8. The main sources for the debate include Trotsky's *Biulleten' oppozitsii* (4 vols., New York, Monad Press Reprint, 1973), and Trotskyist and radical journals published in Europe and the United States. Several interesting books grew out of the debate; some are cited below.
9. Dwight MacDonald, in *Partisan Review*, Winter, 1945, p. 186. He was criticizing an article in the same issue by James Burnham, "Lenin's Heir," which

argued that "under Stalin, the Communist revolution has been, not betrayed, but fulfilled" (p. 70). For a similar methodological point, see Tucker, *Soviet Political Mind*, p. 6.
10. Michael Karpovich, "The Russian Revolution of 1917," *Journal of Modern History*, vol. 2, no. 2 (June, 1930), p. 253.
11. *The Gulag Archipelago*, vols. 1-2 (New York, 1974), p. 137; and his "Understanding Communism," *The New Leader*, August 4, 1975, p. 8.
12. See, respectively, Karpovich in *Partisan Review*, July, 1949, pp. 759-60; *The Soviet Union: Background, Ideology, Reality*, ed. Waldemar Gurian (Notre Dame, Indiana, 1951), p. 7; Reshetar, *Concise History of the Communist Party* (New York, 1960), pp. 218-19; Daniels, *The Conscience of the Revolution: Communist Opposition in Soviet Russia* (Cambridge, Mass., 1960), p. 403; Brzezinski in *The Development of the USSR: An Exchange of Views*, ed. Donald W. Treadgold (Seattle, Wash., 1964), p. 6; McNeal, *The Bolshevik Tradition: Lenin, Stalin, Khrushchev* (Englewood Cliffs, N.J., 1963), pp. 136-37; Ulam, *The Unfinished Revolution* (New York, 1960), p. 198; and *The Bolsheviks* (New York, 1965), p. 477; *Essential Works of Marxism*, ed. Arthur P. Mendel (New York, 1965), p. 199; Azrael in *Authoritarian Politics in Modern Society*, ed. Samuel P. Huntington and Clement H. Moore (New York, 1970), pp. 266-67; Willets in *Survey*, April, 1963, p. 9. See also Alfred G. Meyer, *Leninism* (New York, 1962), pp. 282-83.
13. Waldemar Gurian, *Bolshevism: An Introduction to Soviet Communism* (Notre Dame, Indiana, 1952), p. 3.
14. This has been the customary explanation of collectivization and the purges. Many examples could be cited, but see two standard works: Zbigniew K. Brzezinski, *The Permanent Purge: Politics in Soviet Totalitarianism* (Cambridge, Mass., 1956), p. 50 and *passim*; and Naum Jasny, *The Socialized Agriculture of the USSR* (Stanford, Calif., 1949), p. 18.
15. *How Russia is Ruled* (rev. ed., Cambridge, Mass., 1963), p. 59. One of the best books in Soviet studies, it is marred chiefly by an interpretative perspective of an inexorable process toward a "full-blown totalitarian regime" (pp. 12, 31, 37, 91, 95, 102, 109, 116, 128). For similar allusions, see Tucker, *Soviet Political Mind*, p. 178; Robert V. Daniels, *The Nature of Communism* (New York, 1962), p. 111; Gurian, *Bolshevism*, p. 72; Brzezinski in *Development of the USSR*, p. 6; McNeal, *Bolshevik Tradition*, p. 70; Ulam, *The Bolsheviks*, p. 541; John A. Armstrong, *The Politics of Totalitarianism* (New York, 1961), p. x.
16. Adam B. Ulam, *The New Face of Soviet Totalitarianism* (New York, 1965), pp. 48, 49. Similarly, "The steady advance of the Soviet system to the absolutism, or totalitarianism, of full Stalinism makes the process seem inevitable." Robert G. Wesson, *The Soviet Russian State* (New York, 1972), p. 96.
17. See, for example, Bertram D. Wolfe, *An Ideology in Power: Reflections on the Russian Revolution* (New York, 1969).
18. Milovan Djilas, *The New Class: An Analysis of the Communist System* (New York, 1957), pp. 51, 53, 56, 57, 167-68; and his "Beyond Dogma," *Survey*, Winter, 1971, pp. 181-88. For Burnham, see his *Managerial Revolution* (New York, 1941), pp. 220-21; and above, note 9.
19. Many other ex-Communists contributed to the continuity thesis. On this, see Isaac Deutscher's intemperate but interesting essay, "The Ex-Communist's Conscience," *Russia in Transition*, pp. 223-36. A notable exception is Wolfgang Leonhard, who insists that "Stalinism does not by any means represent the logical or consistent continuation of Leninism" (*The Three Faces of Marxism*, New York, 1974, p. 358). See also his solitary position in a survey on the question in *The Review: A Quarterly of Pluralist Socialism* (Brussels), no. 2-3, 1962, pp. 45-68.
20. For a discussion of Carr and Deutscher, see Walter Laqueur, *The Fate of the Revolution: Interpretations of Soviet History* (New York, 1967), pp. 96-108, 111-33.
21. E. H. Carr, *Studies in Revolution* (New York, 1964), p. 214.

22. "Russia in Transition," *Dissent*, Winter, 1955, p. 24; *Russia in Transition*, pp. 216-18; *Russia after Stalin* (London, 1969), pp. 21-22, 28-29, 33-34, and chap. 2. *passim*; and *The Prophet Unarmed: Trotsky, 1921-1929* (London, 1966), p. 463. Deutscher regarded the "balance between change and continuity" as the "most difficult and complex problem by which the student of the Soviet Union is confronted." He disclaimed having "struck any faultless balance" on the question (*Ironies of History*, London, 1966, p. 234; *Russia in Transition*, p. 217).
23. I am quoting Hannah Arendt. Speaking of participants at a conference in 1967, she continued: "Those who were more or less on the side of Lenin's revolution also justified Stalin, whereas those who were denouncing Stalin's rule were sure that Lenin was not only responsible for Stalin's totalitarianism but actually belongs in the same category, that Stalin was a necessary consequence of Lenin." *Revolutionary Russia*, ed. Richard Pipes (Cambridge, Mass., 1968), p. 345.
　　One other scholarly tradition should be mentioned. Some writers interpreted the Stalin years in the context of Russian historical and cultural traditions. This emphasis on the resurgent Russian-ness of Stalinism might have led them to conceptualize discontinuities between bolshevism and Stalinism. Instead, they blurred dissimilarities by treating both as "communism" and continuous, or by tracing resurgent traditions back to early Soviet history. See, for example, Nicholas S. Timasheff, *The Great Retreat: The Growth and Decline of Communism in Russia* (New York, 1946); Berdyaev, *Origins of Russian Communism*; Dinko Tomasic, *The Impact of Russian Culture on Soviet Communism* (Glencoe, Ill., 1953); and Edward Crankshaw, *Cracks in the Kremlin Wall* (New York, 1951). More recently, Zbigniew Brzezinski has treated Soviet political history in terms of a dominant autocratic "Russian political culture." He interprets bolshevism-Leninism as a "continuation of the dominant tradition," and thus Stalinism as "an extension—rather than an aberration—of what immediately preceded." "Soviet Politics: From the Future to the Past?" (This article will appear in a volume of essays in honor of Merle Fainsod to be published by Harvard University Press. I am grateful to Professor Brzezinski for allowing me to read and cite it in advance.)
24. Maximilien Rubel in *Revolutionary Russia*, p. 316. Similarly, see Cyril E. Black, "The Modernization of Russia," *The Transformation of Russian Society: Aspects of Social Change since 1861*, ed. Cyril E. Black (Cambridge, Mass., 1967), p. 678; Theodore H. Von Laue, *Why Lenin? Why Stalin?* (Philadelphia and New York, 1964), pp. 202, 206; Alec Nove, "Was Stalin Really Necessary?" *Encounter*, April, 1962, pp. 86-92. One advocate of the development approach says that the "most salient fact about the Soviet Revolution . . . is its remarkable history of continuity . . ." Alex Inkeles, *Social Change in Soviet Russia* (New York, 1971), p. 41. Another problem with the modernization approach to the Soviet 1930s is that it obscures other important developments in economic, social, and political life which were not "modern" but traditional and even retrogressive.
25. Among them are Moshe Lewin's *Lenin's Last Struggle* (New York, 1968), *Russian Peasants and Soviet Power: A Study of Collectivization* (Evanston, Ill., 1968), and *Political Undercurrents in Soviet Economic Debates: From Bukharin to the Modern Reformers* (Princeton, N.J., 1974); Robert C. Tucker's *Stalin as Revolutionary, 1879-1929: A Study in History and Personality* (New York, 1973); and my *Bukharin and the Bolshevik Revolution: A Political Biography, 1888-1938* (New York, 1973). An early work that challenged the thesis indirectly was Alexander Erlich, *The Soviet Industrialization Debate, 1924-1938* (Cambridge, Mass., 1960).
26. The first comment is from Adam B. Ulam, *Stalin: The Man and His Era* (New York, 1973), p. 352; see also pp. 282, 294, 362. The other two are from Richard Gregor's intoduction to *Resolutions and Decisions of the Communist Party of the Soviet Union*, vol. 2, ed. Richard Gregor (Toronto, 1974), p. 38. I base this statement on a survey of recent historical writings by scholars of both generations, and of scholarly reviews of five recent books that treat the relationship between bolshevism and Stalinism: Roy Medvedev, *Let History Judge: The Origins and Consequences of*

Stalinism (New York, 1971); Solzhenitsyn, *The Gulag Archipelago*; Ulam, *Stalin*; Tucker, *Stalin as Revolutionary*; Cohen, *Bukharin and the Bolshevik Revolution*. It should be noted here that, unlike an earlier generation of historically minded political scientists, recent political scientists specializing in the Soviet Union, because of their methodological and contemporary interests, have rarely concerned themselves with these questions of Soviet historical development. One exception is Frederick C. Barghoorn. See, for example, his interesting and problematic treatment in "The Post-Khrushchev Campaign to Suppress Dissent," *Dissent in the USSR*, ed. Rudolf L. Tökes (Baltimore, 1975), pp. 38-42.

27. As does, for example, Medvedev, *Let History Judge.*

28. *The New International*, February, 1939, pp. 53-55. On the question of "roots," see also Trotsky, *Stalinism and Bolshevism*, p. 23.

29. Thomas T. Hammond, "Leninist Authoritarianism before the Revolution," *Continuity and Change in Russian and Soviet Thought*, ed. Ernest J. Simmons (Cambridge, Mass., 1955), p. 156.

30. The issue of whether Stalinism can be defined apart from its excesses figures prominently in recent Soviet discussions. Soviet revisionist historians have argued, for example, that the collectivization drive of 1929-33 is incomprehensible apart from its excesses (*peregib*). A Soviet leader then complained that for these historians "collectivization was a whole chain of mistakes, violations, crimes, etc." "Rech 'tov. D.G. Sturua," *Zaria vostoka*, March 10, 1966, p. 2. Answering a *samizdat* writer, Roy Medvedev makes the same point: "The *essence* of Stalinism was those very 'imbecile savage extremes' that Mikhailov regards as a minor detail." *On Socialist Democracy* (New York, 1975), pp. 398-99. For a Western concept of Stalinism without "excessive excesses," see Nove, "Was Stalin Really Necessary?"

31. *Bukharin and the Bolshevik Revolution*, pp. 2-5, and *passim.*

32. For example, Bukharin's writings influenced considerably Leninist and Bolshevik ideology on imperialism and the state. Ibid., pp. 25-43. In *The Bolsheviks Come to Power: The 1917 Revolution in Petrograd* (New York, 1976), Alexander Rabinowitch shows us a Bolshevik party in 1917 dramatically unlike the stereotype of a conspiratorial, disciplined vanguard, a party responding to, and gaining from, grassroots politics. The enormous impact of the civil war remains to be studied.

33. Merle Fainsod in *Continuity and Change in Russian and Soviet Thought*, p. 179.

34. Boris Souvarine, "Stalinism," *Marxism in the Modern World*, ed. Milorad M. Drachkovitch (Stanford, Calif., 1965), p. 102.

35. Jasny, *Socialized Agriculture of the USSR*, p. 18.

36. As has been pointed out before, Isaac Deutscher, "The Future of Russian Society," *Dissent*, Summer, 1954, pp. 227-29; Robert D. Warth, *Lenin* (New York, 1973), p. 171.

37. *Dissent*, January-February, 1953, pp. 581–82.

38. *Let History Judge*, p. 359.

39. Zbigniew Brzezinski in *Development of the USSR*, p. 40. Brzezinski was replying to Robert C. Tucker in an exchange on Soviet political history. Arguing against Brzezinski's continuity thesis, Tucker had suggested that study of Soviet history must start at the beginning, proceeding "layer by layer."

40. *What Is History?* (London, 1964), p. 42.

41. I have learned much from discussions on this point with Moshe Lewin.

42. Solzhenitsyn's theory that the ideology "bears the entire responsibility for all the bloodshed" is only a recent, though somewhat extreme, version. A. Solzhenitsyn, *Pis'mo vozhdiam Sovetskogo Soiuza* (Paris, 1974), p. 41. For academic versions, see, for example, Ulam, *Unfinished Revolution*, p. 198; Donald W. Treadgold, *Twentieth Century Russia* (Chicago, 1959), p. 263; and Zbigniew K. Brzezinski, *Ideology and Power in Soivet Politics* (rev. ed., New York, 1967), p. 42.

43. The interpreter can then define "Stalinism . . . as mature Leninism." Philip Selznick, *The Organizational Weapon: A Study of Bolshevik Strategy and Tactics*

(New York, 1952), pp. 5, 39, 42, 216, and the index entry at p. 348. The movement's "original sin," according to Ulam, was "lust for power." *Stalin*, pp.261, 265.

44.   N. Osinsky in *Deviatyi s'ezd (RKP (b). Mart-aprel 1920 goda*: *Protokoly* (Moscow, 1960), p. 115.

45.   See Timasheff, *The Great Retreat*; Frederick C. Barghoorn, *Soviet Russian Nationalism* (New York, 1956); Robert V. Daniels, "Soviet Thought in the Nineteen-Thirties: An Interpretative Sketch," *Indiana Slavic Studies*, vol. 1, ed. Michael Ginsburg and Joseph T. Shaw (Bloomington, Ind., 1956), pp. 97–135; and Paul Willen, "Soviet Architecture: Progress and Reaction," *Problems of Communism*, no. 6, 1953, pp. 24–34. Soviet scholars have commented on the change in focus from masses to leaders. See M. V. Nechkina in *Istoriia i sotsiologiia* (Moscow, 1964), p. 238. For a vivid illustration, compare the films made to commemorate the tenth and twentieth anniversaries of the 1917 revolution: *October, or Ten Days That Shook the World* (1927) and *Lenin in October* (1937).

46.   Daniels, "Soviet Thought in the Nineteen-Thrities," p. 130. In 1932 Ol'minsky complained that ideological changes in party historiography were leading to a "castrated Leninism." Quoted in L. A. Slepov, *Istoriia KPSS—vazhneishaia obshchestvennaia nauka* (Moscow, 1964), p. 11.

47.   See, for example, Selznick, *The Organizational Weapon*; and S. V. Utechin's introduction to V. I. Lenin, *What Is to Be Done?* (Oxford, 1963), p. 15. For a polemical but effective critique of this theory, see Max Shachtman, *The Bureaucratic Revolution: The Rise of the Stalinist State* (New York, 1962), pp. 202-23. As Shachtman points out, few Western scholars have missed the chance to quote approvingly Trotsky's 1904 prediction: "The organization of the party will take the place of the party; the Central Committee will take the place of the organization; and finally the dictator will take the place of the Central Committee."

48.   See *Ocherki istorii kommunisticheskoi partii Turkmenistana* (2d ed., Askhabad, 1965), p. 495; *Ocherki istorii kommunisticheskoi partii Kazakhstana* (Alma-Alta, 1963), p. 377. And see the evidence in Robert Conquest, *The Great Terror: Stalin's Purge of the Thirties* (New York, 1968), chaps. 8, 13; and Medvedev, *Let History Judge*, chap. 6.

49.   Tucker, *Soviet Political Mind*, chap. 1 and p. 212.

50.   Nikolai Bukharin, *K voprosu o trotskizme* (Moscow and Leningrad, 1925), p. 11. To put this point differently, the infamous 1921 ban on factionalism in the party was not, as most scholars suggest, the culmination of the Bolshevik-Leninist tradition but a quixotic attempt by a panicky leadership to constrain, or legislate away, its own tradition. As official historians have complained over the years, party history has been a history of "factional struggle." M. Gaisinskii, *Bor'ba s uklonami ot general'noi linii partii: Istoricheskii ocherk vnutripartiinoi bor'by posle oktiabr'skogo perioda* (2d ed., Moscow and Leningrad, 1931), p. 4; Slepov, *Istoriia KPSS*, p. 22.

51.   See, for example, Inkeles, *Social Change in Soviet Russia*, p. 41; and Bertram D. Wolfe in *The USSR after 50 years*, Samuel Hendel and Randolph L. Braham (New York, 1967), p. 153.

52.   Tucker in *Development of the USSR*, p. 33; *Soviet Political Mind*, pp. 18, 179.

53.   On "purge" and "class war," for example, see Robert M. Slusser's review of Brzezinski's *The Permanent Purge*, in *American Slavic and East European Review*, vol. 15, no. 4 (December 1956), pp. 543-46; and Tucker, *Soviet Political Mind*, pp. 55-56.

54.   *Soviet Political Mind*, p. 135. See Conquest, *The Great Terror*, chaps. 8, 13; and Medvedev, *Let History Judge*, chap. 6. Conquest calls the crushing of the party "a revolution as complete as, though more disguised than, any previous changes in Russia" (p. 251).

55.   Between 1918 and 1933, there were 10 party congresses, 10 party conferences, and 122 Central Committee plenums. Between 1934 and 1953, there were 3 party

congresses (only 1 after 1939), 1 party conference, and 23 Central Committee plenums (none in 1941-43, 1945-46, 1948, or 1950-51). *Sovetskaia istoricheskaia entsiklopediia*, vol. 8 (Moscow, 1965), p. 275. According to Medvedev, the expression "soldier of the party" was replaced by "soldier of Stalin." *Let History Judge*, p. 419. For an example of the cult of the state, see K. V. Ostrovityanov, *The Role of the State in the Socialist Transformation of the Economy of the USSR* (Moscow, 1950).

56. *Vsesoiuznoe soveshchanie o merakh uluchsheniia podgotovki nauchno-pedagogicheskikh kadrov po istoricheskim naukam, 18-21 dekabria 1962 g.* (Moscow, 1964), p. 242.

57. As Boris Souvarine has argued. "Stalinism," *Marxism in the Modern World*, pp. 90-107. Since Stalin's death, the official euphemism for Stalinism has been, of course, "cult of the personality."

58. Compare, for example, references to the party leadership, the Central Committee, political ideas, etc., at the following gatherings: *XVII konferentsiia vsesoiuznoi kommunisticheskoi partii (b): Stenograficheskii otchet* (Moscow, 1932); *XVII s"ezd vsesoiuznoi kommunisticheskoi partii (b). 26 ianvaria–10 fevralia 1934 g.: Stenograficheskii otchet* (Moscow, 1934); and *XVIII s"ezd vsesoiuznoi kommunisticheskoi partii (b), 10-21 marta 1939 g.: Stenograficheskii otchet* (Moscow, 1939). As time passed, there was a virtual ban on literature about Lenin. *Spravochnik partiinogo rabotnika* (Moscow, 1957), p. 364. The diminishing of Lenin began earlier. On the anniversary of the revolution in November 1933, an American correspondent counted in the shop windows on Gorky Street 103 busts and portraits of Stalin, 58 of Lenin, and 5 of Marx. Eugene Lyons, *Moscow Carrousel* (New York, 1935), pp. 140-41.

59. *XVIII s"ezd*, p. 68; V. K. Oltarzhevskii, *Stroitel'stvo vysotnykh zdanii v Moskve* (Moscow, 1953), pp. 4, 214.

60. The term *Stalinism* appears to have been used privately, by high leaders as as well as others. See *Khrushchev Remembers: The Last Testament* (Boston, 1974), p. 193; Medvedev, *Let History Judge*, pp. 506-7. It has been used widely in *samizdat* literature.

61. "Open Letter to the Central Committee," *Washington Post*, April 27, 1969.

62. See, for example, Treadgold, *Twentieth Century Russia*, p. 165; Ulam, *The Bolsheviks*, pp. 467-68; Paul Craig Roberts, "'War Communism': A Re-examination," *Slavic Review*, June, 1970, pp. 238-61. Craig is arguing against the view that war communism was primarily expediency, which he calls the "prevalent interpretation." This is not my impression.

63. The concluding quotation is from Adam B. Ulam, *The Russian Political System* (New York, 1974), p. 37. The first two are from Arthur E. Adams, *Stalin and His Times* (New York, 1972), p. 7; and John A. Armstrong, *Ideology, Politics and Government in the Soviet Union* (3d ed., New York, 1974), p. 22. Similarly, see Fainsod, *How Russia Is Ruled*, pp. 528-29; Gurian, *Bolshevism*, p. 76; and Solzhenitzyn, *The Gulag Archipelago*, p. 392, where it is said that the "entire NEP was merely a cynical deceit."

64. Treadgold, *Twentieth Century Russia*, pp. 165, 199, 258.

65. *Bukharin and the Bolshevik Revolution*, chap. 3, 5-90;

66. For a fuller discussion, see ibid, pp. 53-57.

67. V. I. Lenin, *Sochineniia*, vol. 22 (Moscow and Leningrad, 1931), pp. 435-68.

68. E. H. Carr, *The Bolshevik Revolution*, vol. 2 (New York, 1952), pp. 51, 53, 98-99.

69. A classic example is Nikolai Bukharin's *Ekonomika perkhodnogo perioda* (Moscow, 1920). For an interesting Soviet study of this question, see E. G. Gimpel'son, *"Voennyi kommunizm": Politika, praktika, ideologiia* (Moscow, 1973).

70. For a discussion of NEP in these terms, see my *Bukharin and the Bolshevik Revolution*, pp. 270-76; and Lewin, *Political Undercurrents*, chap. 4, 5, 12.

71. Alfred G. Meyer, "Lev Davidovich Trotsky," *Problems of Communism*,

November–December 1967, pp. 31, 37, and *passim*. Meyer's is a rather pristine example of the interpretation, but variations run through our literature. See, for example, Leonard Schapiro, "Out of the Dustbin of History," ibid., p. 86, Reshetar, *Concise History of the Communist Party*, pp. 230–31; Basil Dmytryshyn, *USSR: A Concise History* (2d ed., New York, 1971), p. 121; Ulam, *Stalin*, p. 292, n. 3; and Isaac Deutscher, *Stalin: A Political Biography* (2d ed., New York, 1967), p. 295, which seems to be contradicted on p. 318.

72. Cohen, *Bukharin and the Bolshevik Revolution*, pp. 147-48, 186-88. For a different view of Stalin in the 1920s, see Tucker, *Stalin as Revolutionary*, pp. 395-404. Tucker argues that much of Bukharin's programmatic thinking was antithetical to Stalin psychologically, and that Stalin's later policies were already adumbrated in differences of emphasis between the two. Even so, it does not alter the fact that there was no meaningful difference on the level of public policy and factional politics between 1924 and 1927.

73. *XIV s"ezd vsesoiuznoi kommunisticheskoi partii (b). 18-31 dekabria 1925 g.: Stenograficheskii otchet* (Moscow and Leningrad, 1926), pp. 254, 494.

74. Cohen, *Bukharin and the Bolshevik Revolution*, chaps. 6, 8, 9.

75. The economic ideas of Trotsky and the Left are treated elliptically and somewhat inconsistently by Isaac Deutscher, though he does call Trotsky a "reformist" in economic policy. *The Prophet Outcast: Trotsky, 1929-1940* (London, 1963), p. 110. For a fuller study, see Richard B. Day, *Leon Trotsky and the Politics of Economic Isolation* (Cambridge, England, 1973); and Lewin, *Political Undercurrents*, chaps. 1-3.

76. E. Preobrazhensky, *The New Economics* (London, 1965), pp. 110-11; Erlich, *Soviet Industrialization Debate*, pp. 32-59.

77. As Preobrazhensky later pointed out. *XVII s"e zd*, p. 238.

78. See Lewin, *Political Undercurrents*, chaps. 2, 3.

79. Ibid., pp. 68-72; Cohen, *Bukharin and the Bolshevik Revolution*, pp. 347-48.

80. Cohen, *Bukharin and the Bolshevik Revolution*, pp. 328-29. This question is treated in terms of Stalin's leadership role in Tucker, *Stalin as Revolutionary*, chaps. 12-14.

81. *Pravda*, April 28, 1929, p. 1; *Pravda*, March 21, 1931, p. 1.

82. It is true that the Bolshevik economist Iurii Larin was accused of having proposed a "third revolution" against kulak farms in 1925. But Larin was a secondary figure unaffiliated with the leadership factions, whose suggestion was derided by all. Medvedev is mistaken, I think, in suggesting that he was a Trotskyist. *Let History Judge*, p. 97. See also Deutscher, *Stalin*, pp. 318-19.

83. See Tucker's *Stalin as Revolutionary* and *Soviet Political Mind*.

84. I refer here to the internal Soviet order of 1946-53, not to the transformations effected in Eastern Europe. The ahistorical "totalitarianism" approach saw the Stalinist regime of 1946-53 as still being revolutionary and dynamic. For a different approach and conclusion, see Tucker, *Soviet Political Mind*, pp. 174, 186-90. The conservatism of late Stalinism is noted even in official Soviet accounts. See, for example, N. Saushkin, *O kul'te lichnosti i avtoritete* (Moscow, 1962), pp. 26, 32.

85. The Krushchevian theory dated Stalinism's rise from 1934, a fiction preserved even in more detailed accounts. Saushkin, *O kul'te lichnosti i avtoritete*.

86. For a fuller discussion of these two points, see my *Bukharin and the Bolshevik Revolution*, pp. 314-15, 332-33; and Medvedev, *Let History Judge*, pp. 85-86, 89-90, 101, 103. Medvedev points out that many of Stalin's orders came "in *oral* form."

87. Moshe Lewin, "Class, State and Ideology in the *Piatiletka*" (unpublished paper delivered to the conference on "Cultural Revolution in Russia, 1928-1933," Columbia University, November 22-23, 1974). See also Lewin, *Political Undercurrents*, chap. 5; and his "Taking Grain," *Essays in Honour of E. H. Carr*, ed. C. Abramsky (Cambridge, England, 1974), pp. 281-323.

88. See, for example, Medvedev, *Let History Judge*, pp. 314-15; A. F. Khavin,

Kratkii ocherk istorii industrializatsii SSSR (Moscow, 1962), pp. 305-6; and A. Nekrich, *22 iunia 1941* (Moscow, 1965), pt. 2.

89.   Anecdotes about the disaster were rife; the following one circulated in Moscow in the early 1930s. The party leadership was attacked by body lice. Doctors were unable to get rid of the lice. One wit (allegedly Radek, as always) proposed: "Collectivize them, then half of them will die and the other half will run away." Lyons, *Moscow Carrousel*, p. 334.

90.   A survivor tells us that Stalinism "not only destroyed honest people, it corrupted the living," *Vsesoiuznoe soveschchanie*, p. 270. Medvedev also links the growth of the cult to the disasters of the early 1930s. *Let History Judge*, p. 149. The birth of the notion of Stalin's infallibility probably should be dated from his famous article "Dizzy with Success" in March 1930. Despite the objections of some high party leaders, he managed to place full blame for the "excesses" of collectivization on local officials. The fictional, or mythical, character of Stalinist ideology remains to be studied in historical and sociological terms. For a study of its ideological aspects, which unfortunately confuses bolshevism and Stalinism, see Roman Redlikh, *Stalinshchina kak dukhovnyi fenomen: Ocherki bol'skevizmovedeniia*, Book 1 (Frankfurt, 1971).

91.   See, for example, Trotsky, *The Revolution Betrayed*; Shachtman, *The Bureaucratic Revolution*; M. Yvon, *What Has Become of the Russian Revolution* (New York, 1937); Peter Meyer, "The Soviet Union: A New Class Society," *Politics*, March and April, 1944, pp. 48-55, 81-85; Adam Kaufman, "Who Are the Rulers in Russia?" *Dissent*, Spring, 1954, pp. 144-56; Djilas, *The New Class*; and Tony Cliff, *State Capitalism in Russia* (London, 1974). Class-bureaucracy theories of Stalinism are also proposed by some *samizdat* writers. See, for example, S. Zorin and N. Alekseev, "Vremia ne zhdet" (Leningrad, 1969); and *Seiatel'*, no. 1 (September, 1971), in *Novoe russkoe slovo*, December 11, 1972.

92.   Tucker, *Soviet Political Mind*, pp. 133-34.

93.   See, for example, Timasheff, *The Great Retreat*; and above, note 23.

94.   E. H. Carr, "Stalin," *Soviet Studies*, July, 1953, p. 3.

95.   See, for example, Sheila Fitzpatrick, "Cultural Revolution as Class War" (unpublished paper delivered to the conference on "Cultural Revolution in Russia, 1928-1933," Columbia University, November 22-23, 1974).

96.   Medvedev, *Let History Judge*, pp. 415-16, 536. David Schoenbaum's concept of a "revolution of status" in Hitler's Germany may apply here. See his *Hitler's Social Revolution* (Garden City, N.Y., 1967), chaps. 8, 9. Stalin's personal popularity is acknowledged in official critiques of Stalinism. See, for example, *Kratkaia istoriia SSSR*, pt. 2 (Moscow and Leningrad, 1964), p. 271.

97.   Medvedev, *On Socialist Democracy*, p. 346. For similar testimony on this point, see *The Times* (London), May 25, 1937. Medvedev called this popular sentiment "an implicit criticism of bureaucracy." It may have been, however, implicit anti-Communist sentiment.

98.   For similar points, see I. Zuzanek, quoted in Medvedev, *Let History Judge*, p. 529; Hugh Seton-Watson, "The Soviet Ruling Class," *Problems of Communism*, May-June, 1956, p. 12; and Barghoorn, *Soviet Russian Nationalism*, p. 182.

99.   Medvedev, *On Socialist Democracy*, p. 346. Elsewhere Medvedev objects to the theory that the Stalin cult was rooted primarily in traditional village religiosity, arguing that it originated in the city and was strongest among workers, officials, and the intelligentsia. This leaves open, however, the question of the social origins of these city groups. *Let History Judge*, pp. 429-30. There are many other first-hand testimonies to the religious and authentic nature of the cult. See, for example, *In Quest of Justice: Protest and Dissent in the Soviet Union Today*, ed. Abraham Brumberg (New York, 1970), pp. 320, 329. Soviet scholarly studies of religion often read like implicit analysis of Stalinism. See Iu. A. Levada, *Sotsial'naia priroda religii* (Moscow, 1965).

100.   The expression is G. Pomerantz's. *In Quest of Justice*, p. 327.

4. The Totalitarian State and Personal Dictorship

1. Karl Mannheim, *L'uomo e la società in un 'età ricostruzione*, tr. Aldo Devizzi (Milan, 1959), p. 325.

2. Benito Mussolini, *Opera Omnia*, (Florence, 1951 ff) vol. 34, pp. 406-16.

3. Galeazzo Ciano, *Diario*, vol. 1, 1939-1940 (Milan, Rome, 1950), p. 111 (entry of 3 June 1939).

4. Mussolini, *Opera Omnia*, vol. 13, p. 89.

5. For the text of the Lateran Treaty see *Treaty and Concordat between the Holy See and Italy; Official documents* (Washington, D.C., 1929) National Catholic Welfare Conference, [1929]. See also D. A. Binchy, *Church and State in Fascist Italy*, (London, 1970 [1941]).

6. Arturo Carlo Jemolo, "Sulla qualificazione giuridica dello Stato italiano in ordine alle sue relazioni con la chiesa," in *Rivista di diritto publico*, vol. 23, ser. 2 (1931), pt. 1, p. 168.

7. These were the words of Benedetto Croce in his speech to the Senate against the Lateran Treaties, given on March 24, 1929.

8. Augusto del Noce, "Idee per l'interpretazione del fascismo," in *Ordine civile*, vol. 2, no. 8, 15 April 1960, repr. in *Il Fascismo: Antologia di scritti critici a cura di Costanzo Casucci*, pp. 380-81.

9. See Francesco L. Ferrari, *L'Azione Cattolica e il regime* (Florence, 1957), pp. 187-99.

10. Carmen Haider, *Capital and Labor under Fascism*.

11. Stefano Jacini, *Il regime fascista* (Milan, 1947), p. 51.

12. Carlo Ludovico Ragghianti, "Il fascismo e la cultura," in *Storia dell' antifascismo italiano a cura di Luigi Arbizzani e Alberto Caltabiano*, vol. 1 (Rome, 1964), p. 106.

13. Giuseppe Bottai, *Vent'anni e un giorno* (Rome, 1949), p. 43.

14. Ottavio Dinale, *Quarant'anni di colloqui con lui* (Milian, 1953), p. 181.

15. See Alberto Aquarone, "L'altro Mussolini: Il Duce visto dai collaboratori," *Il Mondo*, vol. 15, no. 29, 16 July 1963, pp. 15-16.

16. Giuseppe Bottai, *Vent'anni e un giorno* (Rome, 1949), p. 31.

17. Giuseppe Bastianini, *Uomini cose fatti. Memorie di un ambasciatore* (Milan, 1959), p. 42. See also Dino Alfieri, *Due dittatori di fronte* (Milan, 1948), esp. p. 23.

18. Antonio Raimondi, *Mezzo secolo di magistratura*, p. 323.

19. See Luigi Albertini, *Vita di Luigi Albertini* (Rome, 1945), p. 191.

20. See Guido Leto, *Ovra, Fascismo Antifascismo*, (Bologna, 1952), p. 145. Regarding the effects of Mussolini's mania for personally holding various offices see Attilio Tamaro, *Venti anni di storia*, (Rome, 1954), vol. 2, p. 227; also, see Giuriati's observations concerning the obvious violation of the principle governing the 1925 statute defining the powers of the head of the government.

21. Giuseppe Bottai, *Vent'anni e un giorno*, (Rome, 1949), p. 127.

22. For Italian military unpreparedness, see Carlo Favagrossa, *Perché perdemmo la guerra: Mussolini e la produzione bellica* (Milan, 1946). In addition to the memories of General Armellini, *La crisi: dell'esercito*, see Carlo Silvestri, *I responsabili della catastrofe italiana. Guerra: 1940-43, Armistizio: 8 settembre 1943*, (Milan 1946), esp. pp. 161ff.; and Renzo Montagna, *Mussolini e il processo di Verona* (Milan, 1949), pp. 20ff.

23. Giorgio Pini, *Filo diretto con Palazzo Venezia* (Bologna, 1950) p. 84.

24. See Galeazzo Ciano, *1937-1938, Diario*, (Milan, 1946), p. 265.

25. Allessandro Lessona, *Memorie*, (Florence, 1958), p. 333.

26. Giuseppe Bastianini, *Uomini cose fatti*, (Milan, 1959), p. 39.

27. Sergio Panunzio, *Teoria generale dello stato fascista* (Padua, 1939), p. 568. See also Mussolini, *Opera Omnia*, vol. 32, p. 178.

28. Mussolini, *Opera Omnia*, ibid., p. 177.

5. Totalitarianism: The Concept and the Reality

Some of the concepts in this essay were previously expressed in my essay on "Objective and Subjective Inhibitants in the German Resistance to Hitler," in Franklin Littell and Hubert Locke (eds.), *The German Church Struggle and the Holocaust* (Detroit, 1974), pp. 114-123, but this present essay is newly written, expressly for this book.

1. Hans Buchheim, *Totalitarian Rule: Its Nature and Characteristics*, trans. Ruth Hein (Middletown, Conn., 1968), pp. 11-37, esp. 29f.

2. Herbert J. Spiro, "Totalitarianism," in David L. Sills, ed., *International Encyclopedia of the Social Sciences* (2d ed., 1967) vol. 16, pp. 106ff.

3. Buchheim, *passim*; see also Hannah Arendt, *The Origins of Totalitarianism* (2d ed., New York, 1958) and Carl J. Friedrich and Zbigniew K. Brzezinski, *Totalitarian Dictatorship and Autocracy* (2d ed., New York, 1965).

4. William Kornhauser, *The Politics of Mass Society* (Glencoe, Ill., 1959). Having elsewhere shown that this theory simply does not accord with the data, I will not repeat that point here but refer the reader to my "Appeal of Fascism and the Problem of National Disintegration" in Henry A. Turner, Jr., ed., *Reappraisals of Fascism* (New York, 1975), pp. 44-68.

5. Buchheim, p. 69: "... totalitarian rule and politics stand in the greatest imaginable contrast to each other." But he qualifies this (p. 70) as he also insists that the full totalitarian goal "is never reached and actualized but must remain a trend, a *claim* to power," because it is by definition "impossible to control man's personality and fate completely" (p. 38).

6. Edward N. Peterson, *The Limits of Hitler's Power* (Princeton, 1969). The classic study of competition within the Nazi party remains Sir Hugh Trevor-Roper's *Last Days of Hitler* (3d ed., New York, 1962) while the best theoretical analysis is Joseph Nyomarky, *Charisma and Factionalism in the Nazi Party* (Minneapolis, 1967).

7. Timothy W. Mason, *Sozialpolitik im Dritten Reich: Arbeiterklasse und Volksgemeinschaft* (Opladen, 1977), esp. pp. 15-41.

8. Karl A. Schleunes, *The Twisted Road to Auschwitz: Nazi Policy toward German Jews, 1933-39* (Urbana, Ill., 1971), pp. 72, 80, 86, 93.

9. Fritz K. Ringer, *The Decline of the German Mandarins, 1890-1933* (Cambridge, Mass., 1969).

10. Marlis Steinert, *Hitlers Krieg und die Deutschen: Stimmung und Haltung der deutschen Bevölkerung im zweiten Weltkrieg* (Düsseldorf, 1970). Also available in an abbreviated English translation as *Hitler's War and the Germans.*

11. Sarah A. Gordon, "German Opposition to Nazi Anti-Semitic Measures between 1933 and 1945, with Particular Reference to the Rhine-Ruhr Area," (Ph.D. diss., State University of New York at Buffalo), Feb. 1979, pp. 185ff.

12. William S. Allen, *The Nazi Seizure of Power: The Experience of a Single German Town, 1930-1935* (Chicago, 1965), pp. 213-26.

13. Such is also the conclusion of the authoritative article on totalitarianism in the second edition of the *International Encyclopedia of the Social Sciences* (vol. 16, p. 112): "In many other important respects [Hitler's Germany and Stalin's Russia] resembled nontotalitarian systems."

14. Peterson, *The Limits of Hitler's Power*, chaps. 5, 8.

15. Allen, *The Nazi Seizure of Power.* "Thalburg" was the pseudonym used for "Northeim in Hannover," but since the identity has long since been made public by the German press, there is no need to avoid the town's real name any longer. The new data may be found in the Niedersächsisches Staatsarchiv Hannover and has not yet been assigned an archival number; however, it is here cited as "NSAH, Bestand Hann. 310-I/Nachtrag," followed by the preliminary folder number. It covers primarily the years after 1935. Ernst Girman, Northeim's local Group Leader, was originally given the name "Kurt Aergeyz."

16. NSAH, Best. Hann. 310I/Nachtrag, N-5: "Rundschreiben der Gauleitung u.

Kreisleitung betr. Organisation, 1935-36,"; N-6: "Rundschreiben des Kreisleiters Northeim, 1935-36" (especially Number 53/36, 27.6.36); also N-11, "Veranstaltungen u. Tagungen in Northeim, 1936-37 (I)" and N-21 and 22, "Ortsgruppe Northeim, Korrespondenz, 1935-36."

17. Ibid., folders N-28 to N-30, "Ortsgruppe Northeim, Politische Beurteilungen einzelner Personen, 1935-1943." For comparison, see Hann. 310I/L-3, which suggests that this practice was common to the area. A negative evaluation was exceedingly rare.

18. Ibid., N-17: "Ortsgruppe Northeim, Ausgegangene Schreiben, 1934 (A-M)" Girman to Studienrat Meinecke, 4.12.34: "So werden wir allen Glauben der Pfaffen durch unseren Glauben an Hitler überwinden."

19. NSAH, Best. Hann. 80, Hild. III/2631. Girman's campaign began on 5.IV.37 and the final action of the Regierungs-Präsident Hildesheim came on 23.IV.38. There were an estimated 750 Catholics in Northeim; for their pastor's protest see Fr. Meyer to BM Girman, 9.IV.37.

20. NSAH Hann. 310I/Nachtrag, N-17 and 18, "Ausgegangene Schreiben, 1937." His threatening letters generally went to people who wouldn't contribute money, attend meetings, said improper things, etc. For an example of his retribution against a young man who insulted the Nazi party, see "Ortsgruppe Northeim Parteikorrespondenz, 1936-43 (L-R)". Girman to OGL, 8.11.41.

21. Ibid., N-19 "Ortsgruppe Northeim, Korrespondenz 1935 (A-K)": *Ortsgruppenleiter* to Fräulein Albrecht, 14.5.35.

22. For his defense of a Freemason, see ibid., N-18, "Ausgengangene Schreiben, (N-Z) 1934": memorandum on Pg. Dr. Gerhard Meissner; on Jews see N-15, "Ausgegangene Schreiben (A-M) 1932-33", Ortsgruppenleiter to N. S. Heilpraktiker Fachschaft, 30.9.33 and "Korrespondenz 1936-43 (L04)": Ortsgruppenleiter to Kreisleitung Northeim betr. Bankier Hermann Müller, 21.11.36.

23. Ibid., N-18, "Ausgegangene Schreiben, 1934 (N-Z)," Ortsgruppenleiter to Reichsbahn Oberinspektor Pg. Schulze, 23.8.34.

24. Preussisches geheimes Staats-Archiv, Dahlem, Rep. 90-P/3,4: "Lagebericht des Regierungspräsidenten Hildesheim für die Monate April u. Mai 1935 (1.6.35)." The reporter, Dr. Muhs, was an early and fanatical Nazi, which may account for his pessimism. But for corroborative material from another source see ibid., "Lagebericht der Staatspolizeistelle Hildesheim, 2.12.35 and 7.1.36."

25. NSAH, Best. Hann 310I/Nachtrag, N-11: "Veranstaltungen u. Tagungen in Northeim, 1936-37 (I)." Every *Blockwart* and *Zellenleiter* was given several training sessions with a Walther PK-9 and was later issued a pistol to wear with his uniform.

26. Herbert J. Spiro, "Totalitarianism" in *International Encyclopedia of the Social Sciences* (2d ed. 1967), vol. 16, p. 112.

6. Terrorism and Totalitarianism

1. Wadim Sagladin, *Die Kommunistische Weltbewegung: Abriss der Strategie und Taktik*, (Frankfurt a.M., 1973).

2. Mikhail S. Voslenskii, "Uber die Strategie und Taktik der kommunistischen Weltbewegung," *Osteuropa: Zeitschrift für Gegenwartsfragen des Ostens*, vol. 24, Nov.-Dec. 1974, pp. 844-54.

3. Jean François Revel, *The Totalitarian Temptation*, trans. David Hapgood, (Garden City, N.Y., 1977).

4. Sagladin, op. cit., p. 36.

5. Lenin, *Werke*, vol. 28, p. 293.

6. Voslenskii, op. cit., p. 852.

7. Totalitarianism: A Monolithic Entity

1. Irving Louis Horowitz, *Three Worlds of Development* (New York, 1966), p. 160.

2.   Robert Slusser, *The Berlin Crisis of 1961* (Baltimore, 1973).
3.   Adrian Lyttelton, *The Seizure of Power: Fascism in Italy, 1919-1929* (London, 1973) p. 187.
4.   Ibid., p. 150.
5.   Edward R. Tannenbaum, *Fascism in Italy* (New York, 1972), p. 70.
6.   Ibid., p. 57.
7.   Alberto Aquarone, *L'organizzazione dello Stato totalitario* (Turin, 1965), p. 292.
8.   Tannenbaum, p. 388.
9.   Alastair Hamilton, *The Appeal of Fascism* (London, 1971), p. 67.
10.   Edward Peterson, *The Limits of Hitler's Power* (Princeton, N.J., 1969); Joseph Nyomarkay, *Charisma and Factionalism in the Nazi Party* (Minneapolis, 1967), pp. 31-32.
11.   Christopher R. Browning, "Unterstaatssekretaer Martin Luther and the Ribbentrop Foreign Office," *Journal of Contemporary History* (April 1977), p. 313.
12.   Peterson, p. 102.
13.   Ibid., p. 209.
14.   Tannenbaum, p. 69.
15.   Lyttelton, p. 165.
16.   Peterson, p. 102.
17.   Dietrich Orlow, *The History of the Nazi Party: 1933-1945* (Pittsburgh, 1973), p. 64.
18.   Helmut Krausnick, et al., *Anatomy of the SS State* (New York, 1968), p. 189.
19.   Joseph Stalin, *Foundations of Leninism* (New York, 1932).
20.   Aryeh L. Unger, *The Totalitarian Party: Party and People in Nazi Germany and Soviet Russia* (New York, 1974), pp. 40-43.
21.   Michael Gehlen, *The Communist Party of the Soviet Union: Functional Analysis* (Bloomington, Ind., 1969).
22.   Roy Medvedev and Zhores A. Medvedev, *Khrushchev: The Years in Power* (New York, 1977).
23.   Nikita Khrushchev, *The Last Testament* (Boston, 1974), p. 137.
24.   Jerry F. Hough, *The Soviet Prefects* (Cambridge, 1969), p. 213.
25.   Ibid., pp. 101-2.
26.   Ibid., p. 91.
27.   Ibid., p. 95.

8. "Totalitarianism" Revisited

The author wishes to acknowledge the support of the Institute of International Studies, University of California, Berkeley, for assistance and support in the preparation of this essay.

1.   Leonard Schapiro, *Totalitarianism* (New York, 1972); Juan J. Linz, "Totalitarian and Authoritarian Regimes," in F. I. Greenstein and N. W. Polsby, eds., *Handbook of Political Science* (Reading, Mass., 1975), vol. 3.
2.   Domenico Fisichella, *Analisi del totalitarismo* (Florence, 1976).
3.   Waldemar Gurian, "The Totalitarian State," *Review of Politics*, vol. 40, no. 4 (October, 1978); S. Whitfield, " 'Totalitarianism'–The Disintegration of an Idea," *The American Spectator*, vol. 12, no. 1 (January, 1979).
4.   Cf. Giovanni Gentile, *I fondamenti della filosofia del diritto* (Florence, 1955), p. 118 and chap. 7. While Gentile's specific allusions to "totalitarianism" appear after 1925, it is clear that the concept functions in his first version of *I fondamenti*.
5.   Carl Friedrich and Zbigniew K. Brzezinski, *Totalitarian Dictatorship and Autocracy* (New York, 1956), pp. 3, 9; cf. pp. 8, 10.

6. Cf. A. J. Gregor, *An Introduction to Metapolitics* (New York, 1971), pp. 131-35.
7. Friedrich and Brzezinski, *Totalitarian Dictatorship*, pp. vii, 7.
8. Ibid., pp. 3ff.
9. Robert Burrowes, "Totalitarianism: The Revised Standard Version," *World Politics*, 1969, 21/2: 281,282.
10. Friedrich and Brzezinski, *Totalitarian Dictatorship*, pp. 28, 63, 134, 135, 152 (emphasis supplied), 154 (emphasis supplied).
11. Alexander Groth, "The 'isms' in Totalitarianism," *American Political Science Review*, 1964, 58/4: 888.
12. Friedrich and Brzezinski, *Totalitarian Dictatorship*, p. 6.
13. William Ebenstein, "The Study of Totalitarianism," *World Politics*, 1958, 10/2: 274-88.
14. Otto Stammer, "Aspekte der Totalitarismusforschung," in Bruno Seidel and Siegfried Jenkner, eds., *Wege der Totalitarismus-Forschung* (Darmstadt, 1968); Peter Christian Ludz, "Entwurf einer soziologischen Theorie totalitär verfasster Gesellschaft," in Seidel and Jenkner; Oskar Anweiler, "Totalitäre Erziehung," in Seidel and Jenkner.
15. Ebenstein, op. cit., p. 282; Friedrich and Brzezinski, op. cit., pp. 11 (emphasis supplied) and 264.
16. Frederic J. Fleron, Jr., "Soviet Area Studies and the Social Sciences: Some Methodological Problems in Communist Studies," *Soviet Studies*, 1968, 19/3: 313; cf. Patrick Suppes, "A Comparison of the Meaning and Uses of Models in Mathematics and the Empirical Sciences," in Hans Freudenthal, ed., *The Concept and the Role of the Model in Mathematics and Social Sciences* (Hingham, Mass., 1961).
17. May Brodbeck, "The Philosophy of Science and Educational Research," *Review of Educational Research*, 1957, 27/5:429.
18. Friedrich and Brzezinski, *Totalitarian Dictatorship*, p. 9.
19. Fleron, "Soviet Area Studies," p. 326.
20. Zbigniew K. Brzezinski, *Ideology and Power in Soviet Politics* (New York, 1967), chap. 1; Carl Friedrich, "The Evolving Theory and Practice of Totalitarian Regimes," in Carl J. Friedrich, Michael Curtis, and Benjamin R. Barber, *Totalitarianism in Perspective: Three Views* (New York, 1969), p. 127.
21. Friedrich, "The Evolving Theory," p. ix.
22. Benjamin R. Barber, "Conceptual Foundations of Totalitarianism," in Friedrich, Curtis, and Barber, p. 3.
23. Friedrich and Brzezinski, *Totalitarian Dictatorship*, p. 10.
24. Burrowes, "Totalitarianism," p. 287.
25. Fleron, "Soviet Area Studies," p. 328.
26. Gregor, *Metapolitics*, pp. 127ff.
27. Burrowes, "Totalitarianism," p. 283.
28. Ludz, "Entwurf einer soziologischen Theorie," pp. 533, 535.
29. Burrowes, "Totalitarianism," p. 288.
30. Barber, "Conceptual Foundations of Totalitarianism," p. 5.
31. Herbert Spiro, "Totalitarianism," in David Sills, ed. *International Encyclopedia of the Social Sciences*, vol. 16 (New York, 1965).
32. Robert C. Tucker, "Towards a Comparative Politics of Movement-Regimes," *American Political Science Review*, 1961, 55/2: 281-89.
33. Stammer, "Aspekte der Totalitarismusforschung," pp. 430, 432; Peter Christian Ludz, "Offene Fragen in der Totalitarismusforschung," in Seidel and Jenkner, pp. 470.
34. Michael Curtis, "Retreat from Totalitarianism," in Friedrich, Curtis, and Barber, p. 55.
35. Friedrich and Brzezinski, *Totalitarian Dictatorship*, chap. 27; Friedrich, "The Evolving Theory," pp. 123, 130, 131, 139, 140, 124.
36. Ibid., p. 125.

37. Karl Popper, *The Logic of Scientific Discovery* (New York, 1961), pp. 106ff.
38. J. L. Talmon, *The Origins of Totalitarian Democracy* (London, 1952).
39. A. James Gregor, "Classical Marxism and the Totalitarian Ethic," *Journal of Value Inquiry*, 1968, 2/1: 58-72, *Contemporary Radical Ideologies: Totalitarian Thought in the Twentieth Century* (New York, 1968).
40. Burrowes, "Totalitarianism," pp. 267, 277; Curtis, "Retreat from Totalitarianism," pp. 84ff.
41. Robert C. Tucker, "The Dictator and Totalitarianism," *World Politics*, 1965, 17/4: 555-83.
42. Groth, "The 'isms' in Totalitarianism."
43. Herbert Spiro and Benjamin Barber, "Counter-Ideological Uses of 'Totalitarianism,'" *Politics and Society*, 1970, 1/1: 3-22.
44. Cf. Rodolfo Mondolfo, "Il fascismo in Italia," in Renzo De Felice, ed., *Il fascismo e i partiti Italiani* (Bologna, 1966); Giuseppe Prezzolini, "Ideologia e sentimento," in Felice.
45. Groth, "The isms' in Totalitarianism," pp. 890ff.; Friedrich and Brzezinski, *Totalitarian Dictatorship*, p. 17; Roland Sarti, *Fascism and the Industrial Leadership in Italy, 1919-1940* (Berkeley, Calif., 1971).
46. Linz, op. cit., p. 334.

9. Totalitarian Dictatorship vs Comparative Theory of Fascism

1. Hannah Arendt, *Origins of Totalitarianism* (New York, 1951); Franz L. Neumann, *Behemoth: The Structure and Practice of National Socialism 1933-1943*, 2d ed. (New York, 1944); C. J. Friedrich and Z. K. Brzezinski, *Totalitarian Dictatorship and Autocracy*, 2d ed. (Cambridge, Mass., 1965); Ernst Fraenkel, *The Dual State* (New York, 1941); J. L. Talmon, *The Origins of Totalitarian Democracy* (New York, 1961).
2. Cf. Carl Schmitt, "Die Wendung zum totalen Staat," in *Positionen und Begriffe* (Hamburg, 1940); Ernst Forsthoff, *Der totale Staat* (Hamburg, 1933); Ulrich Scheuner, "Die nationale Revolution: Eine staatsrechtliche Untersuchung," in *Archiv des Offentlichen Rechts*, n.s., 24 (1933-34); cf. Martin Greiffenhagen, "Der Totalitarismusbegriff in der Regimenlehre," in M. Greiffenhagen, Reinhard Kühnl and Johann Baptist Müller, eds., *Totalitarismus: Zur Problematik eines politischen Begriffs* (Munich, 1972), pp. 38ff.
3. In that the conservative teachers of public law first of all labored under the illusion that it should be specifically the transfer of unlimited responsibility to the dictator which would make possible the realization of the principle underlying the state: "For only a state in which there is personal rule also on the lower levels of government, personal rule carried by an initiative bound to the leader, free in principle yet curbed by unlimited responsibility is truly authoritarian and conceivable as a total state" (Forsthoff, *Der totale Staat*, p. 38).
4. Cf. Sigmund Neumann, *Permanent Revolution*, ed. Hans Kohn, 2d ed. (New York, 1965); Karl Loewenstein, *Hitler's Germany* (New York, 1940); Fritz Morstein Marx, *Government in the Third Reich* (New York, 1936). For the unfolding of the theory of totalitarianism, cf. Howard D. Mehlinger, *The Study of Totalitarianism: An Inductive Approach* (Washington, D.C., 1965); Klaus Hildebrand, "Stufen der Totalitarismusforschung," in *PVS*, 9 (1968); Bruno Seidel and Siegfried Jenkner, "Wege der Totalitarismus-Forschung," in *Wege der Forschung*, 140 (Darmstadt, 1968).
5. Cf. Hans Kohn, "Communist and Fascist Dictatorship: A Comparative Sudy," in *Dictatorship in the Modern World*, ed. Guy Stanton Ford (Minneapolis, Minn., 1935); Max Lerner, "The Pattern of Dictatorship," in Ford, pp. 3-25; Carlton J. H. Hayes, "The Novelty of Totalitarianism in the History of Western Civilization," in *Proceeedings of the American Philosophical Society*, 82 (1940); Robert M. McIver, Moritz J. Bonn, and Ralph B. Perry, *The Roots of Totalitarianism: Addresses*

delivered at a Meeting of the American Academy of Political and Social Science (Philadelphia, 1940).

6. Cf. Theodor Pirker, ed., *Komintern und Faschismus, 1920-1940* (Stuttgart, 1965); Iring Fetscher, "Faschismus und Nationalsozialismus: Zur Kritik des sowjetmarxistischen Faschismus-Begriffs," in *PVS*, 3 (Cologne, 1962). Cf. also Hans Mommsen, "Antifascism," in *Marxism, Communism and Western Society I* (New York, 1972), p. 131-141.

7. Cf. also C. J. Friedrich "Totalitarianism: Recent Trends," in *Problems of Communism* 17 (1968), pp. 32ff. and C. J. Friedrich, ed., *Totalitarianism: Proceedings of a Conference Held at the American Academy of Arts and Sciences, March 1953* (Cambridge, Mass., 1954).

8. Zbigniew K. Brzezinski, *The Permanent Purge: Politics in Soviet Totalitarianism* (Cambridge, Mass. 1956); Adam B. Ulam, *The New Face of Soviet Totalitarianism* (Cambridge, Mass., 1963); Merle Fainsod, *How Russia Is Ruled* (Cambridge, Mass., 1953): Bertram D. Wolfe, *Communist Totalitarianism: Keys to the Soviet System* (Boston, 1956).

9. For an attempt to solve this problem, see above all Robert C. Tucker, "Towards a Comparative Politics of Movement-Regimes," *American Political Science Review*, (1961), pp. 281-89. See the review of Peter Wiles, *American Political Science Review*, 4 (1961), pp. 290-93.

10. Cf. Siegfried Bahne, " 'Sozialfaschismus' in Deutschland: Zur Geschichte eines politischen Begriffs," in *IRSH* 10 (1965), pp. 449-61.

11. Cf. Karl Dietrich Bracher, *Zeitgeschichtliche Kontroversen: Um Faschismus, Totalitarismus, Demokratie* (Munich, 1976), p. 85; Hans Buchheim, *Totalitäre Herrschaft: Wesen und Merkmale* (2d ed., Mucnich, 1962), pp. 41f.

12. Cf. J. Nyomarkay, *Charisma and Factionalism in the Nazi Party* (Minneapolis, 1967); Bracher, op. cit., pp. 84ff.

13. Alfred Cobban, *Dictatorship: Its History and Theory* (London, 1939); Eric Voegelin, *Wissenschaft, Politik und Gnosis* (Munich, 1959); cf. Hans Joachim Lieber, "Totalitarismus: Aspekte eines Begriffs," in H. J. Lieber, *Philosophie, Soziologie, Gesellschaft: Gesammelte Studien zum Ideologieproblem* (Berlin, 1965), pp. 213ff.

14. J. C. Talmon, op. cit., see also Talmon, *Political Messianism* (German ed., Cologne, Opladen, 1963). Compare Gerhard Schulz, "Der Begriff des Totalitarismus und der Nationalsozialismus," in Seidel and Jenkner, op. cit., pp. 457ff.

15. Winfried Martini, *Das Ende aller Sicherheit* (Stuttgart, 1954).

16. Compare Otto Bauer, H. Marcuse, and A. Rosenberg, *Faschismus und Kapitalismus: Theorien über die sozialen Ursprünge und die Funktion des Faschismus* (Frankfurt and Vienna, 1967), pp. 9ff.; Gerhard Schulz, *Faschismus—Nationalsozialismus: Versionen und theoretische Kontroversen, 1922-1972* (Frankfurt, 1974), pp. 61ff.

17. Ernst Nolte, *Three Faces of Fascism* (New York, 1966); See also Wolfgang Schieder, "Faschismus und kein Ende," in *Neue Politische Literatur*, 15 (1970), no. 2.

18. Theodor W. Adorno et al., *The Authoritarian Personality* (New York, 1950); Erich Fromm, *Escape from Freedom* (New York, 1941).

19. M. Greiffenhagen et al., op. cit., p. 23.

20. Cf. Johann Baptist Müller, "Kommunismus und Nationalsozialismus: Ein sozio-ökonomischer Vergleich," in Greiffenhagen et al., op. cit., pp. 61ff. In reference to this above all the excellent analysis by Peter Christian Ludz, "Entwurf einer soziologischen Theorie totalitär verfasster Gesellschaft," in Seidel and Jenkner, op. cit., p. 539ff.

21. Compare the comments of Bruno Seidel in Seidel and Jenkner, op. cit., pp. 7f. and 23f.

22. Kark Dietrich Bracher, *Zeitgeschichtliche Kontroversen*, p. 66ff.; This approach was developed systematically by Richard Löwenthal, "Totalitäre und demokratische Revolution," in Seidel and Jenkner, op. cit., continuing along the lines

of Sigmund Neumann, *Permanent Revolution*, loc. cit. However, Löwenthal's interpretation differs from Bracher's in that he does not include the October Revolution under the term *totalitarian revolution* and locates the deviation with the beginning of war communism.

23. Cf. Karl Dietrich Bracher, "Die Krise Europas 1917-1975," *Propyläen Geschichte Europas* (Berlin, 1976), pp. 36ff., 40, 131ff.; Klaus Hildebrand, "Hitlers Ort in der Geschichte des preussisch-deutschen Nationalstaats," in *Historische Zeitschrift* 217 (1973), pp. 621ff.; "Hitlers 'Programm' und seine Realisierung 1939-1942," in Manfred Funke, ed., *Hitler, Deutschland und die Mächte: Materialien zur Aussenpolitik des dritten Reiches* (Düsseldorf, 1976), pp. 92f.; Hans-Adolf Jacobsen, "Zur Struktur der NS-Aussenpolitik 1933-1945," in Funke, op. cit., p. 171; comp. also A. Hillgruber, *Kontinuität und Diskontinuität in der deutschen Aussenpolitik von Bismarck bis Hitler*, 3d ed. (Düsseldoff, 1971). Eugen Weber also doubts whether it is meaningful to burden the discussion by introducing yet another variant to the concept of "conservative revolution." "Revolution? Counterrevolution? What Revolution?" *Journal of Contemporary History* 9 (1974), pp. 3ff.

24. Thus the title of the essay by Timothy W. Mason in *Der Politologe* 7 (1966).

25. Compare Wolfgang Sauer, "National Socialism: Totalitarianism or Fascism?" in *American Historical Review*, 73 (1967). Greiffenhagen et al., op. cit., pp. 50ff. How emphatically the comparative study of fascism has turned away from the theory of totalitarianism is shown by the basic analysis of Juan J. Linz, "Some Notes towards a Comparative Study of Fascism in Sociological Historical Perspective," in Walter Laqueur, *Fascism: A Reader's Guide* (Berkeley, 1976), pp. 3-122).

26. Cf. Hans Mommsen, "National Socialism: Continuity and Change," in Laqueur, op. cit., pp. 182ff. For the problem of depoliticization in the Soviet system compare Peter Christian Ludz, "Offene Fragen in der Totalitarismus-Forschung," in Seidel and Jenkner, op. cit., pp. 493f.

27. Cf. Eberhard Jaeckel, *Hitler's Weltanschauung: A Blueprint for Power* (Middletown, Conn., 1972) as well as the above-cited studies by Jacobsen, Hildebrand and Hillgruber; see also Axel Kuhn, *Hitlers aussenpolitisches Programm* (Stuttgart, 1970). Cf. Hans Mommsen, "Ausnahmezustand als Herrschaftstechnik des NS-Regimes," in Funke, op. cit., pp. 42ff.

28. Henry A. Turner, "Verhalfen die deutschen 'Monopolkapitalisten' Hitler zur Macht?" in Turner, *Faschismus und Kapitalismus in Deutschland* (Göttingen, 1972), pp. 9ff.; Timothy W. Mason, *Arbeiterklasse und Volksgemeinschaft* (Cologne, 1975). An overview of the state of the discussion is given by Alan S. Milward, "Fascism and the Economy," in Laqueur, op. cit. pp. 379-412.

29. Fritz Tobias, *Der Reichstagsbrand: Legende und Wirklichkeit* (Rastatt, 1962); Hans Mommsen, "The Political Effects of the Reichstag Fire," in H. A. Turner, ed., *Nazism and the Third Reich* (New York, 1972).

30. Symptomatic for the emotional perception of this question are the merely polemical publications of the so-called "Internationales Kommittee" zur wissenschaftlichen Erforschung der Ursachen und Folgen des Zweiten Weltkrieges: *Der Reichstagsbrand*, vol. 1 (1972), vol. 2 (1978), as well as the pamphleteering presentation of Eduard Calic, *Der Reichstagsbrand: Die Provokation Des 20. Jahrhunderts* (Luxemburg, 1978). These volumes, produced with great propagandistic effort, do not present truly relevant material contradicting the sole responsibility of van der Lubbe, presented reasonably for the first time by Tobias.

31. K. D. Bracher, *Zeitgeschichtliche Kontroversen*, loc. cit., pp. 17ff., 62ff, and *passim*. See also Bracher's contribution to the present volume.

32. Cf. Klaus Westen, "Communist Party of the Soviet Union, Part II." in *Marxism, Communism and Western Society*, vol. 2 (New York, 1972), pp. 119-136.

33. Hans Mommsen, "National Socialism," op. cit., p. 193.

34. For the structure of the NSDAP, see Wolfgang Horn, *Führerideologie und Parteiorganisation in der NSDAP 1919-1933* (Düsseldorf, 1972); Wolfgang Schaefer, *NSDAP* (Frankfurt, 1956); Dietrich Orlow, *The History of the Nazi Party*, 2 vols.

(Pittsburgh, 1969, 1973) and Peter Diehl-Thiele, *Partei und Staat im Dritten Reich* (Munich, 1969).

35. Cf. Mommsen, "National Socialism," pp. 193ff.; Lothar Gruchmann, "Die 'Reichsregierung' im Führerstaat," in Günther Doeker and Winfried Steffani, eds, *Klassenjustiz und Pluralismus: Festschrift für Ernst Fraenkel* (Hannover, 1973), pp. 197-223. Cf. Jeremy Noakes, *The Nazi Party in Lower Saxony, 1921-1933* (Oxford, 1971), pp. 237f.

36. Cf. Hans Mommsen, *Beamtentum im Dritten Reich* (Stuttgart, 1966), p. 46.

37. Wolfgang Schieder, "Der Strukturwandel der faschistischen Partei Italiens in der Phase der Herrschaftsstabilisierung," in W. Schieder, ed., *Faschismus als soziale Bewegung* (Hamburg, 1976), pp. 89f.

38. Cf. Robert Koehl, "Feudal Aspects of National Socialism," in *American Political Science Review*, 54 (1960).

39. Ernst Fraenkel, *Der Doppelstaat* (German ed., Frankfurt, 1974), pp. 75ff.; Among the first to take up this problem was Zbigniew K. Brzezinski, "Totalitarianism and Rationality," *American Political Science Review*, vol. 50, no. 3 (1956), pp. 751ff. The capacity of the Soviet system for normative-rational measures is emphasized by Ludz, *Entwurf einer soziologischen Theorie*, loc. city. pp. 545f.

40. David Schoenbaum, *Hitler's Social Revolution*, 2d ed. (Garden City, N.Y.: 1967), p. 285f. and *passim*. The same results are found by all more recent monographic research efforts. See also Martin Broszat, "Soziale Motivation und Führerbindung des Nationalsozialismus," *Vierteljahreshefte für Zeitgeschichte* 18 (1970).

41. Karl W. Deutsch first posed the question in terms of systems theory: "Cracks in the Monolith: Possibilities and Patterns of Distintegration in Totalitarian Systems," in *Totalitarianismen*, ed. C. J. Friedrich, p. 308-33. Yet the National Socialist Regime never was a monolith in the sense of the theory of totalitarianism, while one surely cannot deny the Soviet system the capacity for "social learning."

42. Cf. Hans Pfahlmann, *Fremdarbeiter und Kriegsgefangene in der deutschen Kriegswirtschaft, 1939-1945* (Darmstadt, 1968); see also Edward L. Homze, *Foreign Labor in Nazi Germany* (Princeton, 1967).

43. Cf. Martin Broszat, *Der Staat Hitlers: Grundlegung und Entwicklung seiner inneren Verfassung* (Munich, 1969).

44. Cf. Hans Mommsen, "National Socialism: Continuity and Change," and his "Ausnahmezustand als Herrschaftstechnik des NS-Regimes," in Funke, ed., *Hitler, Deutschland, und die Mächte*, pp. 30ff.

45. Cf. Wolfgang Schieder, "Fascism," in *Marxism, Communism and Western Society*, vol. 3 (New York, 1972), pp. 282 ff.

46. Cf. the study by Christian Streit, *Keine Kameraden: Die Wehrmacht und die sowjetischen Kriegsgefangenen, 1941-1945* (Stuttgart, 1978).

47. Cf. Juan J. Linz, *Comparative Study of Fascism*, pp. 15f.

48. Cf. the basic analysis by J. Linz, op. cit., and the contributions of Michael Kater, H. A. Winkler, and Hans Mommsen in Schieder, *Faschismus als soziale Bewegung*.

49. Cf. Wolfgang Michalka, "Die nationalsozialistische Aussenpolitik im Zeichen eines 'Konzeptionen'-Pluralismus," in Funke, *Hitler, Deutschland und die Mächte*, pp. 49f.

50. Cf. K. D. Bracher, "Tradition und Revolution im Nationalsozialismus," in Bracher, *Zeitgeschichtliche Kontroversen*, pp. 62ff.

51. Cf. Peter Christian Ludz, "Entwurf einer soziologischen Theorie totalitär verfasster Gesellschaft," in Seidel and Jenkner, op. cit., pp. 547ff.

52. Cf. Benjamin Barber and Herbert J. Spiro, "The Concept of Totalitarianism as the Foundation of American Counter-Ideology in the Cold War," *Politics and Society*, vol. 1, no. 1 (1970).

53. Maurice Cranston, "Should We Cease to Speak of Totalitarianism?" in *Survey: A Journal of East and West Studies*, 23, (1977-78) pp. 62ff.

10. Despotism–Totalitarianism–Freedom-Oriented Society

1. Paul Hazard, *Die Krise des europäischen Geistes, 1680–1715* (Hamburg, 1939), p. 317.

2. Wilhelm Bolin in the biographical introduction to Ludwig Feuerbach, *Pierre Bayle* (Stuttgart, 1905), p. 47.

3. *Berliner Politisches Wochenblatt*, vol. 1 (1832), p. 192.

4. Alfred Stern, *Geschichte Europas von 1848 bis 1871*, 4 vols., p. 525.

5. For example, Karl Marx and Friedrich Engels, *Werke* (MEW) (Berlin, 1956-), vol. 16, p. 71, vol. 19, p. 29.

6. *Fürst Bismarck als Redner*, ed. Wilhelm Böhm, vol. 9, p. 194 (speech of 17 Sept. 1878).

7. Eugen Dühring, *Die Judenfrage als Frage des Rassencharakters und seiner Schädlichkeiten für Völkerexistenz, Sitte und Kultur* (Berlin, 1905), p. 32.

8. M. Robespierre, *Oeuvres* (Paris, 1840), vol. 2, p. 550. Cited in *Historisches Handwörterbuch der Philosophie*.

9. Waldemar Gurian, *Die politischen und sozialen Ideen des französischen Katholizismus, 1789-1914* (Mönchen-Gladbach, 1929), p. 219.

10. Cf. Ernst Nolte, "Revolution und Reaktion, Exempel einer verdrängten Dialektik," *Frankfurter Allgemeine Zeitung*, 17 Dec. 1977.

11. Alexis de Tocqueville, *Democracy in America*, ed. J. P. Mayer and Max Lerner (new translation by George Lawrence, New York, 1966), vol. 2, p. 666: 'Thus I think that the type of oppression which threatens democracies is different from anything there has ever been in the world before. Our contemporaries will find no prototype of it in their memories. I have myself vainly searched for a word which will exactly express the whole of the conception I have formed. Such old words as 'despotism' and 'tyranny' do not fit. The thing is new, and as I cannot find a word for it, I must try to define it."

12. Milorad M. Drachkovitch, *De Karl Marx a Leon Blum: La crise de La social-démocratie* (Geneva, 1954), p. 66

13. Albert Krebs, *Tendenzen und Gestalten der NSDAP: Erinnerungen aus der Frühzeit der Partei* (Stuttgart, 1959), p. 156 (English trans. *The Infancy of Nazism*, W. S. Allen, New York and London, 1976, p. 162).

14. Ernst Nolte, *Deutschland und der Kalte Krieg* (Munich and Zürich, 1974), pp. 536ff.

15. On the whole, compare Martin Jänicke, *Totalitäre Herrschaft: Anatomie eines politischen Begriffs* (Berlin, 1971), esp. pp. 134ff.

16. Mihail Manoilescu, *Le Parti unique* (Paris, 1936).

17. Ernst Fraenkel, *Deutschland und die westlichen Demokratien* (Stuttgart, 1964), p. 7.

18. Ernst Nolte, *Der Faschismus in seiner Epoche* (Munich, 1963), p. 34.

19. Ibid., p. 544.

20. Ibid., pp. 470-ff.

21. Ernst Nolte, ed., *Theorien über den Faschismus* (Cologne, 1967), p. 47.

22. Especially through the development of concepts such as "relaxed society," "society in tension," "the incomplete European revolution," "party-state-capitalistic-dictatorship of mobilization," as well as through the stress on "left" totalitarianism.

23. Particularly unrestrained and naïve is the contribution by Johann Baptist Müller in Martin Greiffenhagen, Reinhard Kühnl, and Johann Baptist Müller, *Totalitarismus: Zur Problematik eines politischen Begriffs* (Munich, 1972).

11. Totalitarianism of the Center

1. Robert Paxton, *Vichy France: Old Guard and New Order, 1940-44* (New York, 1972) Joel Colton, *Léon Blum: Humanist in Politics* (Cambridge, Mass., 1974).
2. George Mosse, *The Nationalization of the Masses* (New York, 1975).
3. Robert Soucy, "French Fascism as Class Conciliation and Moral Regeneration," *Societas—A Review of Social History*, Autumn 1971, pp. 287-97; Robert Soucy, "The Nature of Fascism in France," *Journal of Contemporary History*, vol. 1, no. 1, 1966, pp. 27-55; Robert Soucy, "France: Veterans' Politics between the Wars," in Stephen Ward, ed., *The War Generation* (Port Washington, N.Y., 1977).
4. Following widespread sitdown strikes by French workers in 1936, representatives of French business made major wage and work concessions to French labor. Henry Ehrmann has described the consequent backlash by French businessmen, especially small businessmen, to these "Matignon accords" in *Organized Business in France* (Princeton, 1957).
5. See Theodor Zeldin, *France, 1848-1945* (Oxford, 1973), pp. 285-364.
6. See Lloyd Garrison, "A Sleeping Monster May Be Waking Up," *New York Times*, Dec. 24, 1967, p. E5; "De Gaulle and the Jews," *Newsweek*, Dec. 11, 1967, p. 47; "France: Ugly Question," *Newsweek*, Jan. 27, 1967, p. 44; G.S., "Le Monstre est réveillé," *L'Express*, Dec. 11-17, 1967, pp. 66-67.

12. Behavioral Study of Obedience

Editor's Introduction

1. Vol. 67, no. 4, pp. 371-78.
2. The progress, scope, and conclusions of Professor Milgram's work on obedience are conveniently summarized in his *Obedience to Authority: An Experimental View* (New York, Evanston, San Francisco, London, 1974). The appendices (pp. 193-205) contain representative selections of commentary on the work's impact.
3. Stanley Milgram, *The Individual in a Social World: Essays and Experiments* (Reading, Mass., 1977).
4. Milgram, *Obedience to Authority*, p. 175.
5. Milgram, *Individual in a Social World*, pp. 92-94.
6. Both the scientific validity and the ethics of Professor Milgram's experiments have been questioned. Regarding the former, Proefessor Milgram took issue with his critics Orne and Holland in "Interpreting Obedience: Error and Evidence," in A. G. Miller, ed., *The Social Psychology of Psychological Research* (New York, 1972), pp. 139-54, repri. in Milgram, *Individual in a Social World*, pp. 124-38. For the Orne and Holland paper, see "The Ecological Validity of Laboratory Deception," *International Journal of Psychology*, 1968, vol. 6, no. 4, pp. 282-93. The ethical issues were raised by Diana Baumrind in "Some Thoughts on Ethics of Research: After Reading Milgram's 'Behavioral Study of Obedience,'" *American Psychologist*, 1964, vol. 19, pp. 421-23. Professor Milgram responded in "Issues in the Study of Obedience: A Reply to Baumrind," *American Psychologist*, 1964, vol. 19, no. 11, pp. 848-52, repri. in Milgram, *Individual in a Social World*, under the title "Ethical Issues in the Study of Obedience," pp. 139-46.
7. Milgram, *The Individual in a Social World*, p. 1.
8. Ibid. The experiments on "The Individual in the City," examine the bystander syndrome, urban anonymity, and the individual's image of the urban environment. The experiments on "The Individual and the Group" constitute studies of group pressure and conformity, and in those dealing with "the individual in a communicative web," communicative acts are used both as tools and as objects of sociopsychological inquiry. All of Milgram's work is concerned with the impact of the social world on individual action and experience.

9. Ibid., pp. 92-94.
10. Milgram, *Obedience to Authority*, p. 123.
11. See, for example, Barrington Moore, Jr., *Injustice: The Social Basis of Obedience and Revolt* (White Plains, New York, 1978), pp. 93-100, 432-33. Though Moore is quite satisfied with the scientific basis of Milgram's experiments, he draws from them much more optimistic conclusions regarding the nature of man.
12. For example, Harold D. Lasswell, "The Psychology of Hitlerism," *Political Quarterly*, vol. 4, July 1933, pp. 373-84; Wilhelm Reich, *Die Massenpsychologie des Faschismus* (Copenhagen, 1933; English trans., *Mass Psychology of Fascism*, 3rd ed., trans. Theodore P. Wolfe, New York, 1946); Erich Fromm, *Escape from Freedom* (New York, 1941); T. W. Adorno et al., *The Authoritarian Personality* (New York, 1950); P. Müller-Hegemann, *Zur Psychologie der deutschen Faschisten* (Rudolstadt, 1966).

Text

1. This research was supported by a grant (NSF G-17916) from the National Science Foundation. Exploratory studies conducted in 1960 were supported by a grant from the Higgins Fund at Yale University. The research assistance of Alan C. Elms and Jon Wayland is gratefully acknowledged.
2. A related technique, making use of a shock generator, was reported by Buss (1961) for the study of aggression in the laboratory. Despite the considerable similarity of technical detail in the experimental procedures, both investigators proceeded in ignorance of the other's work. Milgram provided plans and photographs of his shock generator, experimental procedure, and first results in a report to the National Science Foundation in January 1961. This report received only limited circulation. Buss reported his procedure 6 months later, but to a wider audience. Subsequently, technical information and reports were exchanged. The present article was first received in the Editor's office on December 27, 1961; it was resubmitted with deletions on July 27, 1962.
3. Forty-three subjects, undergraduates at Yale University, were run in the experiment without payment. The results are very similar to those obtained with paid subjects.
4. A series of recently completed experiments employing the obedience paradigm is reported in Milgram (1964).

References

Adorno, T., Frenkel-Brunswik, Else, Levinson, D. J., and Sanford, R. N. *The Authoritarian Personality*. New York, 1950.

Arendt, H. "What Was Authority?" in C. J. Friedrich, ed., *Authority*. Cambridge, Mass., 1958, pp. 81-112.

Binet, A. *La Suggestibilité*. Paris, 1900.

Buss, A. H. *The Psychology of Aggression*. New York, 1961.

Cartwright, S., ed. *Studies in Social Power*. Ann Arbor, Mich., 1959.

Charcot, J. M. *Oeuvres complètes*. Paris, 1881.

Frank J. D. "Experimental Studies of Personal Pressure and Resistance." *J. Gen. Psychol.*, 1944, 30, 23-64.

Friedrich, C. J., ed. *Authority*. Cambridge, Mass., 1958.

Milgram, S. "Dynamics of Obedience." Washington, 25 January 1961. (Mimeo)

Milgram, S. "Some conditions of Obedience and Disobedience to Authority." *Hum. Relat.* ["in press" in 1964].

Rokeach, M. "Authority, authoritarianism, and conformity," in I. A. Berg and B. M. Bass, ed., *Conformity and deviation*. New York, 1961, pp. 230-257.

Snow, C. P. "Either-or." *Progressive*, 1961 (Feb.), p. 24.
Weber, M. *The Theory of Social and Economic Organization*. Oxford, 1947.

13. Death and History

1. Work with Japanese youth is reported in *History and Human Survival* (New York, 1970); and with innovative young American professionals, as discussed in *The Life of the Self* (New York, 1976).
2. Susanne Langer, *Philosophy in a New Key* (Cambridge, Mass., 1942), p. 168.
3. Loren Eiseley, "Man, the Lethal Factor," mimeo., pp. 7-8.
4. Robert Jay Lifton, "The Young and the Old—Notes on a New History," in *History and Human Survival* (New York, 1970), pp. 332-73; "The Postwar War," *Journal of Social Issues* (1976), vol. 31, no. 4, pp. 181-95; and *Home from the War* (New York, 1973).
5. Alexander and Margarete Mitscherlich, *The Inability to Mourn* (New York, 1975). (In a Preface in that book (pp. vii-xiii) I discuss some of the issues stated below.) An abridged version of *The Inability to Mourn* can be found in Lifton and Eric Olson, eds. *Explorations in Psychohistory: The Wellfleet Papers* (New York, 1975), pp. 257-70.
6. Lifton, "Survivor as Creator," *American Poetry Review*, January-February 1973, vol. 2, 1:40-42. See also discussions of greater response to Hiroshima and the European holocaust in *Death in Life: Survivors of Hiroshima* (New York, 1976). Chaps. 10-13.
7. Lifton, "Protean Man," in *Boundaries: Psychological Man in Revolution* (New York, 1977 [1969]), pp. 37-63.
8. Eiseley, op. cit.
9. Lifton, *Thought Reform and the Psychology of Totalism: A Study of "Brainwashing" in China* (New York, 1961), Chaps. 22-24.
10. Ibid., chap. 22.
11. Robert G. Waite, *Vanguard of Nazism: The Free Corps Movement in Postwar Germany, 1918-1923* (New York, 1969), pp. 183, 201.
12. Robert G. Waite, *The Psychopathic God* (New York, 1977), p. 24.
13. Ibid., pp. 17-18.
14. Lifton, *Revolutionary Immortality: Mao Tse-Tung and the Chinese Cultural Revolution* (New York, 1976 [originally published by Random House and Vintage Books, 1968]), pp. 36-37.
15. In C. Vann Woodward, *The Strange Career of Jim Crow* (New York, 1974), p. 64.
16. See *Death in Life*, pp. 511-39.
17. Theordor H. Gaster, *Festivals of the Jewish Year* (New York, 1952), pp. 143-44.
18. Ibid., pp. 144-45.
19. Ibid., p. 142.
20. Mircea Eliade, *The Sacred and the Profane* (New York, 1961), p. 29.
21. James E. Breasted, *The Dawn of Conscience* (New York, 1933), p. 70.
22. Erwin Panofsky, *Tomb Sculpture* (New York, Abrams, undated; [based on lectures delivered at the Institute of Fine Arts of New York University in the fall of 1956]).
23. Eberhard Otto, *Egyptian Art and the Cults of Osiris and Amon* (London, 1968), p. 25.
24. Breasted, op cit., p. 225.
25. Ibid., p. 151.
26. Harold I. Isaacs, *India's Ex-Untouchables* (New York, 1965), pp. 27-28.
27. *Oxford Dictionary of English Etymology*, p. 97. Some believe there is a confusion between the Greek *nekromanteia* (divination by corpses) and the medieval Latin *nigromantia* (black magic) (*American Heritage Dictionary*, pp. 878). But in any case, the association is psychologically important.

28. Sigmund Freud, *Moses and Monotheism*, Standard Edition, vol. 23, pp. 91-92.
29. Ibid., p. 136.
30. Notably those of Lucy S. Dadwidowicz, *The War against the Jews, 1933-1945*, (New York, 1975); J. P. Stern, *Hitler—The Führer and the People* (London, 1975); Karl Dietrich Bracher, *The German Dictatorship* (New York, 1970); and Uriel Tal, "Violence and Defense: The Jewish Experience," *Proceedings of the Seminar on Violence and Defense in Jewish History and Contemporary Life, Held at Tel Aviv University, August 18—September 4, 1974*, and personal communication.
31. Dadwidowicz, *War against the Jews*, p. xiv.
32. Ibid., p. 21.
33. Ibid., p. 22.
34. Rudolf Binion, *Hitler among the Germans* (New York, 1976).
35. Kenneth Burke, *The Rhetoric of Religion: Studies in Logology* (Berkeley, 1970), p. 4.
36. Quoted by Louis Nemzer from Zhdanov, in Carl J. Friedrich, ed., *Totalitarianism* (Cambridge, Mass., 1954), p. 129.
37. Waldemar Gurian, "Totalitarianism as Political Religion," in Friedrich, pp. 122-23.
38. Burke, op. cit., pp. 4-5.
39. Gurian, op cit., p. 128.
40. Albert Camus, *The Rebel* (New York, 1954), p. 163.
41. Ibid., p. 214.
42. Lifton, *Thought Reform . . . and Revolutionary Immortality*.
43. Jean-Paul Sartre, *Anti-Semite and Jew* (New York, 1962), p. 17.
44. Ibid., p. 43.
45. Ibid., pp. 53-54.

Epilogue: Obedience and Human Autonomy

1. Robert Jay Lifton, "Witnessing Survival," *Society*, March–April 1978, pp. 40-44.
2. Stanley Milgram, *Obedience to Authority: An Experimental View* (New York, Evanston, San Francisco, London, 1974), p. 188.
3. Lifton, "Witnessing Survival," op. cit., p. 41.
4. Hannah Arendt, *The Origins of Totalitarianism* (new. ed. with added prefaces, New York, 1973), p. 464.
5. Michael Curtis, "Totalitarianism Reconsidered," paper delivered at the 1977 annual meeting of the American Historical Association in Dallas, p. 2.
6. Arendt, op. cit., p. 437.
7. T. W. Adorno et al., *The Authoritarian Personality* (New York, 1950), p. 971; Bruno Bettelheim, "Eichmann: The System, the Victims," in *Surviving and Other Essays* (New York, 1979), pp. 256-73, 266-67.
8. Michael Selzer, "The Murderous Mind," *New York Times Magazine*, 27 Nov. 1977, pp. 35ff, 140.
9. Hermann Glaser, *Spiesser-Ideologie: Von der Zerstörung des deutschen Geistes im 19. und 20. Jahrhundert* (Freiburg, 1964; 2d ed., Cologne, 1974; I cite from the first edition; English trans., *The Cultural Roots of National Socialism*, London and Austin, Texas, 1978).
10. Ibid., pp. 73-75.
11. Albert Traeger, "Wann, Wann Marschieren Wir 'gen Norden?" *Die Gartenlaube*, 1863, no. 21, p. 328. Pleads the poet fervently, ". . . wann endlich in den heiligen Krieg?" (". . .when, at last, into the holy war?").
12. Louise Mühlbach, "Der Kurfürst und der Geldfürst," *Die Gartenlaube*, 1883, no. 49, pp. 769-72, no. 50, pp. 784-89, no. 51, pp. 801-4. no. 52, pp. 817-23.
13. Robert Koehl, "Feudal Aspects of National Socialism," in Henry A. Turner, Jr., ed., *Nazism and the Third Reich* (New York, 1972), pp. 151-74, 158.

14. Jürgen Habermas, "Hannah Arendt's Communications Concept of Power," *Social Research*, vol. 44 No. 1, Spring 1977, pp. 3–24.

15. Hannah Arendt, *Elemente und Ursprünge totaler Herrschaft* (Frankfurt, 1955), p. 749, quoted in Habermas, "Hannah Arendt's Communications Concept of Power," p. 10.

16. Habermas, "Hannah Arendt's Communications Concept of Power," pp. 21-22.

17. Ibid.

18. Jürgen Habermas, "Umgangssprache, Wissenschaftssprache, Bildungssprache," *Max Planck Gesellschaft Jahrbuch 1977* (Munich, 1977), pp. 36–51, 42 (Sonderdruck). Habermas cites Johan Galtung's "Violence, Peace and Peace Research," *Journal of Peace Research*, vol. 6, 1969, pp. 167-91. The author acknowledges gratefully Professor Habermas's making available the reprint of his article and his helpful suggestions.

19. Ibid.

20. Sigmund Freud, "Massenpsychologie und Ich-Hypnose," *Studienausgabe*, vol. 9, *Fragen der Gesellschaft, Ursprünge der Religion* (Frankfurt, 1974), pp. 61-134, 119.

21. Helmut Schelsky, *Die Arbeit Tun die Anderen: Klassenkampf und Priesterherrschaft der Intellektuellen* (Opladen, 1975), pp. 243-44.

22. Habermas, "Ungangssprache,", pp. 37, 42.

23. Milgram, *Obedience to Authority*, p. 142.

24. Ibid., p. 188.

25. Koehl, op. cit., p. 154.

26. pp. 79-80 of this volume.

27. Robert Jay Lifton, *Thought Reform and the Psychology of Totalism* (New York, 1961), p. 422, cited from Alex Inkels, "The Totalitarian Mystique: Some Impressions of the Dynamics of Totalitarian Society," in C. J. Friedrichs, ed., *Totalitarianism* (Cambridge, Mass., 1953), p. 91.

28. Ibid.

29. Ibid., p. 437.

30. Hannah Arendt, *Eichmann in Jerusalem: A Report on the Banality of Evil* (New York, 1963), p. 231.

31. Ibid., p. 226.

32. Robert Jay Lifton, *The Life of the Self: Toward a New Psychology* (New York, 1976), p. 170.

INDEX